GANGLAND VOLUME 2

The Underworld in
Britain and Ireland

GANGLAND VOLUME 2

The Underworld in Britain and Ireland

James Morton

LITTLE, BROWN AND COMPANY

A *Little, Brown* Book

First published in Great Britain by
Little, Brown and Company in 1994

Copyright © 1994 James Morton

The moral right of the author has been asserted

A CIP catalogue record for this book
is available from the British Library.

Typeset by Hewer Text Composition Services, Edinburgh
Printed in England by Clays Ltd, St Ives plc

ISBN 0 316 90997 1

Little, Brown and Company (UK) Limited
Brettenham House
Lancaster Place
London WC2E 7EN

Contents

For Dock Bateson, with love

Introduction

In the years after the trial of the Kray twins in 1969 the reporter
Brian McConnell was sent around the countryside, on behalf of
the *News of the World* for whom he was then writing, offering up
to £100,000 reward for information which would lead to a
conviction in an unsolved murder in the area. Wherever he
went he saw senior local police officers and was confronted
both with the statement that there were no gangs operating in
the area of the force he was visiting and the belief that there had
to be something seriously amiss with the Metropolitan Police to
have allowed the Krays to have flourished at their peak for as
long as they did – something in the region of five years with one
abortive prosecution in the middle.

It is an attitude which still persists in many forces. That there
have been gangs in the area in the past but certainly there are
none today. Nothing like London. They couldn't possibly
flourish with the control we have of criminals in our town.
We're a small community. We know them all and who's doing
what and what they're capable of.

To a certain extent the comment about the knowledge of the
local hook's capabilities are, or at any rate were, justified. Some
years ago a bank robbery went off in a city in the Midlands and a
client of mine who went on to national notoriety was hauled up
from London as a probable suspect. Chatting with the officers
before the identification parade, I asked why they suspected it

was an out-of-town job. It was easy, they replied. There was only one man in the town capable of such a robbery, 'and he was flattered when we went to see him'.

From my client's point of view the identification parade went off smoothly. He was a stoutish man and, on hearing of his arrest, friends travelled to the Midlands to give help and support. One of them, Peter Hubbard, now deceased, a celebrated horse doper, closely resembled my client particularly in relation to the number of pounds overweight he was carrying. For once the police officer in charge of the parade was prepared to let my client have a friend stand on the parade as a foil or dummy. Naturally he selected the position next to Hubbard and at the last minute changed ties with him. Hubbard was identified and, since he had a deal of trouble even climbing stairs in those days, was quickly eliminated from the inquiry.

The parade had been held in an upstairs room in the police station and on the way down I followed behind the witness and one of the police officers. There were some recriminations going on and the witness said, with some reproach, 'But you told me he was the one with the red tie.'

That night I broke one of my golden rules about not travelling with my clients and their friends. The last train to London had gone and the choice was staying in the town overnight or getting a lift back with my client. Hubbard had an interest in a boy boxing on the undercard at the Albert Hall and was keen to see his protégé in action. It was a foggy night and he drove at breakneck speed passing, for some reason or other, through Newmarket. My client was urging him to slow down but Hubbard was in ebullient form. 'No worse than when I doped that horse before the Guineas,' he said, naming a racing *cause célèbre* and the bookmaker who he maintained had paid him. And as we swished through the fog he pointed out the stables where he had worked his art over the years.

I asked to be let out at the first underground station to which we came. I have no idea whether they reached the Albert Hall in time although I noticed their boy won. I idly followed his career from then on, but he never amounted to much.

The attitude that the police are on top of crime in their area still persists. Last year whilst trying to research professional crime in Dublin, I met a Gardai officer who was keen to impress on me that there was no such thing in Ireland. 'You're wasting your time,' he said. 'Stay and have a good holiday, but you're wasting your time.' The following morning the papers were full of a professional hit which it seems had been directed at the wrong man. The next few days revealed a chapter of crime which the Krays and Richardsons at their peak had never approached.

As with *Gangland*, I have tried to distinguish between crime committed for profit and for political or social motives. I have therefore omitted the details of the dozens of miners who were accused of rioting and other civil disorder offences in Wales during mining disputes with the mine-owners. Nor is there any account of the extortion by some members of Dev Sol and the Kurdish Workers' Party who are said to have been targeting Turkish businesses in London, Hull, York, Harrogate and Liverpool for funds – £100 per worker is reported to be the going rate. Shortly before Christmas 1993, demands ranging from £5,000 to £100,000 were made on Turkish North London shopkeepers. One restaurant owner from Stoke Newington who refused to pay was savagely beaten. A special unit was set up at Stoke Newington police station and the Metropolitan Police had plans to extend this throughout the whole of London.[1] There had been a similar protection racket run on the Cypriot community in the 1960s. Similarly disturbances and quarrels in the cause of religion, even though the participants have often been gangs in all but name, cannot feature and so there will be nothing in the chapter on Liverpool about the death of John Kensit, the founder of the Protestant Truth Society, on 25 September 1902. He was attacked by a large Catholic crowd as he left a meeting, and died after being struck by a file thrown from the crowd. John McKeever was charged with the murder and acquitted.

Domestic crimes have therefore had to be excluded, even though this means the loss of such fascinating cases as that of Ernest Clarke whose conviction at Newcastle Assizes in 1980 of the killing of 16-year-old Eileen McDougall ten years earlier ended in the Court of Appeal in 1986, when Mr Justice Lawton said that it was inconceivable that the murder could have been committed by anyone else.[2] It was a blow for JUSTICE, the organization which had investigated his case and campaigned for

---

[1] *Observer*, 5 December 1993; *Sunday Telegraph*, 2 January 1994.
[2] See F. Bresler, *An Almanac of Murder*, p.37.

his release[3]. Nor can there be any detailed look at Joseph Clarke (no relation) who on 3 February 1929 had one of the shortest murder trials on record. At Liverpool Assizes he was sentenced to death in a case which lasted four and a half minutes. He had strangled his landlady.[4]

Politically motivated crime on the mainland has once again been excluded, hence the Workers' Party of Scotland will not receive the coverage which the activities of its members – Ian Doran, a second-hand-car dealer; William McPherson, professional gambler; Colin Lawson, former monk in a closed order at Nunraw Abbey, West Lothian (later a 'soldier of the proletariat') and their leader, bookseller Matthew Lygate – perhaps deserve. Their aim was to turn the country into a Communist republic. To finance the revolution they committed a series of robberies in 1972, armed with shotguns and ammonia sprays. Lygate, a man of previous good character who defended himself at the trial, received twenty-four years, Doran twenty-five and McPherson twenty-six respectively. Lawson did best of all: he received a mere six years.

Crime in Belfast has been omitted on the basis that it is too intricately connected with political matters. Given the situation in Ireland, this exclusion has not always been possible. The interconnections between organized criminals and major and fringe political groups there have been, at times, almost indissoluble. I have tried, however, to avoid the murders, robberies and kidnappings which can be clearly shown to be the work of political extremists. Even that is not always possible, but sadly I have had to exclude both the Sallins Train Robbery, which was a miscarriage of justice to rank with some of the better British efforts, and the Kerry baby case, a wholly domestic matter but important because it led to a change of attitude by senior officers to the workings of the Gardai.

I had intended that once more the starting point should be the turn of the twentieth century. However, I cannot bring myself to

---

[3] JUSTICE was founded in 1957 following the joint effort of leading lawyers of the three political parties to secure fair trials for those accused of treason in Hungary and South Africa. It is now an all-party association of lawyers (with membership open to non-lawyers) to strengthen and uphold the rule of law in the territories for which the British parliament is directly or ultimately responsible: in particular, to assist in the administration of justice and in the preservation of the fundamental liberties of the individual.
[4] See J. Bland, *True Crime Diary*, p.40.

consign to oblivion without at least a mention the engagingly named Paisley Mohawks, who sound like an ice-hockey team, but were in fact a collection of racecourse bullies in the mid-nineteenth century.

The time scale should also eliminate the so-called High Rip Gang which may or may not have flourished in Liverpool in the mid-1880s. There is no doubt that there was a considerable amount of violence in the Scotland Road area where the police patrolled in couples. It was there the legend of the High Rip Gang grew up, much to the annoyance of the Chief Constable William Nott-Bower:

It was suggested that the large number of crimes of violence in the Scotland Division was due to the work of an organized gang, banded together for purposes of plunder and violence, and executing vengeance on all who ventured to give evidence against them or their nefarious work. And, not content with inventing the Organization, a most euphonious name for it was also invented, and it was stated that this organization was known as the 'High Rip Gang'. Of course all this created considerable, and entirely unjustifiable, alarm, though there was never the very faintest shadow of foundation for the suggestions made. But letters from all sorts of irresponsible persons, Press comment, and a certain sort of public opinion assumed the impossible, and accepted the fact of a 'High Rip Gang'. It was impossible, for such a gang could not have existed without the police ever hearing of it, and the circumstances of the various crimes were such as to render it impossible to assign them to such a cause.[5]

Whether there was such a gang may be open to question, but there were certainly a great number of robberies with violence and woundings in the list for the November Assizes of 1886 presided over by Mr Justice Day. He dealt with them sternly. After each verdict of guilty, and there seem to have been about twenty of them, the defendant was put back to await sentence at the end of the Assize. On the last day he was brought up and sentenced to a term of imprisonment coupled with twenty or

[5] W. Nott-Bower, *Fifty-two Years a Policeman*, p.148.

thirty lashes of the cat. As a reminder, this was to be administered in two instalments, the second just before the man's release from prison. Crimes of violence in Liverpool, High Rip Gang or not, decreased sharply for a time after that.[6]

However, the overall picture of Manchester and its policing would be poorer without an account of the good Inspector Bannister who ran the brothels and probably a good deal more in the 1890s. Nor, even though it occurred in 1895, would it really be possible to omit mention of the theft, and subsequent fate, of the first FA Cup from a Birmingham shop window.

In 1895 Aston Villa won the FA Cup, beating West Bromwich Albion 1–0 at the Crystal Palace ground. On the night of 11 September it was stolen from the window of William Shillcock, football and boot manufacturer, in Newton Row, Birmingham. The shop was a lock-up one and the zinc covering was removed from the roof, allowing a man to be lowered in.

A £10 reward was offered by Shillcock, who also said that if the Cup was returned there would be no questions asked. It was well insured and it was proposed that a new gold Cup should be purchased at a cost not exceeding £200, the insurance money. This suggestion was turned down and it was agreed that another Cup – as closely resembling the old one as possible – should be purchased. Aston Villa was fined £25, the exact cost of the replica.

Nothing was heard of the Cup for over half a century until in February 1958 the *Sunday Pictorial* carried a scoop that Harry Burge, an 83-year-old Birmingham man, had stolen the trophy. Burge said that he and his two companions had jemmied the back door, stolen the Cup, money from the till and some boots, and had then melted it down and used it to fake half-crowns, some of which were passed in a public house belonging to Dennis Hodgetts, the Villa forward. There were a number of discrepan-

---

[6] Certainly the *Daily Telegraph* thought there were High Rips. As part of Mr Justice Day's swingeing sentencing, two lads of 19 said to be High Rips received fifteen years penal servitude for stabbing a member of the Logwood gang. One man, said the newspaper, had had to have police protection because he would not allow the High Rips to use a goods shed of the Lancashire and Yorkshire Railway Company, the keys to which he had been entrusted. (*Daily Telegraph*, 15 November 1886.) There is some oral evidence that there was such a gang. In an interview in the *Liverpool Echo and Express* on 19 October 1960, Elizabeth O'Brien, then aged 86, recalled that, 'There were women in the High Rippers who identified themselves with a flower or plume in their hair. They were more vicious than the men'. She also said that the only control of the High Rippers came from a policeman known as Pins. When he approached the gang scattered, calling, 'Pins is coming.' She would have been nine at the time Mr Justice Day dealt with the gang.

cies in his account, but that may be attributed to a recollection of events which had taken place over sixty years earlier. Burge had been in and out of prison for forty-six years, and two years after the Cup was stolen he was convicted of theft himself, so he had the right pedigree for the job.

Shillcock later wrote in *The Book of Football*, 1906:

It was an incident which seemed to me at the time a great and unprecedented calamity. I pictured myself a ruined man. I seemed to see myself a hated individual – to see my business boycotted. Why, I was the man who lost the English Cup . . . I am not joking when I say that I believed that incident was destined to ruin my connection with football, but happily such has not been the case. But you see that I shall ever be a man with a record unique in the annals of football.[7]

So far as the end of the time scale is concerned, it has become increasingly difficult to separate the history of crime in any major town or city from that of international drug trafficking. However, for the purposes of chronology I have included in chapters on the towns themselves some individual crimes, such as the apparently random killing of Benji Stanley in January 1993 in Moss Side in Manchester, rather than looking on his death as part of the national and international scene.

One of the problems with writing a sequel is that there is bound to be a certain amount of repetition. I hope I have kept this to a minimum. Although in the chapter on London I have referred to the Krays, the Richardsons and the Sabinis, the last at some length, I hope that I have provided new stories about the various gangs and, although presenting a chronology, I have not repeated in too much detail their exploits which have already

---

[7] Not quite unique because on Mothering Sunday, 26 March 1966, the World Cup was stolen from the Stampex exhibition at Westminster Hall. The thieves removed the screws from the plates of padlocked double doors and the lock from the back of the glass-fronted cabinet. Several days later a demand was received, along with the detachable top of the trophy, and following a telephone call a 47-year-old docker was arrested.

Shortly afterwards a Dave Corbett was out with his dog Pickles on Beulah Hill, Streatham, when the animal sniffed out the trophy hidden in the bushes. Pickles was given a year's supply of goodies by a dog food manufacturer and a medal by the National Canine Defence League. Mr Corbett undoubtedly also did well from the recovery of the trophy. Unfortunately, so the story goes, Pickles did not live long to savour the benefits from his triumph; whilst chasing a cat, he strangled himself with his lead.

appeared in *Gangland*. The behaviour of London criminals is crucial to an understanding of the rest of the country. There have been links and exchanges in a series of cases. In the 1960s Glasgow hardmen wanted for crime in their city were sent for rest and recuperation, and possibly to do a job at the same time, in London. For example, when the Krays wantèd to deal with Georgie Cornell, before he was shot, a Scot was recruited to shadow and pay (in the sense of punish) him. Criminals from the provinces would set up the jobs to be carried out by London teams, thereby providing a measure of protection for both, and conversely when a safe needed blowing, London criminals would hire a man from Glasgow or the North East where there were mining communities from which men experienced with explosives could be recruited.

In the case of supergrasses and particularly the Brinks-Mat robbery, I have had to restate the facts of the cases which have appeared in *Gangland* before bringing the stories up to date. In general I have omitted the lives and careers of the great individual jewel thieves such as Peter Scott, Raymond Jones and George 'Taters' Chatham. In a curious way although a part of, they were also apart from, the Underworld and often moved in a completely different society. I had intended to look more closely at some of the great art robberies, but with the exception of the loss of the Beit collection (twice) that subject will have to await another day or another book.

As for this book itself, I would like to claim it is a complete history of what has recently become known as designer crime, but it would be idle of me to do so. As I wrote in the Introduction to *Gangland*:

> Of course much of this book is oral history and the narrators of the tales may not be wholly reliable. Quite genuinely their memories will have faded but also there are axes to grind, scores to be settled, no longer with knives but in print, proving yet again that the pen is mightier than the sword. It also has to be said that some of the reporting in the old days, as since, was not aimed at a sociological study but at the number of copies of the newspapers or magazines to be sold . . . One of the major causes of the break-up of the Spot-Hill partnership was their rivalry over the publication of their respective memoirs. Wearing one of his less

attractive hats, the newspaper reporter Duncan Webb was used by Hill, whose autobiography he ghosted, to discredit and embarrass Spot.

One example of the difficulties faced in writing a social history of crime such as this is that the protagonists played under a variety of different names, often their mothers' maiden ones. Ruby Sparkes, for example, appeared in court as Watson. When I was trying to trace his former girlfriend Lilian Goldstein, I was confidently informed that she was, 'Nona Hayes, you know, the daughter of Timmy, Guv'nor of West Ham'. This was firmly denied by others who knew her and who placed her as coming from North-West London. When eventually I found details of her career in the Public Record Office which seemed to confirm that she was no relation of the Hayes family, I mentioned this to my informant. He was sceptical and suggested she might have been some sort of illegitimate daughter; it was almost as if he wished her to have a legitimate criminal pedigree. Generally speaking Goldstein was thought at the very least to be attractive, and she must have had a good deal of skill and bravery as can be seen from the grudging tributes by officers who followed her in 1940 in the hope she would lead them to Sparkes who had just escaped from Dartmoor.

Contrast this then with the recollection of Val Davies, who wrote a number of books on the pre-war London Underworld:

If we rule out Peter the Painter and the Bonnet gang, a woman has the distinction of being the suspect pioneer of smash-and-grab crime in this country. But I must hasten to add she was by no means a glamorous bobbed-haired bandit. On the contrary, she was an unwashed, foul-mouthed, illiterate, drink-sodden Amazon with a reputation of being able to use her fists as ably as a man, however tough he may be.[8]

You might not think the descriptions could be of the same woman, but it is accepted that there was only one girl smash-and-grab raider at the time so he must have been referring to Goldstein.

Other examples of multiple names include the old villain

---

[8] V. Davis, *Phenomena in Crime*, p.136–7.

Arthur Harding who was also known as Tresidern, whilst Harryboy Sabini was also called Harry Handley and Henry Handley. Jack Spot was variously named Camacho and Comer.

Another problem is the absence of documentation about these heroes. In the early days many could not read and write, and those who could were not too often willing to commit themselves to paper. By the time records are released by the Public Record Office, those to whom they refer will have long passed out of memory. When they did commit themselves to paper the events had happened long before and, even allowing for scores to be settled, recollections could be genuinely faulty and inconsistent. Take Arthur Harding remembering his companion Jack 'Dodger' Mullins. In *East End Underworld* on p.132, Harding refers to Mullins as 'ignorant as bloody hell and brutal with it'. By p.149 Mullins has become 'a thief but not a violent type', but by p.185 he has reverted to being 'one of the biggest terrors in London at the time'.

The final problem is, perhaps, a technical one. We are long past the days when cases were disposed of with anything approaching celerity; now, a simple shoplifting case can take two days and a murder case with two or three defendants will last a month. In 1959 Ronald Marwood was suspected of killing a police officer in a fight outside a dance hall in the Holloway Road. He was not arrested immediately but thirteen of his companions were. In those days there was no such thing as a paper committal; every word of evidence against a defendant had to be taken down, usually in long-hand. This included witnesses such as a plan drawer or photographer, let alone anyone whose evidence might be challenged. The remaining defendants were committed for trial by the end of the year. Marwood gave himself up in early January. His trial at the Old Bailey was in March (after a full committal hearing) and he was executed in April. Now cases which once would have been heard within weeks will take a year or more to come to trial. Juries, where in 1911 they had taken twenty-eight minutes to convict Steinie Morrison[9]

---

[9] Steinie Morrison aka Alexander Petropavloff was charged with the murder of Leon Beron, found dead on New Year's Eve 1909 in some bushes on Clapham Common, London. He received a few shillings a week rent from properties he owned, but lived in a sevenpenny-a-night lodging house. However, Beron did carry on him both jewellery and fairly large sums of money – up to £70, which could then buy a house. The victim's skull had been fractured and he had been stabbed. His money, watch-chain, and a £5 gold piece

against whom the case was never strong, will, following the American example, retire for hours, if not days. As a result it is not possible to give the outcome of cases which have happened in the last year or sometimes even two. There are inevitable lacunae.

All I can really hope is that this book is the most comprehensive so far. When I completed *Gangland* a number of those mentioned telephoned me to say they had acquired – even if they had not actually purchased – copies and pointed out some errors. I hope that there will be even fewer in this book, but of course there will be omissions. Once more, if those who feel unfairly left out, and that they have done better than some of the named participants, care to write to me stating their credits, I will endeavour to ensure they find themselves in any subsequent edition.

As always I am grateful to a considerable number of people for their help and advice and who have allowed me to quote from their books. This time they include, in strictly alphabetical order, Joe Beltrami, Julian Broadhead, Lisa Brownlie, Doug Cluett, Dani Garavalia, Frank Fraser, Frances Hegarty, Brian Hilliard, Dick Hobbs, Cal McCrystal, Brian McConnell, John Morris, James Nicholson, Douglas Skelton, Edda Tasiemka, Stuart Tendler, Leon Williams, Frank Williamson, and Richard Whittington-Egan, to whom I owe a special debt for the references he obtained from his library, as well as the staff at the Public Record Offices both in Chancery Lane and at Kew. There are also a great number of journalists and others who have assisted me but have asked not to be named. Faults and frailties are mine alone. The book could not have been written without the endless support and encouragement of Dock Bateson.

cont'd
he carried were gone, and his forehead was incised with several cuts that looked like the letter 'S'. This was the initial letter of the Russian word for *spic* or double agent. A reward of £500 was offered for information leading to the conviction of his killer.

His death came only a fortnight after the Houndsditch murders by the Russian anarchists who, whilst carrying out a burglary, had been surprised by unarmed police and had shot them dead. Three days into the New Year there had been the famous siege of Sydney Street in which the murderers died in a blazing house after a long gun battle with the Scots Guards. Was there any evidence that Beron knew the Houndsditch murderers? No, said Inspector Frederick Wensley in charge of the investigation. It was, he believed, purely a matter of robbery.

The evidence against Morrison was that he knew Beron and was seen with him in the East End shortly before midnight on the night of his death. He also knew the area; just before his arrest he had obtained work in a bakery at Lavender Hill a few minutes from Clapham Common. He had given a parcel to a waiter in an East End restaurant, saying it *cont'd*

contained a flute, but at Morrison's trial the waiter said it was far too heavy to be a flute and seemed more like an iron bar. Again, there was evidence that Morrison had been thoroughly unpleasant to him and the man had every reason to hold a grudge against him. There were spots of blood on Morrison's collar when he was arrested; he seemed to have come into money just after Beron's death; and in those days, when identification evidence was accepted quite readily, he was identified by two cab-drivers who firmly put him on Clapham Common at the time of the murder.

The trial started at the Old Bailey on 6 March, almost two months from the day of his arrest, before Mr Justice Darling. His defence was an alibi. After midnight he had been in his lodgings. Some of the witnesses called to place him with Beron before midnight were prostitutes, and the waiter who said he had been given an iron bar rather than a flute to mind had tried to commit suicide (then a felony). Morrison's counsel, Edward Abinger, tore into them, ignoring the judge's warning of the consequent damage to Morrison's character in evidence. The identification evidence was not strong; Abinger called a John Greaves, of the Royal Institution of British Architects, to deal with the inadequate lighting at the Clapham Cross cab rank, and he threw considerable doubt on the identification. Also, it was shown that Morrison had at least ten collars and that he was a fastidious dresser. Nor was he a fool. Surely he would not have worn an unwashed collar for a week – particularly one stained with Beron's blood?

The difficulty came when his alibi about seeing two sisters at a music hall was effectively broken. The girls were muddled over their evidence; they could not say who paid for their tickets and, worse, could not remember who was on the bill. Morrison did not help himself when he went in the witness-box. He could not prove that the upturn in his finances had not come from Beron's pockets. Then Abinger's tactics in cross-examining the prostitutes rebounded against his client. Morrison's character was put in evidence – prison record, false names and all.

Darling was not sure of Morrison's guilt and he certainly did not sum up for a conviction. He told the jury that Morrison had no convictions for violence and, more importantly, that a foreigner on trial for his life might do things an English person would not do. Merely because he had concocted a false alibi did not mean he had committed the crime. This did Morrison no good; the jury took only a short time to convict. Morrison now told the court that the money he had came from a bank forgery. It was normal for judges to add that they agreed with a jury's verdict, but instead Darling told Morrison to be advised by his solicitor and learned counsel.

Even though they upheld the verdict it is clear the recently formed Court of Appeal did not like the conviction, but under the terms of the Criminal Appeal Act 1906 there was nothing they could do:

> Even if every member of the Court had been of the opinion that he personally would have acquitted the prisoner the Court must yet have upheld the conviction, unless they were of the opinion that the verdict was so perverse that no reasonable jury would have given it.

Nevertheless it, plus Darling's summing-up, was enough to save Morrison's life. Churchill commuted the death sentence to one of penal servitude on 12 April 1910. Morrison could not accept the verdict, and time and again petitioned the Home Secretary to have his case re-opened. He is also said to have petitioned for the death sentence to be carried out. After starving himself for three months he died in prison on 24 January 1921.

1

London –
The Families

The battles for control of London, in particular the East End and
Soho, have been charted before, albeit from different perspec-
tives.[1] Briefly the history traces through such early gangs in the
East End as the Russian immigrant Bessarabians and Odessians
at the turn of the century, Arthur Harding and his Vendetta boys
in the first few years of this one, running through the Titanics, a
team of pickpockets and burglars destroyed in around 1915, to
the Sabinis, initially a racecourse gang after the First World War,
and their long-lived rule of Little Italy in Clerkenwell and Soho.

The Sabinis, five brothers born of an Italian father and an
English mother named Handley, led by the redoubtable Darby,
had first seen off Billy Kimber and the Brummagen Boys, a
Birmingham-based racecourse gang (but with many members
from around the Elephant and Castle) and later the Camden
Town Mob, led by Fred Gilbert but in which their old rival
Kimber had a considerable interest. The leader was not present
in July 1922 nor was Kimber – he had been shot the previous year
and survived – when the Sabinis visited their regular haunt the
Red Bull on the edge of Clerkenwell to find members of the
Camden Town gang in what they could justifiably call their bar.
There had been a rumble a few weeks earlier, as a result of which
Joseph Sabini would be sentenced to three years' imprisonment.
Now the knives (Sabinis) and guns (Camden Town) were out.

[1] See J. Morton, *Gangland, London's Underworld*, and R. Murphy, *Smash and Grab*.

1

Fortunately, as on other occasions, either the weaponry was faulty or they were extremely bad shots because Detective Constable John Rutherford, who had been in the bar and had followed the Camden Town boys as they chased the Sabinis, was shot at at close range. The bullet missed. In November a number of men were sentenced for this little fracas. Joseph Jackson received seven years and George Baker five years' penal servitude. Birmingham men George Martin and George Hillier were acquitted and presumably went back home.

Then when there should have been peace and prosperity they faced internal difficulties from their senior lieutenants such as the Cortesis, and also from other smaller organizations over the division of the spoils and the allocation of pitches on the racecourses.

The Cortesi brothers were already serving four-year sentences for their assaults on Darby and Harryboy Sabini in the Fratellanza club in Clerkenwell when another ally of the family, Edward Emmanuel, was attacked in September 1924 by which time the Yiddishers, who foolishly and temporarily had aligned themselves with the Cortesis, were back in the Sabini fold.[2]

The prosecution of Alfie Solomon for murder in the Eden Social Club, Hampstead Road, London came about over an incident earlier in the evening when former prize-fighter Barnett 'Barney' Blitz, also known as Buck Emden, set on Emmanuel with a broken glass. He believed Emmanuel had been responsible for grassing him up the year before over an affray at Epsom races. He suggested that Emmanuel, who organized the bookmakers' concessions, had paid the police £20 to have him arrested. Given Emmanuel's 'in' with the police, it seems a perfectly reasonable belief. Solomon came to Emmanuel's aid and stabbed Blitz with a carving knife. The boxer died in hospital some days later and the Sabinis rallied to the assistance of their supporters.

---

[2] Emmanuel had a long-lived history in the East End. At one time, before seeking an alliance with the Sabinis, he had run with Arthur Harding. In his later life he was regarded as being a great 'fixer' with the police. His son, Phillip, was among the first eight stewards appointed in 1921 at a wage of £6 per week each to assist the Racecourse Bookmakers and Backers Protection Association. The other stewards included the Sabini brothers. In 1926 Netley Lucas wrote of the Sabinis in *London and Its Criminals*, '. . . the gang is backed and upheld by one of the best known and most powerful bookmakers on the Turf. A member of all the racing clubs, a man who pays out thousands after each big race, and retains twice as much, he has a smart flat in the West End, several expensive cars and a still more expensive wife.'

It was the strict custom in the 1920s for members of the Bar to see their clients only in their chambers. Not many years previously it had been the custom not to see the clients on capital charges at all, leaving their solicitors to transmit messages of succour and support to the prisoners. Now Darby Sabini and his friends descended on Sir Edward Marshall-Hall KC in his flat in Welbeck Street and, with the help of a bundle of the old white £5 notes, known as Bradburys, and said to total £1,000, persuaded him that he was the only man at the Bar able to save Solomon from the gallows.

They were right to select Marshall-Hall. In one of his most impressive displays of forensic theatricality, he smashed a glass on counsel's bench in front of him and held it so that the jury could see the jagged and dangerous edge. Surely, confronted with this and an enraged boxer, there was every reason for poor Solomon to panic. The jury thought so and returned a verdict of manslaughter. Solomon was sentenced to a term of three years' imprisonment.[3] On his release he asked the police for protection against other race gangs.

The Sabinis' control of matters declined in the 1930s. They were under siege from the up-and-coming White family who had initially been amongst their supporters, and also now from Alfie Solomon to whose defence they had rallied a decade earlier. Darby Sabini could no longer control the disparate Jewish and anti-Semitic factions in his organization. A slashing of a member of the Hoxton mob at Liverpool Street Station led to the fight on 8 June 1936 at Lewes racecourse when Sabini bookmaker Mark Solomons (once acquitted of the attempted murder of Billy Kimber) and his clerk, Mark Frater, were badly beaten. An accommodation was reached.

---

[3] Marshall-Hall was probably the greatest of the old-style advocates of the twentieth century. His behaviour in court was often spectacular and the glass-smashing demonstration at Solomon's trial echoed that of his earlier defence of Marguerite Fahmy, a lady who had married a rich Egyptian, Ali Kamel. Apparently he both treated her with violence and subjected her to sexual brutality. When finally he demanded anal intercourse she shot him. In his speech to the jury, Marshall-Hall, demonstrating to the jury how she snatched the gun to protect herself from this anti-social behaviour, dropped the weapon just as she had described dropping it after shooting her husband. He said later it was by accident, but the effect was described as 'an attack on the nerves as violent as a physical blow'. Mme Fahmy was acquitted to an outburst of cheers and clapping. Hall is the model for the performance by Charles Laughton in the film *Witness for the Prosecution*. In later years the character of Mme Fahmy has undergone something of a downgrading. She was, it now appears, a Parisian prostitute rather than a high-born lady.

Now the Whites took King's Cross whilst the Sabinis retained Clerkenwell and Soho.[4]

During the War the Sabinis were dealt some rough treatment, not only by rival gangs but also by the British government. Some of the brothers were interned as enemy aliens. Darby Sabini was detained in June 1940, and by the November had still not appeared before a tribunal to determine whether the reasons for his detention were justifiable. Harryboy (alias Harry Handley, Henry Handley and a few other names) was detained at the same time. In the War Darby Sabini served a short prison sentence for receiving. Curiously, although he maintained he had been framed possibly either by Alf White or Alfie Solomon, he pleaded guilty. His son was killed in the Battle of Britain and this effectively destroyed him and what power his family had retained.

Like all good gang leaders, Harry's convictions were modest and the evidence of his bad character was minimal. George Cortesi had taken out a summons for assault against Harry, Darby and a number of others. At Clerkenwell Police Court on 22 October 1922 Harry had been fined £3 and £2 costs. The conviction brought into play a bind-over earlier in the year at Marylebone where he had been charged with assaulting a Fred Gilbert at Paddington Railway Station with an automatic pistol. Harry had not been convicted but had been bound over to be of good behaviour, with a surety, each in the sum of £5. Now both he and Edward Emmanuel, his surety, forfeited the money. This was the incident which led to the shooting of Harryboy and Darby by the Cortesis in the Fratellanza Club. There was also evidence that sixteen years later, in 1938, Darby had been seen in Tattersall's enclosure at the Ascot races kicking a Richard Hutton. Harry had gone to give a bit of extra help to Darby who was said to be drunk. Darby was expelled from the meeting

---

[4] The celebrated battle at Lewes racecourse was the last of the big gang racing battles. There are grounds for thinking that the Sabinis tipped off the police who were then able to prevent considerable punishment being dealt to Frater, the clerk. Certainly, according to DCS Greeno, an anonymous telephone call had been received telling the Squad, 'It's going to be off at Lewes on Monday.' (*War on the Underworld*, p.64.) Sixteen men were arrested and the ringleaders drew five years' apiece at the next Lewes Assizes. One of them was Jimmy Spinks, leader of the Upton Park mob. It spelled the end of him as a real contender for the control of the Underworld. It is said that the men's families were supported during the sentences by the founder of one of Britain's largest bookmaking firms.

and a black mark was registered by DI Ted Greeno against Harry, later to be used in evidence against him. Conviction wise, the worst that could be said about the family was that Joseph, another of the brothers, had been sentenced to three years' penal servitude in 1922. There had also been a small matter of the attempted bribery of prison officers whilst he was in Maidstone.

The police report leading to Harryboy's arrest described him as

. . . one of the leading lights of a gang of bullies known as the Sabini gang who under the cover of various rackets have by their blackmailing methods levied toll on bookmakers . . . He is a dangerous man of the most violent temperament and has a heavy following and strong command of a gang of bullies of Italian origin in London.

The report concluded:

We have no knowledge that he has previously engaged in any political activities but . . . he can at best be described as a dangerous gangster and racketeer of the worst type and appears to be a most likely person who would be chosen by enemy agents to create and be a leader of violent internal action.

Harryboy appealed against his detention under regulation 18B. The reasons for his detention were given as 'hostile associations' but more likely he, together with boxer Bert Marsh, also known as Pasquale Papa – who had been acquitted of murder following a fight at Wandsworth Greyhound Stadium in 1934 – had been detained because they were suspected of a successful bullion raid at Croydon Airport. This dated back to the 1920s and was believed to have netted the then very substantial sum of £80,000.

There is no doubt that security at the recently opened Croydon Airport was lax, as was the discipline with the pilots. In theory the buffet-cum-restaurant was open only to passengers and customers, but the pilots kept overcoats in their lockers to wear over their uniforms so as to gain access. Nancy Johnstone, who worked in the buffet, recalls that one pilot, Paddy Flynn, used a code 'a little more sugar this morning' to mean a measure of whisky in his coffee before he flew. He lost a leg in an air crash whilst flying for Imperial Airways in the early 1930s.

Opposite the restaurant was the bullion room in which gold bars, the universal currency, were stored. If a transfer of currency was made between countries then the gold bars were literally moved. The security was in the hands of guards of the Civil Aviation Transport Organization, but from time to time the door to the bullion room was left open with the key in the lock.

The staff noticed that a man was hanging around the airfield, and it is thought that he took a wax impression of the key when one day it was left in the lock. Nancy Johnstone remembers locking up the canteen one afternoon after the last flight – there were no such things as night flights – and when she returned to the premises the next morning she found it in an upheaval. Gold due to be flown to France was gone.

Shortly afterwards a Sabini bookmaker, in tribute to or financed by the robbery, began betting using the name Nick Gold.

The appeal was delayed and so Harryboy, ill-advisedly as it transpired, applied for a writ of *habeus corpus*. He had already offered his house, worth some £15,000, as surety if he could be granted bail. In his affidavit in support of the application for leave to be granted the writ, he said he had never been known as Harry Handley. The evidence of his arrest was that the police had gone to his house at 44 Highbury Park, Highbury New Barn in North London on 20 June 1940 and asked Sabini's wife where Harry Handley was. The reply had been 'upstairs'. It was also successfully argued that he could be described as being of 'hostile origin' even though he had an English mother, Eliza Handley, and his father had died when he was a child. His brother George Sabini had a daughter in the ATS and a son in the RASC who had joined up after war had been declared with Italy. The authorities were none too pleased when Harry was released from detention on 18 March 1941. He was promptly re-arrested for perjury, and on 8 July that year he received a sentence of nine months' imprisonment.[5]

Arthur Swan, himself detained under the wartime 18B measures at what he described as the Ascot Concentration Camp – the authorities later preferred to regard it as an internment camp – remembers them:

---

[5] There is a full and critical account of the regulation 18B process under which the Sabinis and many others were detained in A. W. Brian Simpson's *In the Highest Degree Odious*, Chapters 13 and 14. Home Office papers TS27/496A.

Amongst this diverse community were two men, the Sabinie [sic] brothers, the Soho gangsters who had achieved great notoriety as the result of their raid on Croydon's airport strongroom and the theft of £80,000 of gold bullion. Always with them, but slightly to the rear was a 'Papa' Marsh, a short, stocky individual who, I was informed, carried out the Sabinie orders. I might add that they were held in great awe by the Anglo-Italian section. I recall at one time we were having a spot of bother with the Anglo-Italians and when I was walking around the compound they came up beside me and said, 'If you can get us a bottle of Chianti from the other side of the wire you will have no further trouble from the Italian section.' Shades of Chicago!![6]

One Sabini man who survived the purge was 'Italian Albert' Dimes, who became Billy Hill's right-hand man when he and Jack Spot controlled Soho. Once the anti-Italian orders had been signed, reprisals were taken against the Italian-owned clubs in Soho. Italian-Jewish fights broke out and continued for some time. The main aim was to inflict the maximum damage on the rival club owner's premises. One of the fights was in the Palm Beach Bottle Parties club in Wardour Street. It was there that Antonio 'Babe' Mancini stabbed Harry 'Little Hubby' or 'Scarface' Distleman to death. Rather against the run of evidence and certainly the judge's summing-up, he was convicted of murder. 'Italian' Albert Dimes, an increasingly powerful figure as the years went by, was present and charged with affray. In the second trial for the affray witnesses were becoming increasingly reluctant to identify Dimes or his co-defendants and he was bound over to come up for sentence. On his release he was returned to his unit in the RAF from which he had deserted.

The Whites had an uneasy tenure in office. They were not really hard (or hard enough) men. As early as 1939 their leader, old Alf White, had taken a bad beating at Harringay dog track by some young tearaways from Stoke Newington, and there seems not to have been the expected swift reprisal. Their serious and rapid decline began at the end of the War, first with their

---

[6] Unpublished memoir of Arthur Swan. Swan, who was Mosley's British Union District Treasurer of the Lowestoft Branch, was Camp Leader at Ascot Concentration Camp. There he represented all detainees, not simply Mosley's Blackshirts. He died in 1993.

ousting from control of Yarmouth racecourse in October 1946
when their hardman Eddie Raimo, who had earlier slashed Billy
Hill, backed down in the face of Jack Comer, known sometimes
as Jack Comacho and most often as Jack Spot, who wished to
install a Jewish bookmaker on one of the prime pitches. Later
Spot, with the help of Arthur Skurry of West Ham, took over the
pitches at Ascot from the family.[7] In January the next year they
were comprehensively evicted by Spot in an alliance with Billy
Hill.

Frank Fraser, longtime friend and assistant to Billy Hill,
recalls the family:

> Then [pre-war] they had a good team with men like Jock
> Wyatt and Billy Goller on the strength but now Alf White
> was old and Harry, his son, was a lovely man but with no
> stomach for a fight. Harry was in Wandsworth in 1944.
> He'd hit a geezer with a walking stick and got a few months.
> That was all the time he'd done and he didn't like it. He was
> very big, impressive, full of bonhomie, hail-fellow-well-met.
> And Alf was as well. If you had a crooked copper they were
> the ideal men to handle it. If anyone was in trouble and
> could get a bit of help they were the ones to go to, but as for
> leaders they didn't really have the style. All in all they were a
> weak mob and they were ripe for taking.
>
> Billy Hill didn't really have time for racing people. He
> thought they were phonies, frauds who'd never really done
> any proper bird. He booked them as sort of bullies. So I
> don't think he thought of turning them out but there again
> he didn't have any time for them either. Jack Spot was the
> one who wanted control. Now Spot wasn't a thief. He
> would run a million miles from nicking something himself
> but what he'd do was he'd then nick it off the thief. He was
> what they call a thieves' ponce. What he was was an

---

[7] R. Murphy, *Smash and Grab*. Murphy's always interesting account of the Underworld
is in parts, as he freely admits, the Gospel according to Spot. Neither Murphy nor Spot's
other detractors would claim that the man with a thousand cuts was always completely
accurate in his recall of events. One story on which Spot traded for his working career was
how he had felled the wrestler Roughneck, the bodyguard of the fascist leader Mosley, in
his march down the East End in 1936. In its edition of 23 January 1955 the *Sunday
Chronicle*, which was running Spot's memoirs at the time, published a retraction of the
Roughneck story: 'No attack occurred on Sir Oswald Mosley, or the procession. The
story of Sir Oswald Mosley being attacked is therefore complete fabrication.'

enforcer. His real name was either Comacho or Comer. He reckoned he'd got the name Spot because he was always in the right spot when there was trouble. He'd got great ideas about protection at the races and Bill was friendly with him. Spot could see Bill would be a great asset and when Spot had the row with the Whites he pulled Bill in. Bill had a tremendous amount of respect and clout and that was the overwhelming factor.

Spot had good hard people like Teddy Machin and Franny Daniels, who were on the airport job, solidly behind him then.[8] They were all getting plenty of money where the Whites never had that muscle. They had some good people but not enough. Harry White never fancied a mill and when Spot did White's team at the end of 1946 in Al Burnett's The Nut-House off Regent Street, he hid under a table.[9] That's when Billy Goller got his throat cut. The one who would have been terrific and who would have defended the territory was Alf White's son, also called Alf, but he had died in 1943. The other brothers, Johnny and Billy White, were really racing people and not involved in clubs. The Whites were literally eliminated. I wasn't surprised at all, but they still kept the race meetings. Old Alf and Harry were clever there.[10]

Nothing was too small for Hill.

Jimmy Farrell's father used to sell pigeon food in Trafalgar Square and paid Hill to let him do so. Hill took money off the smudge, off the clip joints. He was like Tony Mella, he took everything off everyone. He says he wasn't involved in

[8] The 'airport job' was a raid in 1948 on London Airport said to have been organized by Jack Spot. It ended in disaster when the police discovered the plot in advance of the raid. Detectives were substituted for the baggage handlers who were to be robbed and a battle took place. Several men were convicted and received up to twelve years' imprisonment. Teddy Machin escaped, as did Franny Daniels who held on to the chassis of a lorry and received severe burns whilst doing so.
[9] Al Burnett owned a number of clubs and night-spots over the years, all of them frequented by the Fancy. When Nipper Read investigated the Krays' hold on the West End, Burnett vehemently denied paying them protection money although it is apparent that he was doing just that. Burnett was a follower of greyhounds, in which he had some success. His dog Pigalle Wonder won the Greyhound Derby, and on retirement was a prepotent force in breeding. Burnett also wrote his memoirs *Ace of Clubs*.
[10] F. Fraser, *Mad Frank*, p.46.

9

vice but he took money off the Messinas to allow them to operate.[11]

Of course, whilst Spot and Hill controlled Soho, the epicentre of crime, there were still other teams who had non-competing interests in inner London. For example Frank Fraser, twenty years later associated with the Richardson brothers in South London, was then operating a small gang of jewel thieves and robbers. Aldgate was another Soho. It was riddled with clubs, including Jack Spot's Green Dragon, catering for East Enders in general and seamen off the ships which had just docked in particular. Prostitutes lined the pavements. In Sanders Street, just off Henriques Street and Berners Street, was a row of brothels run by the emerging force of Maltese.

Running a drinking club was a traditional small- (and sometimes quite large-) time way of making money through illegal sales of drink, illegal gambling, possibly coupled with a certain amount of prostitution and receiving. Clubs and 'parties' had proliferated during and after the War, with the police waging a battle against them. In London, prosecutions had been at the rate of two a week, from the club on the marshes which catered for Pitch-and-Toss punters on the marshes, through the Pavilion Bridge Club in Shepherd's Bush run by a family from its home – the police had moved against it when they received ten complaints, including one from a woman who wrote that her husband gambled away his money and kept her short of food – to a similar Temperance Club in Brighton, up to the Gateways in the King's Road which had 700 members and was 'very tastefully decorated' but which 'unfortunately' had gaming machines, back down again to the Ninety Club in Clapham which was

> . . . frequented by men and women of the lowest order, and troops of the Allied Nations . . . A young woman made spasmodic noises on an accordion . . . anyone could get admittance by giving three rings on the bell, and they could

---

[11] The smudge was a photography racket operated in London and at the seaside. Punters had their photographs 'taken' with a camera with no film. They then paid a ten-shilling deposit for the non-existent photographs. Tony Mella ran clubs in Soho. He was shot in a quarrel by his long-time friend Alf Melvin, who promptly killed himself. See J. Morton, *Gangland*, pp.364–5.

then drink to their hearts' content. The people . . . were mainly of the worst possible type: thieves and women of the lowest order. The conversation was foul, and some dancing went on with women high-kicking in scanty clothing . . . the place was in effect an unlicensed public house. In two previous incarnations as a club it had been struck off the register twice and on the last raid was making a substantial profit.[12]

Another more identifiable gang, however, was the Elephant and Castle mob who had flourished as an amorphous group since the 1920s when they had aligned themselves with Billy Kimber against the Sabinis and had suffered for it.[13] They were credited with being a gang not only with its own slang – a bit of an exaggeration because it was only Cockney back and rhyming slang – but also in allowing women to be members, but again this intelligence seems to have been a bit of reporters' licence.

Now some of the younger male members of the Elephant and Castle team were in extreme difficulty. They were involved in the murder of Alex de Antiquis. On 29 April 1947 a robbery took place at Jay's, a jeweller's near what used to be the Scala Theatre in Charlotte Street where the magicians Maskelyne and Devant played an annual Christmas season. The raid was a failure from the start. The staff was held at gunpoint but one member managed to press the burglar alarm. When a director of the firm, Ernest Stock, leaped over the counter and shut the safe door, he was rewarded with a blow from a revolver. Seventy-year-old Bertram Keates threw a stool at one of the gang and a shot was fired in return. By now the raid was clearly in difficulties

[12] South London Press, 16 October 1942.

[13] 'In a series of lightning raids, the Sabinis proceeded to hit rival gangs where it hurt most. The Irish Mob in Camden Town had seen their most lucrative night club, the Blue Angel, torched to the ground. The Townsend Brothers, the vice lords of Paddington, had two of their brothels visited by the Sabinis, the girls and their clients driven into the street, too terrified to return. And tonight the Sabinis had smashed up six spielers belonging to the Elephant Gang and had helped themselves to the loot;' Edward T. Hart, *Britain's Godfather*, p.103. In July 1922 the police nipped another major fight in the bud with the arrest of Fred Gilbert, said to be the leader of the Camden Town Gang or Brummy Sage's Mob. He had been heard to talk about a raid to be undertaken that evening saying, 'Alf White and the Sabinis will be done for certain.' He was acquitted at the Old Bailey of slashing George Droy and shooting at him and his brother Trixie as well as blackmailing a bookmaker Harry Margules. Efforts, including an offer of £150 to leave the country, were made to get Margules to change his story. On this charge Fred's brother, John, and two others were also acquitted. MEPO3/366.

and the men ran into the street to their car. Because a lorry was blocking the way the three men involved could not reach their getaway car and instead ran off down the street waving their guns.

The men were almost caught at the scene when a surveyor Charles Grimshaw, who was passing, tackled them. Those were the days when members of the public would 'have a go'. He was fortunate to escape with his life.

> At that moment a motor-cyclist drew up in front of me. He more or less stood up from his machine on one leg, as though to dismount, and I heard a shot and saw him fall. I saw two men come round the front of the machine, which had fallen over, still running towards me across Charlotte Street. They were side by side and the taller of the two was removing a white scarf from his face. There seemed to be a third person on the other side of the fallen motor-cyclist.
>
> I stepped off the kerb behind a stationary car and as they drew near me, trip-kicked the shorter man. He fell full length on the pavement and dropped the gun he was carrying. I jumped on top of him, but his companions, who had run on a few paces, turned back and kicked me on the head. That made me release the man as I was dazed, and he pushed me over and stood up . . . He picked up the gun, pointed it at me and said 'Keep off.' I stayed where I was.[14]

The shot motor-cyclist was 34-year-old father of six, Alex de Antiquis. He had tried to block their path by stalling his motor-cycle. As he lay dying in the gutter he said, 'I tried to stop them . . . I did my best.'

The robbers turned out to be Harry Jenkins, his friend Christopher James Geraghty, and 17-year-old Terence Peter Rolt. They were traced through a massive police hunt led by Robert Fabian, the legendary 'Fabian of the Yard'. A raincoat was found in a room in a building in nearby Tottenham Court Road, and in turn that was traced to a shop in Deptford where it was identified as having been sold to Jenkins' brother-in-law.

Jenkins, with a record of assaults on the police and known by his associates as 'The King of Borstal', who had only been

[14] R. Higgins, *In the Name of the Law*, p.126.

released six days earlier, was brought in for questioning. Now he told the police it looked like his coat but that he would say nothing more. His friend, Christopher Geraghty, who had twice escaped from a Borstal with Jenkins, was also picked up. His story was that he had been in bed with an attack of boils; he was released. Rolt was also known as a friend of Jenkins; he too had apparently been ill in bed at time of the raid, and he too was released. Jenkins was also allowed to go after twenty-seven witnesses on an identification parade had failed to pick him out.

The next day, however, Fabian had Jenkins in again. This time he told Fabian that he had lent his raincoat to a man in Southend. This man was eventually found and admitted to a robbery in Queensway, West London, with Jenkins and Geraghty. After that they had all gone to Southend where he, Walsh, had tricked the others out of their money. He admitted casing the premises in Charlotte Street but denied being on the raid. That, he said, was down to Jenkins and Co. He later received five years for the Queensway robbery.

A loaded .45 revolver was then found in the mud at Wapping and ballistic tests showed it was the one which had been fired in Jay's. Jenkins' parents-in-law lived only a quarter of a mile from where the gun was found. Geraghty was the first to be arrested. He made a confession naming Rolt but refused to put Jenkins in the frame. Rolt was next to be pulled in and he too confessed, but this time he named Jenkins. The so-called 'King of Borstal' was arrested within hours.

The whole story came out in dribs and drabs. The bungling of the raid appears to have been largely that of Rolt. He had been told to wait for his colleagues outside the jeweller's but instead blundered in, leaving the others to follow. It was Geraghty who shot de Antiquis as they fled from the scene. Neither Geraghty nor Rolt gave evidence, but Jenkins produced an alibi calling a number of witnesses. His story was not accepted; he and Geraghty were hanged on 19 September 1947. Rolt was ordered to be detained during His Majesty's Pleasure.

The executions of Jenkins and Geraghty had a salutary effect on London's gangland, says ex-Detective Superintendent Robert Higgins:

[The Antiquis case] had the effect of breaking up much of the gang warfare which was brewing in London's Underworld at that time. Many criminals went as far as throwing away their guns when they heard that two young men were destined for the gallows.[15]

When it came to it, the Jenkins family were fortunate that on an earlier occasion both Harry and an older brother, Thomas, had escaped the hangman. On 8 December 1944 they had taken part in a raid on a jeweller's in Birchin Lane in the City. Ronald Hedley, known as 'Silver' because of his blond hair, was the driver who had knocked down Captain Ralph Binney, who ran into the road with arms outstretched to signal the getaway car to halt.

Hedley did not stop and passed right over the gallant retired naval captain. Hedley put the vehicle in reverse and then, with Binney trapped under the car, drove off at high speed. Binney[16] was dragged for over a mile before being dislodged. At the trial Hedley was found guilty of murder and Jenkins of manslaughter. Hedley was sentenced to death, reprieved and released after serving nine years. Thomas Jenkins received eight years.

> Harry Boy wasn't charged. When they took Harry Boy into the police he had this brilliant idea and he chinned the police sergeant, knowing full well he'd be mercilessly beaten up. As a result everyone on the ID parade had to be plastered up with tape and so he wasn't picked out. He eventually got Borstal for the assault on the copper.[17]

For the next seven years peace more or less reigned in the London Underworld as Spot and Billy Hill, with the tacit approval of the police, kept the capital under control. Who was the dominant figure of the ill-assorted pair really depends upon whose version of events is believed. It would seem that at the start Spot was the senior partner. Hill at the time was having some small localized trouble. He was arrested for a warehouse-breaking which, for once, he did not commit. On bail he removed some stolen parachutes from the original thieves and with the

---

[15] Ibid p. 135.
[16] A medal for civilian gallantry was struck in honour of Captain Binney.
[17] F. Fraser, *Mad Frank*, p. 30.

proceeds headed for South Africa. There in Johannesburg and in association with Bobby Ramsey, later to run with the Krays, Hill opened a gaming club, Club Millionaire. This was directly in opposition to the wishes of the South African ex-wrestler Arnold Neville, known as the 'Guv'nor of Guv'nors'. Permission would normally have to be sought from him and, in turn, he would expect a percentage.

Reprisals were swift. Neville and his henchman launched an attack on the club and were badly beaten by Hill, who had been given a gun, and Ramsey. Neville was nearly scalped, needing a hundred stitches, and given a striping by Ramsey for his pains.[18] Hill vanished to Durban where he was arrested; given bail, he again absconded. Ramsey stood his ground and received a sentence of five months for assault. A week later Hill was back in England, hiding under the protection of Arthur Skurry in Upton Park in the East End.

After a job in Manchester in which he, another man, and Teddy Machin netted £9,000 – they had been told the proceeds would be not less than £35,000 – Hill gave himself up on the original warehouse-breaking charge. He received three years and according to Spot was penniless when he was released in 1949. Spot then maintains he allowed him to manage some of his spielers.

Hill and his friends tell it rather differently. The money to finance clubs came not from Spot but from a former brothel-keeper Freddy Field. Hill, who was a fine gambler, had a share in a club with Sammy Samuels who describes his play:

> With Billy Hill the game was the thing, quick and fierce, win or lose that's how he liked it. Where another man would turn nasty over a losing run, Bill simply shrugged. Money was not all that important to him.
>
> I have seen twenty players round a dice table calling bets and when Bill arrived watched those same people play to double the stakes. Players who had hesitated to call on a pound now called to fifty-pound bets. Whatever the amount they knew they would be accommodated.

---

[18] A striping was done not, as might be expected, across the face but across the buttocks. It was also called noughts and crosses. The victim would remember the damage, as for some time he would not be able to sit down.

> B. H. not only livened up a game, he brought the money
> with him to make the play interesting.[19]

By 1952 there was no question whose star was in the ascendancy.
Jack Spot had organized the failed bullion raid on London
Airport, whilst on 21 May of that year Billy Hill pulled off
the stunning Eastcastle Street mailbag robbery which netted him
and his associates some £287,000, closely followed in 1954 by a
bullion raid in Holborn. Hill, now a celebrity both in and outside
the Underworld, never needed to work again. Spot did. Worse,
he saw his old henchmen changing allegiance. Each was courted
by newspapers but Hill, with the shady reporter Duncan Webb[20]
behind him, had the better press and Spot, enraged with Webb's
championing his rival, broke the reporter's arm one night. It cost
him dear: a conviction, damages and later bankruptcy.

In August 1954 came the celebrated fight in Frith Street
between Spot and Albert Dimes, friend to the Sabinis and
now Hill's right-hand man. It was one more battle for control
of social and political supremacy of the West End. Now, it
appears that Spot sought out the relatively amiable Dimes in an
effort to get at Hill. Both Spot and Dimes were acquitted after
considerable shenanigans involving perjured witnesses at the Old
Bailey. It was, however, effectively the end for Spot. A year later
he was badly slashed by Frankie Fraser and others at Hill's
instigation. Later clubs he owned were torched. He dropped out
of the scene whilst Hill assumed the role of 'Godfather', buying
himself a villa in Spain to which he went with a new friend Gypsy
Riley. His wife Aggie stayed behind running a couple of Soho
clubs. Dimes went into betting shops, gaming machines and
another half-dozen dubious enterprises. He was believed to be
the trusted representative in England of the Bruno family from
Philadelphia.

Soho was, it seems, up for grabs and for a time the Nash family
from Islington – six brothers once lovingly described by a
newspaper as the wickedest brothers in England – reigned
supreme. They had started life protecting Cypriot cafés at £2 a
week, and had moved up in the world and into Mayfair where

---

[19] S. Samuels with L. Davis, *Among the Soho Sinners*, p.84.
[20] For further details of the late Mr Webb's escapades, see fn. p.282; J. Morton, *Gangland* and F. Fraser, *Mad Frank*.

they had interests in fashionable clubs including the celebrated Astor nightclub, the beloved haunt of the Underworld on a Friday night. By today's standards their exploits have paled into insignificance and, over the years, several of them have gone on to build respectable businesses.

Seemingly the beginning of the end of the Nashes came over a stupid fight following a minor car accident. Others, such as Bert Wickstead, who rose to become a Commander in the Flying Squad, read it as chance providing an opportunity for a significant move in the power-play for control of the West End.

Selwyn Keith Cooney, manager of the Billy-Aggie Hill-owned New Cabinet Club in Gerrard Street, and no friend of the Nashes, was in a relatively minor car accident with one driven by hostess Vicky James, known as 'Blonde Vicky' and a friend of Ronnie Nash. Cooney, instead of doing the more sensible thing and forgetting about the matter, sent the bill for 54/9d for the damage to the girl. She was not insured and the bill remained unpaid. Quite by chance Cooney met Ronnie Nash in a Notting Hill drinking club. Words were exchanged and each suffered a black eye in the subsequent fight. Two days later Cooney went to the Pen Club, said to have been bought with the proceeds from a robbery at the Parker Pen Company and named as an Underworld joke, in Duvall Street near Spitalfields Market. It was a club which was frequently raided by the police and, almost as regularly, it changed hands.

Reports of the background to the incident on 7 February 1960 vary. Apart from Wickstead's theory one version is that Jimmy 'Trunky' Nash, who worked as a minder at the Astor Club in the West End in which the family had an interest, set out to avenge his brother's beating. Another is that Jimmy, the mildest of the brothers, was sucked into the incident.

Jimmy, together with his red-headed girlfriend, a hostess named Doreen Masters, Joey Pyle and another former boxer, John Read, arrived at the Pen Club a little while after Cooney. According to witnesses Cooney was pointed out to Nash by Doreen Masters and, together with Pyle and Read, he went straight over, broke Cooney's nose with one blow and proceeded to give him a severe beating. 'That will teach you to give little girls a spanking,' he said. Cooney, protesting he had done nothing of the kind, fought back and there was a cry 'He's got a gun.' Two witnesses were adamant that Nash then shot Cooney in the head at point-blank range.

17

Others in the club then attacked Nash and Read, who was hit over the head with a bottle. They ran out of the club and Nash was driven away by Pyle whilst Doreen Masters drove off with Read. Two witnesses in the club were brought in for questioning. The first was Cooney's girlfriend, a 19-year-old barmaid from the New Cabinet, Joan Bending. The second was Johnny Simons, who had hit Read over the head with a bottle. Both were to point the finger at Jimmy Nash, Pyle and Read. Joan Bending had picked out both Pyle and Read at an identification parade.

Two days later James Nash surrendered himself at City Road police station. He, Pyle, Read and Doreen Masters were charged with the capital murder of Selwyn Cooney. What followed was one of the worst examples of post-war witness interference and jury intimidation.

It began on 16 March with a razor attack on Johnny Simons in a Paddington café. His face needed twenty-seven stitches to repair it. The assault was followed by two on his girlfriend, a 23-year-old model, Barbara Ibbotson. On the first occasion she was snatched in broad daylight in Soho, and thrown into a car where her face was slashed four times. Three weeks later she was the victim of another attack when three men broke into her flat whilst she was taking a bath, held her under water and slashed her again. This time she received wounds also requiring twenty-seven stitches. Now Bending and Simons accepted the police protection offered them.

The trial began on 21 April with the public gallery filled with 'faces' including members of the Billy Hill organization, and the Kray twins as well as the Nash family in force. Only Nash, Pyle and Read stood trial; the charges against Doreen Masters had been dismissed.

Of the ten male jurors one, who was later found to have a conviction for dishonesty as a juvenile, had appeared to nod towards Billy Nash in the public gallery. The police overheard a remark that one of the jury was to be nobbled, and a watch was kept on this particular juror. One day after court he was followed by officers who had seen a young man run away from his car. 'You won't catch me putting a foot wrong now,' he said with the emphasis on *now*. Meanwhile it seems that one of the two women on the jury, a Mrs Doris Reed, had a husband on remand in Brixton. He is alleged to have told Nash, Pyle and Read that his wife had made up her mind that Nash was guilty of capital murder.

The facts were reported to the judge by both the prosecution and defence, and on 25 April Mr Justice Gorman discharged the first jury.

In the second trial the defence case was reached and a surprise witness, David Sammons, was called to say that at the time Cooney had been shot Johnny Simons had been drinking in another bar, and that Joan Bending was so drunk she had had to be helped out of the bar before the fight. Pyle and Read were acquitted on 2 May and then next day James Nash gave evidence that he had never had a gun but that he had hit Cooney 'twice on the nose with my fist because of the things he was saying'.

The all-male jury took ninety-eight minutes to acquit Nash of Cooney's murder, but at a second trial which began an hour later he was found guilty of causing grievous bodily harm and was sentenced to five years' imprisonment. For his part in the affair Pyle received a sentence of eighteen months, and that was the last substantial sentence he received for thirty years.

Now with the Nashes seemingly vulnerable, the police mounted a campaign against them which ended when several of the family and friends were found in a club in Queen's Gardens, Bayswater with, so it was said, guns, something they vehemently denied. Prison sentences followed.

On his release from the assault charge Pyle kept well in the background but it was he who advised small-time villain, Michael Perry, to go to *The Times* over his blackmailing by three policemen, which led to the great inquiry of 1969 and the subsequent gaoling of the officers.

In 1971 Pyle's home was searched when the police were looking for Sewell, the killer of Superintendent Richardson in Blackpool, and, it was alleged, a firearm and ammunition had been found there. In the summing-up at his trial, the judge told the jury that to acquit Pyle would mean that the police officers had committed perjury. They did. Some months later one of the officers on the search, Harold Hannigan, was found guilty of trying to bribe a Sussex detective. He was given a conditional discharge by Mr Justice Melford Stevenson, who called him 'a very, very, conceited fool', and advised him to see a psychiatrist.

In 1978 Pyle was suspected of having helped actor John Bindon flee to Dublin after an incident in which John Darke, a small-time thief and police informer, was hacked to death at the Ranelagh Yacht Club, Fulham. Bindon, charged with murder, later returned and was found not guilty. The charge of perverting the course of justice against Pyle was dropped. He now became interested in unlicensed boxing and at one time was said to have had a share in the contract of a prominent South London light-heavyweight.

In 1984 his name surfaced once more when police opposing the granting of a pub licence to a former football star alleged that he was being backed by Pyle who, they said, had been involved with international crime figures. They also alleged he had been building a South London empire of clubs and pubs based on protection. Pyle challenged this, saying, 'I'm no gangster. Of course I know villains but I also know very respectable people.' Later another allegation against him was that he had close links with the Mafia.

In December 1992 time ran out for him. He was admired by many as one of the great masterminds of the London criminal scene, and certainly was a man whom the police wished to see go down. His case also involved drugs and many of the fraternity thought his fourteen years' sentence at the Old Bailey excessive. He was found guilty, along with Reggie Kray's 'adopted' son Peter Gillett, who was sentenced to eight years, in a conspiracy to supply £175,000 of opium and heroin substitute.[21] A third man, 62-year-old Frank Tyson, also received a sentence of eight years.

In June 1991 their trial had begun with a plea from the police that the jury at Southwark Crown Court should be given round-the-clock protection. Judge Gerald Butler refused the request, but after three jurors alleged they had received threats or were offered bribes the case was stopped and transferred to the Old Bailey for a re-trial. This time the jury received protection.

The evidence against Pyle had come from a 'businessman' Richard Green aka Ledingham who, needing money, had borrowed £20,000 from Pyle to be repaid with interest at £500

---

[21] Whilst serving a sentence for conspiracy to rob, Peter Gillett became the protégé and later 'adopted son' of Reggie Kray. On his release he endeavoured to build himself a career as a pop singer and TV celebrity. He was partially successful and cut some records including 'Closet Queen' and 'Masquerade'. A visit to an island off Sri Lanka for Network Seven with former tennis player turned TV presenter Annabel Croft and others was not a noted success. Ms Croft was less than complimentary about his behaviour and he faded from the screen. There is a perceptive interview with him in Duncan Campbell's *That Was Business, This Is Personal*.

per week. 'Standard in the motor trade' said Pyle, according to Green. Green managed to repay the £20,000 but still owed the interest and, he claimed, Pyle asked him if he would sell on some heroin at £28,000 a kilo. Green, who at the time of the trial was said to have a contract of £50,000 on his head, went to the police. Over a period of six months undercover officers, including one who became a secretary at Pyle's offices at Pinewood Studios, then taped the series of conversations which led to his conviction and sentence.

John Bindon also left the scene. He died in October 1993, it was said of cancer, but, more probably, of an AIDS-related illness – the death certificate said broncho-pneumonia – from which he had been suffering for some time. A small-time criminal with convictions for petty violence and living off immoral earnings, he had starred with Carol White in *Poor Cow*, one of the kitchen-sink dramas beloved in the 1960s. His greatest claim to fame had been the number of beautiful women with whom he had associated, maintaining that Princess Margaret had been one of them. There is little supporting evidence for this claim, save that they were on the West Indian island of Mustique at the same time and that Her Royal Highness came across Bindon whilst he was posing naked on the beach. There is a photograph of them together, with Bindon wearing a tee-shirt emblazoned 'Enjoy Cocaine'. Certainly model Vicki Hodge, the baronet's daughter with whom Bindon lived on and off for a stormy ten years, was in the number and proud of it.

It was during their relationship that he came to the aid – with a machete, so he told the court – of his friend, Roy Dennis, who was being attacked by Johnny Darke, one of the well-known family, at the Ranelagh Yacht Club on 21 November 1978. This was not the version of the prosecution, who maintained Darke's death was a contract killing by Bindon for a fee of £10,000 said to have been put up by a John Twomey. It was difficult for the police to establish the pattern of things because by the time they reached the yacht club most of the debris had been stowed away. Darke, acquitted of a wages snatch at BOAC in 1969 and the leader of the South London Wild Bunch, had been a police informer for some years. He had been paid £850 for information about men arrested for armed robbery in October 1977. The previous year he had been acquitted of murder. In 1978 there had been a contract of £5,000 on his life after he had spirited

21

away a consignment of marijuana. It was thought he was about
to rip off another drugs dealer when he died. An associate said of
him, 'He was the type of man who would carry a knife into
church.'

Aided, so said the police, by Joey Pyle and Lennie Osborne,
the severely wounded Bindon fled to Dublin, wrapped in a red
blanket to hide the blood, accompanied by a girlfriend, a former
Bunny girl and friend of football manager Malcolm Allison.
Others suggested the flight was with the connivance of the police
in return for help given. Some witnesses suggested it was the girl
who had given Bindon the 10-inch knife with which he killed
Darke. He had it, so he said, for protection from a mysterious
Mr X, 'an 18-stone lunatic', who knew about his previous
existence and threatened him in some unspecified way. For fear
of prejudicing the outcome, an episode of the popular TV series
Hazell, in which Bindon played a heavy, was postponed until
after his trial. He returned of his own accord to face the charges
and was charged with murder and affray along with Raymond
Bohm and George Galbraith, friends of Darke. Lennie Osborne
and Ernest Begbe, who were also charged, failed to appear at the
Central Criminal Court. Meanwhile rival factions staged benefits; Flash Harry Hayward, landlord of the Harp of Erin and
brother of Billy who had been involved in the Richardson fight at
Mr Smith and the Witchdoctor's Club, supported Darke's
widow, whilst Dave Barry, a long-time friend of Spot and Billy
Hill, organized one for Bindon.

The evidence that it was a contract killing came from the
familiar source of a cell-mate to whom Bindon was said to have
confessed. The £10,000 contract was the story of prisoner William
Murphy, also on trial for murder. Asked why he grassed Bindon,
he piously replied, 'I don't think it's right people should go
around killing other people and getting paid for it.'

In giving evidence in his defence Bindon described the incident
as 'almost like a ballet', presumably from *Gayaneh*. Bindon was
stabbed in the chest and eye and, so he said, Darke was
threatening him saying, 'I'll cut your head off.' 'I held my arm
out with my knife in it. I was trying to keep him off me . . .' said
Bindon.

For a time after his acquittal in December 1979 Bindon – for
whom actor Bob Hoskins had given evidence, calling him 'Biffo
the Bear' and so obtaining a rebuke from the trial judge – was

temporarily lionized by London's café society. One of his party tricks was to get down on all fours and thump the floor asking, 'What's it like down there, Darkey?' His particular trick, however, was to balance a number of half-pint beer glasses on his erect penis; this was done by inserting the member through the handles rather than balancing them budgerigar style.

Bohm and Galbraith were not so fortunate. They received three and four years respectively for their part in the affray.

As the years passed Bindon faded from the scene. In the long run the case had done his television career no good and he appeared in magistrates' courts throughout London on minor charges on an irregular basis. He had always been a 'Jack the Lad' and there is a story that a journalist found him near his home in Chelsea at the wrong end of the attentions of a George Wright. Mr Wright, who died in 1976, had apparently pointed a gun at Bindon's head and said, 'Go on, John, now lick the sole of my other shoe.' He was, he said, trying to teach Bindon some discipline.

By the end of his life Bindon[22] was in a sorry state, racked with pain and drawing social security. 'I couldn't go and see him,' says one London face, 'he'd see it in my eyes, no matter how I tried to hide it.'

If Bindon ended his life alone, Lennie Osborne ended his in disgrace. After such a good start, he went bent on his former friends and colleagues and became a supergrass.

Meanwhile, back in the 1960s, with the Nashes out of the way the path was clear for two brothers who were to some extent their protégés. Ronnie and Reggie Kray built an empire in the East and West End.[23]

The East End had always had a series of 'Guv'nors,' most of whom had flourished over a period of years with little or nothing to show for it at the end. They had, however, never thought to extend their territories, or if they had they were not capable of it. John Pearson describes some of them:

Jimmy Spinks, Timmy Hayes, old Dodger Mullins: none of them admirable men, but they were recognized for what

[22] John McVicar paid a tribute to John Bindon in *Lucky For Some* in the *Evening Standard* reprinted in *Prison Writing*, No.4 1994.
[23] John Pearson, *The Profession of Violence*, p.31. Reg Kray pays tribute to a number of these men in *Villains We Have Known*.

they were and did what many better men would like to have done. They never worked. They'd scare money out of bookmakers, publicans and successful shopkeepers. Dodger would work his own protection racket round all the small-time bookmakers calling each Monday for his 'pension'. Shopkeepers paid him something too; sort of insurance to keep the lesser tappers away.[24]

Even their brutality was memorable: 'Jimmy Spinks ordered some fish and chips, and when they cut up rough because he wouldn't pay, he threw the fish-shop cat in the frier.'

There were also the families who ran the London docks, such as the Butlers, and who did not need to extend their territory. An East End Londoner says:

The London Docks were No.6 and No.7 at Wapping and Bermondsey. If as a new boy I went onto a ship and there was thieving of say Ronson lighters, then I might be allowed to steal six. Everyone clubbed together to give the ship worker his cut. If you stole you had to chip in to Jimmy Butler who ran Scruttons, a big docking firm, or you paid the Collins or the Maddens. I reckon on the docks out of 3,000 then 2,000 was thieving.

Meanwhile in South-East London Charlie Richardson with his brother Eddie, said by some to be even smarter than his sibling, were also erecting a series of companies and an organization which set them apart from the other powerful South-East families of the time such as the Haywards, the Hennesseys and the Frenches. In Canning Town in the early 1960s there was what was derisorily known as the Brown Boot Gang. Members and affiliates dressed snappily, so they thought, in 50-guinea suits, but spoiled the image by wearing brown boots and the white stock favoured by East Enders. They did however prosper, and moved out to Noak Hill near Romford and points further East.

Even less known are some of the families who have controlled sections of West London, a more or less unchronicled hive of activity, including the Mills brothers one of whom, Alan, gave

[24] John Pearson, *The Profession of Violence*, pp.28–9.

evidence for the prosecution over the death of McVitie, and the Cannons, of whom Joey was the best known but not the most favoured amongst the fraternity.[25] Other well-known faces from South and North London, such as Ray Rosa and Bert Rossi, had clubs there.

Some of the families were involved in running prostitutes as well as club protection, but, 'The brasses weren't the sort of scrubber you saw in Park Lane, they were more film-star-like looking. I couldn't believe they were on the game,' recalls one habitué.

The Krays have had far more publicity than the head-below-the-parapet Richardsons which, if anything, may point to how much more intelligent the latter family was. Certainly their interests were better organized and their public profile less clear. They were perhaps unlucky to meet their downfall as they did – another fight in a club.

The lucky venue was Mr Smith and the Witchdoctor's, a barn of a place with cabaret and gambling in Catford. Again versions as to the reasons for the fight vary. The official version is that the Fraser–Eddie Richardson axis had been asked to take over what could be euphemistically described as security for the premises. Unfortunately no one had told the present incumbents, the Haywards and Hennesseys, that this was to happen. Another version is a splendid conspiracy theory that this was an attempt by the Krays – with whom the Richardsons were, at the time, in serious disagreement over the rights to provide security for a blue-film racket in the West End – to dispose of their rivals once and for all.

Frank Fraser in his memoirs suggests that, as is often the case, it may have been nothing more than domestic feuding:

> What I heard years later, and I think it's right, is what they were afraid of was really a domestic matter. Roy Porritt had worked for us, me and Eddie, on the machines. He was a great mechanic. He'd left us to go on his own but we were still friendly. Billy Hayward had been having it off with Roy's wife. Roy had found out and told her to drop it out

---

[25] Cannon gives a graphic account of running prostitutes in his book *Tough Guys Don't Cry*. He fell foul of a number of people in West London and was the subject of attacks in prison by men who suspected him of being too close to the authorities.

otherwise he'd tell us and there's no doubt we'd have been cross with Billy.[26]

Whatever the cause or causes may have been, fighting broke out about 3.30 a.m. A small-time villain and friend of the twins, Dickie Hart, produced a gun and shot Henry Rawlings. In turn Hart was shot dead. Fraser, who himself was badly injured with a bullet in his thigh, was acquitted of his murder. Eddie Richardson, Fraser, Billy Hayward and a number of others were convicted of affray and each received five years' imprisonment. Now the police, led by Gerald McArthur who earlier had been a leading investigator into the Great Train Robbery, made inroads into an empire of long-firm frauds, protection and violence. Charlie Richardson received ten years, as did Eddie and Fraser. Charlie Richardson also received five years for conspiracy to pervert the course of justice; he had tried to bribe a juror during the trial of his brother on the affray charge.

Was the meeting with the Haywards and Hennesseys for a show-down over control of the club planned? Probably not. If it was, where was the fearless East End hardman George Cornell, now a close friend of Fraser? It was he who had called Ronnie Kray 'a big fat poof' in what was meant to be a meeting of reconciliation at the Astor Club. Three days after the affray at Mr Smith's, Cornell was shot in the Blind Beggar in Whitechapel. He had been visiting another friend, Jimmy Andrews, who was in hospital having had his leg blown off in another shooting incident. It is unlikely that the Fraser–Richardson axis would have been without Cornell if they had planned trouble that night.

Ronnie Kray has it that he and his brother owned a small share of Mr Smith's.

---

[26] F. Fraser, *Mad Frank*, p. xi. There have been many accounts of the rise of the Kray twins and the Richardson family. Perhaps the best are John Pearson's *The Profession of Violence* and Robert Parker's *Rough Justice* describing the Krays and the Richardsons respectively. Another example of a domestic dispute is that of Ray Moore, brother of Charlie Kray's ex-wife Dolly. In October 1984 he was shot at close range by Thomas Murphy shortly after leaving the home of a relative in Eltham. For a time it was believed to be in connection with the Brinks–Mat robbery, and the police were also investigating Moore in relation to a lump fraud during the building of the £500 million Thames flood barrier. It turned out to be more prosaic: Murphy believed Moore had been involved with his wife.

. . . nothing heavy, nothing serious. Some said that the Richardsons had been tipped off that Reggie and I and half our firm would be in the club that night, and that was why they hit it. But only one member of our firm was there at the time – a young guy called Richard Hart, who was having a quiet drink. He was an extremely nice fellow, with a wife and little kids, but they shot him dead.

Richard Hart had to be avenged. No one could kill a member of the Kray gang and expect to get away with it. The problem was both of the Richardsons and Mad Frankie Fraser were in custody and likely to remain so. That left Cornell. He would have to pay the price. And let's face it, who better?[27]

One member of the Richardsons who survived the fight in Mr Smith's and the subsequent trial, and who later went on to far greater things, was James Alfred Moody. He helped carry the wounded Fraser out of the club and Eddie Richardson to hospital, and was acquitted of affray after a retrial.

Moody had always been a shadowy figure in the London Underworld. He was known as a hard man – his first conviction in 1967 was for manslaughter of a young Merchant Navy steward William Day, at a South London party, for which, along with Moody's brother, Richard, he received a six-years' sentence. It was his last conviction but by no means his last involvement in crime.

At school in Hackney he was said to be a mother's boy but later, a committed body-builder, he was enormously fit and strong. He became an invaluable member of the so-called Chainsaw Gang – and also of Billy Tobin's Thursday Gang – of the late 1970s, which specialized in hi-jacking, often with considerable violence, security vans in the South-East London area. On one occasion Moody, dressed as a policeman, jumped out of a car in the Blackwall Tunnel and forced a security van to stop. To prevent the alarm being given he took the keys from a

---

[27] R. and R. Kray, *Our Story*, pp. 71–2. Ronnie Kray is wrong; Charlie Richardson was not at that time in custody. He was in South Africa from where he returned to try to assist in his brother's defence. There have been numerous other suggestions over the reason for the fight. One is that it was set up by another South-East London family with feet in both camps who saw the chance to divide and rule. Given the volatility of members of the Underworld, particularly when in drink, there may be a bit of truth in each of them.

number of nearby motorists. The end for Tobin, and in a way Moody, came when he was arrested at Dulwich in the act of hijacking a security van with a mobile crane.[28] The ever-resourceful Moody escaped and hid out in a lock-up garage which he furnished with books, food, body-building equipment and a chemical toilet. Caught when he visited his son's flat in Brixton, he was charged with a series of robberies totalling £930,000 and sent to Brixton prison to await trial. In the 1980s it was still possible for remand prisoners to have food, wine and beer brought in by friends and relatives. Moody's brother Richard brought, with the Sunday lunches, hacksaw blades, drill bits and other tools.[29]

Moody had noticed that outside his cell was a flat roof and it was to this that he and cell-mates Gerard Tuite, a Provisional IRA bomb-maker, and Stanley Thompson, veteran of the Parkhurst prison riot of 1969 and now charged with armed robbery, cut through the brickwork. Every morning the rubble was removed in their chamber-pots at slopping-out time. On 16 December 1980 they pushed out the loosened brickwork of their cell, stepped on to the roof where a ladder had been left by roofers and were away.

Thompson need not have bothered. The escape took place whilst the jury was out in his trial at St Albans and, in his absence, they found him not guilty. Tuite was later arrested in Dublin, becoming the first person to be charged in Ireland with criminal offences committed in England. He received ten years. Richard received two years for the help he had given his brother.

And James Moody? He simply vanished. Some Underworld faces say they received irregular Christmas cards from him but, apart from that and an unsuccessful raid on a flat in West London where his fingerprints – and nothing else – were found, there was no sign at all for the next thirteen years.

[28] Billy Tobin had led a charmed life. He had been acquitted of a gin robbery in 1974, and a year later, despite the identification evidence of eight police officers, had been acquitted of a warehouse robbery. In March 1977 he was acquitted of a £115,000 robbery at the Express Dairy, Wembley and in 1978 was acquitted on ten counts of conspiracy to rob and possession of firearms with intent in relation to the £197,000 raid at the *Daily Mirror* offices during which a security guard was shot. It was in this case that Tobin alleged he had paid Hugh Moore, later Assistant Chief Constable for the City of London, for help. The allegation led to *Operation Countryman*. Finally Tobin received sixteen years for the Dulwich hi-jack.
[29] There is a full account of Moody's life and death in Cal McCrystal's 'The Hit at the Royal Hotel', *Independent on Sunday*, 8 August 1993.

Then on the night of 1 June 1993 while drinking at the bar of the Royal Hotel, Hackney, where he was known as Mick, he was shot dead by a man described as in his early forties and wearing a leather jacket. The man had ordered a pint of Foster's lager and put two coins down on the bar to pay for it. Then he had moved towards Moody and fired three shots. As Moody slumped to the floor, a fourth was fired into his back before the man was driven away in a stolen white Ford Fiesta XR2.

Where had he been and why was he shot? As to the first, there were suggestions that he had been hidden out by the Provisionals, but clearly he returned to England some years ago, if indeed he ever left. At the time of his death he had been living in Wadeson Street, a back alley off Mare Street in Hackney. As to why, one theory was that it was a killing done on behalf of a cuckolded husband, for Moody was very much a ladies' man – he is said to have required the services of a different woman each evening. A second version is that it was a part of the long-drawn-out struggle for power between the Arif family and other South London interests, and that it was in revenge for the killing of David Brindle in the Bell public house in Walworth in August 1991.

According to the prosecution evidence, on 11 March 1991 Patrick and Tony Brindle allegedly shot Ahmet Abdullah, known as Turkish Abbi, in a Walworth betting shop. They were both charged with the murder. This, it was said, followed the shooting of a Stephen Dalligan, a nephew of a senior London figure, Tony White.[30]

The killing of the Brindles' brother, David, was said to be in revenge for the death of Ahmet. The brothers were wrongly said to be the nephews of the old villain Frankie Fraser, and this led credence to the story that it was all part and parcel of a gang war. In fact Grace Brindle, their mother, is at pains to deny any family connection with the famous Frasers or Brindles. Now that he is dead the most convenient name in the frame for the killing of David is that of Jimmy Moody. Moody is also fancied for the killings of Terry Gooderham and his girlfriend Maxine Arnold in Epping Forest in December 1989, and antique and cocaine dealer Peter Rasini in Palmers

[30] One theory is that Dalligan had gone to the Connoisseur Club to act as a peacemaker following a quarrel between his brother Mark and Ahmet Abdullah.

29

Green in March 1991.[31] There is also speculation that he carried out the killing of Peter and Gwenda Dixon, whose bodies were found near an arms cache in 1989. It is thought that they stumbled upon him accidentally. Attributing all these deaths to Moody may, however, be another way of clearing up crimes.

As for Tony and Patrick Brindle, neither of whom had any convictions, they were both acquitted of Abdullah's murder after an extraordinary trial at the Central Criminal Court in which screens were fitted so that witnesses, who were identified by numbers and not by name, could not be seen by the defendants. Tony gave evidence that he had been playing cards in the Bell. Patrick did not give evidence. Their mother told the newspapers how they cried when their budgie had died, and of their partiality for helping old ladies cross busy roads. In their enigmatic way the police said that the inquiry into Turkish Abbi's death was now closed.

There is, however, another theory over David Brindle's death which fits the facts but has nothing to do with the overall game plan of the South London warlords. It was simply a personal matter:

It now turns out that Jimmy Moody was working in a pub at the back of Walworth under the name Tom. He'd been in

[31] On 24 March 1991, 47-year-old antiques dealer and cocaine user Peter Rasini was shot in the garden of his home in River Avenue, Palmers Green. A solo gunman had come behind him as he walked down his garden path and had shot him four times in the back. Loyally his family said they knew he had no enemies in the world. Maxine Arnold and her boyfriend Terry Gooderham were found shot dead in their black Mercedes in Epping Forest on 22 December 1989. Most likely she was a bystander; he may have been more of a player which resulted in what was certainly a gangland execution. As always a variety of suggestions were offered. Terry had an active life for he shared it with Maxine part of the week and another blonde woman, for the remainder. One suggestion was that there was a third Ms Gooderham in the background and she had organized the hit, but enquiries came to nothing. Nor did they in relation to the theory that he was involved with Brinks-Mat monies. Gooderham had been a stocktaker for a number of clubs and pubs in London and Hertfordshire and one anonymous friend put it, 'It is nothing to do with his love life or his own business but a lot of money is involved.'

There were claims that he had been the victim of part of a drugs war and indeed a small amount of drugs were found in the car, but the police became convinced these had been planted and were a red herring. Then there was a claim in the *Daily Mirror* on 4 January 1990 that he had tried to muscle-in on the lucrative Spanish ice-cream market and had so upset suppliers that a £50,000 contract was put out on him. Finally there was yet another solution offered. This time it was that the killing was over £150,000, euphemistically described as having been 'redirected'.

the area for ten years. He wasn't an out-and-out night-clubber so he could have been there and very, very few people would know who he was. He'd done quite a bit of bird and now he took it as a personal thing to keep out. It was a personal challenge for him. There's a lot of other guys been in that position and they've been out nightclubbing it and soon got caught. Jim did have that determination and single-mindedness to keep that low profile and trust no one. He could be stubborn and obstinate, a good man but a loner. He'd be content to do his work and watch the telly knowing that every day was a winner. That's how he would look at it. I think David had had a row with the publican and Jimmy had crept behind him and done him with a baseball bat. David was badly knocked about and told Jimmy it wouldn't be forgotten. Next night or a couple of nights later Moody and another man went into the Bell in East Street and shot David and a bystander. Immediately afterwards he went over to the East End.

Much as I knew Jim well, I can understand the feelings about David's death and that it was one that had to be done. I suppose if someone who knew it was going off had really pleaded for him it might have made some difference but I doubt it.[32]

Once Moody had been traced to Hackney it became common knowledge in South-East London that reprisals were to be taken, and Fraser absented himself from London on the night of the killing. No doubt a number of others did so as well.

As might be expected reaction to Moody's death was mixed. His son, Jason, an actor, told the *Sun*: 'I'm not ashamed of my dad, because he did what he did for his own reasons. All I know is he'd be proud I didn't turn out like him.'

David Brindle's mother appears to have been convinced her son was killed by Moody.

I'm glad Moody's dead. My family is overjoyed. The police rang to tell us this morning. He got it the way he gave it out. I'm glad he didn't die straight away – nor did David. That man was evil and I hope he rots in hell.[33]

[32] F. Fraser, *Mad Frank*, p. 221.
[33] *Sun*, 3 June 1993.

The Richardson empire toppled in 1965 and the Kray one some four years later. Theirs had been an endlessly recounted story of protection, long-firm frauds and a murder each. Ronnie had carried out his promise and shot down George Cornell in the Blind Beggar. Reggie had removed Jack 'The Hat' McVitie, a long term hardman now drinking heavily who, given money and orders to kill Leslie Payne, one-time financial adviser to the Firm, had not only conspicuously failed to do so but also had boasted about ripping off the twins.[34]

Another suggestion for the quarrel with the Richardsons is the refusal of that family to give up a lucrative car-park racket at Heathrow Airport. In fact Heathrow, or Thiefrow as it came to be known, was a long-time haven of criminal activities. In the 1960s and 1970s property was stolen almost at will. Part of the reason for the thefts was that at the time the Universal Postal Union required that registered mailbags had a distinguishing label so that special care could be taken for their protection – at the same time, giving special notice to a thief. Some thought the thieves were unfortunately amateurs with no real network for disposing of the millions which passed through their hands. An old-time villain laments:

> One time I dived in the river for a load of industrial diamonds which had just been chucked. £38,000 it came to. The people who'd nicked them didn't know what to do with them.

This was not the view of the authorities. In an investigation carried out by Captain John Gorman, then head of BOAC security, he found that the dead letter-box beloved of the spy story was being used. Thieves would put the stolen industrial diamonds in prearranged hiding places one of which was, rather chancily, under a stone beside the Great West Road. These would be collected later and the thief would receive £1,000 a few days later.[35]

Once the Krays were out of the way the police were keen to ensure no upstarts took over their patch. Certainly they had their

---

[34] There are a number of stories of McVitie in his heyday in F. Fraser, *Mad Frank*.
[35] P. Gladstone Smith, *The Crime Explosion*, p. 86. In 1970 Smith wrote that the annual loss in diamonds, jewellery etc. at Heathrow was £500,000, 30 per cent of which came from passengers' luggage, with only 20 per cent recovered.

eyes on a potential return by the Nash family but none materialized. Nipper Read recalls:

The work done by Harry Mooney [an officer on Read's squad] to put the lid on the East End had been so effective that no one was daring to occupy the vacuum left by the dismemberment of the Kray Firm. However, I was now to look at target criminals, and one North London gang fell neatly into my catchment area. They were the obvious first choice and we looked at them intently for a period of time, but they certainly weren't doing the things you would expect them to be doing if they had taken over from the Krays. They had one or two clubs in the West End who were paying them money but it was being done in a very different way from the Krays' regime of terror. It was really rather a friendly business with this gang – almost a two-way operation with benefits to both sides. We thought they would jump in and occupy the vacuum, but it never happened. I think they sensed that if they had done that they would have let themselves in for a major investigation and consequently all sorts of troubles. It was a good example of preventive policing.[36]

It was not until April 1972 that the Dixon brothers – also from the East End, and who had been fringe members of the Kray coterie – met their match in Commander Bert Wickstead, and it was he who brought down James Tibbs and members of his family six months later. In the latter trial particularly it appears that the complainants could just as easily have stood in the dock, and there are still many in the East End who believe that the Tibbs family was merely defending itself rather than making any pro-active moves towards domination of the East End.

Curiously that seems to have been the last prosecution of any protection racket in either the East or the West End by families or even individuals until 1990. That year Frank Salmon, a market trader from Dagenham who ran a small-time racket covering wine-bars, saunas and clubs, received seven and a half years at the Old Bailey.

South-East London was, however, a different proposition. It

---

[36] L. Read and J. Morton, *Nipper*, p.266.

was here that the powerful families controlled the Underworld community more or less untroubled by authority in their day-to-day life. It was over this world that the Arif family, Turkish Cypriots who settled in Rotherhithe, wielded substantial influence. They were the 'most heavily investigated criminal "firm" since the Krays.'[37] The Arif empire extended to clubs, pubs and restaurants – 'it doesn't matter whose name it is over the door of the pub in some areas, it's the Arifs who own it' – and for a time the head of the family (though the third brother), Dogan (born February 1949), owned the Gola League club, Fisher United. Principally their art-form was the armed robbery. The list of their convictions and unsuccessful prosecutions is a history of the 1970s and 1980s, as is the genealogy of the Arif family in which few of the brothers have not swum into the notice of the police.

Ozer's (b. September 1947) principal claim to fame was his acquittal in 1977 on a charge of the murder of security guard, David Cross, on the A2 near Dartford during an attack on a Securicor van in which £103,000 was stolen. Bekir (b. September 1953) was convicted of disposing of the guns used in the robbery and received five years. Ozer had already been convicted of a minor part in a West London bank robbery in 1975.

In 1981 under surveillance during the so-called police Operation Kate, Michael McAvoy, sentenced to twenty-five years' imprisonment in the Brinks-Mat robbery which netted £26 million of gold bullion in London on 26 November 1983, was photographed with a member of the family. At the end of Operation Kate, Dennis (b. April 1956) and Bekir were convicted of conspiracy to rob when they were seen too near another Securicor van, this time in Bromley.

On 27 November 1990 the police ambushed the Arifs in another raid on yet another Securicor vehicle as it toured the Reigate area delivering £750,000 to branches of Barclay's Bank. Kenny Baker, Dennis Arif, Mehmet (b. December 1950) and Anthony Downer (a close friend of sister Susan) were cornered when the police vehicle rammed their van. Dennis and Downer threw down their weapons; Mehmet and Kenny Baker did not. Baker was shot dead and Mehmet wounded.

At the trial, at which Mehmet and Downer pleaded guilty and received eighteen years apiece, Dennis Arif ran the ingenious – if

---

[37] N. Darbyshire with B. Hilliard, *The Flying Squad*, p.5.

difficult to establish – defence of duress. He owed Baker £60,000 in gaming debts and Baker had threatened to shoot him if he did not pay it back. As a result he had taken part in the raid. This defence was not a great success; the police had been able to show that both he and the late Mr Baker had been at a family wedding at the Savoy earlier in the year. Dennis Arif received a sentence of twenty-two years.

Dogan was already in gaol serving fourteen years for his involvement in an £8.5 million drug-smuggling plot for which Eddie Richardson received twenty-five years. In 1983 Dogan had been acquitted of taking part in a bogus arms deal designed to separate the Ayatollah Khomeni from £34 million. Bekir followed shortly after Mehmet and Dennis when he was caught in another police trap, this time in Norwood.

The Arifs had integrated well with the South-East London community. Apart from their sister Susan's relationship with Anthony Downer, Dogan's brothers-in-law include Peter and Terry Cunningham, serving eight and sixteen years respectively for conspiracy to steal and rob and firearms offences. James Coleman, another brother-in-law, had been acquitted of the murder of Peter Hennessey, one of the brothers who owned the Dog and Bell in Peckham.

Meanwhile the North London teams seem to have been keeping their heads out of the range of police fire. Reports are that nothing much has changed in the territory, with the two most powerful families seeming to have reached at least a temporary accommodation. The East End, thought perhaps to be unified under Kray control in the 1960s, is now split into areas with one family and friends in control of Canning Town and another masterminding operations in Barking. Others operate in Bow and Stepney. In part they are based on school acquaintance-ships, as well as allegiance to football clubs and in particular Millwall.

2

London –
the Robbers and the Others

Crime in London is not, and never has been, purely family-controlled. There have always been a number of individuals and joint enterprises which have worked either independently of, or in conjunction with, the fraternal businesses. Nevertheless family ties do bind more than friendship. A traditional way of solving crime has been through the use of the informer, or by persuading a minor member of the operation that he, or sometimes she, is better off in the witness box than in the dock. The annals of criminal trials are littered with witnesses who have shared cells with prisoners and who have heard from them a valuable and timely confession denied to the police. One instance of the former is the Kray case, where Read was successful in persuading a number of fringe players to 'go QE'. Indeed, a good part of the art of detective work is turning or bending the small fry as it is known. Curiously, if the defence attempts to bend back that same small fry it is known as conspiracy to pervert. The Bindon trial is an example of the use of the cell-mate who has heard the hitherto silent defendant cough his lot.

In the 1970s, however, a new breed of witness was born. It was the era of the supergrass; usually an armed robber who had seen daylight fading through the prospect of prison bars and had decided to tell all he knew about his former colleagues in return for a nominal sentence, served very often in a police station and accompanied by booze, television, evenings out with his minding officers and sometimes conjugal visits. The first of these re-formed villains was Bertie Smalls, who gave his name to the

phrase 'to do a Bertie' or to inform.[1] He secured the best deal of
them all. Much to the fury of Mr Justice Lawton he was never
prosecuted. He was followed in quick succession by Maurice
O'Mahoney, who wrote a book about his life and time, Charlie
Lowe, Billy Amies, Leroy Davies and dozens of others. All were
keen to repent at the expense of their friends and, for a time, with
lawyers not knowing how to cross-examine them effectively and
with help from the trial judges, very successful they were too.
Instead of the fifteen and twenty years' imprisonment terms they
merited, and which were handed to their former friends, they
received fives. Then as the years went by, and the convictions
mounted, juries became more sceptical. It was apparent that
some of the behaviour of the Crown's witnesses was infinitely
worse than that of the driver on a minor bank robbery. Billy
Amies who, dressed as a policeman, had threatened his victim
with castration and had the man's daughter stripped to her
underwear, asking, 'How would you like to see your daughter
raped?', could not have appealed very much to jurors. He named
fifty-eight criminals but was responsible for the conviction of less
than half a dozen.

It also became clear that these men were not completely born
again. A number of them returned to their old trade. Donald
Barrett was allowed to become a supergrass on two occasions
and survived to tell the tale, but David Smith, who had actually
killed a man and received five years for his part in over sixty
robberies, soon took up where he had left off. On 29 September
1986 he was caught in a raid on a Securicor vehicle in Golders
Green and five days after his birthday on 8 October, in a cell still
festooned with balloons to mark the occasion, he cut his throat
with a razor-blade.

Some, however, were much tougher. One figure from the 1970s
who re-surfaced and survived, in a little reported case, was Bertie
Smalls' immediate successor in the supergrass stakes, the self-styled
'King of the Squealers' Maurice O'Mahoney, now known as Peter
Davies. In the summer of 1993 he was to be found in the dock at the
Old Bailey flaunting a Flying Squad tie and charged with robbery.

---

[1] At the time when Smalls dictated his epoch-making statement, a 'very senior detective
who knows the form book backwards' estimated that there was a pool of some 3,000
criminals in London readily available for bank robberies. J.A. Mack, *The Crime Industry*,
p.60. Recruiting for jobs was often done on an *ad hoc* basis in such clubs as the A&R and
the Log Cabin in Wardour Street, see J. Morton, *Gangland*, p. 230.

Following his successful career as a bank robber, and a subsequent equally gratifying one as a supergrass, O'Mahoney kept out of public vision until he was arrested in Reading in 1990 on a charge of shoplifting. He had been found, along with his young son, pushing a shopping trolley out of a store. His defence was that he was on his way to the electrical department to obtain some guarantees before paying. The case was stopped by magistrates at the committal proceedings.

Three years later his defence to a charge of robbery was that it was a snatch carried out on the instructions of the police to incriminate another man. In the witness-box he told a strange story. After his acquittal at Reading, when curiously his custody record had disappeared, his cover was blown. He now tried to see a senior officer whose job it had been to protect supergrasses, and received no substantial help. In the November he went to see a DI whom he knew at Brixton police station, and asked what help he could have. Again there was a negative response, but this time O'Mahoney asked when and where the station's Christmas party would be held. He entered the raffle, which carried the first prize of a ticket to Paris.

According to O'Mahoney he was later contacted by a DI, the man whom he had seen at Brixton police station, and asked to carry out a small commission for him. What the police wanted, said O'Mahoney, was for him to carry out a smash-and-grab at a sub-post office, leave behind the main money and instead take a money-bag containing £250 worth of 20p pieces from outside a post office in Shepherd's Bush. The robbery was to take place on 30 June. The idea was that when O'Mahoney handed the bag over to the police they would then plant the money on another man.

O'Mahoney went on to say that, since he had packed in the job of supergrass, or more probably it had packed him in, and he had served his five-year sentence in Chiswick police station, he was a frequent visitor to Briefs wine bar, a popular haunt of villains, barristers, solicitors and the police, not necessarily in that order, which was opposite Inner London Crown Court in Newington Causeway. Briefs had been opened by three police officers who had subsequently left the Metropolitan Police, along with solicitor Michael Relton who later had received twelve years' imprisonment for his part in laundering the money from the Brinks-Mat robbery. O'Mahoney told the court he spent much of his time in Briefs, and his function in life was collecting and laundering money and generally helping Relton. The wine bar was one which, from time to time, had been placed off-limits by Commissioners.

According to O'Mahoney's evidence he was introduced at the Brixton party to an officer known as Basher, whom he said had acquired the nickname because, every time he was drunk, he started to fight. It was then the proposition was put to him and it was suggested he should recruit someone who was clean to carry out the raid with him.

O'Mahoney found a man in Bristol and duly appeared in Shepherd's Bush. A white Ford Escort car was, he said, to be near the shop and a red one for the getaway outside a local public house, the Fox and Hounds. As he looked round the area before the robbery he saw a Rover motor vehicle with three officers in it, as well as two mounted police officers near by. Something, he told the court, was wrong. He had intended to do the snatch himself but now he sent the other man in. It was completed but the alarm went off. The man got back into O'Mahoney's car, and as he did so the police started shooting.

In the car provided by the police, according to O'Mahoney, was a bag of guns – one a starting pistol, a second which had been tampered with – and cartridges which had been sprayed with oil. The effect of this would make them extremely unreliable. He maintained, and there was no evidence to contradict him, that neither he nor his friend ever shot back.

According to the Home Office expert eight shots were fired, all by the police. O'Mahoney never attempted to reach the exchange getaway car; instead he took to his feet, was caught and taken to Shepherd's Bush police station where DS Fuller, who had looked after O'Mahoney when he was in custody in Chiswick in his supergrass days, arrived. The custody record showed that no one knew who O'Mahoney was, and that Fuller took his prints to identify him. According to O'Mahoney, Fuller told him that everything would be sorted out.

In the witness-box O'Mahoney listed the officers with whom, he said, he had had corrupt dealings going back as far as the early 1970s. Efforts to suggest that he had turned up uninvited to the Christmas party and had been summarily booted out foundered when he produced his winning raffle ticket which, sensibly, he had not cashed.

It was, wrote Duncan Campbell of his behaviour in the witness-box, '. . . a virtuoso performance. The prosecution dismissed his case as rubbish but the jury acquitted him.'[2]

As Campbell went on to write, this has left Mahoney in something of a dilemma and his lawyer, Adrian Neale, wrote to the Home Office and indeed went to see the Home Secretary, Kenneth Baker, asking for a guarantee of his client's safety. He has been given no promises. An inquiry by the Police Complaints Authority carried out before the trial exonerated the officers involved in the Shepherd's Bush case.

Certainly the greatest British robbery in terms of money obtained rather than in public interest had been the 26 November 1983 Brinks-Mat case. With £26 million, even allowing for inflation, it dwarfed the Great Train Robbery as the most successful operation of its kind, but neither it nor its perpetrators ever captured the imagination of the public in the same way. A good deal of this has to do with the reporting restrictions imposed by the Criminal Justice Act 1967. Before then, every week when defendants in custody were brought before the court the prosecution would outline the facts of the case to the magistrates, particularly the most unattractive ones from the defence point of view. They would be duly reported in the early editions of the evening papers. The 1967 Act imposed substantial restrictions on what could be reported in the papers without the consent of the defendants. In a flash all the fun went out of local court reporting, and people who week by week had been front-page national figures were relegated to a small paragraph on page seven.

The Brinks-Mat robbery was another example of the escalation in violence offered to victims. At 6.40 a.m. the robbers, wearing balaclavas and armed with machine guns, burst into the vaults of the Brinks-Mat security company near Heathrow and terrorized the guards. Two had the crotches of their trousers cut open and petrol poured on them; the team leader then threatened to set fire to them or to cut off their penises. £26 million, in the form of 6,800 gold bars waiting to be sent to the Middle and Far East, was loaded and transferred into waiting vans.

[2] *Guardian*, 16 July 1993.

It was really only a matter of days before the police latched on to the last guard to arrive that morning – Tony Black – who had missed the robbery because he was ten minutes late for work. Black confessed. His sister was living with Brian Robinson, one of a number of villains over the years known as 'The Colonel'. Robinson had been on the Williams & Glyn's robbery in 1978 and in 1981 had benefited through the mistakes of the No.5 Regional Crime Squad.[3] Black identified two more of the team, Tony White and Michael McAvoy.

In December 1984 Robinson and McAvoy received twenty-five years each; White was acquitted. Later there was said to be £50,000 on offer to free McAvoy and Robinson. Black, who had given evidence for the Crown, was handed a six-year sentence. 'Never again will your life be safe. You will be segregated at all times and you and your family will forever be fugitives from those you so stupidly and wickedly helped,' said the judge, the late Mr Justice David Tudor-Price, in another of the homilies senior judges like to hand down, for the benefit more of the press than the defendants who no doubt know it already.

That still left a number of villains at large and a very large amount of property missing. The gold had been in marked ingots of extremely high quality. It could not be offered to legitimate dealers; instead it was being smelted by a small bullion firm, Scadlynn, on the outskirts of Bristol.

A surveillance operation on another suspect, Kenneth Noye, ended in disaster. An undercover police officer, John Fordham, clad in a balaclava helmet, was stabbed to death in the grounds of Noye's home at West Kingsdowne in Kent. Noye, charged with the murder of Fordham, gave evidence that, 'I just froze with horror. All I saw when I flashed my torch on this masked man was just the two eye-holes and the mask. I thought that was my lot. I thought I was going to be a dead man.'

---

[3] Robinson was one of a number of criminals who were known as 'The Colonel'. The most famous example is Ronnie Kray and another is George Copley. It was Copley who was instrumental in sabotaging the efforts of the No.5 Regional Crime Squad when in June 1981 he and Frankie Fraser junior, a nephew of 'the great man', were on trial at Oxford on charges of robbery. Three months previously a Sergeant Pook visited him in Reading gaol and was secretly taped by Copley in a conversation in which Pook confirmed an offer that if Copley was to admit his part in the Williams & Glyn's robbery (another problem for the City of London Police) and also give evidence of corruption against certain London detectives, he would receive only a five-year sentence. The tape was produced at the trial and the case was stopped. It was 'hopelessly compromised' said Stephen Wooler for the Director of Public Prosecutions.

And, as the jury found, in self-defence he stabbed Fordham eleven times. In November 1985, Noye and Brian Reader, who was with him at the time, were acquitted of murder. In July of 1986 both were convicted of handling the Brinks-Mat gold, along with Garth Chappell, a Scadlynn director. Reader received nine years and Noye, whose defence was that he was a gold smuggler and VAT fraudster as opposed to being a thief and receiver, ended up with fourteen years. However, there are still plenty of figures in the Underworld who believe that his defence was correct. No Brinks-Mat gold was ever found on his premises and, although £100,000 of gold was discovered, tests showed this could not have been from the Brinks-Mat robbery. Garth Chappell received ten years, whilst Matteo Constantino, 68, a long-standing Hatton Garden villain who had allowed his company to be used in a false VAT claim, received a suspended sentence of twelve months for conspiracy to evade VAT on the gold. After being melted down it had then been delivered in small parcels to London. The gold was sold on the legitimate market, mainly to dishonest dealers who were charged VAT at 15 per cent. Constantino had been acquitted of dishonest handling and was suffering from cancer at the time.

The convictions of Noye and Reader were the greatest successes the police had on the Scadlynn side of things. The next year John Palmer, a former director of Scadlynn who had been invited to leave Spain by the authorities and who chose to be deported to Britain from Rio de Janeiro, was put on trial at the Old Bailey. Charged that he conspired with Noye and Reader to dishonestly handle the gold, he was acquitted and went to live off the proceeds of his time-share business in Tenerife.

Nor was there any greater success in the case of John Fleming who was deported from Florida in 1986. In March of the next year, with evidence given against him by a new supergrass, Patrick Diamond, Fleming was charged with dishonestly handling nearly £500,000 of the Brinks-Mat proceeds. At the committal proceedings at Horseferry Road Magistrates' Court, he was found to have no case to answer. Fleming told reporters, 'I feel a great relief. It has been a bad year,' before he returned to Spain where he was involved in a car accident and again deported. He was back in London in December 1993 when he was attacked in the Horseferry Road near Victoria Station, receiving wounds which required some forty stitches.

1991 had been a fatal year for Noye's former friend, 43-year-old Nick Whiting, who ran a garage at Wrotham in Kent. Whiting had been questioned back in 1983 over a Range Rover sold to Noye and bought back. Now on 6 June Whiting vanished from the garage along with five cars. At first it seemed to be a straightforward kidnapping, but when all the cars stolen in the raid on his garage were recovered within a few days unkind suggestions came on offer, including one that Whiting had staged his own disappearance over the Brinks-Mat spoils and that he had gone on the run with a friend of his, Lennie 'Little Lew', who was also wanted in connection with Brinks-Mat.

Ex-racing driver Whiting had secured a plot of land during the period of falling property prices and had borrowed bent money to finance a building deal. One suggestion was that the mortgagor wanted his money back. A variation on the theme is that Whiting owed money on the cars. At the beginning of June his body was found in marshland in Essex, nearly a month after his abduction; it appeared he had been beaten up, bound hand and foot, and stuffed in a car boot. He had then been shot in the back of the head, seemingly after being frog-marched across at least three miles of boggy ground.

As for McAvoy and Robinson, they were awaiting the hearing of their appeals when Fordham was stabbed and realized that, without a substantial sweetener, any slim chance they had of getting a few years off their twenty-five years had evaporated with his death. They put up a deal to DAC Brian Worth. If they gave back half their share of the bullion, then a good word could be put in to the Court of Appeal. The proposition foundered when they found their friends on the outside and in possession would ante up perhaps a million or two, but nothing like the required amount required for any possible reduction. McAvoy, in particular, was annoyed. He wrote from Leicester prison in November 1986 that he was considering informing, he was not going to be 'fucked for my money and still do the sentence'. But when it came to it he was not prepared to turn informer.[4]

The Brinks-Mat laundering trials continued into the 1990s, by which time several of those convicted early on in the proceedings, such as solicitor Michael Relton, had been released. In November 1991, after five months of evidence, the trial of McAvoy's ex-

---

[4] N. Darbyshire with B. Hilliard, *The Flying Squad*, p.232.

wife Jacqueline, Gordon Parry, Brian Perry, Jean Savage, Patrick Clark and his son, Stephen, was halted by Judge Henry Pownall who would not reveal the reason but told the jury, 'Believe me, it is a proper reason.'

By 1993 Noye was in Latchmere House in Richmond, Surrey, once a boys' remand centre but now a resettlement centre for villains coming to the end of their sentences. The regime is fairly relaxed, with the men allowed out to work during the day and being given extensive weekend leave. It was believed that Noye had been involved in a plan to import cocaine from America as well as laundering dirty money. Unfortunately it appears that a detective may have tipped off one of Noye's partners in the operation, as a result of which a shipment of drugs was cancelled. It is said that Noye paid £500 to the police officer for the information.

It is not the first time that Noye has been involved in bribery since his imprisonment. In 1988 he is said to have offered £1 million to a senior officer who, in turn, was cleared of any misconduct.[5]

In real terms little of the Brinks-Mat money has been recovered, and civil actions have been started to try to retrieve some of the outstanding losses. Several actions have already been settled by those convicted.

McAvoy was probably right when he decided to observe the code of silence. In recent years, and in contrast to the days when Smalls and the others walked about seemingly impervious to the large prices said to be on their heads, informers have had a hard time. In turn the police have gone to lengths to try to convict those they suspect of killing them. After all, if they do not, then potential informers may get discouraged.

In February 1989 informer Alan 'Chalky' White was killed. He was last seen walking to the off-licence in Minchington, Gloucestershire to get some lager. Three months later his body, wrapped in a blue tarpaulin, was spotted by a family at the Cotswold Water Park near Cirencester. He had been stabbed in the heart.

White, who had several minor convictions, was due to give evidence against a Danny Gardiner with whom, so White said, he had robbed a petrol station in Stroud netting £4,800 in 1986.

---

[5] *Sunday Times*, 5 December 1993.

White, who had a drug problem, had declined the police offer of a new identity. He was given a 'panic button' to use if he felt threatened, but most nights he could be found in the local Crown public house. With the death of White, the case against Danny Gardiner collapsed and he went abroad.

With the help of Interpol the police conducted inquiries in Egypt – where Mr Gardiner was wrongly reported to have died in Cairo – France, Spain, Morocco and Israel. On 4 January 1991 Mr Gardiner flew back voluntarily from Tel Aviv. He had been found there working in a tourist hotel, having apparently entered the country under a false name. Gardiner was later convicted of White's murder.

In 1990 another informer was killed. He had previously told the police of a planned contract killing resulting in the arrest of the hit-man. Before the trial the judge accepted the argument of the defence that it needed access to police information; this would have meant a disclosure of the identity of the informant, and the trial was abandoned by the prosecution. At the time of his death, the man had been resettled in Germany – the cost of relocating an informer, names, passports and driving licences for him and his family, is around £100,000 – and he was murdered shortly afterwards.

A second killing occurred in Amsterdam and involved a man who had given police information about a gang of drug traffickers; and the third, early in 1993, was in Ireland. It seems the link to the identification of the informant had come about through the withdrawal of the case by the prosecution.

In May 1993 the trial of four men, whom the prosecution alleged brought over hired killers from Northern Ireland to dispose of supergrass David Norris, collapsed with little publicity at the Old Bailey. Indeed, for such an important case the press had been remarkably silent. After nearly six weeks the trial, which had cost almost £1 million, was halted when the Recorder of London, Judge Lawrence Verney, ruled that the evidence of the two main prosecution witnesses, Renwick Dennison and Stuart Warne, was unsafe for the jury to rely on. Patrick Doherty, George McMahon (both from South London), Terence McCrory from Belfast and John Green from Falkirk, were all acquitted.

The prosecution had outlined a curious but ultimately not compelling story of hitmen hired through Northern Ireland drug dealers who were promised cheap cannabis in return for the completion of the contracts. Two men who were never arrested, Thomas McCreery and Stephen Pollock from Kent, were said by the prosecution to have helped organize the murder squad. McCreery, so the prosecution said, had come to London from Belfast after he had been shot for supplying Catholics with drugs.[6]

At an earlier trial Warne, the link between the English drug dealers and the Irish, and Dennison, one of the hitmen, had been sentenced to life imprisonment after admitting conspiracy to murder. Warne had told the jury how one of the defendants, Patrick Doherty, had met him in a South London public house and had whistled up £20,000 in half an hour by using his mobile phone. This was, he said, the price for the unsuccessful killing of a second man, John Dale, 'the object of dislike and hatred apparently because he was in the habit of ripping people off in drug deals', said Timothy Langdale QC for the prosecution. Dennison took over the contract and shot him in the back outside his London home in April 1991, and then missed at point-blank range when he shot at his head. So far as Norris was concerned, the 45-year-old informer was shot as he begged for mercy with his wife watching helplessly.

Norris' death was just another in the series where the prosecution had inadvertently blown their man's cover by dropping the case. He was shot in July 1992 at his home in Belvedere by a motorcycle-riding killer.

In 1987 the *Sun* newspaper, in one of its more public-spirited displays, had a photograph taken of five supergrasses in Bedford Gaol. The men, David Medin, Clifford Barnes, Fred Scott, Steven Henry and John Davies, were photographed at exercise. The *Sun* pointed out that if their photographer could take a camera shot of them, with a reported £1.8 million on offer for their collective deaths, then a hitman could just as easily take a real shot at them.

Nevertheless, some still thought it was worthwhile to exchange

---

[6] McCreery seems to have had a chequered and eventful life. According to evidence given in the case he had been active in the Belfast Loyalist Underworld since the middle 1970s as both a drug dealer and the recruiter of Protestant hitmen. At one time he was on the run and thought to be in Spain after he had been shot in a car outside a social club in the Shankhill Road area. The IRA had indicated that he was under sentence of death. He had been lucky to survive for so long for he was thought to have had contacts with the IRA and INLA. A close relative of his, Ned McCreery, was killed by the UDA in 1992.

twenty-two years inside for a lifetime of looking over their shoulders. Lawrence Cain, known as 'The Snake' and said – a trifle optimistically, given the going rate – to have a £250,000 contract on him, was one of them when, in 1991, he received just seven years for armed robbery. He had given 'valuable help' to the police after admitting taking part in twenty-seven raids in South-East London over an eight-year period. The money had gone on foreign travel and a £300-a-day heroin habit. Amongst those who went down as a result of his evidence were his former partner Alan Condon, who drew twenty-one years, Cain's best man when he married a Thai girl who collected sixteen, and William Harding who netted a year less. Cain's counsel told the court that he had turned informer for the highly praiseworthy reason of divorcing himself from the criminal community. 'No one will come near me unless it is to kill me', said Cain whilst giving evidence.

Two spectacular snatches, if not quite of the magnitude of the Brinks-Mat raid, seem to have been carried out by the same man. The first in December 1990 happened when Eddie Maher was apparently a victim. Maher was a Securicor guard when thugs burst into his driving partner's home, held him and his wife hostage for fourteen hours and told him she would be killed unless the money was handed over. The guard together with Maher drove to the Securicor depot, collected £2 million and handed it over in Rotherhithe. They were then put in the back of the van and later released. The other man's wife was subsequently released in Epping Forest. Securicor offered £100,000 as a reward leading to information and conviction of the robbers but it was never claimed.

Then on 22 January 1993 Eddie Maher disappeared with £1,327,500 packed in fifty white Securicor bags. The 'robbery' had taken place outside a bank in Felixstowe. Maher and his regular colleague delivered cash to a branch of Lloyds bank; whilst the other man was inside the police allege Maher drove off in the two-ton van, which was found an hour later a mile away, with the secured cash compartment empty. Maher's lover, Debbie Brett, and her son had left their rented home in Woodham Ferrers near Chelmsford a week before the Felixstowe robbery. It is possible that this second 'hi-jacking' was the work of one man working alone.

Another more or less solo effort was by the man the newspapers named 'Florida Phil' Wells. He was thought to have decamped to the warmer climes of that State with something approaching £1 million taken from his security van at Heathrow in July 1989. The van, from which he should have delivered the money to a branch of Thomas Cook, was found forty-eight hours later at the Colnebrook estate near Heathrow. Also gone was his wage packet; those of his colleagues were still in the van. It was a crime which captured the imagination of the public.

In 1991 Wells telephoned from France that he was on the run both from the law and gangsters. In March 1993 he – or at least someone closely resembling him – surfaced in the pages of the *Sunday Mirror*.[7] The robbery, he (or his doppelganger) said, had been forced on him when he was threatened by West Indians who had poured petrol on his son Christopher. No, he had not gone to Florida. He had been hidden in a caravan park at Clacton, been on the Norfolk Broads, lived on a canal barge near Shrewsbury. He had also had a heart attack, and he believed there was an £80,000 contract out on his life. Indeed at one time it had been thought he was dead. The police were reported to be furious that they had not been tipped off.[8]

Wells did not last long on the outside after that. In May another daily newspaper, this time the *Sun*, was approached by an intermediary and invited to buy an interview for £25,000. The police were alerted and Wells was caught in a trap; he had only £4 on him. On 9 December 1993, after a two-week trial at Isleworth Crown Court, he was found guilty of stealing £928,000 in foreign currency. The story now came out. The £2.50-an-hour security guard had collected the money in nine shoe-box-shaped bags from an aeroplane and loaded them into his Ford Fiesta van which he had dumped only a few miles away; to cloud the trail he had telephoned a relative to say he was off to Florida. His story to the *Sunday Mirror* was not wholly accurate; the Norfolk Broads and the caravan park at Clacton had not featured all that prominently. He had certainly stayed in Clacton – indeed the police had raided the park and missed him by a few hours – but his real base had been in Malta where he landed first in October 1989. He was on and off the island constantly, visiting Hungary, Tunisia, Bulgaria, Sicily and finally Russia where he married his

[7] *Sunday Mirror*, 14 March 1993.
[8] *News of the World*, 24 January 1993.

third wife, Olga (described variously as a gymnast/night-club stripper) in Uzbekistan. He had told her he was a wealthy greengrocer. He seems to have forgotten about another wife in America. After the trial she announced she wished to have nothing more to do with him.

On 14 January 1994 he received a sentence of six years. Neither the police nor the trial judge were by any means convinced he had acted alone. Prior to the theft he had, it seems, been bragging about his employment in East End public houses.

If blue, or black, plaques were to be awarded to houses and flats for their significance in crime, then a candidate would be Welbeck Mansions in Marylebone. It was here that Bert Wilkins, convicted of the manslaughter of the Montecolumbo brother at Wandsworth dogs in 1934 and later a shadowy but influential figure in Soho, lived until his retirement to the South Coast. It was also here that businessman Donald Urquhart lived with his Thai girlfriend, Pat Lamspithone, until he was gunned down in Marylebone High Street on 2 Jan 1993. The millionaire property tycoon and owner of Elstree Golf Club was on his way home from a meal in a local restaurant when a man in a white crash helmet walked up, pulled out a .32 pistol and shot him twice in the head. The man then jumped on a black Yamaha 250 motorcycle and disappeared. Urquhart's killing was said to have been worth £20,000 and, according to persistent newspaper reports, the assassin was said to be an ex-boxer who worked for a South London gang.

The police were able to trace the bike. It had been advertised in the 23 November 1992 issue of *Loot* magazine for £275, and sold for £200. A similar ten-year-old bike had been used by the killer of ex-boxer Roger 'The Growler' Wilson, then manager of an off-licence and a jewellery fence. He had been shot in the head as he got out of his Mercedes in Kensington on 5 March 1992. Again the motorbike which the killer used had been advertised in *Loot*.

Another motorcycle killing came on 21 June 1993 when Tommy Roche (42) was shot three times as he worked in a lay-by near Heathrow Airport, said to be over a drug deal which went wrong. Roche had been the minder to Donald Urquhart and was also said to have been a grass. As a teenager he had tried to work with the Krays.

The technique of murder by motorbike comes from Columbia where teenage hitmen were first hired in the 1980s, but the London version seems to have been cut-price in the extreme.

'What's amazing is that they're using ten-year-old clapped-out bikes to flee the scene. Obviously they are really cutting costs,' said Detective Superintendent Bill Scholes.[9]

At the other end of the scale, by the early 1990s patterns of crime had also changed. Gone were the days when a handbag was merely snatched. Now, too often, the victim is stabbed as well, often for the fun of it. Nineteen-year-old crack addict Duane Daniels led a team of muggers through the streets of South London in general and, in particular, on the notorious William Bonney Estate in Clapham. By the time his criminal career was suspended at the Old Bailey in December 1993 he had committed 959 identifiable offences to finance his habit, which was said at his trial to be a daily intake of half an ounce of cannabis, twenty rocks of crack, ten pints of extra-strength lager, two doses of LSD, a quarter of a bottle of spirits and handfuls of tranquillisers.[10] At his arrest Daniels, whose rocks of crack cost £25 a rock, had nothing to show for his crimes except the clothes in which he stood. His team, the 28 Posse, recognized by a special mark in their closely cropped hair, was a motley assortment of both willing and frightened recruits. One boy who declined to join had his coat set on fire.

In one month alone Daniels stole £100,000 worth of television and video sets in burglaries, but before the end of this part of his career he and his gang had turned to a much more sinister form of crime. His victims were kidnapped and tortured to reveal their personal identification numbers which would allow Daniels to obtain money from the cashholders at banks.

One victim was working alone in the evening in the offices of a building contractor's when Daniels tricked him into opening the door, claiming he was a cleaner. The man was hit on the head with a bottle and tied with telephone wire before being stabbed in the legs to make him reveal the PIN number. Daniels and other members of his gang fled and the victim then threw himself through a window in an effort to get help. Another, a woman

---

[9] *News of the World*, 14 February 1993.

[10] This was not the largest number of offences taken into consideration at the Central Criminal Court. Brian Reece wrote to *The Times* saying that in the 1970s he recalled a case of a man who had had 1,187 offences taken into consideration. They had all arisen from a nationwide operation to defraud banks by cashing stolen cheques each to the value of £30. The man had received a sentence of two years' imprisonment suspended for two years. *The Times*, 5 January 1993.

who was attacked in a veterinary surgery, was threatened with the decapitation of her guinea-pig. In 1991 he had been jailed for three and a half years for a series of similar violent crimes.[11] Now he received nine years.

Another victim of an indiscriminate shooting was barrister's clerk Amaranath Bandaratilleka who was gunned down by Avie Andrews, aged 16, the middle-class son of an actor. His victim was in a newsagent's shop in Hammersmith when Andrews, together with Sam Perman aged 18, son of an antiques dealer and director of the Poetry Society, robbed it. Mr Bandaratilleka was shot in the stomach after being ordered to turn out his pockets and revealed he had only 26 pence, a pocket calculator and an office organizer on him. Andrews, the father of a five-month-old baby by a 20-year-old girl – and who was being supported by another middle-class girl – also admitted robbing drug dealers of £650 of cannabis with a sawn-off shotgun bought from Underworld contacts for £200 as a defence weapon for his bogus drug racket – a thriving trade in cold cure pills crushed to resemble Ecstasy tablets, to pay for his heroin addiction. He later confessed to his sister and then to his father. He had, said Edward Quist-Arcton for the defence, started taking cannabis at 11, and was addicted to heroin by the age of 15. Now the Court was told that during his time on remand he had tried to commit suicide but had, after an escape from a secure unit, kicked the heroin habit. 'The Avie Andrews before the court now is a far, far different person from the drugged, befuddled teenager of earlier this year. He has manfully accepted full responsibility for the death and nobody regrets the senseless waste of life more than he does.' Apart from Mr Bandaratilleka's family and friends presumably.

The 1990s saw the continued rise of the contract killer. The targets, apart from Moody, included those involved in drugs deals which had gone sour, and supergrasses. There was also the suggestion that one killing had been a community action with the death of a drug dealer who had been warned off a territory. Of course, contract killing is not a new phenomenon. Earlier examples included the killing of Paddy O'Nione and Tony Zomparelli.

In April 1993 Judge Michael Coombe sentenced James Brooker and his brother Mark to terms of nine and eight years

[11] *Sunday Times*, 5 December 1993; *The Times*, 24 December 1993.

following an attack on a mechanic, Thomas Kennedy, in the Simla public house in Thornton Heath. They had been acquitted of charges of attempted murder. Kennedy required more than a hundred stitches after being attacked with a knife, a cosh, a beer glass and a bar stool. The subsequent trial was littered with missing witnesses. The judge said:

> I haven't the slightest doubt that there has been interference with witnesses in this case. It is proved to my satisfaction that certain witnesses had been put in fear, a grave fear. It is an indication of the violence surrounding this case that the terror which began on June 20 [1992] could extend all these months later.[12]

By the end of the trial two witnesses were still missing, another had changed her statement and a fourth had been declared 'hostile' by the judge. At first he had been seen as an important witness, but later claimed he could not remember the incident.

The intimidation of witnesses and, in particular, the victim, is nothing new but with the time between arrest and trial in serious cases now up to a year, it is much easier for offers and threats to be made. Nationwide, over twenty major trials involving serious violence have collapsed and some three hundred investigations, including murder hunts, have been abandoned during 1992–3. In June 1993 a pregnant woman received a month's imprisonment at Newcastle Crown Court for failing to give evidence at the murder trial of her former boyfriend; she said threats had been made against both her and other witnesses. It was slightly different in Merthyr Tydfil when Ali Khan, a shopkeeper whose shop had been under siege in a racist attack, declined to give evidence. The men were convicted when local residents told the court they had heard the men threatening to burn Mr Khan's shop. In 1992 a trial in Manchester collapsed when a woman who had named several people she said were involved in a machete attack on Carl Stapleton, disappeared. She had insisted on anonymity in court, but the judge had refused. As a result the prosecution offered no evidence. There have been other instances in both Manchester and Liverpool.

It is not always private witnesses who seek protection. In

---

[12] *Sunday Times*, 11 April 1993.

December 1993 the much vaunted Operation Mensa trial collapsed at the committal stage when the officer who had allegedly infiltrated the gang told the court he wished to be shielded from the view of the public gallery and to give a false name. When this was refused the prosecution had the charges dismissed by the stipendiary magistrate, Mr David Fingleton, saying they were intending to apply for a voluntary bill of indictment.

The great individual jewel thieves are men of the past. George 'Taters' Chatham is in his eighties; Peter Scott is a tennis coach; Raymond Jones, once said to be the greatest climber in the country, is retired. Jewel thefts have never had great attraction for the run-of-the-mill criminal.

> Whoever you go to to sell, it will always be, 'Oh how difficult this particular jewellery is. It will require resetting and cutting and this will devalue it because there's been such a hue and cry about it.' And there's no challenge to this type of market. The thief has to put up with whatever price comes up unless he finds someone who personally fancies a piece or pieces of the jewellery for his own personal use, and that man would have to go to the expense of having it altered. If you're not lucky enough to find that person you're lumbered. But jewel raids will always go on. It's easy to carry away and you might be lucky to get that particular diamond or two which could come to a lot of money. That's the chance you're looking for. It is a very precarious commodity to sell. Sometimes you can get a commission, that's the better thing because you know exactly what you're going for and what you're going to get for it.
>
> A few years ago a pal of mine did a jeweller's, a tie-up, and I believe officially it was said that nearly £2 million pounds worth of jewellery was stolen. I think about five of them were engaged on this endeavour and my friend who took a leading part, which meant that he would have at least an equal share, he received £7,500 altogether. That was getting it in dribs and drabs as well. They just couldn't sell the tom.[13]

As Fraser says, there will always be thieves who are prepared to try their luck at a snatch and resale. For example, 13 July 1993

---

[13] F. Fraser, *Mad Frank*, p.30.

saw the end of one the world's best professional safe-breakers, Roy Saunders, who had opened locks on behalf of Scotland Yard, and another locksmith, Robert French. They had led a five-man team including Robert Reed on a raid on the New English Artworks workshop, which manufactures watches for Cartiers in New Bond Street. It had been a highly professional job with one of the gang, posing as a window-cleaner, checking the fire alarm the day before. Bugging devices had been planted to deal with video cameras. Unfortunately they ran into a police surveillance unit which was watching the area, not for them but as a result of a series of lesser burglaries. Two men escaped by abseiling down the back of a five-storey building in New Bond Street, but the others were caught in the basement of a nearby shoe shop. Saunders was unable to tell the police what either he or his equipment were doing on the premises. He and French told the police that by chance Reed had wandered into the shop to urinate after finding the door open. Equipment worth several thousands of pounds was found in his car. At the trial Saunders said he had been too drunk to remember anything of the evening. It was not a defence which appealed to the jury. Sentencing them to four years each in prison, Judge Fabyan Evans said on 6 August 1993, 'This must have been one of the most sophisticated burglaries of commercial property that has taken place in recent years. It is rare nowadays that an offence of this kind that involves such considerable profit involved no violence. Quite why men of your age became involved in an offence like this is a mystery to me.' The target had been £1 million, but it would have been likely to fetch only one-fifth in the market. The answer is both money and excitement. Anyway, older men than they had been at it for years.

On 28 November 1924 some wild colonial boys Dennis Harris and John James, along with John Russell and Edward Flood, were charged with breaking into Ewarts in Euston Road. They were seen coming out of the premises and promptly arrested. Scotland Yard's records describe them as 'a gang of dangerous warehouse breakers, safebreakers'. Harris, known as 'Dare Devil Dennis', was 64 at the time and received three years' penal servitude, as did the 60-year-old James. Both had convictions in Australia and South Africa where they had ridden as steeplechase jockeys. Only three years earlier Harris had received four years for receiving stolen property from big London robberies.

But when one door shuts another opens, and a recent example of a well-researched target was in July 1993 when, in a snatch lasting ten minutes, three thieves raided Graff jeweller's in Hatton Garden, said, 'Don't move or we'll shoot' to the staff whom they forced to lie on the floor, and escaped with diamonds, rubies and sapphires totalling some £7 million.

It took place in the middle of the morning rush hour when the thieves, who had the codes to the security room doors, took one £2-million diamond intended to be the centrepiece for a brooch and a £1-million ruby and diamond necklace. They were interrupted by another member of the staff who had been out for a cup of coffee, and left behind another diamond valued at £2.5 million before escaping into Farringdon station. This was the second attack on a store owned by victim Laurence Graff. In March 1993 the West End branch of his firm was robbed of jewellery worth £2 million.

Nevertheless by now drugs were the mainspring of the whole of the Underworld, both London and nationwide.

3

Glasgow

Perceived wisdom has it that there were no gangs in Glasgow until after the First World War. Sir Percy Sillitoe, the Chief Constable of the 1920s, chronicles the Redskins and the Black Hand gangs with their 'childish names' as being the first of many[1], whilst the old *Daily Mirror* crime writer, Norman Lucas, with a fine disregard for such worthies as Arthur Harding, Darby Sabini, Billy Kimber and a whole host of Londoners, suggested that Peter Williamson was the 'first true gangleader in Britain'.[2]

Quite apart from the racecourse gangs which flourished in the nineteenth century and which operated out of the city[3], both seem to have overlooked the existence of the Penny Mob which operated in the 1880s in Townhead and the East End of Glasgow.

> This gang had a common fund to which all contributed, and when members were fined at the police courts, the money was always forthcoming – hence the name 'Penny Mob'. Their picturesque name should not disguise the fact that

---

[1] Sir Percy Sillitoe, *Cloak Without Dagger*, p.140.
[2] Norman Lucas, *Britain's Gangland*, p.5. Others, including John Mack in *Crime in Glasgow*, agree with him.
[3] In 1848 the *Renfrewshire Advertiser* noted that the Glasgow Fancy had attended Paisley Races and had used brute force to obtain a levy from the owners of stalls at the meetings. In the early part of this century the Redskins, so known because of the razor slashes on their faces, roamed the Scottish racecourses in much the same way. See Carl Chinn, *Better Betting with a Decent Fellow*.

they were 'a gang of hooligans, who for long were a source of serious annoyance to the community'.[4]

But the Penny Mob whose leaders, as was common at the time, were known as Chairmen, was not alone. There were at least three other fighting gangs, the boys of the Wee Do'e Hill and the Big Do'e Hill along with the Drygate Youths. Twenty years later there were two rivals in central Glasgow, the San Toy Boys and the Tim Malloys. The former had the helpful chant:

We are the young San Toys,
  and we can fight the Tim Malloys.

After them came the Mealy Boys, the McGlynn Push, the Village Boys and a few years later the Gold Dust Gang. They all seem to have operated in much the same way, fighting being the principal ambition coupled with a certain amount of leaning on local shopkeepers for protection money to pay off the inevitable fines.

The Redskins came a little later, flourishing during the First World War, but this gang, reckoned at one time to be over 1,000 strong, was far better organized than its rivals such as the Kelly Boys from Govan, the Baltic Fleet from Baltic Street, the Beehive Corner Boys, the Waverley Boys, the Cowboys and the Bell On Boys. Again the members' speciality was inter-gang fighting, but they also demanded protection money from shopkeepers whose premises were otherwise ransacked. The unfortunate owners would find all their goods mixed in a heap on the floor with, if they were extremely unfortunate, themselves deposited in the middle of the debris. On the way out the gang would break the shop windows.

Robert Colquhoun, who later became a detective chief super-intendent and who was then a young beat constable, thought 1923 was a vintage year for Glasgow gangs, citing the Cheeky Forty and the Black Diamonds in the St Rolox area as his immediate concern:

They were street corner thugs, who fought one another in head-on clashes a hundred strong or more – though they usually preferred it if some unsuspecting rival gangster

---

[4] *The Times*, 19 January, 1920.

strayed alone into their territory and could be 'done up' in the appropriate tradition. Sometimes girls attached to a gang would provide the necessary lure to achieve the catch.[5]

From time to time fights were more straightforward, one-on-one, affairs and there seems to have been no disgrace in recruiting a champion to promote your cause. Colquhoun recounts the story of two hardmen who fought each other with razors, then stopped and went to hospital together to be patched up.

> That night had been enough for Jacko. He still kept up his quarrel with Chopper, but he hired a strong-arm man from the Gorbals to fight the next round of the battle. In gangland code, Jacko's standing didn't suffer by his decision to employ a deputy. After all, it was argued, he was still willing to continue the quarrel – and that was the important thing.[6]

It was, however, the Beehive Corner Boys, later abbreviated to the Beehive Boys or Gang, who moved up a gear. Under the leadership of Peter Williamson, described by Sillitoe as powerfully built and coming from a respectable family, who was aided by his lieutenant Harry M'Menemy and a man called Howie, they were into straightforward theft, burglary, armed robbery and, with the help of a London criminal recruited for the purpose, safebreaking.

Williamson, who apparently preferred one-to-one fights rather than gang battles and who had the ability to spot a policeman a mile away, could often be seen at the end of a gang fight appealing to the brawlers to behave. For some time it stood him in good stead but eventually the convictions began to pile up and M'Menemy, true lieutenant that he was, served a nine-month sentence for Williamson. He allowed himself to be put forward as the attacker of a man whom Williamson and a Dan Cronin had assaulted. His captain would undoubtedly have earned a term of years rather than months on conviction. Later the gang moved away from being a traditional fighting gang and into theft, safeblowing, house-breaking and armed robbery.

[5] R. Colquhoun, *Life Begins at Midnight*, p.18.
[6] Ibid p.77.

In 1924, at a time when there was open warfare between the South Side Stickers and the long-lasting San Toy Gang, one of the major gangland fights of the era took place in the Bedford Parlour Dance Hall in Celtic Street not far from the football ground. It was, however, between two of the smaller affiliated teams, and James Dalziel, the leader of the Parlour Boys, died in it.

Dalziel, aged 26 and described as snub-nosed and sturdy, was known to his friends as Razzle-Dazzle. Although traditionally Glasgow gangs had many 'queens' or girl hangers-on who could be used to secrete weapons if the police arrived, Dalziel, whose favourite weapon was a pickshaft which weighed nearly three pounds and was three and a half foot in length, considered it effeminate to dance with them; he would only take the floor with the other male members of the gang. The Parlour Boys, as befitted its name, had proprietorial rights over the dance hall and did not have to pay admission. Instead members observed a two-part ritual. They would troop past the cashier saying they 'knew the boss'; the second and equally important part of this quasi-masonic ritual was to wipe their boots.

On 2 March 1924 the Bedford Boys went into the hall, to be followed in the early hours of the morning by the Bridgegate Boys, a group affiliated to the San Toys. Possibly they had merely come in to avoid the heavy rain, but it is more likely that to pass their rivals' headquarters without a murmur would have been a major loss of face. They cleared the first hurdle of the ritual muttering that they 'knew the boss', but when they failed to wipe their boots the cashier, Mrs Stevenson, sounded the alarm.

In the traditional phrase of the police, 'Fighting broke out', and during it Dalziel was stabbed in the throat by a youth, Collins. Later at the Assizes the jury acquitted him of Dalziel's murder and he received a twelve-months' sentence for affray. Fines imposed on those convicted of affray were paid for by a levy on local shopkeepers. Immediately the convicted men were elevated to the status of hero.

Many of the fighting gangs had junior sections, just as today the Crips and the Bloods of Los Angeles and other gangs have wannabees and graduating ranks for pre-teen children. In 1928, four years after the Dalziel murder, another gang killing ended with heavy sentences. This time the participants were from the junior division, and the fight broke out over a minor injury to one of the queens belonging to the South Side Stickers, sustained in a cinema fight. Now three girls went to see Frank Kerney, the 16-year-old leader of the Calton Entry gang, to say that Abraham Zemmil of the Stickers challenged him to a fight on the Albert Bridge. For once, instead of all-out warfare the terms were that the battle should be five-a-side. Lining up with Zemmil were Alexander McCaughey and James McCluskey. McCaughey had a sword, as did Kerney. McCluskey, who had a dagger, hit James Tait of the Calton gang supporting Kerney. Kerney and his team then attacked McCluskey, who stabbed Tait in the back.

McCluskey, Zemmil and McCaughey, along with Archibald Gaughan, James Walker and George Stokes, appeared at the Assizes charged with causing the death of Tait. They were between 15 and 17 years old. Unsurprisingly and unfortunately, none of them could explain how Tait had come to be stabbed in the back. The charges against Walker and Gaughan were withdrawn. Zemmil and Stokes each received a year inside. McCaughey, who pleaded guilty to rioting, received eighteen months' imprisonment and McCluskey, who pleaded guilty to mobbing, rioting and culpable homicide (an equivalent to manslaughter), was sentenced to a term of five years.

That was the year when the very powerful Billy Boys were born. There has long been a sectarian element in Glasgow life, let alone street life. For example, the major football clubs in the city were, until the 1980s, conducted on strictly religious lines. Only Catholics played for Celtic; only Protestants for Rangers. The Billy Boys, taking their name from William of Orange, the persecutor of the Irish Catholics and victor at the Battle of the Boyne, faced up to the Norman Conquerors, known as the Norman Conks, who came from Norman Street and were Catholics.

The leader of the Billy Boys was William Fullerton, a fighting man who worked in Gilmours Club in Olympia Street and who tended to leave the thefts undertaken by the gang to other members. The Conks were led by Bill Bowman, who saw the march of the Communist-led National Unemployed Workers' Movement on 19 January 1932 as a splendid way of invading the Boys' territory. Fullerton and his gang diverted the march into Abercrombie Street where rioting took place. In accordance with local tradition, the fines levied were paid for by the local shopkeepers who had already had their plate-glass windows broken.

At one time the eight hundred members of the Billy Boys had membership cards on which a weekly payment of 2d a week was marked. The money, which once totalled £1,200, went into a Bridgeton bank. Even in church the members were armed; in the 1920s Fullerton attended the wedding of one of his gang:

> The bridegroom stood before the minister with a sword concealed in his morning dress. The best man had a gun in his pocket . . . I'll never forget the scene as they left the Church. The gang waiting outside threw bottles instead of confetti.[7]

Sunday was church parade day, when the Billy Boys would march through their enemies' territory to the Church of Scotland in French Street. Participation in the service was not obligatory for the members who, satisfied with their efforts, returned home. Later, in 1934, Fullerton organized a fife-and-drum band to accompany them on all Catholic Holy Days. The band would march playing Loyalist tunes such as 'The Sash My Father Wore' until they encountered the Conks. The end of these parades came when the Chief Constable, Sir Percy Sillitoe, decided enough was enough. Sillitoe, who had already been responsible for treading with some brutality on the Gavin-Mooney gangs in Sheffield before his move to Scotland, now organized what came to be called Sillitoe's Cossacks.

When one day the band marched towards Celtic Park along Norman Street, two officers ordered them to turn around. As they were brushed aside two police vans emptied officers, armed with long riot batons, on to the streets. The whole band was arrested and charged with assaults and disturbances. Only one of the players escaped injury. According to legend, Elijah Copper dived into his own bass drum and hid there until the fighting had ended.

That was the beginning of the end for the Billy Boys and their eclipse came shortly afterwards when a drunken Fullerton, carrying a three-year-old child, was leading his men towards the Toll Gate. Two police officers tried to remove the child and were pushed aside. They followed the gang at a distance until they saw a Sergeant Tommy Morrison, known as 'Big Tom' from Toll Gate. By now the march was a little over a quarter of a mile

[7] *Evening Citizen*, 17 January 1955.

away from the Toll Gate police station. The gang was allowed to turn a corner and then Morrison and the two officers intervened. Fullerton, told he was being arrested for being drunk in charge of a child, struck the sergeant who 'drew his baton to defend himself'. Billy Fullerton received twelve months' imprisonment, and when he was released his leadership was over. The Conks, with no Billy Boys to fight, also seem to have gone into decline and pined away.[8]

What Sillitoe optimistically saw as the end of Glasgow gangsterdom as such came in April 1935. John M'Namee, his brother Andrew and a third man, Kennedy, set on a John M'Allister. Andrew M'Namee had an iron bar, the other two had knives. According to Sillitoe, M'Allister said, 'If that is your way, then we will fight it out man to man, one at a time. There are three of you.' M'Namee is said to have answered, 'There are no fair fights here.' A passer-by, Angus Doherty, tried to help M'Allister and was set about by Andrew and his iron bar. Then Charles Smith, outside whose house the fight was taking place, came home from work. He stopped to help Doherty, and as he did so John M'Namee ran back and stabbed him through the shoulder-blade. Smith died instantly.

In the witness-box Doherty was unable to identify his attacker, but not so Mary Smith, the 15-year-old daughter of Charles, waiting and watching for her father's return. John M'Namee received fifteen years' imprisonment for culpable homicide, Andrew M'Namee four and Kennedy three.

Just as he is credited, partly through self-proclamation, for cleaning up Sheffield, Sillitoe did the same for Glasgow. His technique was simple. John MacLean, a constable for thirty years in the City of Glasgow Police, recalls:

> He got together the biggest and hardest men in the force, and ordered them to go out and batter the living shite out of every Ned who scratched his balls without permission. I'm telling you we didn't have to be asked twice.[9]

---

[8] In 1939 Billy Fullerton joined the Army and, it seems, served with distinction. Later he worked in a Clydebank shipyard. After his death in 1962 some 600 people followed his coffin, laden with floral tributes including a cushion of marigolds, to Riddrie Cemetery. Massed flute bands played 'Onward, Christian Soldiers' with which his 1930s band had always ended their tour of Catholic territory.

[9] John MacLean, quoted by Jonathan Goodman and Ian Will in *Underworld*, p.76.

When they heard of a gang fight, the technique was now for the police to trundle along in nondescript vans – the aim was certainly not to break it up in advance – watch the participants battle each other and then beat and kick the survivors. As in Sheffield, Sillitoe's conduct in Glasgow has been severely criticized:

> Before long, the batter squads acquired a reputation for violence that was quite as high as that of any of the gangs. But just how effective they were in reducing the number of street battles is open to question: they certainly had *some* effect, but nothing like as much as Sillitoe claimed. It is possible that, in the long term, they gave a sort of seal of approval to acts of violence, for the only apparent difference between them and the gangs was that they were paid to cause physical harm. If the guardians of the law used strong-arm tactics, didn't it show that might was right? Whenever Sillitoe boasted of his success against the people he described as 'unemployable louts', he stated that his purpose was to make them *heed* the law; he never said anything about getting them to *respect* it.[10]

But the gallant Sir Percy was deceiving himself and others if he thought that the M'Namee case was the end of the Glasgow fighting gangs. In reality the continuity of the gangs has survived two World Wars and flourishes today. Rather, it is the chronicling of them that has faded.

Over the years Glasgow juries have proved resistant to convicting men charged with capital murder, and from 1928 to 1946 there was no single person executed. The fights, however, went on.

However, on 20 October 1945 John Patrick Smyth was walking along Argyle Street around 10 p.m., when eight men approached him, asking, 'Where are the Dougie Boys?' Smyth, seeing a bayonet under one of the men's coats, tried to leap on to a passing tram, decided that it was going too slowly, leaped off and ran for it, leaving behind the girls with whom he had been walking. He also left behind 19-year-old John Brady, who had simply been out walking and who had no connection with the Dougie Boys. Brady, who had been discharged from the Navy

[10] Ibid., p.76.

only four days previously, was stabbed to death. Four men appeared in the North Court in Glasgow charged with his murder; one of them was only seventeen years old at the time, and under the prevailing rule he could not be sentenced to death if the trial ended before his eighteenth birthday. It did not; the jury retired that day. He and two others were convicted, but in the end he and one man were reprieved. Twenty-one-year-old John Lyon was hanged on 9 February 1946 at Barlinnie prison, the first man to go to the scaffold for eighteen years.

He was, however, soon followed by another fighting man, Patrick 'Carry' Carraher. He had been the fortunate recipient of the benefit of a Glasgow jury's dislike of the death penalty when, in October 1938, he had been acquitted of the murder of a regular soldier, James Shaw. By then Carraher, who would fight without fear using boots, fists or weapons alike, had already racked up eleven convictions including assault, housebreaking and carrying explosives. On 13 August 1938 he had sent a message via a young girl to a prostitute that he wanted her company. She refused to go with him and ran to her protector, James Drurie, on whom Carraher, unused to disobedience, pulled a knife. The men faced each other and then suddenly Carraher turned away.

By chance, they met later that night and again matters might have quietened down until Shaw bravely, if foolishly, butted in and tried to act as a peacemaker. He was unsuccessful. Peter Howard, one of the men who had been with Drurie, told the court: 'Suddenly I heard a scuffle. When I turned around, Carraher had disappeared and Shaw was holding his neck.'

His jugular vein had been slashed and he died on the way to the Royal Infirmary. Howard was taken to the police station and Carraher, when he heard of his arrest, said to a girl: 'I stabbed Shaw – he was very cheeky. But I won't let Howard swing for it. I'll give myself up.'

In fact he didn't. A Detective Sergeant, John Johnson, found him sitting by the fireside in a house in Florence Street in the Gorbals. Carraher had already thrown away the knife.

In what was described at the time as a brilliant defence, Carraher's counsel made much of the fact that in the few seconds before the blow was struck none of the witnesses could actually say what had happened. Carraher received three years for culpable homicide.

Now he rejoiced in the soubriquet 'Killer' and was back in

prison in 1943, this time for slashing a man with a razor, for which he received another three years. Two years later he went to the assistance of his brother-in-law, whom he had been told was in a fight at a public house in Rottenrow. There he saw John Gordon, an ex-Seaforth Highlander, who had been captured at Dunkirk and who had recently been released from a prisoner-of-war camp in Germany. Gordon, a bystander, was thought wrongly by Carraher to have been one of his brother's attackers. He cut Gordon behind the left ear, a wound measuring four inches deep. The soldier died almost immediately after he was admitted to the Royal Infirmary. Curiously, it was John Johnson who again found Carraher; this time the man was fast asleep in bed. The blade of Carraher's knife was only two and a half inches long and therefore, said the defence, it could not have caused a four-inch-deep cut. Medical evidence for the prosecution convinced the jury that it could. Carraher's appeal was dismissed and his petition for a reprieve refused. He was hanged at Barlinnie on 6 April 1946 and according to Patrick Meehan, safebreaker and Glasgow hardman who would himself be convicted of murder, fought all the way to the gallows.

After the Second World War the city planners began moving Gorbals' dwellers from that slum to high-rise estates on the edge of the city. One, unintended, effect was for gangs to name themselves after areas rather than mere streets.

In the 1950s there was a youth gang called the Bingo Boys in Govan, but again fighting rather than theft seems to have been their main activity, just as it was in the late 1960s when James Patrick – the pseudonym of a teacher who, for social research purposes, joined a juvenile fighting gang, the Young Team from Castlemilk – was able to list twenty youth gangs in the city. Several called themselves Tongs as a mark of respect for the old-time Calton Entry or Calton Tongs. But by the end of the 1950s there had already been the Torran Toi, the Bal Toi and the Bar-L (a diminutive of Barlinnie) on the new Easterhouse estate.

According to the writers Goodman and Will, the old-fashioned weapon the cut-throat razor, faced with obsolescence because of an increase in the use of its safety counterpart, was now at a premium. Flick-knives and steel knitting needles were the choice weapons of the time, replacing ice-picks, meat-cleavers and the spud-grenades (potatoes studded with razor-blades) of earlier times.

If there were any lingering hopes that the fighting gangs had disbanded by the 1960s, James Patrick's book should swiftly dispel them. There is also evidence that by now the older members of the gangs had moved into illegal money-lending or loan-sharking, as opposed to say the London and Dublin sport of club and pub protection. Ronald Maxwell wrote:

> Big money for protection of clubs, casinos and book-makers, does not exist in Glasgow. Most gangsters live from illegal money-lending. The interest rate is 4–5/s in the £ per week. So someone who borrows £5 must repay £6 the next week.[11]

Maxwell recounted the story of one man who borrowed £10 and could not keep up the interest payments. He eventually owed £100 after paying back £30. The debt was cancelled on the understanding that he paid £2 per week for life.

Sometimes it was hard to tell whether the accounts by players were genuine and, if they were, should they actually be included in a list of gangs since they clearly saw themselves as 'White Angels'. In 1965, *News of the World* reporter Ron Mount interviewed what could be described as such a band who operated from a fifth-floor office next door to Wendy's Restaurant in West George Street, Glasgow. The decor was bizarre, with a stuffed stag's head in a corner on the floor and a shrunken head on the mantelpiece. Ranged around were a number of ancient guns, spears and daggers. More usefully there was a large tape-recorder. There John Muir Lindsay, Lieutenant in the Royal Marines Reserve, sometime estate agent, sometime insurance claims investigator, ran a commando outfit which promised to do anything required. They had placed an advertisement in the *Sunday Times*;

> Have Gun, still travelling. We are a rather unusual firm. Our service is world wide and strictly confidential. In our ranks we have commandos, parachutists, snipers, lawyers and insurance claims investigators. We will go anywhere anytime.
> We will try anything. James Bond has nothing on us. If

---

[11] *Sunday Mirror*, 18 February 1968.

you are a corporation and want a difficult job well done, contact us. If you are an individual with a problem or are in trouble or just plain desperate, drop us a line. It will probably surprise you how we can help. Our fees are – well, let's say it again, depends on how we like the job.

Lindsay told Mount that he had about fifty former officers on call in the UK and 250 agents worldwide. Letters had poured in and the firm had now been going for a year. The requests had included demands to murder the Prime Minister, which they had not taken seriously, and one from three men in Africa who had written about a comrade's dying wishes to find and kill a man who had raped his wife. The woman was still in a mental hospital because of the experience. They had taken this seriously and made inquiries, tracing the man to Israel where it was thought he had already died.

Most of their work, as reported to Mount, seems to have been along the lines of assisting women of whom advantage had been taken following a laced drink to obtain retribution from their violators. One poignant tale concerned a vicar's wife who many years earlier had had an illegitimate child. Now quite by chance the father turned up in the town and recognized her. He required her to submit to him every Friday afternoon and, Lindsay told Mount:

> . . . after a few weeks of hell she wrote to us. We sent two lads who told the man that unless he left her alone we would deal with him and his own mother would not recognise him afterwards. That stopped him and his nasty little game.

In Lindsay's pile of mail the morning Mount interviewed him was a letter from a 'distraught father who alleged his daughter was being kept in a Home Counties' convent against her will'. The man had enclosed a map of the place, asking Lindsay and his men to raid it and kidnap her.[12]

And if that seems just too fantastic to believe, think now of the retrieval and the subsequent de-programming of children who have joined the Moonies and other out-of-the way sects.

The year 1967 saw the break-up of the definitely serious

[12] *News of the World*, 16 June 1965.

Tallymen. The violence which led to the demise of that gang began on 14 July, Glasgow Fair week. A pimp, 'Babs' Rooney – who had fallen behind with his repayments – and Sadie Cairney were celebrating the Fair in Kinning Park when Rooney was knifed to death over the £7 debt. James 'Babyface' Boyle and William Wilson, brother of the gang boss Frank 'Tarzan' Wilson, were charged. Jimmy Boyle received life imprisonment, with a recommendation that he serve fifteen years' minimum for the murder. Wilson was found not guilty of Rooney's murder but received twenty-one months for theft and assault.

Later that year Frank 'Tarzan' Wilson, along with his chauffeur John 'Bandit' Rooney and the crooked Glasgow lawyer, James Latta, were jailed for a total of twenty-four years for plotting to have the two men freed. All three were found guilty of inducing people to give false evidence at the trial of Boyle and William Wilson. Frank Wilson, who had wanted to do better than be a simple loan-shark – to further his education he had borrowed books from the public library on Sicily and the Mafia – was jailed for twelve years and Rooney for four. The third man in the dock, James Latta, had been on a retainer from the gang; he was a frequenter of the Hi-Hi bar in the Gorbals where he discussed the fabrication of alibis, bribery and the suborning of witnesses and the jury. The gang had not been wholly successful in their efforts in the Boyle-Wilson case, although Sadie Cairney left the witness-box at the High Court saying she was in fear of her life, and a bomb exploded in the front room of another witness, 15-year-old Eddie McGill, in Hutcheson Town Court. Before sentencing Latta the trial judge, Lord Grant, commented that he believed because of the lawyer's activities the administration of justice in Glasgow had been seriously compromised over a long period.

The demise of the gang soon followed. With the leaders gone, the police were able to make swift and considerable inroads into the affairs of the Tallymen who apart from their six-for-five loan-sharking had been into safe-breaking and extortion. Owners of businesses in the financial district of the city had been pleased to pay protection money rather than go to the expense of having the aerosol paint removed from their office façades. Said one Scottish judge:

Crime in Glasgow is dominated by money-lending. It is an unspoken theme. These so-called motiveless crimes – slashings and beatings – are not motiveless at all. The victim is very often in debt and he is trying to dodge the column. The last thing he'll do is go to the police and tell the real story.

James Boyle's earlier career was in the best tradition of the Glasgow hardmen. His father had been one of Peter Williamson's lieutenants in the pre-war Beehive Gang, and before the Rooney stabbing James Boyle had accumulated a formidable record of assault both on the police and civilians. He attended St Bonaventure's school, from which eight former pupils were serving life sentences in the 1970s, and almost all of the old boys at that time had, at the very least, been on probation. Between 1965 and the 1970s he was acquitted of one murder and the charge in another case was dropped. The police had had considerable difficulty in obtaining witnesses. In two cases, parcels of gelignite had been dropped through their letterboxes.

It was never expected that Boyle would be a model prisoner, and at first he kept up his reputation. Within a year he had eighteen months added to his sentence for assault on a prison officer, and in October 1967 he received a further four years for attacking two more officers. In 1973 he was acquitted of the murder of a fellow inmate in Porterfield. The same year he was one of several prisoners convicted of attacking prison officers, for which he received another six years consecutive to his existing sentence. Amongst the cognoscenti he was not thought to be likely to live out the initial sentence anyway; he had received a beating from the Porterfield batter-squad of prison officers and it was believed that another bad beating would do for him. Even if it did not, he was always at risk from another inmate from a rival gang.

Then came the transformation scene. Boyle was selected to be sent to an experimental unit in Barlinnie where he was encouraged to indulge in 'self-examination, self-awareness and self-expression'. Given a knife for wood-carving, he never abused his privilege. A prison visitor Sarah Trevelyan, daughter of Sir John, the former film censor, married him during the latter part of his imprisonment. He was released in the early 1980s and has subsequently spent much of his time in social work with young people. On Friday 13 May 1994, Boyle's son, twenty-seven-year-old James Boyle junior, was found dead from stab wounds near a tenement block in the Oatlands district of Glasgow. Police refused to comment on suggestions that local people had complained of drug dealing in the area.

The decline and fall of one gang is exemplified by the Y Y Shamrock (Young Young Shamrock) which could boast about 150 members in 1968. One boy said he joined because he couldn't walk in town without being attacked. Now the YYS were on top of the pile with Real Mental Shamrock, the parent group (note the same structure of the Crips and Bloods in Los Angeles, with its ranking organization). The Shamrock gang, or 'team' as it was called by its members, began as the Emeralds Football club which failed through apathy.[13]

By 1968, of the original founders of the Shamrocks eight years earlier, two were serving life, one six years for attempted murder, another member three years for attempted murder; three were in prison for a serious assault, and three were detained at Her Majesty's pleasure. Their arch-enemies were the Fleet from Maryhill. A Fleet member was killed and the Fleet grassed the Shamrock, hence the sentences and a perfectly good reason for the continuance of warfare but, as Voltaire might have said, if reasons did not exist they would have been invented.[14]

A total of eighty-three years' imprisonment was handed out by Lord Cameron following the death of 17-year-old John Muir who strayed into a fight between the Spur and the Nunny gangs. There was a shout of 'get that one' and William Bonner put a blade through Muir's arm. Bonner received twelve years' detention and William Donnelly the same. He had convictions for theft, attempted housebreaking and attempting to pervert the course of justice. After this incident, whilst on bail, he had been in trouble again. By the early 1970s the once powerful Shamrock Gang had gone, according to Glasgow's Assistant Chief Constable, William Ratcliffe.

By now it was thought that there were probably about twenty-five gangs in the city, each with a hard core of six or seven boys. Glasgow was rated the most violent city in the United Kingdom, and ranked among the six most violent in the world in company with Mexico City, New York, Chicago, Palermo and Bogota.

A short-lived gang flourished briefly in the autumn of 1969, and they were certainly not boys. Two of the four were ex-Glasgow police officers. On 16 July 1969, dressed as businessmen, they were each carrying a briefcase before they reached the

---

[13] Ken Martin, *Observer*, 1 December 1968.
[14] *News of the World*, 24 June 1968.

doors of the British Linen Bank in Williamswood, Renfrewshire. There they put on nylon masks and held up the staff, blindfolding and tying them all up except the manager who was forced to open the safe and hand over £21,000.

Three of them tried again on 30 December 1969, and this time successfully robbed the Clydesdale Bank in Bridge Street, Linwood of £14,212 which they put into two suitcases. They also took a quantity of silver and this they put in a metal box. It was as they reached safety, the flat in Allison Street where Howard Wilson (who had served ten years in the force) lived, that they were approached by Police Inspector Andrew Hyslop. He had recognized Wilson, seen the box and along with Constable John Sellars went over to investigate. By the time they went into the back court of the flats Wilson had disappeared. Hyslop called for reinforcements and met Wilson again in Allison Street. The man denied having a box or suitcase and Hyslop asked if he could search the flat. There in the living-room were the two suitcases full of money. He went to look for the box, could not find it and returned to the front room where Wilson shot him at point-blank range, taking away most of the left-hand side of his face. He also shot through the head Constable Edward Barnett, who had joined the search, and Acting Detective Constable McKenzie who was shot a second time whilst he was on the ground. One officer locked himself in the lavatory to use his mobile radio to call for assistance and another, Detective Constable John Campbell, with enormous courage, tackled Wilson, knocking him to the ground and capturing the gun. A second robber in the flat took no part in the shooting and a third escaped only to be retrieved later.

Wilson accepted full responsibility for the shooting. There was no question of joint enterprise, so although at first charges of the murder of DC Barnett were preferred against the other two men, it was accepted they should only stand trial on the charges of robbery. Each received twelve years' imprisonment. Wilson received life, with a twenty-five-year minimum recommendation. The fourth man at the July raid was never found; the police had reason to believe he was dead.[15]

Nor were Walter Norval and his team, known as Norval's Criminal Syndicate, by any means a boy's gang. For a time he

---

[15] Joe Beltrami gives a full account of the legal aspects of the case in his *The Defender*, pp.125 et seq.

was at least one of the Kings of the Glasgow Underworld. In November 1977 he and eleven others stood trial for a series of armed robberies. The trial was delayed when the Glasgow High Court building was damaged by petrol bombs; it was thought the attack had been carried out by supporters of the team with the aim of destroying the documentary evidence against them. Norval's daughter was charged with conspiracy to destroy the building, but was acquitted.

Again the case was surrounded with accusations of witness intimidation. Norval's son-in-law was sentenced to five years' imprisonment for threatening to kill a man who was due to give evidence against Walter. A leading prosecution witness, although kept under guard and in solitary confinement, had scalding water thrown over him. Round-the-clock surveillance was provided for the jurors and an armed bodyguard for the judge and prosecuting counsel.

Norval received the modest sentence of fourteen years. At least it was modest in comparison with those meted out to the Workers' Party of Scotland some five years earlier (see p.73). The Norval trial did not break the gang; the remaining members recruited suitable candidates to fill the temporary vacancies.

Shortly after the Workers' Party of Scotland had been broken up with heavy prison sentences, there was a straightforward criminal enterprise, an armed robbery, which went tragically wrong. On 21 December 1973 a team of robbers stole £20,000 from the British Engineering works in Charles Street, Townhead, Glasgow and when tackled by Jim Kennedy, a security guard, a member of the gang shot him in the stomach. The Glasgow police learned the men were travelling back to London.

In theory it had been a well-planned job organized by Robert Marley at the Railway Tavern in Cowlairs. He had anticipated that the take, swollen by Christmas bonus pay packets, would be over £50,000. He approached James Aitken and in turn they recruited heavies including Steve Doran and Jim Murphy. Murphy then contacted two more young men, Sid Draper and Alan Brown. Members of the squad travelled to Glasgow from London and met on Friday 21 December.

Equipped with high-powered binoculars and a two-way radio, Aitken stayed in a multi-storey car park which commanded a view of the works' yard. Brown, Murphy, Marley and Draper, together with another man, armed with two sawn-off shotguns, an automatic pistol and two pistols, hid themselves by the entrance. As other security guards began transferring money boxes from the strongroom to a fork-lift truck Aitken gave the signal. The fork-lift driver was squirted with ammonia and both guards were shot in the arm and back. Jim Kennedy ran to challenge the robbery, was clubbed to the ground and tried once more to prevent the theft. This time he was shot.

The gang was traced because one of its members had mentioned the name 'Big Jim' on the raid. An anonymous caller provided another name. Glasgow police travelled to London to mount a joint operation with London officers led by Detective Chief Superintendent Jack Slipper (who later chased Ronnie Biggs, the Train Robber, to Brazil). They staked out the flat of Robert Marley's girlfriend and he was arrested within hours. He soon made an eleven-page statement giving details of the preparation for the crime; the gang had held what amounted to board meetings to determine in what way the robbery should be carried out, and whether they should have guns.

Within twenty-four hours all but one of the robbers had been arrested; the last was arrested some weeks later in Brighton. The team received a total of 119 years. Brown received a life sentence with a twenty-five-year minimum recommendation. Steve Doran's brother Ian had already been jailed the previous year for twenty-five years for the more politically motivated bank robberies of the Workers' Party. The police believed that they had been part of a 'travel anywhere' Robbery Inc. whose other members had carried out robberies including one in Dundee (£11,000 from the Royal Bank of Scotland) and another in Erskine, Renfrewshire, where bank raiders had taken £2,000, as well as at least one other robbery in Glasgow.[16]

One of the great Glasgow gang wars took place in the 1980s, culminating in the murder of six members of the Doyle family including an 18-month-old baby in April 1984 when the door of their flat at 29 Bankend Street was soaked in petrol and then fired.[17]

---

[16] There is a full account of the police work leading to the arrest of the men in J. Slipper, *Slipper of the Yard*, Chapter 10. Draper escaped from Gartree prison by helicopter on 10 December 1987. Andrew Russell had hi-jacked the helicopter and forced the pilot to land in the prison's exercise yard. Draper and 38-year-old John Kendall climbed aboard and escaped. The helicopter was obliged to put down in poor weather on a nearby industrial estate and the men held up car drivers to get clear of the area. Draper was later caught in Enfield, North London.

[17] There is a very full account of the case, and comprehensive analysis is put forward as to why the convictions were unsafe, in Douglas Skelton and Lisa Brownlie's *Frightener*.

The war was over territorial rights to ice-cream concessions. Much of the post-war troubles in Glasgow originated in the housing schemes. There had been a policy to shift the Inner City slums to the outskirts and building had commenced by the beginning of the Second World War but had then been suspended. One of these was Carntyre in the East End. Unfortunately the building work was not always of the highest quality. The houses and flats were invaded by rot; on the other hand the allotments bloomed. It was here and on estates like it throughout Scotland and the rest of the country that the mobile ice-cream van flourished.

The ice-cream – like the hot-dog – trade has always attracted competition, and not infrequently violent competition. Traditionally, the tricks employed to temporarily disable the opposition have been at a fairly low level such as squirting raspberry flavouring on to a rival's windscreen or stopping either directly in front of or behind a rival and so creating instant competition. Extreme examples could, however, include putting nails under a van's tyres. Fights between rival drivers were not all that infrequent. Other ploys adopted to deter or maim the competition were for drivers to damage their own vans and then report the incident as criminal damage by their rivals.

Youths could be hired for a few pounds or even a drink to carry out an attack on the opposition, and it was not unknown for a driver to pay someone to threaten him in the presence of a witness so that the matter could be reported to the police. This could then be stored up as a kind of goodwill with the police against the day when allegations would be made against that driver.

In Dundee there was considerable trouble between rival van owners and drivers, whilst Edinburgh had introduced a licensing system based on zones. A driver found in the wrong zone could lose his licence. The Glasgow Council knew of the ice-cream troubles and in the 1970s did have some control over them, but this lapsed with the Civil Government (Scotland) Act 1982. Glasgow estates became an open city, with escalating violence being used to increase the market share. The violence which followed has been ascribed to a war over the drug trade, but in their book Douglas Skelton and Lisa Brownlie maintain that this particular quarrel in 1983–4 had nothing to do with drugs but was purely and simply over the profit which could be made – £200 a week more or less tax-free, or up to £800 if the driver sold stolen cigarettes and soft drink – on a lucrative van round.

Drivers could either be owners of their vans and pay the ice-cream distributors such as Fifti Ices for garaging space, or lease the van on a weekly basis. The big companies which offered this facility included the Marchetti brothers, who were connected by marriage to Fifti Ices.

Instead of a squirt of strawberry on the windscreen, or deflated tyres, the early 1980s saw the use of the baseball bat, then firearms and finally the petrol bomb. The troubles were not between the owners of Marchetti (although it was their vans which suffered) and Fifti, but between the drivers. By the end of 1983 vans operating in the Garthamlock area would return to their depot with the windows and headlights smashed, as did the vans which lodged at Fifti. By then it was on a twice-weekly basis. Helpers were recruited and Andrew 'Fat Boy' Doyle was given a Marchetti van rent-free to try to run the opposition off the road.

The first use of firearms in what came to be known as the ice-cream wars seems to have occurred around 8 p.m. on 29 February 1984, when shots were fired at driver Doyle and his 15-year-old assistant Anne Wilson as they made the rounds in Garthamlock. A shotgun was fired by a man who had climbed out of a Volvo car and the pellets broke the windscreen of Doyle's van. Earlier that month there had been an attempt to set fire to the Marchetti building in Glentanar Road.

The attacks continued throughout the month and in the middle of March a police sergeant who knew the warring drivers spoke to James Mitchell, a Marchetti man, and Agnes Lafferty and Tony Capuano (Fifti Ices). Marchetti would agree to nothing except an unconditional surrender in the shape of the withdrawal of Fifti Ices from Garthamlock. Lafferty and Capuano said that although they would not be frightened away, if Mitchell would agree to a compromise they would. Unfortunately, as it turned out, the name of a major Glasgow hardman was mentioned by Agnes' brother Thomas who was with her. The name was Thomas Campbell known as 'TC' – partly because those were his initials, partly because he wore steel-capped Big T boots, but also after the cartoon character 'Top Cat.' The last thing wanted, said Lafferty, was for 'TC' to be involved.

Campbell was the brother of one of the Marchetti drivers, Sadie, who was paying protection money. If she gave credit it was never repaid; if she refused credit her van was attacked. Campbell was a genuine Glasgow hardman who ran the Goucho gang with a razor of iron. He was sentenced to ten years for mobbing and rioting after a fight in a car park at a Glasgow dog-track. After his release he associated with the Barlanark Team, which then numbered about forty and worked in groups 'tanning' or robbing post offices and cash-and-carries throughout Scotland. He was acquitted of complicity in a prison-break from Barlinnie in 1980. Escapers included John and James Steele, the brother of Joseph who would stand trial with Campbell for the Doyle murders. Later Campbell bought a van with his wife Liz and worked the route. Attacks continued both ways and spread to an attack on a Viking Ices van in Castlemilk, an area also used by Fifti Ices drivers. In one incident a van operated by two girls was attacked and a minder, John Shepherd, travelling in it was stabbed.

The fire occurred at 2 a.m. on 16 April, the night – as many of the witnesses recalled over the years – Tommy Cooper died on television. During it or shortly afterwards Christine Halleron, Anthony Doyle (aged 14), Mark Halleron (aged 18 months), James Doyle junior, Andrew Doyle and James Doyle died. Stephen Doyle jumped with his dog from a window, Lilian Doyle was rescued from a window-ledge. Daniel Doyle survived when he managed to get his head out of a broken window and so avoided inhaling the fumes.

There were two possible eyewitnesses to the fire-raisers. One, John Whitefield, described four young fellows aged 15–16 running past him, and another said he thought he might recognize the men involved. Neither was asked to attend an identification parade.

At first the police considered whether the fire might have been started because of the Doyle brothers' work in the nightclubs, where they were thought to have upset punters. However, slowly but surely they hardened on the theory that it was to do with the ice-cream wars. They came to this conclusion in part because as Andrew Doyle lay in the ambulance in Bankend Street he said to a police officer, 'I told you the bastards would torch me. If this is because of the ice-cream hassle I'll get the bastards.' Apparently on an earlier occasion he had said to the same policeman, 'Look, they've battered me, shot me, all I'm waiting on now is the petrol bomb.' The officer duly reported the second conversation to a superior.

The first man arrested to confess was Joe Grainger, who admitted that he, Thomas Campbell and others had been keeping clock, or look-out, whilst Joseph Steele and others actually started the fire. He retracted his evidence at the trial and as a result served five years for his pains and perjury. He appealed successfully to the European Court of Human Rights, which ruled that he had not had a fair trial, but the Scottish Office took no action. The second plank of evidence on which the prosecution would base its case was that of Billy Love, who said he had been in the Netherfield bar when Thomas Campbell had asked for volunteers to firebomb the Doyle household. Steele had been with them.

The other evidence against Steele and Campbell amounted to little more than one sentence of verbal admissions. Campbell was alleged to have said that he intended the fire only to be a frightener, whilst Steele had said it wasn't he who had lit the match. A further piece of supporting evidence was the finding of a map in a briefcase belonging to Campbell which circled Bankfield Street and marked the Doyle flat with a cross. Steele and Campbell supporters point out that there was no need for their clients to have such a map: they both lived in the area and knew it like the backs of their hands. Steele's alibi was that he was home in bed with the flu; his mother was his witness. Campbell said he had been watching a video with his wife, Liz. Both men were convicted. Campbell received a life sentence with a recommendation that he serve at least twenty years. Steele's sentence carried no recommendation.

After the trial the press had a field day. After all, here were two men both of whose families had been involved in heavy gang crime in Glasgow for years. There were suggestions that instead of raspberry ripple in the cones there had been heroin at £10 a bag, something which had not been mentioned at the trial. It is a claim which Campbell fervently denies. The fighting between Fifti Ices and Marchetti did not end with the convictions. There were even allegations, again denied, that Campbell was controlling things from his cell.

Since the trial there have been persistent attempts to re-open the case. Billy Love has from time to time changed his story back and forth. In the latest version given to a BBC journalist in 1993 on his release from Dartmoor, he said, 'I couldn't even ask Thomas Campbell or Joe Steele to forgive me for what they've been through. I know I've shortened their lives.' Campbell has said he will neither shave nor cut his hair until his release. Filmed in Barlinnie prison, he spoke bitterly of the Serious Crime Squad which he called the Serious Fit-Up Squad. 'They're called in to assess of all villains in the area who has the least defence. Then if they've no alibi or only one witness they'll do.' Steele has escaped three times, once glueing himself to the railings at Buckingham Palace. On his last escape on 25 May 1993 he spoke to the BBC reporter, saying that although he was now nearly eligible for parole he would not apply. 'Only guilty men take parole.' He surrendered by climbing a scaffolding tower in front of the prison, staying there for an hour to be filmed by the press.

The chances of either Campbell or Steele winning their hoped-for re-trial are slim. Two of the senior officers in the case are dead; one committed suicide shortly after the case. All they can hope for is a pardon, or that the case will be referred back to the Court of Appeal. One of the defence counsel in the case who referred to the evidence brought against the men as 'rotten to the core' is now an Appeal Court judge, and the men and their supporters hope he will somehow intervene on their behalf. One difficulty regarding Love's retraction is, as a Scots lawyer put it, 'Technically it is not what the Appeal Court would base any decision on. They have said before they will not entertain an appeal merely because a witness changes his story.'

Steele believes that unless he wins a re-trial he will only leave prison in a box. 'If I don't win my case, I don't think I'll get out.'

In March 1992 a man who had a genuine claim to be the King of Glasgow's Gangland, possibly even that of Britain, died peacefully. Arthur Thompson, who had survived countless attacks and attempts on his life, died of a heart attack. The weekend before his death he had been out dancing with his wife and friends. Perhaps of all Glasgow hardmen he could be said to have been a genuine Gangland Boss in the old traditional style. His lawyer, Joe Beltrami, who said that Thompson had 'gun-metal eyes', wrote:

[Thompson] was an impressive-looking figure – about five feet ten inches tall and weighing about 12 stones. He was well-built, in a not-so-obvious way – his suits were well-cut and sober, his ties and shirts conservative. Distinguished-looking and slightly older than I, his face displayed small marks of by-gone conflicts. He had more acquittals to his name than most.[18]

Thompson was born in 1931, the year of the introduction of the Means Test. His parents lived in a tenement in Glasgow's North Side and were eventually rehoused in Blackhill. His brothers became barmen-cum-bouncers in the Provanmill Inn near the family home, but Thompson himself had greater ambition; he wished to be a landlord and not merely a bouncer. His efforts to acquire the necessary capital foundered when he and Paddy Meehan, a noted peterman who had learned his trade with the legendary Johnny Ramensky, blew the safe at the Commercial Bank in Beauly, Inverness-shire.[19] The raid was not a success. The bank contained five safes, one of which housed a sixth. There was little in them except for documents and £400. On the way back to Glasgow they stopped for petrol and the garage owner took the number of the Humber Snipe because it was 'not the sort of car one usually associates with such men'. They were further out of luck, for the key to Thompson's house was found in the road where he had dropped it on leaving the bank. Meehan, convicted on a majority verdict, was sentenced to six years and Thompson to half that.

In the 1950s and 1960s he built up a reputation as a hardman dealing with villains such as Gorbals street baron, Teddy Martin – described as having the Italian looks which drove women wild, and a ferocious temper – who was shot on 25 March 1961, and Algie Earns who was beaten up at Glasgow Cross. Both had run protection rackets involving clubs, pubs and street bookies.

Thompson was described by Meehan as:

> . . . at least as tough [as Martin] and one of the most single-minded men I have ever known. He is happily married,

---

[18] J. Beltrami, *A Deadly Innocence*, pp.58–9.

[19] Ramensky, Glasgow-born of Lithuanian parents, was a brilliant cracksman. He was employed behind enemy lines during the Second World War and awarded a Distinguished Conduct Medal. Another safebreaker used in the war was the Englishman Eddie Chapman, later a close friend of Billy Hill. Glasgow has always had a tradition of providing class safebreakers. In *Life Begins at Midnight*, p.85, Colquhoun wrote, 'Petermen are commonplace in Glasgow. In fact, if I was asked to name the type of specialist criminal most often produced by the city, I'd plump for the safeblower. There's a strong suggestion that a school for safeblowers, where novices can learn their trade from experts, has more than once been organised in the city.'

dotes on his children, and never drinks anything stronger
than a bottle of beer. He is, however, not a man to cross . . .
Both Teddy [Miller] and MacTampson were quite capable
of cool, extreme violence but, I hasten to add, only within a
very strict set of rules. Neither, for instance, would attack
an ordinary member of the public, either on a job or in one
of the pub brawls which are not an uncommon feature of
Glasgow life. Neither would countenance violence towards
a woman, or to a man whose womenfolk were present. But
they were leading members of a very hard society and would
protect their position in that society with any force they
considered necessary. Other criminals who 'crossed' them
did so at their peril. An insult, delivered to them personally,
or to a friend, would be quickly and forcefully avenged.[20]

Thompson had had an uneasy relationship with Martin for some
years and the shooting seems to have been over an initial
suggestion that Thompson was tight with his money. This was
rather harsh since Thompson had, in part and along with
Meehan, engineered Martin's escape from Peterhead prison in
1954, which had been the first successful escape from the jail.
Meehan and John Harvey collected Martin when he came over
the wall, whilst Thompson put up a diversionary scheme. He
arranged for prison clothing to be smuggled out of Barlinnie and
had it marked with Martin's Peterhead number. Once Martin
was out of prison and in fact drinking in a nearby hotel, he made
an anonymous call to the police telling them that the man was
hiding in a loft at Blackhill. It was there the police found the
clothing and presumed he must already be in Glasgow. Now
Martin was safe to take the road from the Highlands to home,
secure in the knowledge that there would be no police blocks on
the way.

The quarrel was over the financing of a robbery at the
Westminster Bank at the junction of the City Road and Old
Street in London. The idea had been promoted by a London
criminal and was to be a safeblowing. Meehan and Martin had
been down in London reconnoitring the situation, and had

---

[20] P. Meehan, *Innocent Villain*, Chapters 3, 4 and 5. Thompson is described as
MacTampson. Teddy Miller appears under his own name. For the prison break Meehan
received fifteen months; Thompson was never charged.

expended a certain amount of money on the enterprise. Thompson was due to go on the raid with them and, as a full partner, was expected by Martin to put up his share of the capital required for the expenses. When he produced a £100 note in a public house, Martin changed tack and suggested that Thompson was trying to set them up, a far worse insult. The implication was that a £100 note, rare at the time, could have come from a robbery and therefore its serial number could be traced if Martin tried to cash it. A week before the robbery was due to take place, Thompson shot Martin in Meehan's flat.

Meehan's wife Betty, who was nine months' pregnant, ran into the room. Now, according to the code of the Samurai, Martin, who was bleeding heavily, could not be touched again. The standard practice would have been for him to be given a coaxy (or piggy-back), put in a van and dumped. Instead Meehan called an ambulance and Martin was taken to hospital in a coma.

The next day he was, however, fighting fit and so far as he was concerned the robbery could go ahead. Thompson was clearly out and so another Glasgow safebreaker was recruited. The robbery was a disaster; Martin and the second man were caught *in flagrante* when an office worker heard the safe blown. Meehan escaped only to look around for another job. The London contact Billy suggested that a Co-op store in Edmonton would be suitable. Meehan appears to have been reluctant but the job went ahead and, at the last minute, Meehan was persuaded to actually blow the safes. He was standing over them unpacking dynamite, of which far too liberal a use had been made, when the police walked in. Billy received five years and Meehan eight. Meehan believed he had been grassed by the woman, Sheila, with whom he had been staying.

Thompson had effectively been apprenticed to bookmaker and gambler, Morris Mendel, who also had an interest in nightclubs, betting offices and casinos for which at the time only a drinks licence was necessary. He became a partner and when Mendel retired to England Thompson took over. He rarely served a sentence. In 1951 he received three years for assault and robbery, in 1953 eighteen months for extortion, and in 1955 three years for the Beauly bank. From the 1950s he maintained links with English criminals. He was a friend of Billy Hill, and visited Frank Fraser when he was in prison serving seven years for the attack on rival gangleader Jack Spot.

When Robert 'Andy' Anderson escaped (rather by chance with Ronnie Biggs, the Train Robber) and appeared on the doorstep of Atlantic Machines, run in Tottenham Court Road by Eddie Richardson and Francis Fraser, looking for assistance, it was to Thompson that Fraser turned for help. Within forty-eight hours Thompson met Fraser and Anderson in Edinburgh and found the escapee work for a period of months until Fraser arranged for Anderson to move south to Manchester to join Bobby McDermott.

Fraser recalls admiringly:

There was a lot of trade between Glasgow and London; a lot of help and friendship. If a Scottish fellow was in London who needed help we'd put him up. It was a two-way thing but it showed the strength of the friendship. You wouldn't get too many people who could get on the phone and ask if they could put up someone who had escaped doing 12 years. Not only that, he'd escaped with Biggs. They never blinked an eyelid. The answer immediately was 'Yes'. It was not for financial gain. They wouldn't take one penny.

But it was over his twenty-five-year-long war that he and his family had with the powerful Welsh family, also from Blackhill – five times as long as the London feud between the Brindles and the Carters – that Thompson really made his mark. First, Patrick Welsh and his friend James Goldie died when their van hit a wall and then a lamp-post. Thompson was charged with causing their deaths by running them off the road and was acquitted after the jury retired for rather less than an hour. The original charge of murder had been reduced to one of unjustifiable homicide. Three months later Thompson and his mother-in-law, Maggie Johnstone, climbed into his MG parked outside his house in Provanmill Road. When he started the car there was an explosion; she was killed, he was injured. Three of the Welshes were later acquitted. In July 1967 Rita Thompson went to prison after admitting leading a raid on the Welsh family's home. The police, if not actually frightened, were certainly wary of Thompson. One senior officer evacuated his family from his home during the prosecution for the deaths of Welsh and Goldie, fearing it would be bombed. Another officer emigrated after the case.

Through his son Arthur Jr, known as the Fat Boy, and some of his London contacts, Thompson reluctantly moved into drugs, operating from a base in Blackpool. But by the end of the 1980s attempts to overthrow him were coming thick and fast. In November 1989 he was shot whilst washing his car in front of a lock-up garage. He booked himself into the private Nuffield Alpine Clinic and told police and the doctor who removed the bullet that he had injured himself with a drill bit which had sheared off during use. Three years later he was run down outside his council house home which by now he had converted into something like a luxury fortress – two houses knocked into one, and heavily barricaded with steel doors. Again he survived.

Arthur Jr did not survive, however. Drugs proved to be his downfall. In 1985 he went to prison for eleven years on heroin dealing charges. The case was a curious one and until his death the Fat Boy maintained his innocence, claiming he had been framed by a Jonah McKenzie. For a time Arthur Jr was able to demand a cut from his team, the Barlanark Gang, but he was by no means a popular leader and a rival organization was in place within the year. Although he may have assisted his son, Arthur Snr was no more anxious to join him in the drug trade than the Godfather, Don Corleone, had been keen to join Sollazo. Thompson firmly denied that his daughter Margaret had died from a drugs overdose in June 1989. Instead it was put about that she had choked to death on her own vomit after a drinking bout. Her drug addict boyfriend fled Scotland. Nevertheless, Thompson loyally protected his son against drug-dealing allegations, maintaining that the Fat Boy had been framed by the police. 'The trouble for young Arthur has been that the cops have long memories,' he told the *Sunday Times*. 'When they couldn't get me they took my son.'

By 1991 it was estimated that up to £200,000 a week was being generated in gang money by the manufacture, supply and distribution of cheap drugs. But so far as the Fat Boy was concerned he was isolated when the gang fractured. His percentage had dried up. Meanwhile, a hand-grenade had been thrown into a public house where the Barlanark team once drank. Before he came out on home leave as part of a parole plan in 1991, he vowed to kill the five men he said had ripped off his earnings. The circumstances of his death were curious. Released on weekend home leave after serving some seven years of his sentence, he arranged to have a meal with his sister in an Italian restaurant. Although the house in which he lived was part of Thompson's fortress, the Fat Boy apparently took no great protective measures for his safety. Almost at the last minute the venue was changed and he went to Café India, a smart Indian restaurant in the centre of the city, with his mother and common-law wife, Catherine. Shortly before he arrived at the restaurant a man, later said to be a Paul Ferris, had approached the manager, asked if there was a Thompson there and insisted on searching the dining area with its two hundred plus customers before he was satisfied there was not. After his meal Thompson returned to the fortress, had a word with his father, and then walked to the end house to check whether his brother, Billy, was recording a film on the video set. He rang the bell and a woman in the house, who went to the door, sensed something was wrong. She saw the Fat Boy staggering away, shot. One bullet had grazed his cheek, one fractured two ribs and the third hit his heart. His last words were, 'I've been shot, hen.[21] I'm going to collapse.' The family did not wait for an ambulance but drove him to hospital where he was found to be dead on arrival.

The police and Arthur Thompson had various theories about the killers. From the point of view of the police, the killing must have smelled of an inside job. Who knew at which restaurant Arthur would be? Or when he would return home? Would outsiders really linger outside the well-protected house awaiting his return? Could a message have been sent to them from the time he left the restaurant?

Now, say Underworld acquaintances, it was the moment for Thompson to show who really was the master. As his son's cortège went to the graveyard it passed a car in which the bodies of the two men Joe 'Bananas' Hanlon and Robert Glover, suspected of Arthur junior's killing and shot in the head with a .22 pistol, had been left. Overall, Hanlon had not led a lucky life. A car he owned had been blown up, his ice-cream van from which he also sold heroin had been torched and he had been shot on two occasions, once in the penis.

Stephen Guy, a friend of the Fat Boy, had been charged over the torching of the van but was acquitted. However, Guy's troubles did not end there. Within the week shots had been

---

[21] A term of endearment sometimes used ironically.

fired at his house and a lodger Robert Johnstone, who had nothing at all to do with Guy, was hit in the neck.

The obligatory police swoop on Fortress Thompson, real name Southfork, over the deaths of Hanlon and Glover, came to nothing. The family was arrested, released and returned to what was now a compound kitted out with surveillance cameras and floodlighting.

In 1992, after a trial lasting fifty-four days, a third man, Paul Ferris, suspected of being one of Thompson junior's murderers, was acquitted. The thread of the case – possibly not the best ever handled by the prosecution – was that all three men had been involved in the killing. It may be that the prosecution had followed, too closely, Arthur Thompson's thought processes, reconstructed the case and found the evidence which would fit the theory. Much of that evidence was from a fellow-prisoner and supergrass Dennis Woodman, a Geordie, who told the jury Ferris had confessed to him in prison. Woodman and his then common-law wife and her brother had been involved in a nasty kidnapping of a farmer in Dumfriesshire in an effort to get him to withdraw money from his bank accounts. How had Ferris made the confession? Shouting through the bars of his cell to Woodman, conveniently in the next cell, whom he had never seen? How had Woodman been placed in the next cell? Well, apparently when he had been in another prison he had been found with escaping tools in his cell, something he, Woodman, said had been planted by the authorities, and as a result he had been transferred. Woodman, cross-examined by Donald Findlay,[22] told of the tragic death of his children in a road accident, something for which everyone had sympathy for several days until it was revealed that the children were alive and well and living in England and, indeed, Woodman had sent them a Christmas card from prison after their 'death'. Most of his evidence about the case could be traced, almost word for word, to pages from the Scottish editions of the *Sun* newspaper. As the trial went on the normally pro-active Findlay quietly demolished Woodman, who became more and more

[22] Findlay, a flamboyant lawyer, is a director of Glasgow Rangers and a known and committed Protestant. According to some observers the trial with the Thompson family, at least nominally Catholic, took on a sectarian dimension.

wild in his allegations, including a suggestion that Ferris's solicitor had endeavoured to bribe him. It was evidence which badly backfired on the prosecution for Woodman was not believed, something which by the end of his two weeks in the witness-box surprised few. Indeed, the surprise was that the prosecution still clung to his evidence instead of chucking their supergrass overboard and relying on the other evidence. And what was that?

Partly, another odd piece from a former girlfriend of Robert Glover who said that he, Glover, had called her in the middle of the night saying he had to see her. At the time she was living with another man, but Glover came round and they sat in a parked car for some hours during which time he told her of his and Ferris's involvement.

This presented something of a problem. Glover was dead and could not be cross-examined on the veracity of his statement. It was admitted into evidence but with considerable warnings from the trial judge, Lord McCluskey, as was the identification evidence that it had been Ferris in the restaurant combing the tables to find the Fat Boy.

There is little doubt that at the very least Ferris had been in the wrong city at the wrong time. Coming from a spectacularly criminal family he had moved to London where, as one Scots lawyer put it, there was evidence he had been 'repotting' himself. Nevertheless he had admittedly flown to Glasgow on the day of the killing to buy clothes for his child by a woman in the city, heard of the shooting and had absented himself smartly, hiring a car and driving south throughout the night.

Ferris – 'clever, articulate and passionate', says one trial observer who adds, 'the most convincing accused are either those who are innocent or those who are guilty but who know the police have manufactured the case against them' – was also cleared of charges of supplying drugs, knee-capping a former member of the Barlanark team, Willie Gillen, and attempting to murder Arthur Thompson himself.

Ferris's defence was, in part, that the killer of young Arthur was in fact 'Blind' Jonah McKenzie, a man who at the age of 37 had acquired thirty-six stab wounds and who had been blinded by 'Bananas' Hanlon in an attack in May 1991. This it was said was as a reprisal for the attack on the ice-cream/heroin van.

McKenzie, a staunch Thompson man, who had received seven years when young Arthur picked up his eleven, vehemently denied the allegation. The jury accepted Ferris's alibi for the murder and the shooting of Willie Gillen; he had sensibly written on sixty-three pages of a notebook before his arrest. The reason for doing this was that he had, so he said, been fitted up by the police on a previous occasion and as a result kept a detailed account of his movements. He had, he said, been assisting another man in Glasgow who had been slashed: 'There was blood spattered all over his face – that's when I noticed his right hand. You could actually see the white muscle tissue and the blood streaming from it.'

Curiously, part of the defence was also to prove that the dead men, Glover and Hanlon, were also innocent and a substantial number of witnesses were found who, if they could not completely alibi the men, could go a long way towards doing so.

So far as the attempt on Arthur senior's life was concerned, this could not possibly have been done by Ferris for Arthur himself, a great performer, went into the witness-box to say he regarded Ferris almost as a son.

After Ferris's acquittal the *Daily Record* reported there was a £30,000 contract on his life. Indeed, in the ensuing troubles Ferris's family had not escaped unscathed. Willie Ferris, his father, required over a hundred stitches following an attack. He was beaten with a hammer and baseball bat and his car, bought with a disability pension, had its tyres slashed and was later set on fire. Ferris's brother Billy, himself convicted of murder, asked to be moved to a prison nearer to his father.

The Fat Boy's funeral itself was graced by the attendance of lawyers, MPs and entertainers. 'What a stroke,' said a South-East London friend of the Thompsons with approbation of the killing of Glover and Hanlon. 'And what a send-off for the boy.'

By now Arthur Thompson senior, who owned a holiday home in Rothesay as well as one in Spain, was moving into the role of businessman, making donations to charity and mixing with prominent political figures. As was befitting, his own funeral in March 1993, an all-day and night affair, was a splendid one with another full turnout by sportsmen and politicians as well as more than one criminal. First, there had been a scare that there was a suspicious device at the cemetery and an Army bomb disposal unit carried out a controlled explosion of what turned out to be a hoax device. After a quiet service at the home for family and friends, it was off to the cemetery, and then to the Provomills Public House where those who had not been able to attend the religious formalities were able to pay tribute to the family.

Meanwhile what had been happening to Thompson's old mate Patrick Meehan? He had certainly been in the wars and had barely survived. Many of his problems stemmed back to Thompson waving the £100 note about in the Glasgow public house.

Meehan had not settled down to do his eight years' preventive detention, imposed by Judge John Maud at the Old Bailey, the easy way. His wife, the long-suffering Betty, had decided enough was enough and began divorce proceedings. In prison Meehan had refused to work and had quarrelled with officers. In December 1962 he tried unsuccessfully to escape from Nottingham prison and his efforts had been rewarded with 180 days' loss of remission, along with cellular confinement and nine days' bread and water. Even before his sentence he had had an unnerving experience. According to his memoirs, whilst changing down the £100 note to more manageable proportions he had been approached by a man who had suggested that, in view of his success with Martin's escape he, Meehan, might be able to assist with the springing of the spy George Blake from prison. It was suggested that Meehan would probably have to go to East Berlin for further instructions.

Meehan succeeded in his escape, again from Nottingham, on 20 August 1963 when, during a diversion in a cricket match, he and three other prisoners escaped through a fence to a waiting car. He and a prisoner named Hogan went to Glasgow, from where Meehan caught a flight to Dublin and then another to Germany, where he recounts that he was questioned about his ability to help to free certain Russian spies including George Blake.

What is absolutely clear is that in early 1967 the recaptured Meehan was transferred from Blundeston prison in Suffolk to Parkhurst on the Isle of Wight. It was there he met a man who was nearly his nemesis, 32-year-old Lancastrian James Griffiths, whose early claim to fame was that he was the first man to escape from a prison on the Isle of Wight and actually get off the island.[23] He and Meehan became friends, along with another Glasgow villain, Roy Fontaine.

Out of prison in August 1968 Meehan, who had served seven of his eight years, returned to Glasgow. He went through a variety of jobs until in the spring of 1969 he started a little business installing spy-holes in front doors at £1 a time. That summer Griffiths turned up in Glasgow selling stolen antiques; he stayed with Meehan on and off during the next weeks, and on Saturday 5 July went to Stranraer to look over a possible burglary at the motor taxation office there.

On 8 July 72-year-old Rachel Ross died at the County Hospital, Ayrshire. She had been the victim of a tie-up robbery off Racecourse Road, Ayr, and one of the robbers had knelt on her chest. Her 67-year-old husband, Abraham, had been hit with an iron bar and stabbed in the neck. Very much in the frame for the robbery and killing were Meehan and Griffiths. One reason was that Abraham Ross said that the two men involved had called themselves Pat and Jim. It was also accepted by Meehan that he and Griffiths had been in the area. At a voice identification parade in which Meehan was the only one who spoke, Mr Ross identified him. He had been asked to say, 'Shut up, shut up, we'll send for an ambulance.'

Two girls to whom Griffiths and Meehan had given a lift also identified Meehan in another identification parade. Griffiths could not be identified; he was already dead. Whilst in prison he had been one of the subjects of a BBC documentary in which he had said he would never do another sentence. He was proved right.

Shortly after Meehan's arrest at 10.30 a.m., the police went to 14 Holyrood Crescent, Griffiths' home. The reason was simple: Meehan had given them Griffiths' name and address as an alibi witness. When there was no reply to their knockings, they kicked the door down and were faced with Griffiths wearing bandoliers

[23] Griffiths was taken before the Rochdale Juvenile Court by his mother as being out of control at the age of nine. Following a career of relatively minor crime, he took part in a nasty armed robbery in Blackpool in 1963 for which he received four years. His escape from Parkhurst in December 1965 was simple. He walked away from an outside working party, caught a bus to Ryde and boarded the ferry to Portsmouth from where he caught a train to Scunthorpe where he lived in a caravan. His time on the outside did not last long. He took part in other armed robberies and eventually, in March 1966, he received a further four years' imprisonment at Lindsey Quarter Sessions for housebreaking and theft. This was consecutive to the sentence which he had left unfinished.

of ammunition about his body and firing at them. A Detective Constable William Walker was hit. The other officers retreated, taking Walker with them and pursued by Griffiths firing at them from the window. By the time Griffiths left Holyrood Crescent four more officers had been injured. He then shot a man, Jim Kerr, who was getting into his car, and when Kerr collapsed out of the vehicle Griffiths took it and drove off to the Round Toll Bar in Possil Road, where he fired two shots into the ceiling and with the third killed William Hughes who had moved only to put down his drink.

Griffiths was chased out of the bar by the extremely brave chargehand, John Connelly. He then shot two more men during his escape until he holed up in 26 Kay Street off the Springburn Road. It was there that Chief Superintendent Malcolm Finlayson, peering through the letter-box, saw Griffiths aiming at the door: 'It was either Griffiths or myself. I took my .38 and aimed it through the letter-box and fired at his shoulder.'

Griffiths, hit in the chest, died after firing further shots at the officers as they burst through the door. That day one civilian was killed and eleven were injured, along with five police officers.

Meanwhile there were rumours in the Underworld that despite Griffiths' suicidal behaviour and his record for unpleasant robberies, he and Meehan had not been responsible for those robberies. The name to come up regularly was that of Ian Waddell. Joe Beltrami, the veteran and probably best-known Scottish solicitor, who acted for Meehan, recalled:

> As one detective told me, 'Waddell's name is mentioned a lot.' A client said, 'The dogs in the street are barking the names of Waddell and Dick. Even they know Meehan's innocent. The police must know too.'[24]

Under Scottish procedure, if a defendant alleges that another has committed the crime then he must impeach or name him in pre-trial procedures and Waddell and another man were duly impeached by Beltrami. At the trial Waddell was invited to repeat the words, 'Shut up, shut up . . .' and Ross, hearing him, said that although he was not sure it was like the voice.

In his book Beltrami complains of the trial judge Lord Grant

---

[24] J. Beltrami, A *Deadly Innocence*, p.62.

whom he believed rescued the Crown whenever necessary. The prosecution was 'rescued' now when he asked Ross, 'Is your recollection as clear now, three months later, as it was when you went to the parade?'

Waddell had been on the Crown's list of witnesses but was not called and so had to be called for the defence. He admitted that he was one of the first people questioned after the murder, but denied that he had paid the substantial sum of £200 to a solicitor to attend the police station with him. Later he denied that he had given the money to the solicitor, John Carlin. The reply would later earn him a sentence of three years' imprisonment for perjury.

Meehan's legal team – Beltrami had briefed Nicholas Fairbairn and John Smith, now the leader of the Labour Party, for him – were hopeful, if not confident, that a verdict of not proven, that intermediate verdict available to a Scottish court, would be the worst that could happen. They were wrong. A majority (and in Scotland a bare 8–7 majority of the 15-member jury will suffice) found him guilty.

Beltrami never gave up. A solicitor with the greatest experience of the Underworld, he used his contacts, notably the influential Arthur Thompson, to discover the real killers in an endeavour to have the conviction set aside.

Beltrami had been half correct in having Waddell and the other man impeached. The correct half was Waddell. His actual partner turned out to be an unlikely one, the noted hardman William 'Tank' McGuinness. He had been a client of Beltrami's for some fifteen years (as had almost every other self-respecting Glaswegian villain at one time or another) and was known for his partiality for tie-ups along with his penchant for violence. In 1968, along with John Farrell, he had been accused and acquitted of the murder of a man named Richards. At first sight Waddell, thought to be something of a blabbermouth in drink, would not seem a likely partner for the very canny and experienced McGuinness, the latter's name not being one to be bandied about lightly. Although not at present on a charge McGuinness began to pay visits to Beltrami's office on an informal basis, leaking more and more clues about the robbery. By the time of his last visit he had admitted that it had been Waddell's responsibility to telephone the police to get the Rosses released. He had also taken the lawyer and Ludovic Kennedy, of the Free Meehan Campaign, around the drainage system of Ayr trying to find rings and keys from the robbery. Beltrami's problem was that these were confidential statements by a client. Without his express permission to use them, he was bound by the lawyer's equivalent of the seal of the confessional. To do so could easily have meant his being struck off the roll of solicitors.

In early 1975 McGuinness' home was broken into late one night by two masked men armed with a sawn-off shotgun. He was not there but his wife and daughter were; they were terrified as the shotgun was fired into a cupboard. On 12 March 1976 he was found in a coma in Janefield Street close to the Celtic football ground. He had been beaten unconscious and died thirteen days later in the Royal Infirmary. He had never recovered consciousness. Although it was never proved, it was put about that McGuinness had been killed over his involvement in the Ross murder.[25]

The death of McGuinness did at least release Beltrami from the confidentiality of the statements made to him by the man. It was established that Waddell's alibi was false and that although he was unemployed at the time, shortly after the Ayr robbery he had been in possession of substantial funds. Meehan was pardoned in May 1976. Now Ian Waddell was charged with the murder of Mrs Ross and put forward the defence of impeachment against Meehan and Griffiths. He was acquitted by a majority verdict of the jury who retired for just over an hour.

His acquittal brought him little fortune, however. In 1982 he was murdered in Blackthorn Street, Glasgow by his friend, Andy Gentle, who received a sentence of life imprisonment. The men had been involved in the death of Mrs Josephine Chipperfield, and the prosecution's case was that Gentle felt that Waddell might turn him over to the police.

'Gipsy' Winning had already gone. In 1980 he had picked a

---

[25] In June 1976, shortly after Meehan's pardon, John 'Gypsy' Winning, another of Beltrami's clients, was charged with the murder of McGuinness, his close friend. In 1962 he and McGuinness had escaped from Barlinnie together and had later stood trial in Glasgow for safeblowing at a Dalry bank. McGuinness was acquitted and Winning received a sentence for reset (dishonest handling of stolen goods). Each received nine months for the prison break. Some of the evidence against Winning was that he had blood of McGuinness' rare type on his coat. Evidence was given that it could have come from a previous instance when Winning broke up a fight between McGuinness and James Bruce in the Braemar Bar in London Road. There were also evidential difficulties about the taking of the blood sample from McGuinness. The jury was directed to return a verdict of not guilty.

fight with James McLellan, yet another of Beltrami's clients, when drunk at a house in Rosebank Cottage, Dunfermline. McLellan was more than a match. His father had been a well-known Glasgow cobbles fighter and had passed on his talents. McLellan's plea to culpable homicide on the grounds of provocation was accepted and he received a sentence of thirty months.

In due course there was an inquiry into the Meehan case undertaken by Lord Hunter. Published in 1982, it offered a new and curious theory that all four men, Griffiths, Meehan, Waddell and McGuinness, had been involved. Meehan finally received the sum of £50,500 in compensation. Beltrami had been hoping for £100,000 and had to work quite hard to persuade Meehan that this was a reasonable sum.

It would be pleasant, but inaccurate, to record that Meehan was grateful for Beltrami's efforts over the years on his behalf. Perhaps understandably given the pressures of prison life, Meehan's letters to Beltrami during his sentence were filled with recriminations. After his release and compensation he appears to have been only marginally more grateful. There is a photograph of him being shown the dotted line by Beltrami as he signs for his compensation, in which he looks reasonably happy. His gratitude did not last. In 1990 he produced a book which was highly critical of Beltrami and partly blamed him for his conviction. After some thought Beltrami decided not to apply for an interdict (injunction). The book was not on general sale.

At the lower end of the scale, in 1992 David McDermott argued with Alan Auld over the loan of £5. McDermott hit Auld twice with a machete, for which he received a sentence of nine years and three months for attempted murder. It was unremarkable. Knives had been the weapons used in 382 attempted murders in 1992 in Strathclyde, and in slightly over half the 92 murders. Once, said David Bryce, a former member of the Calton Tongs, it was about areas. 'You couldn't go from Barrowfield into Calton – you might get killed. Now people go from Barrowfield into Calton to score.'[26] Drugs have taken over once more.

---

[26] Stewart Hennessey, *Slice of Life*, in *The Times*, 15 May 1993.

4

Liverpool
and the North West

The century started badly for the Birkenhead police. On 9
September 1900 the third robbery of the year took place at the
Birkenhead Post Office. George Fell, shoemaker, auxiliary postman and caretaker, failed to answer the gate when other postmen
arrived for the evening shift at about 4.50 p.m. They forced the
door and discovered a pool of blood inside the doorway. Fell was
found in the postmaster's room, his face covered with a postbag.
A broken poker lay on the floor and a coal shovel had several
dents in it. It seemed as though Fell had used it as a shield against
the blows from the poker. £19.15s.2d had been taken from the
safe, along with £50 in £10 notes and three postal orders.
Although details of the notes were circulated and their numbers
printed in the national newspapers, no single one was ever
tendered.

Nor was the killer ever found. One theory is that he may have
had the gate opened to him by Fell sometime during the day and
immediately attacked him, which would account for the blood in
the doorway. Another is that he may even have hidden himself in
the cellar amongst postal baskets whilst the office was open, and
was later surprised by Fell. Fell had a great send-off, with the
Post Office band playing the 'Dead March' from *Saul* and a
crowd of 10,000 mourners at Flaybrick Cemetery. A trust fund
was set up for his widow. The robber was never caught despite
inquiries nationwide and indeed in Australia. At one time the
Birkenhead police fastened on a man in the Grimsby area, but
that line of inquiry came to nothing.

On the two previous occasions when the Post Office had been robbed, the employees were made to make good the loss. Each had a small amount stopped from his weekly pay until the money had been repaid. This does not seem to have been done the third time.

Probably the robbery was committed by an individual rather than a gang. If so it would conform to the consensus of police, lawyers' and sociologists' opinion that on balance there has been no organized crime in Liverpool; certainly not on the scale seen in London.

It is a secondary economy, the economy of the streets with relatively low class crime. Most Liverpool crime relates to casual employment. There are gangs of kids who do a bit of thieving one day, a bit of violence the next and a bit of shoplifting the third. It relates to the economy of the City. Apart from the docks there's nothing worth stealing.
Mike Brogden, Professor of Law, John Moore's University

The criminal classes in Liverpool are mainly deprived children who've grown up in overcrowded Catholic homes – mainly of Irish extraction.
E. Rex Makin, Liverpool solicitor

It is essentially small time, haphazard, lacking in central organization and carried out by individual villains each working more or less alone and for his own nefarious purposes.[1]

It is a view which may partly be true if one ignores that at one time in the early part of the century half the Chinese community was estimated to be actively concerned in the manufacture of opium, that there was dock related crime – including the rolling of drunken seamen – in the days when 18,000 men were employed there, that there have been such active gangs as the Kellys, the Brodies and the Throstles, and that at present there is a thriving drug connection and there appears to be a drug-linked protection war centred on the provision of bouncers for the discos and nightclubs. It may be played down as minor league compared with the great days of the Richardsons and the Krays

[1] R. Whittington-Egan, *Liverpool Roundabout*, p.175.

95

in London, but it isn't particularly small-time when we are speaking of drug deals in the sum of £67 million.

There is also little doubt that the Liverpool City Police were regarded as the toughest of the tough, and that they controlled the street bookmaking, the shebeens and the drinking clubs. But again a view is that their protection rackets were strictly second rate.

It only amounted to a bottle here, 200 cigarettes there. Not proper money. There wasn't any about.

Mike Brogden

They were also protecting their snouts, warning them of raids by the uniformed police. The amount of actual detection was very low. I should think 95% depended upon the snouts.

E. Rex Makin

When on 11 February 1901 the Chief Constable of the Liverpool City Police reported to the Watch Committee he was quietly self-congratulatory. True there had been a slight increase in the number of indictable offences, 3,742 compared with 3,504 the previous year, but twenty years earlier it had been, with a much smaller population, 6,236. Crimes of violence at thirty-five in number were three less than the previous year, burglary and house-breaking four less and forty-four fewer than five years earlier.

The increase in larcenies was due, he wrote, to minor thefts of loose cotton, rope, sugar on the Dock estate. A new class of offence was emerging, however: the theft of bicycles from office doors, passages and shops. In fact so great had been the decrease in crime that the previous year the strength of the force had been reduced by 100 and had worked 'without loss of efficiency'. There was 'no better tribute to the improved conditions in Liverpool'. Thirteen constables received medals, clasps or votes of thanks for stopping runaway horses.

The next year the Chief Constable was even happier. 'Serious crimes of robbery with violence and assaults with intent to rob, seem to be practically stamped out, there being only eight of these crimes during the year compared with 28 the previous year. Some years ago from 80 to 120 cases per annum was a common number.'

By 1911 Liverpool was 'the most criminal, the most drunken, the most lawless city in the United Kingdom. Why is this?' demanded an anonymous writer in a long-forgotten publication of the time. There was a tendency to blame 'those Irish' but this was not borne out statistically. The Chief Constable lamented, 'There is a general decline of personal honesty in many relations of life. Every year I am more convinced of the fact and every year the remedy seems harder to find.'

The writer went on to show that per 100,000 of the population in 1909 Leeds had 182 tried for indictable offences, London 212, Birmingham 250, Cardiff 264 and Liverpool nearly double London's score with 456. There was an enormous rise in crimes against the person.

In 1929 over 900 bicycles were reported as stolen and the Chief Constable now had this to say about a newer form of transport:

> Owing possibly to the mistaken notion that a motor car may be taken from the street, used and afterwards abandoned without the risk of prosecution, we have had a continuance of so-called joy-riding. In all 75 motor cars were reported as stolen. All these cars were recovered, several within minutes of their being reported missing, and the police obtained sufficient evidence to prosecute in 22 cases for larceny of the car, and in 11 cases for larceny of petrol.[2]

Shortly before the War there was an outbreak of protection in 1937 at the Grand National meeting, always a Mecca for outside criminals. A gang led by another of the so-called Colonels and unusually for the time including two Australians were in operation. Herbert Balmer, then a relatively young officer who later became Deputy Chief Constable, was on duty at the racecourse when he noticed the Colonel and his squad. He reasoned that any trouble would occur after the National was run, at a time when the crowds would begin to leave the course without waiting to see the remaining races. He was right. He and his men found two bookmakers who had been slashed. One had eighteen stitches and the other fifteen. Initially they refused to talk, saying that the

---

[2] Report on the Police Establishment and the State of Crime, for the year ending 31 December 1929.

fault was theirs and they should have paid. According to his memoirs, which appeared over a lengthy period in the *Liverpool Echo* on his retirement in 1967, Balmer arrested the Colonel after a struggle in which Balmer's coat was slashed to pieces. The Colonel received four years' imprisonment after asking Balmer merely to charge him with an offence triable only in the magistrates' court which would have meant a maximum of six months.

Where there are docks there is crime should be one of the easiest of maxims for a sociologist to memorize. Or is it a stereo-typical generalization? Whichever it is

> . . . the war brought an increase in Sailor Town in Liver-pool [which] had gangs of youths indulging in inter-gang warfare – coshes, tapes, with the radius of operations around Park Lane, Paradise Street and Back George Street. Sailors were being lured out of the safe haven of milk bars and the YMCA with the offers of visits to illegal drinking clubs and being rolled on the way to a girl's flat. There were allegations by the Recorder of Liverpool of Police Brutality. H. B. Balmer, a sergeant who acted as police court advocate, told magistrates that the US forces had found it necessary to organize a special corps of soldiers to stop pilfering mainly of cigarettes which were being stolen from American stores and ending up on the Black Market.[3]

Balmer had done rather better than that. He had infiltrated a ring of men stealing from the American PX stores. In fact there was a huge trade in watches and jewellery and Balmer and a colleague made arrangements for sale to him of two jeeps and five cases of watches and jewellery for £10,000. When he arrived at the rendezvous with the money he was told they had been outbid. Balmer and his friend appeared to leave but, in fact, climbed through a window at the back of the premises and when the other buyers arrived they were arrested.

At the end of 1945 the Report on the Police Establishment and the State of Crime for the seven years from 1938 commented:

---

[3] *News Review*, 11 March 1943.

Crime had increased 68.9 per cent since 1938. The raids on the City left many premises very easy to break into, and premises made unfit for occupation provided cover from which to attack adjoining premises and also for hiding stolen goods. The shortages of all kinds of food and clothing made it easy for thieves to dispose of stolen property and also made it worthwhile to steal what before the war would not have repaid the trouble and risk. Crimes on a large scale were often instigated by operators in the black market and on many occasions a whole lorry load of goods was stolen. Many such large scale operations were detected by the police and successful prosecutions resulted but it was seldom possible to obtain the evidence necessary to establish the guilt of the principal offender. Deserters from the Forces and Mercantile Marine were responsible for many offences and were not easy to catch as their visits were often of short duration. The darkened streets provided opportunities for 'hold ups' and snatch thieves but the number of such offences was surprisingly small considering the unusual opportunities.

Two years later, dock thefts were up by 10 per cent and seventeen of the people prosecuted – who came, said the Chief Constable's Report, from all walks of life – were watchmen.

And after the War there was a further great influx of prostitutes to assist the spending of money earned by sailors. Liverpool became a big post-war city of murder and violence. Twenty men and four women received substantial sentences for rolling. The *Daily Herald* returned to the theme of violence and crime on 27 July 1950. 'What makes it our wickedest city?' asked Alan Clarke. (Runners-up were Manchester and Blackpool.) Outside the station Clarke had a cup of tea; it cost 8d including a 5d deposit on the cup (no saucer). The stallholder told him that even with the deposit he lost five dozen cups a week. Goods were scarce on the home market. There were pretty girls who could be used in come-on operations. He heard of one eight-year-old leading a gang of housebreakers armed with a blowlamp. Lime Street was thronged with pimps and prostitutes. However, the Kelly conviction had split up the great organized criminal gangs such as the Swallows who had the eponymous bird tattooed on their wrists. In 1948 it was reckoned there had been over 200 juvenile gangs. There were still dozens in 1950 including the Peanut Gang, so-called because they began their career by splitting open bags of peanuts on the docks, before they graduated to splitting open the heads of seamen decoyed into alleys off Lime Street for their wage packets. There was, said Clarke, a well-established cover system by which a wanted criminal was smuggled from family to family. There was still ingrained mistrust of the law – old-timers could remember the police baton charges in motor-cycle chariots. However, the article ended on an encouraging note. By fairness and intelligent public relations, the police were breaking down the old hostility. There were fewer tensions between Catholics and Protestants, for example.

One crime which had been running since the 1920s was grid-lifting to get into cellars and so burgle houses. In 1947, 115 such entries were reported. It seems the householders either did not have them mended when the grids rusted, or that coalmen failed to put them properly back in place after delivering.

But the implication of one paragraph of the Report was that the black population was to blame for much of the disarray:

> I visited a coloured men's 'social' club within a stone's throw of the cathedral. In a room about 15 feet square, I counted 60 black men and white women – packed together and jiving strenuously on the steel-reinforced floor which pulsated with their weight. A Negro drummer beat time on the mantelpiece.

This was clearly particularly wicked.[4]

In 1951, 72 people were proceeded against for brothel-keeping and/or living off immoral earnings. More sinister was the fact that one-third of all dangerous drugs prosecutions throughout the country came from Liverpool.

Things hadn't improved by the year 1952. Liverpool was 'Crime City – and nobody really seems to care,' said Douglas Howell in the *Daily Mirror*. Edward Devlin and Alfred Burns had just been hanged for the murder of Beatrice Rimmer, a middle-aged widow.

---

[4] It was however a view which prevailed at the time. The part of Liverpool by the Cathedral where the black community lived was known as The Jungle.

Four months may be a long time in journalism, but nothing had changed when 'Our Crime Reporter' from *Reynolds News* went to investigate 'The Quiet City – where terror stalks as night falls'. The town was quiet by 11 p.m., probably because the police went down the streets stick-swinging and in pairs. It was a delusion that the gangs who were the successors to the Devlins, the Burns, and the Kellys had been wiped out by the now Chief Superintendent Balmer. Gangs paraded the streets marking out territories to be invaded only in disputes over women. The crime schools were now in the inappropriately named Hope Street and Upper Parliament Street.

After the War there was an outbreak of rolling in the Lime Street area, near the station and known for prostitution.[5] Rolling, or mugging as we now call it, had always been a known Liverpudlian sport.

Rolling has had a long tradition in Liverpool and been traditionally associated with sailors and prostitution and the taking of the pay packet which was flashed around too openly.[6]

This time, however, it was businessmen who were being rolled and subsequently blackmailed. The Throstle Gang operated with a girl who it was said had once been a model in London. She would pick up men in hotel bars and then on the way back to her flat they would be attacked and robbed. Again Balmer was involved, allowing himself to be picked up by the girl who asked him to walk home with her. On the way, in Benson Street, she asked for a light for her cigarette. This was the signal for the robbery, but Balmer had men following him and after a fight in which he engagingly recounts, 'X had to strike him with his truncheon', the Throstles were arrested. The girl, who first denied all knowledge of the men and then later alleged that they had forced her into the scam, received twelve months and the men up to seven years. It was thought they had committed up to eighteen similar offences during their career. Two of the victims were still being blackmailed by the gang at the time of the arrests,

---

[5] The Liverpool ballad *Maggie May* includes the line, 'She'll never walk down Lime Street any more.'
[6] *Crime in the City*: Report of the Steering Group, November 1974.

but despite the arrests they refused to give evidence against them.

Balmer rose steadily through the police and his three finest cases came in the period between 1949 and 1951. The first of them was the Cameo Cinema murder which broke the so-called Kelly gang.

George Kelly had had a life of petty crime. His first conviction had been at the age of 10 when he was discharged under the Probation Act for breaking and entering. It was the first of a long list he acquired before he joined the Royal Navy, from which he deserted five times. In 1943 he was sentenced to nine months' imprisonment for assault. In 1945 he received a sentence for what is now dishonest handling, and the same year three years' penal servitude for desertion along with a year's hard labour.

On his release he worked in a café, as a street trader and as the barker for an escapologist. Then he took up pimping and ran a small string of prostitutes. His gang was a pretty pathetic affair by today's standards. His henchman was Charles Connolly, also a Royal Naval deserter and, after the War, a one-time railway porter. He was a capable amateur boxer who was always looking for a street fight. There were also two girls involved.

According to Norman Lucas, gang leaders such as Kelly were using their cars as mobile brothels with the girls under their control obliged to hand over up to 75 per cent of the night's takings. The girls were also expected to steer punters into clip joints where the men would be overcharged for their drinks but, in contradistinction to the London clip-joint, there would be at least a chance that sex would be available. Usually a couple of rooms were set aside for the girls to take their clients.[7]

One of the girls in the Kelly milieu was Jackie Dickson, who may well have had tuberculosis and who after the War was befriended by Jimmy Northam, known as 'Stuttie' from a speech impediment suffered as a result of an accident in the War, during a part of which he had been involved in a gang which rolled servicemen. Dickson had married a sailor who had deserted her immediately after the wedding. She was summoned by Kelly, and the party was joined in the public house by Marjorie Dawson, known as 'Norwegian Marjorie'.

Kelly, it seems, put up a number of propositions including the waylaying of a taxi driver known to be a police informer, a

---

[7] N. Lucas, *Britain's Gangland*, pp.30–31.

shopbreaking expedition and the robbing of the fun-fair in New Brighton.

It seems to have been Connolly who originally suggested the theft of the takings from the Cameo Cinema in Wavertree. It was agreed that a gun would be needed to frighten the manager and one was produced without difficulty by Kelly. 'Norwegian Marjorie' told him to put it away in case it was seen by other people in the pub, but Kelly calmly loaded it. There was some discussion about a disguise, and Dawson was made to hand over a small green apron for Kelly to use as a mask, whilst Northam surrendered his overcoat.

The next evening Kelly and Connolly went to the cinema. Connolly remained outside, whilst a little after 9 p.m. Kelly climbed the stairs to the office and demanded the takings from the manager, Leonard Thomas. He refused to hand over the takings and Kelly shot him, as he did Leonard Catterall, the assistant manager. Now he panicked and dropped the bag of money he had snatched. On his way out he was seen by Patrick Griffin, the cinema fireman.

Connolly was long gone by the time Kelly reappeared; he had left at the sound of the first shot. Kelly then started to compile an alibi, going into the Leigh Arms and buying a drink for a James Currie, a man whom he hardly knew. Currie would later give evidence that Kelly seemed nervous and out of breath; he asked him what was the matter and whether he had been in a fight. Kelly agreed he had. Connolly had gone off separately to join his wife and sisters in a local dance hall.

The next day the papers were full of the news and Connolly, a very frightened man, said he was going to leave the country, something for which Kelly roundly denounced him. He also threatened 'Stuttie' Northam and Jackie Dickson with a seeing-to from his brothers if they should open their mouths. Shortly after this, Norwegian Marjorie committed suicide.

A month after the murders Northam and Dickson decided to write to the police. Northam, helped by the girl, printed the anonymous letter which read:

THIS LETTER IS NOT A CRANK'S LETTER OR SUCHLIKE. NOR AM I TURNING INFORMER FOR GAIN. I KNOW THREE MEN AND A GIRL, NOT INCLUDING MYSELF, WHO HEARD ABOUT THIS PLAN FOR ROBBERY. I WOULD HAVE

NOTHING TO DO WITH IT AND I DON'T THINK THE GIRL
DID. WHEN I MET HER ON SUNDAY, SHE HAD NOT BEEN
OUT WITH THEM. ANOTHER MAN DROPPED OUT ON AC-
COUNT HE WANTED TO UNLOAD THE REVOLVER BEFORE
THEY WENT. THERE WERE ONLY TWO MEN WENT. THE
MAN HE TOOK WITH HIM LOST HIS NERVE AND WOULD
NOT GO IN WITH HIM, BUT SAID HE WOULD WAIT OUTSIDE
BUT DID NOT.

It was not wholly accurate but it was something for the police to
go on.

The reference to 'another man who dropped out' was to a
window-cleaner, whom Kelly had tried to recruit but who had
refused the offer to participate when he heard of the loaded gun.

The letter continued to the effect that the writer could give
more details of the murder if the police put an advertisement in
the local newspaper offering immunity from prosecution. By the
time they did place a notice in the personal column of the
Liverpool Echo, 'Letter received. Promise definitely given',
Northam and Dickson had disappeared in the direction of
Manchester.

The one outstanding recollection Griffin had of the gunman
was of his dark eyebrows, a feature of Kelly's face, and even
before the letter Herbert Balmer had pulled Kelly in for questioning but his alibi stuck. His girlfriend Doris O'Malley swore
that before he went to the Leigh Arms he had been with her in
another pub, the Coach and Horses.

Balmer eventually heard the story that Jackie Dickson had
been involved, and after a huge search over the North of England
she was retrieved from Manchester. So was Northam, but it was
not until six months after the robbery that he gave up the names
of Kelly and Connolly. When they, in turn, were arrested, they
denied knowing each other and Kelly said, 'I never had a gun in
my life. I don't know how to handle or fire one . . .'

Kelly was by no means pleased to find he was being defended
by Rose Heilbron (who later became a High Court Judge), the
first time a woman had led in a murder case. 'I want no Judy
defending me,' was said to be Kelly's opening gambit. It wasn't
as if Miss Heilbron was making a fortune; she was receiving 15
guineas under the Poor Persons Defence Act, with her junior 10
guineas and her solicitor 2 guineas a day and expenses.

There really wasn't much evidence against Kelly and certainly less against Connolly: an identification witness against the former and the tainted evidence of Dickson and Northam against both. Help was at hand, however, in the shape of a serving prisoner, Robert Graham, doing six months for receiving stolen property. He bolstered the prosecution's case with the evidence that Kelly had told him of the sixty witnesses he had in the Leigh Arms to give him an alibi. Connolly was even less discreet; he apparently told Graham he had had nothing to do with the murders, but admitted he had been to the cinema with the man who did them. He said he had run away when hearing the shots.

All three witnesses, Northam, Dickson and Graham, told the court how frightened they were of reprisals from Kelly's family and friends. 'Stuttie' and his girlfriend, who were now rehoused and living under assumed names, even refused to write them on a piece of paper for the judge.

Worse was to come for Connolly when his alibi was broken. He said he had been at a dance hall from about 8.20 in the evening, and that his wife had joined him twenty minutes later. He also said he had entered a rhumba competition and his wife, two of his sisters and their friends all put him in the dance hall before the murder was committed. Unfortunately it all went wrong. The Master of Ceremonies was sure that Connolly had not arrived until after the pubs closed. He remembered the man specifically because he had been wearing his hat on the dance floor and had been asked to remove it.

Even so the jury was unconvinced. After the thirteen-day trial, the then longest in an English court, they disagreed, were sent out again and failed to reach a verdict after another four hours. This time the prosecution had the idea of trying the men separately and, much to Miss Heilbron's unease, the re-trial was fixed for a week later. She made a series of applications to both Mr Justice Oliver and Mr Justice Cassels, who was to take the second trial, and merely had her ears boxed for her pains because she had made the application without her client being present. One of the reasons for the urgency was that Jackie Dickson was said to be suffering from a fatal and progressive disease.

This time Kelly was found guilty of murder – a decision in which the judge heartily concurred – with the jury retiring for only fifty-five minutes. As Kelly left the dock he said, 'Get

Balmer and I'll . . .' No one heard how he intended to complete the sentence. Northam and Dickson each received £20 reward from the court, with the thoughtful Mr Justice Cassels saying, 'There might be a Liverpool lady or ladies who could show a real act of kindness' – whatever that meant. Miss Heilbron took the case to the Court of Criminal Appeal with a novel if ultimately unsuccessful point. She argued that because there was a juryman who had a felony conviction the trial was a nullity and the conviction should be quashed. It was not an argument which Lord Goddard, the Lord Chief Justice, found attractive. Kelly's appeal was dismissed and he was hanged on 28 March 1950 at Walton Prison. No evidence on the murder charge was offered against Connolly in his separate re-trial, and he pleaded guilty to the robbery of the £50 takings and was sentenced to ten years' imprisonment.

Balmer received a series of threatening letters, but these died away. He was sent to police college, and on his return it was decided he should have a bodyguard. In his memoirs published in the *Liverpool Echo* over a three-month period, he wrote that he did not think much of this idea and did a round of the pubs such as the Beehive where Kelly and his gang had hung out. He had no trouble except that on one evening in Park Street two men alighted from a taxi and ran towards him. Three others de-taxied and hauled them back to the cab.

One of the members of another team at the time of Kelly's trial, the Brodie Gang, boasted a wife who was known as the 'Strong Arm Man', as opposed to woman. She took umbrage at the evidence given in a case and as the witness left court, attacked her with a razor. She received four years' imprisonment and the gang lost its heart.

Balmer's second famous case involved the murder of Beatrice Rimmer, a middle-aged widow who was reputed to have a cache of money in her house. Edward Devlin and Alfred Burns had known each other for some years before August 1951 when Burns was on the run and being harboured by his friend. In one of the all-night cafés in Liverpool frequented by young criminals, Devlin and Burns explained to Marie Milne the opportunity there was for robbing Mrs Rimmer without too much difficulty. Milne, a 16-year-old who had been recruited by June Bury, Devlin's girlfriend, was not completely enthusiastic; she said she would think about it. The next day the men explained the plan to the girls. June Bury said she wanted nothing to do with it but Milne, thoroughly frightened, hedged her bets. Burns and Devlin then recruited George MacLoughlin, a youth who had spent eleven of his 20 years inside, and who at 14 was the youngest person admitted to Walton jail. The plan was simple enough in theory. It is one which has been operated over the years with great success by con-men, gypsies and even young children. Marie Milne was to keep watch until she was sure Mrs Rimmer was in, knock and then engage her in conversation whilst Burns, Devlin and MacLoughlin broke in at the rear.

Things went wrong almost from the start. MacLoughlin was fortunate enough to be arrested for burglary two days before the planned robbery of the 19th. Milne was still not happy with her role. Thoroughly frightened of her part in the robbery, and more so when Devlin pulled a knife from his pocket and threatened her, she was still more frightened about what might happen if she went to the police.

Burns and Devlin decided to go ahead without waiting for MacLoughlin's release – which might have been quite some time in the future – and on the 19th went by taxi with Milne to Cranbourne Street where Mrs Rimmer lived. When they arrived she appeared to be out and Milne was sent to a local cinema and told to wait outside. The men broke the kitchen window and were searching the premises when Mrs Rimmer returned. They attacked her, beating her with a piece of wood, and left her to die on the floor; she had fifteen wounds in her head. When they met up with Milne, she refused to go back to Manchester with them but she still did not inform on them. That was done by MacLoughlin who, whilst serving his sentence in Walton, discussed the crime with other prisoners. Word was passed to the Governor and then to Balmer. In court he justified his informing on the basis that he was a professional burglar and did not approve of violence.

The girls were traced – June Bury was now pregnant – and then the taxi-driver. Milne told them that when she had met the men after the burglary Devlin had asked, 'Will the woman live?' and Burns had replied, 'To hell with the woman. We will be out of Liverpool before long.' Devlin was arrested inside twenty-four hours and Burns three days later.

Richard Whittington-Egan, then one of the leading crime reporters in Liverpool, told barrister Fenton Bresler:

I was present at the magistrates' court during the committal proceedings. Devlin was insolent – whispering and sniggering to his companion in the dock. I never saw two people on a serious charge so unaffected by the circumstances in which they found themselves. I was later to see them at the trial. I expected to see a change in their demeanour after their long weeks in prison. But they were still as cocky as ever. They saw themselves as gangster heroes.[8]

They ran an interesting if not unique defence at the Assizes, claiming that they had been engaged in a robbery at a clothing warehouse in Manchester from which they had stolen raincoats, suits and trousers, and had spent the night at the home of a Joan Downey. Another man gave evidence that he was on the warehouse breaking with them but Mrs Downey flatly denied their story. The factory had been broken into some time between midday Saturday and early Monday morning when the crime was discovered. The trial judge pointed out that there was no reason why the men could not have committed the burglary to which they admitted and the murder to which they did not.

It was after the jury had found them guilty and the Court of Criminal Appeal had rejected their appeals that Rose Heilbron, who had defended Devlin, produced a statement from a 15-year-old Elizabeth Rooke that she had heard June Bury say the men were innocent and that the real killer was the father-to-be of Bury's baby. This caused considerable upset. Lord Goddard refused to admit new evidence.

> What was urged upon us was that we should hear fresh evidence of a most important character . . . and it went to show that June Bury, the importance of whose evidence I have already emphasized, had committed perjury and had admitted that she had committed perjury, and, secondly, that another man had admitted that he had committed the murder.
>
> We declined to consider that evidence, and we declined for very good reasons. Matters of this sort have often previously been before the Court of Criminal Appeal, who have always in these circumstances refused to hear

[8] F. Bresler, *Scales of Justice*, p.43.

such evidence mainly on the ground that they have no power to order a new trial.[9]

So the matter went to the Home Secretary. He appointed Albert Garrard QC and Commander Harold Hawkyard of Scotland Yard to inquire whether a possible miscarriage of justice had taken place. They found that the man named had been away from Liverpool at the time of the Rimmer killing, and that the story of Elizabeth Rooke could not stand up. Both men were hanged on 25 April 1952; both affirming their innocence.

There were reprisals in the Liverpool Underworld. It was decided that Marie Milne should have her throat cut, but in the end she was merely beaten unconscious in a back alley and needed thirty stitches. June Bury was beaten up in an all-night café and later was the subject of a further six beatings. She went to London, underwent plastic surgery and returned to Liverpool secure in the knowledge that she could not be recognized. She could; and was beaten yet again. MacLoughlin, correctly regarded in Underworld terms as a grass, was continually beaten both in and out of prison. Joan Downey, who had refused to corroborate the Burns-Devlin alibi, had her home set on fire.

Even the minor witnesses suffered. The taxi-driver who had taken the trio to Cranbourne Street was beaten up; another prosecution witness was shot and dumped in Blackpool. It was, wrote Norman Lucas, five years before the witnesses felt safe from the wrath of the remaining members of the Burns-Devlin gang.[10]

The third of the famous murder cases in which Balmer was involved at the time was the killing of the semi-crippled junk dealer-cum-recluse, 82-year-old George Hugh 'Daddy' Walker, on 14 January 1953. This time it was not a gang matter but the maniac work of unemployed labourer John Lawrence Todd who hit Walker thirty-two times with an axe. After the death in 1944 of his wife Madam Pepper, a dancing teacher, Walker, who had been a master tailor, lived in a twelve-roomed house at Warbreck Road near Aintree, increasingly surrounded by junk. When his

---

[9] Lord Goddard speaking on a House of Lords' motion that the Court of Appeal should have the power to order a retrial. (*Hansard*, Lords, 8 May 1952, cols 745 *et seq.*) The power was not granted to them until the Criminal Justice Act 1967, since when it has been sparingly used.
[10] N. Lucas, *Britain's Gangland*, p.45.

dog would not stop howling, neighbours went to investigate and found his battered body. The axe had been clumsily hidden in a chimney. Todd went to the police to explain why he might have been seen in the area, but he was identified through a watch stolen in the robbery which he had sold. He was hanged at Walton jail on 19 May 1953.

Even so Balmer was not without his critics. There were allegations both in and outside the police that he had stitched up Kelly as well as Devlin-Burns. Doyen of the Liverpool criminal solicitors, E. Rex Makin, recalls:

> After those cases I used to give a lift to a Detective Sergeant who was involved in them. He wasn't an ordinary sort of copper, a supercilious type of man, and when I told him I wasn't happy with the Devlin-Burns case, he replied, 'Does it matter? They're scum.' That was his attitude and it's stuck with me all my life.
>
> Balmer had been a ship's carpenter. He was a publicity seeker and a bully. His methods were purely verballing. He was the archetypal detective who believed the best evidence was a cough whether genuine, forced, induced or voluntary.

By 1957 there was a general clean-up of the city in anticipation of its 750th birthday. The drinking clubs could be raided on one warrant three times a night. But three years later *Today*, in the form of John Godwin, reported: 'This is Liverpool . . . City of Violence', and included such gems as the tailor who 'includes automatically a special cosh pocket in all suits he makes for teenagers; . . . the Liverpool kiss gripping lapels and ramming the forehead into the nose'.[11]

Violent crime was up: murders from nil to four; cases of robbery with violence from 47 to 69; there were attacks on policeman every two days. According to Godwin, a police inspector told him:

> Our chief problem here? Same as it's always been – violence. We've just about licked the drug traffic, we've chased the prostitutes off the streets, we've closed down most of the shebeens and we've never had much trouble with gambling.

[11] 20 August 1960.

Goodbye to:

Shirley Pitts
(above)

Arthur Thompson
(below)
(*Glasgow Herald and Evening Times*)

Goodbye to:

David Brindle
(above)
(*Martin Goodwin*)

Lee Duffy
(below)
(*North News and Pictures*)

The end of:

Jimmy Moody
(above)
(*S&G Press*)

Thomas Roche
(below)
(*Topham*)

**The six faces of
Howard Marks**
(above)
(*Enterprise News*)

**Billy Hill attends
the funeral of
Billy Blythe**
(right)
(*Hulton Deutsch*)

Albert Dimes celebrates his acquittal in the Jack Spot case (above) (*Topham*)

Arthur Thompson , the 'king of Glasgow' (right) (*Glasgow Herald and Evening News*)

Eugenio Messina arrives handcuffed to a police escort at the start of his trial in Belgium
(*Associated Press*)

**The man they call the
General
(and who denies it)
in disguise**
(*Russell Banks*)

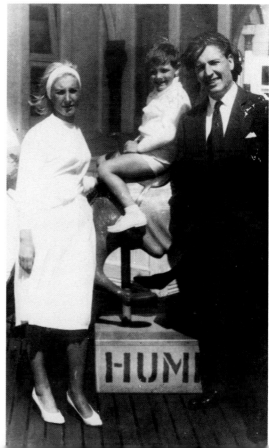

**Family man:
'Mad' Frank Fraser and
family**
(*S&G Press*)

Another family: Jack Spot and Rita
(*Syndication International*)

A flashback to the days of the Sabinis: Joseph Jackson

But we can't stop people from bashing each other over the head.

Nightlife shifted sharply to the east of the city around Parliament Street, Park Road and Grove Street.

The only Underworld boss in Liverpool in recent years, thought Godwin, was Rudolph 'Bull' Gardner who arrived as a stowaway with £11 from Jamaica. He began operating, buying marijuana from American seamen and selling it in the black community (known, in the days when such a phrase could be used without even the slightest lift of an eyebrow, as Jungle Town) near the cathedral. He opened a shebeen and then the Fortune Club in Princes Road on which he spent over £8,000. It was estimated he was earning £50 a night. But he forgot to have front men, and when in 1955 the Fortune was raided he took the fall of two years personally. He returned to Liverpool after his sentence, but was no longer any sort of power and was effectively run out by the police. He then went to London where at the Inner London Quarter Sessions on 12 October 1959, then aged 36, he received another two years for possessing 4lb 3oz of marijuana.

Probably the popularity in the 1960s of the Beatles had as much as anything to do with cutting youth crime in Liverpool. The sociological argument runs that crime is most prevalent amongst middle-teenagers, and that as youths get older they will pair off with girls who will lead them out of the gang. Friday night was fight night and there had been splendid fights with such gangs as the Holly Road and Park Gang. Then members of the gangs began to play instruments. A boy who fought was now regarded as just a man without a woman. Status was no longer dependent on winning a rumble but on how the band within the group had performed. This is to a certain extent the same today when drugs gangs adopt a reggae band of their own.

Suddenly Liverpool became OK. The cathedral was built, the docks were gentrified. On the back of the Beatles came a whole Merseyside culture, much of which has endured – Cilla Black, Alan Plater, George Melly, the Barrow poets. But as the Garden of Britain was planted, the flowers of the city withered.

With the new prosperity came a taxi-war which was waged intermittently for ten years, with licensed taxis being sprayed with graffiti and private vehicles having their tyres slashed. Two of the early casualties were two brothers who on 1 July 1966 received three years each for conspiracy and demanding with menaces – they were acquitted of setting fire to the Stretton Club in Wood Street. They had tried to take over taxi-cab services in the city, setting up the so-called Private Hire Association whose aim was 'to bring together all the private firms in Liverpool'.

Again where there is money to spend crime is almost invariably organized to skim off part of it. By 1979 it was believed there were twelve crime families who ran nearly fifty pubs and clubs in the centre of town. The police believed that the clubs, which ran from the back-street shebeen to smart nightclubs, were being used to launder money and also to generate the capital for more ambitious enterprises outside the city. The calendar of crime for a year in the city was impressive.

On 16 May 1978 fifteen men raided five houses in the Fazakerley, Dovecot, Walton and Bootle areas. They were carrying an arsenal of weapons including sawn-off shotguns, baseball bats, swords, axes and hammers. Their three victims included a man whose ankles were repeatedly hit with one of the axes in an endeavour to cut off his feet; he needed 107 stitches. Another was found in his underwear hiding in a cupboard; his underpants were taken from him and he was striped, before he escaped naked through the streets, by the men in two cars and a taxi. The raid was thought to have been over skimmed takings of a club in which one family held an interest.

In September 1978 three brothers, Colin, Robert and Brian Fitzgerald, were involved in a bottle and knife fight with two other men in the Indiana Club, Berry Street. One of the men received wounds requiring 48 stitches, and in February 1979 Colin began two years' imprisonment to go alongside the three years he was already serving following a fight in the Babalou Club in which two men and a woman were slashed. In the same month a shotgun was fired in a fight in the QT Club in Manstys Lane. The manager, Peter Stockley, received shoulder wounds. In May that year three men were acquitted at the Crown Court of possessing the shotgun and ammunition and causing £400 worth of damage.

In the meantime there had been a couple of arson attacks. The Knightsbridge Club in Duke Street had gone up in flames after an explosion on 1 November 1978, and three months later the Palatine Club in Dale Street was gutted by what the police were convinced was an arson attack. No one was charged with either offence.[12]

But, so far as the police were concerned, the most serious incident had involved the Flying Squad's Detective Sergeant Bernard Craven, who suffered brain damage in an attack on him whilst guarding the London supergrass Billy Amies. Versions of what exactly happened and how vary.

Amies, it will be recalled, was one of the more unpleasant of armed robbers. Amongst his other roles, he was the 'policeman' who had threatened one of his victims with castration and the rape of his daughter. He had also been at work on Merseyside. In the first of his three cases there a middle-aged woman had been repeatedly punched in the face; in the second another middle-aged woman, her Down's Syndrome daughter and her son had all been tied up; the latter had also been threatened with castration. In the third incident a garage owner and his family had been tied up, and the owner had had his testicles bitten to persuade him to open his safe.

Tony Lundy, who turned Amies into a supergrass, described him as follows:

> In some ways Billy was a nutter. He was also known as Billy the Queer because he's a raving homosexual. A big hard man, over six foot, a real animal, a compulsive armed robber who was really feared, but clever too.

Amies was in serious difficulties. He was caught out of his territory and had been arrested with one of Liverpool's real hardmen John Tremarco. Lundy was told by another supergrass, David Smith, that Amies wanted help because he feared a corrupt Liverpool police officer, John Keating, was trying to lighten Tremarco's load by placing it on Amies' shoulders. It appears Amies was being pressured into pleading guilty. Lundy went incognito to Walton jail and saw Amies who, once he had read Smith's statements involving him, decided that the path to safety was for him to turn supergrass. Much to the fury of the Merseyside police Amies was transferred to Brixton on Rule 43 and then to Acton police station. There he told his version of his life of crime, implicating Tremarco and also Keating.

---

[12] *Guardian*, 2 July 1979.

In October 1977, he went back to Liverpool to plead guilty. His statement was then shown to the solicitors for the other defendants who, as soon as Amies walked into the witness-box, in turn were forced to put their hands up. The public gallery howled revenge and the case was adjourned until the Monday for the sentencing of everyone including Amies.

The new and reformed supergrass was, unsurprisingly, unhappy about staying in the North West for the weekend. He wanted to do the round trip to the safety of London. It was agreed he should be returned on the Sunday night to be lodged overnight in a Liverpool police station. So far so good, except that on the Sunday night the London sergeants who had custody of Amies could not find him a home; nor could they manage to contact the local Serious Crimes Officers. They turned up with Amies in tow at the hotel in Liverpool where Lundy was staying. Further efforts to find Amies a bed in a cell failed, so he was booked into the hotel along with his guarding officers Craven and O'Rourke. On a toss of the coin it was decided that Craven should sleep in the room with Amies, and O'Rourke outside.

Unfortunately Amies thought it would be a good idea to go out for a last drink. This was by no means an uncommon situation with supergrasses, and the officer agreed. Off he and Craven went to a pub in the docks called the Crow's Nest. Even more unfortunately it was the haunt of Tremarco's friends. Lundy seems to have been full of admiration for his protégé.

> Typical of the fearless animal he is, off goes Amies with Craven into the lions' den. But as soon as they walk in, they're set upon! Amies, big strong beast, fights his way out and escapes, but Bernie Craven gets an almighty kicking. He's almost kicked to death but he manages to stagger out of the pub, he's found in the front garden of a nearby house and he's rushed to hospital.[13]

Amies was badly cut and had a broken arm by the time he returned to the safety of the hotel. Craven was not so fortunate; he had severe concussion, a broken nose and a fractured

---

[13] The quotations are from M. Short's *Lundy*, pp.51–2. There is a full account of Amies' career in Chapter 4 of the book. An alternative view is expressed in A. Jennings and others, *Scotland Yard's Cocaine Connection*. They point out that apart from the two men in Liverpool, Amies' evidence only served to convict three more people.

cheekbone. He never really recovered, and retired from the force on health grounds. The next morning Lundy managed to have Amies' case remitted to London where he could be sentenced for all his offences. Tremarco received fifteen years. Back in London Amies served only two. Two years later Keating was convicted of attempting to extort half the money an insurance company had paid to a police informer. He received two and a half years.

The story in the Underworld was that Amies had been punished in the pub by a Liverpool hardman, Billy Grim-wood, assisted by two London brothers from a well-known and influential family. The mystery remains as to why Amies chose the Crow's Nest, of all Liverpool pubs, in which to drink.

One outcome was a purge on the Liverpool drinking clubs. The Chief Constable, Kenneth Oxford, objected to the renewal of the licences of twenty-five establishments. They were suspended for one month, after which Mr Oxford withdrew his objections.

> We felt the little fish were going to go under. While they had transgressed, they weren't the people we were really looking for. But the effect has been to say to the club-owners and licensees: 'You have been warned.'[14]

Peace was at least temporarily restored, although the Merseyside police were well aware that many clubs were operated by front men, that there were two sets of books being kept and that the proceeds from the bar takings were going to finance heavy crime committed by Liverpool criminals throughout the country. Now with the recession the great days of the clubs are over and the powerful families have moved into international credit-card frauds.

Meanwhile the Triads had finally been successful in establishing something more than a foothold in the community. There had been a large Chinese community in the city dating from mid-Victorian times and in 1927 the *Echo and Daily Post* had trumpeted, 'What the police found in a Liverpool Chinaman's premises'.[15] By today's standards it was pretty tame, but the bags of opium and morphine (let alone the gun with two hundred

[14] *Guardian, 2 July 1979.*
[15] 10 November 1927.

115

rounds of ammunition) was sufficient to kill 10,000 people, said the city analyst. A year later the community was in the news again. This time there had been raids on the gambling joints, and thirty-nine Chinamen appeared before the city's magistrates. By and large they were a stable and well-respected community; however, there was one celebrated murder case involving a Chinese businessman, which was by no means a gangland killing although it had its origins in a club fight.

Lock Ah Tam had come to England as a ship's steward in the 1890s. He had settled in Liverpool and become a wealthy man through restaurants and clubs. He was thought to be the most respected Chinaman in England and was European representative of a Chinese dockers' union. Unfortunately, in 1918 he was hit on the head with a billiard cue by a drunken Russian sailor and underwent a personality change. He took to drinking heavily, flew into terrifying rages, lost his business and went bankrupt. On 1 December 1925 he gave a party for his son, but when the guests had gone began to abuse his family. His son went for the police, but by the time he returned Lock Ah Tam had shot his wife and daughters before telephoning the police to say, 'Send you folks please, I have killed my wife and children.'

He was defended by Sir Edward Marshall-Hall QC, paid for by the Chinese community, and offered a plea of insanity. It was rejected by the jury in twelve minutes. He was hanged on 23 March 1926.

In 1980 Fenton Bresler reported that a former head of the Drugs Squad in Merseyside had 'no knowledge of any criminal Triads working in the Merseyside area'.[16]

By 1986 however, the picture had changed and, it has emerged, there had been a Wo Sing Wo – a powerful Triad gang – presence on Merseyside for some time. Lau Kam Keung, a relatively minor member of the operation, moved up a grade or two when his immediate boss left for the richer pickings of Soho. Now Lau Kam Keung, or Freddie Lau as he was known, decided it would be a good idea if Wong Mai Cheung, the owner of a restaurant in Nelson Street, paid him £200 a week protection money. To emphasize the seriousness of the suggestion, various of Lau's friends would sit all day in the restaurant over a single bowl of rice. Wong agreed a figure of £100 and paid this for two years

[16] F. Bresler, *The Trail of the Triads*, p. 151.

until he rebelled. He was beaten with rice flails and went to the police. He was given a tape-recorder, and taped conversations when it was suggested that Lau should buy his restaurant to pay off some wholly imaginary debts to Lau. Lau eventually pleaded guilty and received a sentence of ten years' imprisonment.

It came out later that Lau had been operating a loan-sharking arrangement offering Chinese gamblers credit in the north of England casinos. Minimum repayments were £100 a week to keep the interest at bay. As with all good loan-sharkers, the nut or capital sum owed was never touched. One case showed that over two years a punter had paid £4,000 in respect of a £350 debt. The unfortunate men could, however, join Wo Sing Wo as a way out of clearing the interest; though the capital debt was still never voided.[17]

By the early 1980s Liverpool was racked with political scandals with widespread allegations of corruption against officials, councillors and political leaders. A decade later the story in the city was much the same as in the rest of the country. Although with the recession much of the club scene has faded there was a battle, if not a war, between groups of bouncers over who should mind the clubs and the lucrative drug trade that goes with the control of the door. Indeed, drugs were once again paramount although officers maintain, almost certainly correctly, that the trade is minor compared with that of Manchester from where, in the main, the local dealers get their supplies.

Nevertheless it has proved too much for some. Jean Larkin, who ran a company selling window-blinds, and her boyfriend Gary Pettitt, who ran an enterprise selling drugs, left their flat in Aigburth on 27 April 1993. The television was left on and her dog, Bruff, unfed. Pettitt had had a call to a meeting in a McDonald's in Markey Street, Chorley, some 25 miles away, and Jean Larkin went with him. It seems they kept the rendez-vous because a van marked 'Calypso Blinds' had been seen in the neighbourhood. It was later found at Manchester Airport.

On 1 June the police began digging in woods at Coppull, three miles outside Chorley. Some jewellery belonging to the couple was found, as was burned clothing. The police were convinced they had been killed and their bodies burned. Two men had been seen camping in the area the week Pettitt and Jean Larkin had

[17] D. Black, *Triad Takeover*, pp. 86–8.

disappeared; it was believed the men had a brown Rover 213 and a silver Accord which had been seen in the Gateshead area. The Rover was later found in Barry, South Glamorgan. There was no suggestion, said the police, that Miss Larkin had been anything other than an innocent bystander in what appears to have been a drugs deal which went wrong. Two men have been charged with the killing of Pettitt and Larkin.

So, in 1994 Liverpool is like almost all of the other cities. Drugs are the main source of criminal behaviour. Says one senior detective:

At the bottom end 10-year-olds with a habit break into your house or my car to feed their habit; in the middle there is a battle for control of the clubs to see whose drugs go in, and at the top end there is major distribution.

5

—

Newcastle
and the North East

In his novel *Jack's Return Home*[1], Ted Lewis – who was brought
up in the North East – paints a portrait of club life in Newcastle
in the 1960s when in the evenings the winnings from one-armed
bandits spilled on to the carpets of the plush nightclubs and
prosperous working men's clubs, and at dead of night into the
pockets – with a rake-off to the barman or club steward – of the
collectors who were skimming from the machines they had been
sent to empty. His was an accurate picture of local hardmen and
violence linked to London gangsters. At one time, said BBC
producer David Seymour, '. . . it was a bit like the Wild West in
Newcastle . . . the London gangs squabbled and three nightclubs
were burned down.'[2]

On 7 January 1967 two company directors were accused of
murdering a fellow director in a fruit machine business who had
been found shot dead in his car. It became a complete *cause célèbre*
and has featured in many compilations of miscarriages of justice
in the British legal system. Dennis Stafford, aged 23, and Michael
Luvaglio, 29, who appeared at Peterlee magistrates' court in Co.
Durham, were charged with murdering 33-year-old Angus Sibbett
who had been found shot the previous Thursday in the back seat
of his car parked beneath a bridge at South Hetton.

Sibbett, burly, bearded and handsome, had been a key figure in
one of the biggest gambling set-ups in the country. His territory

---

[1] Filmed as *Get Carter*.
[2] *Daily Express*, 28 March 1980.

was in the North East, at that time stuffed full of one-armed bandits, which at that stage were a major source of Underworld income.[3] He had served his apprenticeship in London with one of the biggest gangs, and this connection lasted until his death. He was a larger than life character who had served in Korea, been a shoe salesman, run a Chinese restaurant and done twelve months for receiving before gravitating to Newcastle where he worked for Vince Landa, otherwise Vincente Luvaglio,[4] who had set up Social Club Services Ltd, a company with many subsidiaries which installed gaming machines, then mainly the old-fashioned one-armed bandits, in clubs.

Dennis Stafford, one of the two men charged with the murder, had led what can most charitably be described as an interesting life. His father Joe Stafford, whose real name was Siegenberg, had been, and indeed still was, one of the great go-betweens and fixers for criminals who wanted to do business with the police over bail or the dropping of charges. The good-looking, if also brilliantined and spiv-like, Stafford junior made his name in the Underworld as a high class con-man, burglar and prison escaper.

At the Inner London Sessions on 26 July 1956, he was sentenced to a seven-year term for breaking and entering and being in possession of a loaded revolver. He had pleaded guilty. Four months later on a wet and windy 8 November he escaped over the wall from Wormwood Scrubs, along with Anthony Hawkes, another con-man who in previous metamorphoses had been a cavalry officer, an Irish peer, a foreign trade attaché and a Rumanian butler. Hawkes was serving a six-year sentence for false pretences over a textile swindle which curiously he had been operating in his own name. It is idle to think the pair did not have substantial outside help, because exactly twenty days later they both turned up in Newcastle if not loaded with money then at least presentably dressed, and with enough cash to pay for rooms, offices and the necessary props to open a wholesale cloth long-firm fraud, which they operated successfully until the balloon went up in February 1957. By this time Stafford had a fiancée, Sandra, a 19-year-old model in a make-up fashion house.

---

[3] Frank Fraser gives a long account of the troubles he and Eddie Richardson had in installing their machines in preference to other people's around the country in *Mad Frank*.
[4] *News of the World*, 19 March 1967.

As with all well-organized operators of long-firm frauds, by the time the creditors moved in Hawkes and Stafford were gone. Just as the police had been tipped off that the morose Mr Whelby and the nice Mr Hutton were Hawkes and Stafford respectively, so someone had tipped off the pair that the police were in close pursuit.

Whelby had once more become Mr Hawkes when he was found in the King's Hotel off the Bayswater Road in London ten days later, but of Mr Hutton there was no sign. He had become Wally Birch[5] and had gone to Port of Spain, Trinidad. Unfortunately, as was always the case with Stafford, he was irresistible to women. In the time he was out and about in London before he fled, he had acquired another fiancée, an actress, Eileen. Before taking the boat from Liverpool he told her where he was going and when she sent a telegram to say she was joining him the police, who had been watching her, made four. DI George Mullen and DS Jack Huntley retrieved him – watched, it was said, by a silent crowd of 500 people including several pretty girls.

Stafford was properly and righteously penitent. In an exclusive story he wrote for the *News of the World* whilst in a Port of Spain prison awaiting his extradition, he had this to say:

I'm most sorry for the friends I let down and grateful to the friends who didn't let me down. Most of all I'm sorry for my parents – they never let me down. I only wish I could do something for them. But of course, I can do something for them – from here on I promise them solemnly that I will go straight and stay out of trouble.[6]

Meanwhile his father, Joe, once a landlord of an East End pub and now described as a Soho commission agent, said of his son:

It all began in the War. He was evacuated to Cornwall and I

---

[5] The choice of the name Birch was interesting and should have been a dead giveaway. Wally Birch and Stafford had been involved in a fight with the Kray twins in their teens outside the Mayfair Ballroom in Tottenham. The Krays had been acquitted but Ronnie Kray never forgave Stafford for grassing on him. The real Wally Birch went into clubs in Soho with Joe Wilkins, nephew of Bert who had been acquitted of the murder of Massimo Montecolumbo at Wandsworth Greyhound Stadium in 1934.
[6] *News of the World*, 20 October 1957.

was in the Army. He missed his father's right hand. His big trouble is his big ideas . . . After school he began as a waiter but before he was 17 he was in the fruit business with his own office and doing well until someone let him down over money.[7]

On his return he was sent to Durham Assizes, where he received an additional eighteen months for the Newcastle long-firm.

He settled down for a while in Dartmoor until Monday 5 January 1959, when he escaped along with William Day, a house- and garage-breaker, also serving seven years. It was his third attempt at escape. By the Wednesday it was thought that Stafford, armed with a new passport, was already abroad. An admirer said that the break had been planned with extreme care:

That's the mark Stafford gives to all his work. He is admired by the real criminal element which makes up about 10 per cent of the prison population. They look up to him as a man with a brain, always waging war on the law, and often winning – and a man who doesn't give up when he loses one contest and lands in prison . . . he can always get someone to tip him off about prison routine and events which he, as a man under closer guard, couldn't obtain.[8]

Unfortunately Day did not make it off the Moor. He was found drowned in a reservoir. It seems he had blundered into the water and Stafford had thrown him a lifebelt but had not raised the alarm.

Stafford had not made it out of the country however. On 20 February, forty-four days after his escape, he was arrested in Leicester Square and returned to Dartmoor where he was regarded with something less than critical favour by the other prisoners who held him responsible for the death of Day. He was put in solitary confinement and allowed out by the Governor, George Brown-Smith, to reassure his father that he was not being victimized over Day. Stafford said that he had not merely thrown him a lifebelt but had gone in the water after him and grabbed him, but had lost hold in the dark.

[7] *Daily Mail*, 18 October 1957.
[8] *Daily Mail*, 1 January 1959.

But the original case of housebreaking and possessing an offensive weapon was far from over. In August 1960 John 'Happy' Sambridge swore a statement that it was he who had planted the gun in Stafford's car.

Sambridge, who later was shot by Frankie Fraser over an incident at Brighton Races in 1955,[9] said that on the day of Stafford's arrest he had been approached by a detective who told him he had the needle to Stafford and wanted him nicked. Sambridge had been given a gun by the officer and left it on the shelf under the dashboard. For this service he had received £5. The statement was passed to Lord Stoneham at the Home Office. Joe Stafford, who throughout his son's escapades always campaigned totally on his behalf, said he thought that the finding of the gun might have been an influence on the judge who passed the sentence on the housebreaking charge. As so often happens with statements and confessions and petitions, it was a false dawn. Nothing came of the inquiry.

Stafford was released on 23 March 1961 to join a catering firm as assistant – an ideas man earning the then handsome four-figure sum plus car and expenses – to one of the directors. Again a bright future was prophesied. 'He got into trouble originally because he lived above his income, but now with responsibilities I am sure he will settle down,' said a friend.[10]

Wrong. He lost the job and then worked as a chauffeur to a London car hire firm. After that he was jailed for three months for being in possession of a Browning automatic, and then under the name of Fielding he was back inside for a year after pleading guilty to stealing a car from a car park in Brighton. On his release in 1965 he made his way to Newcastle where he too joined the employment of Vince Landa, working as booking agent for the cabarets playing the clubs. He was now earning a basic £25 per week and could possibly double it with commission.

Landa, whose younger brother was Michael Luvaglio, the other defendant in the Sibbett killing, had at one time been an officer in

---

[9] Fraser was working a pitch on the free course at Brighton owned by Albert Dimes, then in custody over the Spot fight in Soho, when he was arrested by Chief Superintendent Greeno and questioned over suggestions that he was in Brighton to kill one of Spot's men. Fraser was released without charge but believed that Sambridge had identified him to the police. When Fraser was released from prison in 1962 he sought out Sambridge and shot him in the leg.

[10] *Sunday Express*, 22 March 1961.

the RAF police before he had moved to the North East and established a gambling empire. At one stage he was in the multi-millionaire category; he owned a substantial country house with thirty acres near Bishop Auckland, he had a villa in Majorca and he ran a Rolls-Royce, a Jaguar and half a dozen other cars. In a gesture of family solidarity he moved his parents and Michael to the North East. Michael also became an employee of Social Club Services Ltd and its myriad of interlocked companies.

Sibbett's body was found at about 5.15 a.m. on 5 January 1967 in a Mark X Jaguar badly parked near Pesspool Bridge, Front Street at South Hetton. He had been shot at close range. A pit worker had seen there was someone in the vehicle, thought he was asleep and opened the door to wake him and tell him to move.

Stafford was not lucky with informants in the North East. Someone had tipped off the police about his long-firm in 1957. Now ten years later someone told the police that a damaged red E-Type Jaguar was in a Sunderland garage to which it had been taken for repair.

In what became an increasingly misty case, one thing was clear. Michael Luvaglio had driven the red E-type on 3 January. He had been to his brother's home in Majorca with his parents, Stafford and their respective girlfriends. Everyone had flown back to London, then all except Landa had flown up to Newcastle. Landa had stayed behind to see his accountant and then had returned to Majorca. On 4 January Luvaglio had telephoned his brother who told Stafford to use the E-type as his own car was in for repair.

The evidence against Stafford and Luvaglio ran as follows. The red E-type Jaguar had been in some sort of collision with the Mark X. It was common ground that Stafford and Luvaglio had arranged to meet Sibbett that night. They said he had not turned up for the meeting and whilst they waited at the Bird Cage Club, Stafford went outside to the Jaguar to get some duty-free cigarettes he had brought back from Majorca. He noticed that the E-type was damaged and drew it to the attention of a Matthew Dean, the acting doorman. There were tyre marks in the snow which suggested a vehicle had collided with the E-type and had then reversed away. Both men were well alibied by their girlfriends Pat Burgess and Selena Jones, the singer. Much of the prosecution case depended on the time of death and whether the defendants could have driven from the club, killed Sibbett, dumped his body and driven back within three-quarters of an hour.

The trial judge Sir Patrick O'Connor QC, in his summing-up, did not assist the defence and, in one of those pieces of rubric so favoured by judges, offered this little homily.

> Luvaglio has told you that Angus Sibbett was his friend and it is a matter which you will give careful consideration to. As human beings you will, of course, know that friends are of two types. True friends and false. Today [March 15] is the exact anniversary of that famous cry, which has run down the ages, when Julius Caesar lay dying, 'And you, Brutus', whose dagger was in his heart; his friend. Seventy-five years later one greater than Caesar was betrayed by Judas with a kiss.

The jury was out three hours before returning a guilty verdict. The Court of Appeal was unsympathetic and although in March 1972 Reginald Maudling, the then Home Secretary, referred the matter back to that court for a re-hearing of the appeal, there was no joy there. Luvaglio's parents stuck loyally by him, instructing Sir David Napley (soon to be president of the Law Society) on their son's behalf. In his book Napley firmly maintains his belief in Luvaglio's innocence.

> I had then been practising for over thirty years, and was not unfamiliar with the questioning in and out of court, but not one of us – or, for that matter, any of the other experienced lawyers and non-lawyers who afterwards questioned Luvaglio – was ever able to catch him out or fault him. Jimmy Comyn (later Mr Justice Comyn) shared the belief that Luvaglio was innocent of the murder. John Mathew, a Senior Treasury Counsel at the Central Criminal Court, who at the time spent almost his entire time prosecuting, while unwilling to commit himself to the view that he was convinced of his innocence, was far from convinced of his guilt, and was abundantly satisfied that on the evidence a jury ought not to be satisfied beyond reasonable doubt that he was guilty.[11]

---

[11] Sir David Napley, *Not Without Prejudice*, p.289. There is a very full account of the Luvaglio case in Sir David's book in Chapter 21. David Lewis and Peter Hughman, then an articled clerk and now a solicitor, wrote what must be the definitive account of the case – *Most Unnatural: An Inquiry into the Stafford Case*.

In turn Joe Stafford did what he could, approaching such diverse people as the police officer Nipper Read – offering assistance with the Kray case if help could be given to his son – and to the then Prime Minister, Harold Wilson. In January 1973, in an echo of the 'Happy' Sambridge statement, two men swore statements which were handed to the *People* alleging they had been offered £5,000 to kill Sibbett. George Shotton, a Newcastle car dealer with a long criminal record including convictions for violence, said he had been approached in the Bird Cage Club by a man who seemed to be Italian. A second man, whose name was not given, said the man who approached him appeared to be Greek.

But, despite representations by MPs, lawyers, newspapers and by JUSTICE, Stafford and Luvaglio languished in prison. In October 1973 their appeal to the House of Lords was rejected. This was the end of the matter so far as legal avenues were concerned. Both men were paroled in 1979 and the next year Stafford did neither of them a favour. In an exclusive interview with David Mertens in the *News of the World* for a reported fee of £10,000, he confessed, 'I did it'.[12] He said he had committed the crime whilst Luvaglio was in bed. Once more he was out of favour with the Underworld, and to compound his problems he was on the run for a drink-driving offence, and was also wanted in connection with some credit-card frauds. Luvaglio, unavailable for comment, was said to be in Oberammagau with his mother to see the Passion Play. During his stay in prison he had obtained an Open University degree, and since his release he had been working with handicapped children. Later he and Sir David Napley issued a statement pointing out discrepancies in Stafford's account.

Stafford back-tracked quickly. He clearly could not retract to the *News of the World* and so he did the next best thing. He made a statement to the *Sunday People* for their edition of 28 September, saying his confession was a lie and he had only made it for financial reasons and '. . . to prove how hypocritical the system is and how people will believe what they want to believe. We did not commit the murder and the evidence and the facts of the case remain as they were.' Earlier he had told the *Guardian* that Luvaglio had nothing to do with the shooting. In 1989 the *Mail on Sunday* reported Stafford as being under arrest, along with South African banker Gotz Gunterhoner, over a

---

[12] *News of the World*, 7 September 1980.

multi-million-pound international fraud on the Trust Bank of Johannesburg.[13]

What was the truth behind the killing of Sibbett? Was it over his continuing womanizing? Or was it over the machines? It later emerged that he had been skimming substantial profits from the gaming machines he was minding for Landa.

That was certainly the theory advanced, immediately after the trial, by Patricia Sacre, an old friend of both the Luvaglio brothers and Sibbett: 'The trouble was so many people were on the fiddle. Everybody was setting up their own private companies and milking the kitty in various ways.'[14]

Landa's empire collapsed after the trial. It emerged that Sibbett had been organizing thefts on a wholesale basis from the clubs which had rented machines from Coinamatic, a subsidiary of Social Club Services Ltd, to the tune of £1,600 a week. Landa, it was said, knew of the thefts and had turned a blind eye to them. When the police went to his home in Bishop Auckland they found him gone – to his villa in Majorca.[15] For the next few years he led a peripatetic life, wandering like a second division Flying Dutchman around the Mediterranean. In 1977 he was still abroad living in poor circumstances in Malta. He was held twice by the police; once in Italy after the sinking of his yacht in Sicily. Two years later he surrendered himself on charges of fraud to the police in Chester-le-Street. He now had a fiancée, 19-year-old Julie Hamblin, who was standing by him. On 22 February 1980 Landa pleaded guilty to seven frauds on the working men's clubs. The judge, taking into account the time he had spent in prison abroad awaiting extradition, fined him £2,750 with £1,000 costs. On his release Landa told the press that, had he known the outcome of the case, he would have surrendered himself much earlier. He still lives in some style near Durham.

The Stafford-Luvaglio affair was on any reckoning by far the most important case in the North East for decades. Life there generally progresses at a level almost divorced from the more vibrant and wealthy areas of the country. Says Professor Dick Hobbs of the University of Durham:

It's a very run-down area with a very sparse population and a very small market centred on Newcastle City centre where

---

[13] *Mail on Sunday*, 30 April 1989.
[14] *News of the World*, 19 March 1967.
[15] *People*, 20 August 1967.

127

the amount of drinking establishments is quite phenomenal. On a Friday and Saturday people just flock in and get pissed. They queue half an hour in their party clothes to get in a pub in freezing weather.

There is no economic mobility. You go down the pit at 15 and come up at 65. Culturally they are used to that even though it last happened two generations ago. There is no opportunity for people to move around. In some cases by the age of 25 you have gone through economic cycles but it isn't the case in the North East.

The traditional jobs have been the pits, shipbuilding and engineering. People in the workplace were restricted to these masculine stereotypes and the same thing applies to crime in the North East. All you need is cropped hair and big shoulders.

In the rural areas there is still dog-fighting in the villages, and in an evening you can see men in camouflage clothing leading three lurchers out. The gamekeepers shoot the dogs with guns with infra-red sights.

Nevertheless, says one local solicitor:

Although there is a twenty per cent unemployment figure, the remaining 80 per cent do very nicely. They earn their money and they spend it. The cost of housing is low and beer is £1.25 a pint. In Newcastle there is a lot of night life both high and low. There is the Royal Shakespeare Company here for three months, the Scottish National Opera and then there are the wine bars and the clubs. They spend their money and a proportion of it is going to be spent illicitly. Drugs are professionally operated, the amateur approach has been swept aside even in Hartlepool. The drugs come in from everywhere but particularly from the ports such as Newcastle and Middlesborough.

There have been a number of celebrated murder cases in the North East including the unsolved murder of Evelyn Foster in 1931.[16] This, however, was a domestic matter and murders

---

[16] Evelyn Foster was found on 6 January 1931 lying beside the burning wreck of her car. She had suffered appalling burns and died a few hours later. Before she died she accused a bowler-hatted man of setting fire to her. No one was ever arrested for the crime or really even suspected, although Jonathon Goodman puts up a plausible argument naming a possible murderer in *The Burning of Evelyn Foster*.

committed in the course of theft or robbery in the area included that of Police Constable Shiell, in which the evidence was remarkably similar to that of the case of Craig and Bentley. The murder was committed by two young men. Ostler, himself the son of a Leeds police officer, and Appleby were found by Shiell breaking into the Co-op store at Coxhoe, County Durham on 29 February 1940. He chased them into Westley Place where he was shot. He had already blown his whistle to summon help and he was soon found; he was taken to the local hospital where he said to his Superintendent, 'They've finished me Super.' The local justices' clerk was called to take a dying declaration from the gravely injured Shiell: 'I cornered them. One pulled a revolver and the other said, "Let him have it, he is all alone," and he shot me, just one shot in the stomach at the side.'

The men ran a cut-throat defence which was inevitably to bring down both of them. Ostler ran the defence of an alibi, whilst Appleby said he was present when Ostler fired the fatal shot and gave evidence to that effect. Appleby denied saying, 'Let him have it. He is all alone.' His version was that he had said, 'Come on, let's give him a clout.' Mr Justice Hilbery in summing up said:

> If you accept the deceased's account, you may have to ask yourselves if it were not for Appleby's remark, 'Let him have it, he is all alone', the foul hand of Ostler might not have pulled the trigger.

Both were convicted at Leeds' Assizes and sentenced to death.

According to Professor Hobbs:

> So far only Ecstasy appears to be a problem on the drug scene in the North East. There is really no cocaine in general use up here. There is a general conservative culture. Legitimate fashions reach the North-East late. Ecstasy took off two and a half to three years after it did in London.
>
> You can get cocaine in Middlesborough at £50 a gramme, the same price as in London. It's still a yuppie drug here.
>
> Part of the reason is that there is no real ethnic minority community. There is a very small Asian community in Newcastle and an enormous Hassidic community in Gateshead, but 'they're invisible'.

129

There is little doubt that cocaine will arrive and that crack is the ideal substance for a depressed inner city estate where nothing has happened for 25 years. But as yet there is no demand. Crack is a ghetto drug and there are plenty of white ghettos which have no economic vitality legitimate or illegitimate.

This trailing behind the fashions of the remainder of the country seems to be echoed in the attitude in the North East to crime. The Chief Constable's annual reports mark a depressing but relatively slow upward progression in the use of firearms – in 1987 the use of the shotgun doubled and that of the sawn-off shotgun was up by a third – and of attacks on the elderly. There have been instances of force by career criminals, as when in 26/27 April 1977 a customs officer was tortured to make him reveal the whereabouts of his money. Three men later received sentences of up to five years.

There have been sporadic incidents of gang violence, such as the 1980 Saturday lunch-time fight when the West Denton gang took on the Benton gang in the Eldon Square shopping precinct. The victim had cuts running the length of his spine, and the ringleader of twelve received three years. A year later a fish and chip shop in West End was petrol-bombed on 23 April 1981, earning nine years for the ringleaders. That year, at the more professional end of things, it was discovered that forged American $20 bills were being printed in the Newcastle area. Eight men including three from Newcastle were found guilty and given three years each. Generally speaking, however, the Chief Constable's report on interesting crimes in his annual survey was devoted more to domestic incidents than to the activities of the career criminal.

By the middle of the 1980s there were rumours that the various warring Newcastle factions had joined together into what would be a formidable alliance; but, if a temporary alliance was formed, it soon splintered. There had always been some solidarity amongst North East criminals. It is said that when the Kray twins wished to explore the possibility of taking an interest in the North East, and indeed took Joe Louis, the former world heavyweight champion, on a tour there, locals explained that their continued presence was unnecessary. From time to time North Easterners have been recruited for their ability to handle gelignite on one-off operations in the South, but generally they have remained a league apart.

One of Newcastle's most famous criminal sons is the independent safebreaker, Eddie Chapman, now in his late seventies. He had been apprenticed in the shipbuilding trade and then had joined the Guards before, on his first leave, he deserted and received 112 days in the guardhouse. On his release and back in prison, he joined up with Jimmy Hunt who took him on a break-in at Fyffe's, the banana importers. Now he learned how to open safes, and Odeon cinemas became his principal target; there was always a substantial sum kept overnight. His technique involved the use of a condom which was filled with gelignite and water and then pushed through a lock. This stopped the gelignite dropping into the safe.

Eventually Chapman was captured in Jersey, where he had fled while on bail in Newcastle. He had been arrested there following an escape from Scotland where he and his partners were caught blowing a safe in a local Co-op. He was sentenced in Jersey to two years' imprisonment and while serving them the Germans invaded the Channel Islands. He was recruited as an agent but immediately became a double one, working for British Intelligence and being parachuted into Germany. He was allowed to keep his German earnings, and there would be no prosecution over the forty or more safes he had blown. He wrote his memoirs and his story was made into the film *Triple Cross*. In later life he ran a health club and hotel in Hertfordshire, and spent some time trying to prove that a senior Metropolitan police officer was crooked. He finally retired to Spain, one of the very few criminals of the old school who actually held on to their money.[17]

In August 1993 a bizarre crime was committed. In a scenario reminiscent of the 1870s in Arizona, a gang took over the remote town of Rothbury, Berwick-on-Tweed, to steal £15,000 from the post office there.

Early on Monday 23 August five men, dressed in camouflage clothing and wearing ski-masks, appeared in the village, cut the telephone wires and threatened some of the 2,000 residents with crowbars. They took over the main street with a stolen council

---

[17] Apart from his own memoirs, there is an account of his exploits and capture in E. Greeno, *War on the Underworld*, Chapter 10, in which Chapman is referred to as Mike.

van and told the residents who were looking out of their windows to go back to bed and stay there. They then forced their way into the post office and escaped with £15,000 in cash, pension books and stamps.

It was not the first attack on this tiny village. In 1992 the village store had been the subject of a ram-raid, a popular form of sport which had originated in the North East in the 1970s.

The last months of 1993 were not a happy time for Newcastle hardmen and bystanders alike. From the middle of October six men were shot in nightclubs and discos, and two men, rumoured to be connected to the city's leading families involved in drugs, disappeared. It was part of a continuing story that, however isolated the North East may be and however 'behind' in fashion, it is not always immune from the crime problems which beset the other areas of the country. The shooting of Viv Graham has its roots in the late 1980s; the cause was almost certainly drugs. There was a bouncers' war in 1988. As Hobbs says:

Here the bouncers are weightlifters and ex-boxers, huge men and they are used for their size. Some have been on steroids. In other places it's their hardness. The clubs are involved in Ecstasy. It's easy to make your name here. You don't get the challenges you would in Manchester or Liverpool.

Apart from the truth, one of the first casualties was Robert Bell, builder and bouncer of Gateshead. On 22 August 1988, he was dining in Santino's Restaurant in Newcastle's Cloth Market when two men burst in. One man, who was never identified, cut the telephone lines, and it was alleged by the prosecution that a Peter Donnelly went to the table where Bell was sitting and pointed a shotgun at him. Fighting broke out and the gun was taken from Donnelly by Viv Graham who was at the table; he smashed it against the wall and told Donnelly not to be so stupid. According to the prosecution, Donnelly, of Lemington, Newcastle, and the second man then fought Bell who was stabbed first in the shoulder and then in the chest, penetrating the heart. He was saved by emergency surgery. Graham had again intervened and given Donnelly a good beating before the police arrived.

The motive, said David Wood, prosecuting, was revenge for a

fight earlier in the evening between Bell and Donnelly over two girls, which had been broken up by the police who arrested one of Donnelly's friends. The prosecution's case was that Donnelly had then gone home, changed his clothes and come out looking for Bell armed with a gun and carving knife. In a written statement made after the fight, Bell claimed that Donnelly was his attacker. At the trial the following April, when Donnelly was charged with attempted murder and various ancillary offences, Bell changed his story. On reflection he could now not be sure that it was Donnelly who attacked him nor how his injuries occurred. Nor could Bell's brother, Ian, help in the question of identification. He had chased the second man who had tried to take another customer hostage.

There were cheers from the public gallery when Donnelly, who had declined to answer police questions and to give evidence, was acquitted by the jury after a retirement of forty-five minutes.

Graham was not long out of the news. Before the trial of Donnelly, he and his friend Rob Armstrong had been the victims of a drive-by shooting outside Newcastle's Manhattan nightclub in April 1989. At about 1.30 a.m. the rear window of their Bluebird Nissan was shot out, and four other shots put sixty pellets into Armstrong. Graham escaped unhurt. Both men, unable to identify their assailants, denounced them. Rob Armstrong said:

> We are the good guys. We try to keep the peace. I am no angel but I can say outright I haven't done anything to anybody to warrant being shot at. I know I have more friends than enemies in Newcastle. Licensees ask us to keep an eye on their premises during the weekend in case there is an outbreak of trouble. I would only use a reasonable amount of force to eject troublemakers.
>
> I have heard it suggested we were shot at because of some sort of protection war. That is pie in the sky. Newcastle is too small for anybody to operate protection. Licensees ask us to help them out. I have heard it said that an outside operator from Leeds is moving in to slap a protection racket on Newcastle pubs but to me that is just stupid talk.

Viv Graham added:

We are not doormen. Doormen stand outside and try to prevent potential troublemakers from entering the pub.

If a situation gets out of hand, which can happen in packed city pubs and clubs when people have had too much to drink, we will try and calm it down.

A 'city centre pub landlady' was sure there was no protection:

There are good doormen and bad doormen. Just as there are some good police officers and some who go in heavy-handed.

You pay for security because Newcastle is a rough city, but nobody is demanding money by threats. I know of no protection racket.

But the police were not so convinced. A spokesman said that intelligence units had been moved into premises named by licensees as being under protection: 'We know who these gangsters are. This situation will not be allowed to get out of control ... We will not tolerate gang warfare or intimidation on the streets of Newcastle.'[18]

Initially they were not notably successful in their efforts. Two months later, doorman Mark Stephenson had his ear bitten off at Idols, a club in the seaside town of Whitley Bay. It was stitched back on and five men were charged. Then in the July of that year former championship contender boxer Howard Mills, who was now working as a doorman at Hanrahan's Bar, was shot in the leg which he had to have amputated. Two months after the attack on Mills, Billy Robinson, the under-manager of the Cotton Club, was shot at a party in Felling; hours earlier he had been threatened at Bentley's nightclub. Another man, Paul Basey, was also shot simply because he got in the way. Amid cheers and handshakes Alan Swindon, also of Felling, was acquitted of wounding with intent. William Robinson had told the jury at the Newcastle Crown Court that he could not identify his attacker.

The next year Viv Graham received three years for wounding Stuart Watson, the doorman of Hobo. Along with him were members of some of the North East's powerful families. Alan

[18] Neil McKay and John Merry in *Sunday Sun*, 7 May 1989.

134

Tams received two and a half years, as did Stephen Sayers. David Lancaster and Viv's friend Rob Armstrong also went down for a similar period. This had been a high-profile police exercise, with up to fifty officers cordoning off the magistrates' court when the defendants were brought in. Members of the Sayers and Tams families had been up in court only a few weeks earlier when John Henry Sayers, along with Stephen Sayers, was charged with a variety of offences including conspiracy to handle stolen vending machines. Alan Tams was charged with a variety of assaults. Tams, who admitted biting a policeman on the arm – he threatened to bite his nose off if he came any closer – had a month added to his two-and-a-half-year sentence. The policeman had intervened in a food fight in the Elswick Road where eight men had been throwing eggs, flour and ketchup at each other. Tams was seen walking from a general shop with a tray of eggs whilst the others continued fighting. The defence, at one time, suggested the police officer had over-reacted.

At the end of the Watson trial the doorman said he was sorry for what had happened, and went on to accuse the Regional Crime Squad of using him as bait to get Graham and the others. There had been an undercover officer posing as a customer when the incident took place, who had been under orders not to intervene. Unsurprisingly, he came under heavy fire from the defence lawyers and was asked whether when he realized one of the men had a spiked weapon he should have stepped in. 'No,' replied the officer, 'I had been briefed and instructed not to.' A security video of the incident had been a 'chilling picture', said Judge Mary MacMurray.

In November 1991 Alan Swindon left circulation after he took too much Ecstasy once too often, and was given twenty-four years for the murder of Paul Furness with a hunting knife. Swindon and Roy Storey had been stabbed in their stomachs in April 1990 in the Rockshots area, where they had been at an Easter pyjama party.

The troubles had led to a registration scheme for nightclub doormen. Organized in May 1992 by the Northumbria police, and the first of its kind in the country, it required the vetting of all doormen at premises which held a public entertainments licence. 'Incidents involving door supervisors have nose-dived. As well as violence, the registration scheme has addressed the problem of protection rackets and drugs,' said Superintendent Peter Durham towards the end of 1993.[19]

Not everyone had received the message, however. Paul Short suffered a fractured skull, two fractures to his left wrist, two broken ribs and a broken right wrist when he was dropped over a balcony twenty feet on to a concrete floor, allegedly by a bouncer at the Sirocco nightclub in Washington. Magistrates at the court there were told that he did not wish to press charges against his attacker. In fact it was Short who appeared in court. On 22 June 1991 he was fined £50 and ordered to pay £140 for smashing the windows of the nightclub before the bouncers dealt with him.

Now, in the last hours of 1993, Viv Graham was killed by three shots from a .357 Magnum handgun as he walked to his car in the Wallsend district. It seems his attackers had been shadowing him for most of the evening. Graham had been drinking for most of New Year's Eve in the Anchor and Queen's Head public houses. He crawled thirty yards before collapsing outside a newsagent's shop.

Graham had also been credited unofficially with the attack in September 1991 in Walkers, yet another Newcastle club, on the footballer Paul 'Gazza' Gascoigne which damaged his knee and nearly ended his career. The police were unable to find witnesses to give evidence and the inquiry was ended after Gascoigne told them he wanted the matter dropped. The near killing of a pub customer who failed to drink up sufficiently quickly is also attributed to Graham. Whilst he was serving the sentence for the attack on Stuart Watson, he is said to have calmed a riot in Durham prison.

Just about the only unchallenged facet of the killing is that Graham is indeed dead. The permutations of reasons proffered are seemingly endless and depend upon whether the speaker has a pro- or anti-Graham stance. He is thought to have been negotiating with black dealers in Leeds – he was seen in the Hilton there in the summer of 1993 – and there had been attempts by a Yorkshire team to muscle in on the North-Eastern trade. Alternative suggestions have been that the killers came from suppliers in Liverpool or London, or that the men were Italians brought up from London on contract to do the business.

One neutral observer offers the thought that Graham had been

---

[19] Quoted in the Newcastle *Journal*, 3 January 1994.

crossing-up North-Eastern criminal families in general and South Shields ones in particular for far too long. He also suggests, more interestingly, that it may have been related to the death of a young girl in a club which Graham was minding at the time. His third offer had been mooted in the papers; that it relates to the death of Graham's arch-rival Andy Winder who died in Tenerife in 1993.

The 34-year-old Andy Winder, who had previously run a modelling agency in Darlington before leaving in 1986 to go into a time-share scheme, was in charge of the touts for a major time-share company in Los Cristanos, Tenerife. Winder, who had taken over touting in Lanzarote and Gran Canaria, now wanted control of South Tenerife, an area which had been the fiefdom of another hardman who was said to have bitten off a rival's nose and had subsquently left for Portugal.[20]

One version of that story is that there had been a savage bare-knuckle fight between Graham and Winder after which Graham, who had needed substantial surgery, had placed a £10,000 contract on the body-builder. Winder is said to have taken out a bizarre form of insurance, or at least revenge, in the form of a £30,000 contract on Graham only to be executed after his death, which came in late September 1993.

There had been a fight involving four other 'very large men' at a time-share in Tenerife. It appears that Winder tried to stab 26-year-old Richard Cashman from Teesside and, when others intervened, he stabbed them as well. A shot was fired and Winder fell dead. David Coates, from Stockton-on-Tees, was stabbed and broke his arm jumping from a balcony.

Another North-East hardman is also suggested to have been offered substantial terms to deal with Graham. Lee Duffy, from Eston near Middlesborough, who already controlled lucrative protection rackets in Cleveland, had been offered a large stake in organized crime in the North East. Duffy had survived three attempts on his life and had apparently tried to meet Graham on a number of occasions before he himself was killed, stabbed to death in a fight with David Allison in Middlesborough. After

---

[20] Along with the Costa del Crime, Portugal has been a haunt of English gangsters. According to a report in the *Guardian* a group arrived in the late 1980s and 'until recently' were taking £1,000 a week off the managers of Vale Vavio in Portugal on the promise of not breaking the legs of their timeshare salesmen. Nick Davies, 'Who killed Rachel?', in *Guardian Weekend*, 14 August 1993.

being told that Allison had been fighting for his life, the jury acquitted him.

Then there was the question of whether Graham was indeed in the rackets. His father, Jack, was convinced he was not. Citing the fact that he was being taken to court over the repossession of his son's car, he argued that if Graham had been in the drug and protection scene he would not have allowed this to happen. On the other hand, this was not the view taken by New Year's Eve partygoers who on hearing of Graham's death toasted the event saying, 'Viv no more for '94.' A pub landlady told the Newcastle *Journal and Echo* that his protection racket had made the life of a pub owner a misery.

> Pubs were forced to pay £200 a week to him or there would be some sort of trouble. If you refused to hand over the cash someone would be planted and a fight would break out on the premises. There was no way landlords could stop drugs being sold on the premises. He was a hard man, a bully, who threatened both men and women.

But another pub manager said:

> I have never heard anything bad about Viv. You didn't see him much, but if any of the pubs had bother they would give him a ring and he would sort it out. He was a gentle giant really.

'People are upset because Viv was much loved round here,' said one lady, referring to the theft of flowers left at the murder scene. One wreath left behind said: 'Uncle Viv: Our hero. You will always be in our hearts.' Journalists were chased away from the scene by heavily-built men.

Within a week of Graham's death £50,000 reward money was on offer and there were reports that it might soon be doubled, as it was by his fiancée and long-time companion Anna Connelly. Two other claimants for Mr Graham's affections surfaced. In addition to a wife and two children, and Ms Connelly, it was discovered he had had a red-headed lady friend by whom he had another two children.

In the meantime something approaching anarchy was said to be rife amongst the clubs, with Graham's competitors demanding £100 a night to protect the bars he used to control.[21] Whether this was newspaper hype remains to be seen. In the first few weeks following Graham's death there was no apparent take-over of his empire, if indeed one existed.

[21] See Howard Foster, 'Gangland war looms after drug killing' in the *Sunday Times*, 9 January 1994.

6

Manchester

The history of crime in Manchester over the last hundred years resembles a clockwork doll whose mechanism has broken and is now running around in all directions, creating mayhem as it does so. The officers who retired perhaps twenty years ago, when professional crime was the old-fashioned theft, robbery, a little prostitution and a little protection, would have trouble recognizing parts of the city today.

Perhaps it is cheating a little to stretch back a decade before the end of the century to begin the account of crime in Manchester, but it is also instructive to see the state of the police at the time. It was in something approaching disarray, at least 'D' division was. The public inquiry into 'allegations bearing upon the efficiency and discipline of the Manchester City Police' ordered by the Home Secretary began on 24 May 1897 at the City Sessions courthouse before J.S. Dugdale, Recorder of Birmingham. It particularly related to the retired and disgraced William Bannister.

The now ex-Superintendent William Bannister had been a constable in 1871, a sergeant in 1875, an inspector in 1880 and a superintendent in 1882. In the 1890s he was in charge of 'D' district in which there was an abnormally high number of brothels and disorderly houses. In particular in Shepley Street, houses were kept by a woman named Sarah 'Mother' Wilson, and a man named Taylor. These were, said Mr Sutton, appearing at the inquiry for the Solicitor to the Treasury, houses which should have been suppressed. Bannister was a close friend of

140

'Mother' Taylor; he not only drew up her will but also was a beneficiary. After her death the houses continued to be used for immoral purposes, and there was evidence from constables that Bannister was the one who carried on the management of them. This was a problem which had been raised in the early 1890s. When challenged then, Bannister had explained that his father and Sarah Wilson had been intimate friends, that he was the executor and that he had disposed of his interest in one of the houses for £12.

In 1893 Bannister had been brought before the Watch Committee on two charges of misconduct, and at one time in the debate it seemed as though he might be dismissed. Some members of the committee then protested that this would mean the loss of his pension, and a reprimand was substituted for dismissal.

All the constables involved with the 1897 inquiry gave the seeming protection of Bannister by the Watch Committee as a reason why they were afraid to move against him. They were also afraid of being 'swamped by their colleagues', and in the case of one senior officer he too did not want to be responsible for Bannister losing his pension. Others said that 'D' division was no worse than other divisions.

In the Chief Constable's report for 1896, the number of brothels was listed as twelve and houses of accommodation as three. The Chief Constable of Liverpool had commented that he could find fifty in the Oxford Road area alone. Brothels apparently were only regarded as such when it was 'fully proved to have been so'.

Bannister was also seen in company with a Mrs Julia Davis, separated from her husband, in the Falstaff public house in Hulme, behaving in a way which 'if true would have degraded him'. This was the evidence of a Constable Wilkinson before the Watch Committee. Bannister had told the Committee that he was in the pub for the purposes of making a will – he seems to have had a healthy sideline in this occupation – and anyway that there had been a robbery committed which he was investigating. Wilkinson had resigned.

In 1893 Julia Davis took another public house, the Derby Arms in Vine Street. She must have given this up after she had troubles with her licence, because in 1895 she was living at 34 Greenheys Lane. Bannister was regularly seen coming out of the back passage of the house at 8.30 in the morning, and once constables had seen Davis hitting him with her umbrella in the street.

Bannister, described as a bold bad man, had also brought an action against the Reverend John Kelty for defamation. Kelty had complained to Bannister's superior officers that Bannister had gone in a cab, drunk, with two prostitutes to Braby Street police station. At a slander trial at Carlisle Assizes the words had been held to be privileged, but Mr Justice Kennedy had whitewashed Bannister, telling him he left the court without a stain on his character. Bannister had, in effect, won the action and a celebratory testimonial dinner for him was paid for with £200 donated by local licensees. Constables had been invited to sign a testimonial and had been charged sixpence for 'meat and potatoes and plenty of beer'. One officer had become so drunk that when he tried to sing, cymbals had to be brought to 'knock him off'.

How many constables were present? asked R.B. Batty at the inquiry.

'I could hardly see any one absent,' replied Constable Thomas M'Dermott.

Officers gave evidence that they were afraid to make a report to the Chief Constable, making excuses such as that by Constable P. Lacy who feared 'being shifted'.

Q: Is it looked upon as a disgrace in the force to be shifted?

A: The man is looked upon as a mug for interfering.

'All applications for the Watch Committee or the Chief Constable must be submitted through your superintendent, and you are not allowed to write on official subjects to any personage whatsoever without the permission of the Chief Constable,' Lacy added.

There were complaints about the number of prostitutes who frequented the annual police ball. 'The policeman would not have a very happy time if he had no amusements at all,' replied the Commissioner. There were also allegations that the Chief Constable had received £60 or £70 (sensation) as part of a testimonial from local brewers. One witness complained that he was being charged with being given two guineas, when the Commissioner's subscription list reached a thousand pounds. The Chief Constable tired of the complaints and was content to let Bannister wait until he could draw his pension and then he would go.

Inspector Burroughes had made a complaint about a beer-house, and in turn the keeper complained about him. When the licensee was convicted Burroughes wished to go and see the Chief Constable to have the complaint expunged, but Bannister merely deleted it from the charge book. Burroughes went on to say that he believed Bannister had warned prostitutes of raids.

On 7 December 1896 Bannister resigned before the Watch Committee. His last act had been to help his old friend William Taylor escape a charge of brothel-keeping.

According to Dugdale's report, issued on 19 July 1897:

> [He] must have had friends on the Committee who per-suaded the majority, probably out of good nature, to retain him in his position and override the opinion of the sub-committee and the Chief Constable without any risk of any individual responsibility being fastened on themselves.

The report also stated that Bannister had been promoted over four other inspectors and against the recommendation of the Chief Constable:

> This false step was the starting point of all subsequent mischief. A superintendent of police commanding a division of more than 200 men must necessarily exercise very great power; his good word or disapprobation would naturally have great effect in regulating the promotion of the men . . .

In sharp contrast to Bannister was Jerome Caminada, regarded as the father of the Manchester police, who joined the force in 1868 at the age of 24 at a time when the worst areas for crime were the Ancoats and Angel meadow districts. By 1874 Caminada had racked up a staggering 20,000 arrests.

Crime figures are notoriously difficult to explain and justify. A difference may arise because one force cautions all shoplifters on the first occasion they are caught, another may not even document domestic assaults; nevertheless it is difficult to satisfactorily explain the 60 per cent rise in crime in Manchester between 1944 and 1945 (against a London rise of 25 per cent and a Leeds rise of 4.3 per cent) and a tenfold rise in the value of property stolen from £26,375 in 1938, of which half was recovered, to £262,432 in 1946 with £76,985 retrieved – unless someone was, to use a phrase, well at it. And not just someone: several people. The reports of the Chief Constable were silent on an explanation but housebreaking, shopbreaking and warehouse raids showed the greatest increase, conforming to the London pattern. What lay behind both, suggests Edward Smithies, was the insatiable demands of the black market. Manchester's geographical position at the centre of the textile trade made it particularly vulnerable. What was worse was the almost complete collapse of the clear-up rate, down by 32.9 per cent from the 1942 figure of 63.8 per cent.[1]

As with the other major cities the black market flourished during the War in Manchester, with petrol and stolen clothing coupons as favourite commodities. A Manchester syndicate was able to distribute forged clothing coupons to nearly forty firms both there and in London. In fact the forgeries seem to have been pretty amateur ones. The forger had failed to note that most genuine coupons were torn off a sheet; his were cut from it. The ring was broken up by a tip-off and the police found the owner of a London factory with the coupons. Others were traced when a Manchester man was found giving others into a post office in exchange for vouchers. It seems that the word was that if you wanted coupons in Manchester they were freely (well, for payment) available in Great Ducie Street. Twenty-two people found themselves in the dock, mostly charged with handling, and most maintaining they did not know the coupons were forged. The rich defendants had counsel who were able to argue the technicalities, and only ten were eventually convicted. The forger received four years' imprisonment.[2]

It was also a time when, because of the perilous state of the economy, forgery was treated very seriously. Towards the end of the War well-made forged notes had been circulating in the north of England, and it must have seemed to the police that a major counterfeiting gang had been broken when in June 1945 Herbert Winstanley was discovered passing a forged £1 note at the Albion Greyhound Stadium in Salford. When they raided his home there were 2,498 forged £5 notes and 6,651 £1 notes stacked up awaiting distribution. It turned out, however, not to be the work of a major crime syndicate, rather a cottage

[1] E. Smithies, *Crime in Wartime*, p.189.
[2] *Manchester Guardian*, 13 May 1942.

industry. The work was entirely that of Mr Winstanley, who told the police that he had been passing notes for about seven years.

> I was practising on the £1 notes for 11 years before I issued a single one. I started it as a hobby [said the 60-year-old signwriter]. I have done everything myself. With regard to the £5 and £10 notes I have never tried to pass a single one as they are not good enough yet.

He was sentenced to 10 years' imprisonment.

Policing was tough in the 1940s. Sir Robert Mark recalls:

> I can remember a very successful, fairly senior detective in Manchester, who, when dealing with hardened criminals had his own version of the Judges' Rules. It consisted of greeting the prisoner with the blunt enquiry, 'Will you talk or be tanned?' If the reply was in the negative, sometimes colourfully so, the prisoner was removed smartly to the lavatory where he was upended and his head jammed down the bowl. It usually took two to hold him, whilst a third repeatedly pulled the chain until a waggling of the feet indicated a more compliant attitude. He then signed a form headed by the usual caution against self-incrimination. My point in relating this is to make it clear that practices such as this were perfectly well known to solicitors, to counsel, to judges and to the Press, but that no one did anything about them because there seemed no obvious way to achieve a fair balance between the public interest and the rights of wrongdoers. To pretend that knowledge of such malpractices was confined to the police alone, as people occasionally do, is sheer hypocrisy.[3]

After the war there grew up a now legendary collection of characters including the Black Prince, Chuck Taylor, who wore a wig and had a dance trio in which he played the bongo drums, and in the summer used to steal ladies' handbags from the park; and Bobby Critchley who had a bullet-proof car. According to Manchester legend it was Critchley who saw off Jack Spot when he came to the city in search of a nightclub to mind. Critchley

---

[3] Sir Robert Mark, *In the Office of Constable*, pp. 52–3.

had himself been involved in racecourse protection, and the club Spot fancied was his Jacaranda in the Stretford Road.

'When God made heaven he made Manchester,' recalls an old-time face. 'Do you know where you could drink all afternoon? In the Crown Court. They had a bar open there the whole time.'

Old-time police officers are keen to impress that there was little, if any, organized crime in Manchester. 'It was still villagey enough for people to notice. We never had anything which hadn't had someone as a witness,' says one former Detective Chief Inspector.

There was prostitution, of course, run by the Camilleris, a Maltese family. Street bookmaking before the Betting Act was unofficially tolerated. Everyone came before the courts in their turn, and there were no complaints from the bookmakers as long as no one was left out.

Clubs abounded, but it seems to have been fairly harmless entertainment. Clients were sold sponges for 2/6d and encouraged to throw them at the stripper, who collected them at the end of her act for re-sale. The ex-wrestler 'Big' Bill Benny[4] owned clubs including the Cabaret Club – 'The South of France comes to Manchester' – and Chez Joey with roulette and blackjack tables at the back. 'When the police came the doorman would delay them a while to give breathing space for the punters.' According to folklore Benny, who had a hairlip and was by all accounts a genial giant, died in bed and had to be lifted off the girl. The cabarets themselves were fairly homely at the beginning of the sixties, perhaps a wrestling bout, a bit of striptease, and sometimes a freak act such as Tom Jacobsen the armless wonder who shaved punters with a cutthroat razor and his feet, opened beer bottles and played the piano. Later came the top-line acts, the expense of which would close many of the clubs.

The view of some police officers is that the small spielers catered for the Jewish immigrant community in particular:

They were real workers. They raincoated the world. You'd see them from 6 a.m. until midnight. Then when their children were 18 or 19 and off to University, the last thing

---

[4] One of his regular opponents was the Geordie, Charlie Scott, and the billing would read: 'Big' Bill Benny [Afraid of no one not even 'Big Boy' Charlie Scott] *v* 'Big Boy' Charlie Scott [Afraid of no one not even 'Big' Bill Benny].

they wanted was to be seen over a hot sewing machine. That first generation went to clubs, private illegal gambling clubs, to play chemmy and baccarat.

The legalization of gambling ruined clubs such as Chez Joey. Once Mecca opened in the city, no one wanted to go to the smaller clubs. The middle sixties saw the end of the teenage coffee bars where soft drugs had been freely available.

That period also saw the last executions 'in the manner prescribed by the law'. Two relatively minor criminals, Peter Anthony Allen and Gwynne Owen Evans, young Preston dairymen, were hanged on 13 August 1964 for the murder of John Alan West.

The murder had been committed in the drab mining town of Workington. West, who worked for the local laundry, lived in a semi-detached house in Seaton, one of the suburbs. He was killed, hit by a poker and stabbed, in a robbery which went wrong and in which Evans left behind his macintosh together with a Royal Life Saving Society medallion bearing his name and initials. Apparently Evans had known West for some five years. At the time of the murder Evans had been living with Allen and his family and they had been behind with the rent and rates. They had also been on a small crime spree together, committing a series of shopbreakings and other thefts for which they were fined by Preston Borough Magistrates. It seems they committed their murder, in part, to pay their £10 fines. Evans told Allen that West had money lying around, and they drove to Workington. Evans went in to see West in the early hours of the morning and in turn he let Allen in about 3 a.m. Each blamed the other for hitting West with an iron bar, and the jury convicted both after a retirement of three and a quarter hours. It cannot have helped that it came out that Mrs Allen had been 'more than a landlady' to Evans. Their appeals and applications for a reprieve were refused. The letters signing their death warrants were sent on Tuesday 11 August. The Permanent Under-Secretary of State at the Home Office said, 'It seems kinder to let the prisoner go on hoping until the last possible moment.' Allen was hanged at Walton, Liverpool and Evans at Strangeways, Manchester. At the last meeting Allen had with his wife he 'went berserk, really berserk. He was strong, you know, and the glass in there,

147

they say it's supposed to be bullet-proof, but he smashed it. He went berserk.'[5]

It depends on one's outlook whether by the 1960s Manchester crime was free of protection or was firmly controlled by the so-called Quality Street Gang which included the redoubtable ex-boxer Jimmy Swords. The police view is that they were a group of minders and enforcers who, as the years passed and they grew older, had moved into the more respectable lines of club and restaurant owning. Even their critics do not rate them highly. 'They are given credit they didn't deserve.' On the other hand, as property developer and local Conservative Party chairman, Kevin Taylor, recalls:

There was never any such gang, but several Manchester characters had styled themselves that way as a joke, in commemoration of a Quality Street TV advertisement of the 1960s depicting rather suave debonair crooks. In fact, they worked hard almost every day on their car sales pitches, in all weathers, which is hardly to be expected if they were indeed criminals.[6]

The local faces had a good relationship with the police, to whom they could turn if they were threatened by outsiders. There are various versions of the story of what happened when the Kray twins came to Manchester in one of their forays to find a club outside London, and it was on the Cromford Club that they set their sights.

One variation is that they were met on the platform at Piccadilly station and put on the first train back. Frank Williamson, who was in charge, recalls it slightly differently:

Owen Ratcliffe was a charming man. He was a great gambler. He owned the Cromford Club at which Jack London [the ex-heavyweight champion], who by this time was nearly punch-drunk, was the doorman.

---

[5] Mary Allen quoted in E. Jones, *The Last Two to Hang*, p.100. 13 August seems to have been a popular day for hanging celebrated criminals. In 1868 the first so-called private hanging took place when Thomas Wells, aged 18, was hanged after being convicted of the murder of Edward Walshe. He had been sacked for poor work and within minutes returned with a gun to shoot the Dover Priory stationmaster. In 1915 George Joseph Smith, the 'Brides in the Bath' murderer, was hanged by John Ellis at Maidstone.

[6] K. Taylor, *The Poisoned Tree*, p.21.

I went to the Midland with Douglas Nimmo, my sergeant. It was no later than 1961. A house detective, Tabby Booth, who'd been a sergeant in the railway police, alerted me. He rang me at home saying he'd got boxers called Gray from the East End of London who were being difficult and throwing their weight about. He also told me that Owen Ratcliffe had been in the Midland earlier in the evening with a large meat cleaver under his Crombie coat. They'd knocked poor old Jack London down the stairs of the Cromford and there was no need. He was no menace by then. I rang the police in London and asked about the Grays. They told me they had nothing on them. This was patently false because Grays from the East End who were boxers was an easy link. It was only the next letter in the alphabet.

Douglas Nimmo, my sergeant, and I waltzed into the Midland, told them to get on the next train and we never saw them again in Manchester. Len 'The Barber' Carter who had a strong link with London teams was with them. Nimmo just dismissed him. Told him to go away.

The Cromford Club was certainly an object of police attention.

It was the only one which caused us any trouble; not that it wasn't well appointed and well run. It was who went in there and the amount of money gambled there we were interested in. The gaming was run by a man called The Aga because he looked like the Aga Khan.

One person on whom everyone is agreed, however, is that Bobby McDermott was the King of the Barrow Boys and, the police believe, was the King of the Fences. Possibly if Manchester had anyone in the 1950s, '60s and '70s who could be regarded as approaching major criminal status, it was he. According to Frank Williamson, 'We looked at him long and often but we could never pin anything on him.' From McDermott's Cellar in New Barn Street near the Cromford Club, he rented out a series of barrows to the stallholders across the city and would provide work for any man who approached him on his release from prison. He was also regarded as being a high-class receiver, was certainly well connected with major crime figures in both

London and Glasgow and could be relied upon to provide safe
lodgings for prison escapees. When Robert Anderson escaped by
chance with Ronnie Biggs from Wandsworth, it was to McDermott that his London connections later turned for help.

McDermott was also loyal to Manchester officers. At the
height of the investigation into the Flying Squad in 1969, in
an effort to discredit Frank Williamson who was overseeing the
inquiry, officers from London were sent to sniff out any dirt that
might be clinging to his uniform: 'These two officers went to see
McDermott and tried to get him to say something about me
being dishonest but he wouldn't.'[7]

Kevin Taylor, himself once a successful businessman, fell foul
of the police. Amidst political manoeuvrings, allegations,
counter-allegations and certainly a multitude of recriminations, John Stalker, the Deputy Chief Constable of Greater
Manchester, had been suspended and then reinstated before he
finally resigned. His acquaintance Taylor, himself a friend of the
so-called Quality Street Gang (if it existed), and who had built his
fortunes on his skill as a professional card player, had been
ruined by a prosecution which eventually collapsed.

In May 1984 John Stalker was appointed to lead an inquiry
into the shooting of six unarmed men in 1982 by the Royal Ulster
Constabulary, an appointment which if it was by no means
welcomed enthusiastically by the RUC Constable, Sir John
Hermon, was certainly not welcomed at all by others.

Within the year Stalker had made substantial progress in his
inquiry. By February 1985 he was chasing what was known as
'the Hayshed' tape, which, if genuine, he believed would prove
that RUC officers had shot an unarmed teenager without
warning and in cold blood. Despite requests and assurances,
he was never to see the tape, and fifteen months later he was told
that a squad had been set up to investigate a Manchester
policeman. Simultaneously Greater Manchester police were
beginning their investigation into Kevin Taylor.

The inquiry was pursued ruthlessly. Surveillance equipment
had been set up to spy on his palatial Bury home. Friends and
relations were being quizzed by senior detectives. His phones
were being tapped, his mail opened and (on one occasion) his
accountant's office burgled. His bankers all over the world were

---

[7] Frank Williamson, quoted in J. Morton, *Bent Coppers*, p.138.

getting requests from Manchester detectives for confidential documents. Taylor asked his lawyers to find out what the police wanted. They would not say. Taylor told the police he was ready and willing to talk to them at any time they wanted. He got a promise from the Chief Constable James Anderton that if the police ever wanted to speak to him, they would get in touch with his lawyers. That was not the way it happened. When Taylor's house was raided in May 1986 there was no advance warning. The police took away a few old papers from the 1970s – and the real loot: three photographs of John Stalker.[8]

Inquiries continued into the working of Taylor's bank accounts. Certainly he had borrowed £1 million, but the properties were valued at £1.6 million and no customer or client ever suggested that Taylor was involved in fraud. Nor did bank officials. The next step was to approach the Crown Court and ask for access orders to seize Taylor's accounts. In a sworn statement to Judge Preest, DI Arthur Stephenson suggested that Taylor was involved with drugs. Preest granted the orders. The statement was kept in a sealed envelope for over two years. In the trial, counsel for the Crown was to admit there was no evidence at all on which the application was based.

Now Taylor was charged, along with his accountant, a Co-op bank official and a surveyor, with conspiracy to defraud the bank by over-valuing the property. The result was a disaster for him. His companies collapsed, as did the prosecution, but not before Taylor was effectively ruined.

Senior police officers told lie after lie, and were exposed as telling countless others in the course of their investigation. The two chief investigating officers committed a blatant contempt of court for which many an ordinary citizen would have been fined or imprisoned. They were fortunate to escape with a reprimand.[9]

As the trial progressed Stephenson, one of the officers to be reprimanded, was under severe cross-examination by Taylor's counsel, David Hood. Driven ever deeper into damaging admissions over the conduct of the case and, in particular, into the evidence given on the application before Judge Preest, Stephenson's credibility in the case was destroyed. At lunchtime on 18 January 1990 Michael Corkery, a London barrister who had

[8] Paul Foot, *Spectator*, 9 June 1990.
[9] ibid.

unexpectedly been instructed on behalf of the Crown rather than a local member of the Manchester Bar, received instructions from the Director of Public Prosecutions to offer no further evidence.

As for Stalker, by this time he had resigned. He had been removed from the Northern Ireland inquiry on 29 May 1986, and had been given extended leave pending the outcome of disciplinary offences. Inquiries into his relationship with Kevin Taylor continued for the next three months until after a 36–6 vote by the Police Committee he was reinstated on 23 August of that year. At worst the allegations were reduced to the use of a police car for his own purposes. On his reinstatement he maintained an unhappy relationship with the Chief Constable James Anderton who had, by all accounts, been smitten with religion. It was clear to Stalker that he had no future in the force, particularly when Peter Topping was appointed Chief Superintendent in preference to Stalker's choice, John Thorburn. It was Topping who had been the senior officer in the unhappy prosecution of Kevin Taylor. Stalker retired on 13 March 1987.[10]

Police supporters have been keen to point out that Taylor's writ for malicious prosecution has never been actively pursued, adding by way of explanation that Taylor is an incorrigible gambler spending much of his time playing kalooki in Greek-owned gaming clubs. Others know just how much it would cost to pursue a claim without the benefit of legal aid. Stalker went into journalism which was, perhaps, his first love. There is little doubt he had been treated badly by the force. His legal costs for defending himself before the Police Committee had amounted to something over £21,000. Despite his reinstatement without charges, the Police Authority refused to make any contribution to the costs, which were paid for largely by public subscription and a concert organized by a Frankie 'Frou-Frou' Davies.

But putting the Stalker-Taylor problems to one side, at last there was a triumph. In May 1989 came a great feather in the force's cap. It had rooted out from its ranks the 'bullying and crooked' police officer, Thomas Gerald 'Ged' Corley, a constable with wide-ranging contacts in the Underworld. The list of complaints compiled against Corley, described as a 19-stone

---

[10] There are three basic accounts of the two cases. *Stalker*, and *The Poisoned Tree*, are in one pan of the scales, *Topping* is in the other. All are intensely personal.

thug, and certainly a 6ft-4in. weightlifter, included conspiracy to rob and supplying a firearm. It was alleged that for a decade he had conducted a regime of crime and intimidation whilst serving in Greater Manchester. His superiors had failed to act despite there having been twenty-four complaints from the public. Now in 1987 Chief Inspector Peter Jackson was ordered to investigate Corley after a report that whilst off-duty sick he had been working as a nightclub bouncer. It was then Jackson discovered that Corley had devised cruel initiation routines for new police recruits.

At Manchester Crown Court, on a charge of conspiracy to rob – an attack on a security guard at Walkden near Manchester in 1987 – and transferring a firearm, despite his continued protestations of innocence and that he was being fitted-up, Corley was found guilty and received a sentence of seventeen years' imprisonment.

Within a matter of weeks, the cream on the top of the milk had soured. An inquiry began into the investigation which led to Corley's conviction, and it became clear that two officers had trawled criminals for evidence, offering incentives for assistance. Corley was identified after criminals were shown photographs, and then picked him out on an ID parade. In return for this valuable information charges were reduced to simple robbery, and they received sentences of ten years reduced to six on appeal when the court was told of their great assistance. Another criminal who had implicated Corley in the supply of a gun was given bail and committed more robberies. Jackson made a complaint into the conduct of officers in the inquiry – notably the conduct of the man in overall charge, Chief Superintendent Arthur Roberts. An outside force from West Yorkshire, led by Assistant Chief Constable Colin Bailey, was called in to investigate.

The basis of the complaint was that the original investigation into Corley and his behaviour had shown that other police officers may have had potentially unlawful contact with criminals. Jackson had, it appears, repeatedly requested senior officers in the Greater Manchester police to check out this information as thoroughly as the investigation into Corley was being conducted. He maintained this had not been done. After the Corley trial he sent a memorandum to Roberts, then another which insisted on a decision from an assistant chief constable. He was promised the matter would be taken up with the deputy chief constable. Then he found that not only had there been no progress on his memorandum but that his conduct during the Corley inquiry was being investigated. He went to his solicitor and made a formal complaint against Roberts.

The complaint was, in effect, fourfold. First, after the Corley conviction two criminals had said they knew certain officers, one a senior one, had consorted with criminals and they planned to blackmail the officers. The second strand concerned a conversation between Jackson and another informant who said that officers sympathetic to Corley had colluded in an attempt to discredit evidence given against him at his trial. The third was that a member of the Regional Crime Squad had arranged for the police to see defence documents removed secretly from the defence solicitor's office. The fourth suggested that a criminal who was an important witness at the Corley trial had revealed a plot the basis of which was to frame a police officer by planting evidence on him. Apparently it was decided not to make this evidence available at the trial, where it might have damaged the witness. Jackson was concerned that an attempt might be made to say the evidence had come to light after, and not before, the trial.

At the end of August 1992 Roberts, along with a Sergeant Bob Meek, was suspended, not because of Jackson's complaint but because of an earlier one by Corley against the whole team which investigated him. There were then rumours that Jackson himself would be suspended. If this happened what, asked *Police Review*, would be the effect on Jackson's complaint against Roberts and indeed the Corley conviction?[11]

What did happen was that in March 1990 'Ged' Corley who, when one considers the treatment meted out to convicted police officers, rightly described his last two years as a nightmare, was acquitted by the Court of Appeal who described his trial as having been a travesty of justice. He had previously been released on bail by the Court of Appeal in the autumn of 1989, not something which that court does regularly or lightly. If the Crown Prosecution Service had known only a quarter of what had emerged since the trial, Corley would never have appeared in court, said Lord Lane, the Lord Chief Justice.

---

[11] Stephen Cook, *The Inquiry Goes On, and On, and On*, 6 October 1989.

The evidence against Corley had been implication by three men who had admitted their part in the £11,000 wages snatch. Another criminal had claimed the officer had supplied him with the sawn-off shotgun used in the raid. Now the Court of Appeal heard that inducements, including reduced charges, bail and cash, had been offered to the criminals to persuade them to name Corley.

By this time Jackson had resigned from the force and had retired on medical grounds. He claimed that his complaint against Chief Superintendent Arthur Roberts had been followed by a 'vicious campaign' against his sanity and his integrity by a small group of officers. He declared:

> It must be a matter of concern to the public that there are people in the police service who find it unacceptable for an officer to raise doubts about an investigation and consequent conviction. It is the kind of unhealthy atmosphere which makes possible such cases as the Guildford Four.[12]

On 24 January 1992 Salford robber Brian Sands, said to have devised the set-up against Corley, received seven years' consecutive to a sentence of eight years he was already serving.

In May 1992 summonses of perjury and perverting the course of justice were issued against Roberts, Jackson and a Detective Sergeant Kevin Ryan. A month earlier Corley had received the massive sum of £230,000 compensation for wrongful imprisonment from the insurers of the Greater Manchester police. Part of the money was spent on a green Rolls-Royce, in which he drove to watch the men involved in the investigation against him arrive for the remand hearings of their own case.

At Leeds Crown Court in March 1994 the former Chief Superintendent Roberts was acquitted of two charges of misconduct and received a nine month sentence suspended for two years on a third. Inspector Jackson was in hospital receiving treatment for a mental illness and was unable to stand trial.

Criminals grew younger. In July 1992 a boy was sentenced to fifteen years' youth custody for armed robbery. He and a team had not known that the old-fashioned bank robbery would surely lead to arrest. They had been smashing the security

[12] *Police Review*, 12 January 1990.

screens. Still, sometimes variations on the old methods were the best. On 6 May 1993, at least four men were involved in a wages snatch at Armaguard at an industrial estate at Carlisle. The first man is believed to have acted as a decoy by feigning problems with his car which stalled, causing a tailback of traffic around 7 p.m. at a roundabout on the outskirts of the city and causing the crew of a Security Express vehicle to stop. It is thought that whilst the van was stationary two others attached themselves to the chassis of the vehicle and were driven on to the estate by the unsuspecting crew. Once inside Armaguard, the gang seized around £1 million. The fourth member then drove the robbers away in a white Transit van. The men apparently had worn a special harness to attach themselves to the van, a none-too-far cry from the days when Teddy Machin escaped in a similar manner, but using only his hands and feet, after the abortive London Airport bullion raid in 1948.

Until the 1970s one of the more rare forms of crime in Britain was kidnapping. Generally when it occurred it was not for money, but of children as pawns in the custody game played by their parents. When it broadened out again it was not always for ransom as such but to enable a relation (often a bank or building society manager) of the kidnapped person to produce the keys to the safe vault or produce not his own money but that of his employers.

August 1992 saw a Mancunian example of an old-style kidnapping when Elizabeth Kerr, whose husband Derek managed a branch of Barclays Bank in Sale, Greater Manchester, found a man wearing a police officer's uniform at her door telling her that her husband had been injured in a road accident. She went with him, as she thought to the hospital, but the man drove off the road and into a field. He got out, hit her in the face and then after taping her mouth bundled her into the boot of the car. Derek Kerr then received a call demanding £40,000 and telling him that his wife would suffer extreme harm if he did not do so. He took the money towards a junction of the M63 motorway where it was collected by the kidnapper. Mrs Kerr was left tied up in a wood at Over Alderley in Cheshire.

The kidnapper turned out to be soldier turned financial adviser, Tony Bosson-Williams. He was identified when fourteen months after the incident a palm print of Bosson-Williams was found on a piece of paper in the Kerrs' home. At first he denied the matter but then admitted having spent the ransom – giving his wife £1,800 a month, taking holidays in America and Lanzarote and buying a speedboat.

A week before the Kerr kidnap, Bosson-Williams had attempted a similar one involving a Solihull bank manager, but he had gone to the wrong house. On 14 January 1994 at Chester Crown Court he was jailed for twelve years for the kidnapping of Mrs Kerr and two years for the attempt to run consecutively.

A year earlier it was not so much a question of kidnapping, more of hostage taking when on 6 March members of the Wilson family were held in their home outside Chorley. The attack took place shortly after 9 p.m. when Mrs Wilson, one of her daughters, Lisa, and Lisa's boyfriend went to visit a friend. Within minutes two men wearing balaclava masks and surgical gloves burst into the house, knocking aside the remaining daughter Michelle. On their return Mrs Wilson and her family who had been joined by her accountant husband, David, were tied up and made to lie on the floor. David Wilson was ordered outside and the family assumed he was being taken hostage. When they heard two bangs they concluded it was a car backfiring. It was not.

When they later freed themselves they found the telephone wires had been cut and they drove to get help from a neighbour. On their return they found David Wilson's body face down. He had been shot at point-blank range.

Initially the police said they knew of nothing to the detriment of Mr Wilson, who had been a partner in a local firm of accountants, was the owner of a former cotton mill and printing firm as well as being the sleeping partner in a number of other businesses. Then newspapers began to speculate about links with such diverse interests as Underworld and drug gangs and the IRA. It was noted that he had been concerned in an investigation into a shipping fraud. Just over eighteen months later the full story came out at the trial of Stephen Schepke, a former art restorer, charged with conspiracy to murder Mr Wilson. The shipping fraud over a non-existent cargo of cigarettes had involved £26.5 million. The original plan had been to pass off cheap Mexican cigarettes as Marlboros but Hector Portillo, alleged by the Crown Prosecution Service to be Michael Austin, with whom Wilson had been dealing, pulled a double cross. There were no cigarettes. Wilson, who had been involved with Portillo in deals relating to the sale of 90 tonnes of gold bars from

Mexico to an Isle of Man company engagingly known as Fergie Ltd – the gold, along with the cigarettes, failed to appear – was furious and had spoken to the Crown Prosecution Service about his role in the affair.

Portillo then wanted Wilson silenced. The man was far too dangerous to have as a loose cannon sounding off. Probably he contacted Schepke. Six days before his death Wilson, who had been warned earlier in the year that Portillo wanted him dead, had himself fired off a salvo by fax complaining to Portillo that he had 'set him up', saying he would never forgive him and threatening that one day he would 'have his day'. Schepke had stood to make some £60,000 out of the deal if it had gone through. The contract had been carried out by two professional hit-men and it was not suggested that Schepke had been other than an influential cog in the wheel.

On 20 October Schepke was found guilty of aiding and abetting Wilson's murder. The jury was unable to agree a verdict that he had conspired to have Wilson killed. He received life imprisonment.

Now the major action focuses on the infamous Moss Side district, barely a mile from the city centre, home of the drug gangs with an estimated turnover of £20 million plus a year, which bedevil the community and which, for a number of reasons, the police seem to be unable to control let alone eradicate.

Like so many other inner city areas, Moss Side has come down in the world. In the 1850s, when it was known as Twenty Pits, it was wet with pit-like indentations. In the great expansion of Manchester the land was drained and substantial houses built. Then came the large terraced houses which until the 1930s were owned by teachers, bank clerks, and what ex-officer Tony Fletcher describes as 'comfortable' tradesmen.

During the years of the Depression, more and more of these people found it necessary to take in what were at first termed genteel guests, then lodgers, in order to make ends meet. In some cases rooms were let with the provision of meals, or partly furnished for self-catering.

After the War those who wished to move and could do so made their escape to the more salubrious parts, nearer the Cheshire boundary, and the whole area began to deteriorate. Eventually entire houses, often with twelve or fourteen rooms, including cellars and attics, were let room by room to individual tenants.[13] At first the tenants were immigrants from Europe and then from the West Indies. Finally the Alexandra Park estate was built. It was planned as a neighbourhood community, protected from through traffic with little clusters of brick houses facing on to cul-de-sacs and connected by what the planners fondly believed would be companionable footpaths. But it turned out to be an area extremely difficult to police, a warren of rat-runs into which fleeing hoodlums and drug dealers could easily escape. As mob rule took hold and the estate deteriorated, families began to move out. Vacated houses were quickly vandalized, adding to the aura of despair that now pervades the area.[14]

The first death was that of Ivan Preston, the doorman of a shebeen, who was shot in 1987. From then on it seemed that much easier for the drug dealers to kill those who stood in their way.

The major dealer in the Ordsall end of Salford, on the other hand – who has the overall control of the supply of designer drugs, amphetamines and Ecstasy – is a man who, whilst dealing in substantial blocks of cocaine, publicly denounces its supply and use. He has a network of both youngsters and older dealers. 'He is practically untouchable,' says one officer. 'He has kids who will shoot you.' Ordsall is an estate built in the 1970s and – with streets truncated into cul-de-sacs so that criminals could not escape through them – is now covered in graffiti. The local park has been ringed with fencing to keep out stolen cars. This was the scene of the troubles and riots in July 1992 and the *Sunday Telegraph* postulated that the Mr Big of Salford who had a posse of fifty youths at his command could be blamed for fanning them. It was then that a woman found an AK-47 gun in her son's bedroom. Guns brought back from the Gulf War as souvenirs are now coming into circulation. In the area a handgun could go for as little as £70.

Much of the trouble in the inner city area stems from the employment of doormen in the nightclubs and discos. The aim of the drug dealers is to have one of their own men on the door, to enable their dealers to get in to the exclusion of other dealers. So there is a form of both protection and extortion in evidence. The nightclub or disco will be protected from the trouble which would ensue if there was a free drug market, the sponsor gets

<hr>

[13] T. Fletcher, *Memories of Murder*, pp. 45–6.
[14] Russell Miller and Peter Warren, 'A Cry From the Streets' in *Sunday Times*, 7 March 1993.

a clear run at the distribution of his product. When the Cheetham Hill-based Thunderdome Club decided to hire its bouncers from an out-of-town firm in June 1990, revenge was swift. Three of the bouncers were knee-capped in full view of more than 300 people by masked men wearing shotguns. Seven people were later arrested, but the Crown Prosecution Service decided there was insufficient evidence on which to mount a successful prosecution.

Moss Side and Cheetham Hill, Salford are the main drug and gang districts, with Moss Side divided into segments. Pepperhill no longer exists since the pub of that name closed and its members have now regrouped at Doddington. The Gooch Gang suffered a substantial blow to its pride when twenty-one members were caught in Operation China during which undercover police had filmed them selling drugs to members of the public. In a series of raids on forty addresses in the Alexandra Park area, drugs, a loaded semi-automatic weapon and a crossbow were seized.

The police operation came at a time when the Pepperhill-Gooch feud, in which Cheetham Hill aligned themselves with the Gooch, had become more or less totally out of control. Later, sentences ranging from three years' youth custody to eight years for possession of a loaded firearm were handed down at Manchester Crown Court. The Gooch Gang was dead. Children could now play football on the estate without the fear of walking into sniper fire. Peace reigned for about four months. Then – long live the Young Gooch. Seven or eight of the younger members of the Gooch who had not been involved in the swoop reformed. In fact the Gooch Gang itself was not dead at all – it was merely sleeping until it realigned itself in prison, putting pressure on prison officers and governors by demanding, in return for co-operation, such privileges as exclusive use of the gymnasia.[15]

---

[15] Prisons have always been controlled by powerful figures and gangs. At the time of the Parkhurst Riot in 1969 the cinema show could not start until the leader of the prison had taken his seat in the audience. In 1993 Judge Stephen Tumim, the Chief Inspector of Prisons, said that drug-taking including heroin had been an epidemic at Long Lartin prison in Gloucestershire, where prisoners drank their home-made hooch in front of staff. There were protection rackets with weaker prisoners paying insurance in drugs, tobacco or cash. A-wing was dominated by white prisoners, mostly London gangsters, who permitted only non-threatening ethnic minority prisoners, usually Asian, to join them. Even these were only tolerated if they were prepared to carry out menial tasks.

The ascending scale of juvenile and young adult crime in the area ran from theft *from* cars to theft *of* cars, then racing round the streets daring the police to chase them. The next step was into a different league. Across the road from the Moss Side estate is a red light area, and the teenagers then put the arm on prostitutes to take their clients to a certain area where they could be attacked. In one case the client was forced, at knifepoint, to divulge his telephone number, and when he returned home the Gooch Gang member telephoned and threatened to contact the man's wife unless he came to meet him with his cashpoint card. From there, it was on to dealing in heroin and crack.

The catalogue of violence dealt by one gang to the members of another is astounding for such young people – a gang on mountain bikes circling a 19-year-old in his BMW before opening fire, two men jumping from a bedroom window after being shot by a gunman from the doorway, a young man on a mountain bike firing indiscriminately in the street. As the Gooch estate has steadily been evacuated the violence has spread to nearby Old Trafford where on 26 April 1993, in an incident in which five houses were hit with bullets, an 18-year-old student Andrea Mairs was shot in the stomach by a stray bullet as she pulled back the curtains from her bedroom window. Although severely traumatised she lived. Some were not so lucky. On 29 October 1991 Darren Smith tried to escape a gang on mountain bikes by running into a baker's shop; he was killed when six shots were fired at him as he leaped the counter. The men charged were acquitted. A principal prosecution witness had taken a drug overdose rather than appear at the trial. Between January and November 1992 there were six murders.

There is, of course, a steady trade on the estate in guns with the going price of a clean pistol (one which has not been used) anything from £500 to £800 depending upon how urgently it is needed. As for a used weapon – 'anything you care to offer' says one police officer.

Cont'd

Lynne Bowles, the No. 3 Governor at Whitemoor Prison at March, Cambridgeshire, spoke of criminals winning control of the prisons. Calling for a tough regime where criminals had to earn privileges such as television in their cells, she said that the 'senior prisoner and his rent-a-mob are selling drugs, booze and the benefits of refusal to cooperate' and organizing mass disobedience over issues such as the price of chicken in the prison shop. *Daily Mail*, 18 August 1993.

At the adult level a feud developed between senior members from Moss Side and a highly organized team of good professional armed robbers led by yet another military gent, 'The General', from Cheetham Hill. The problem first arose in 1989 when a team from Moss Side came to do an armed robbery and found The General and his men *in situ* bent on the same target.

One of the most appalling pieces of gratuitous violence which exceeded almost anything the London armed robbers have had to offer in recent times came, when in 1989, an armed robbery in Royton, Oldham at the Coin Controls factory went seriously wrong. Just after 10 a.m. the robbers struck when the Security Express van was making a wages delivery. They were approached by two armed robbers who demanded the money and, when told that the chute which contained the cash was jammed, attacked them. In November 1990, at Manchester Crown Court, Judge Rhys Davies was told that Chinadu Igheawara attacked one guard with a machete. As the man lifted his arms to defend himself he was knocked to the ground and then tried to crawl under the van. Stephen Julian then shot the other guard in the groin shearing off the top of his left thigh. Unfortunately the first guard had not crawled far enough under the van and Julian shot his ankle which was protruding, almost blowing it off. His leg was amputated from below the knee. As the second guard tried to escape he was shot in the back at almost point blank range. Amazingly both survived.

Stephen Julian had fled to Jamaica assisted by a Raymond Odoha. Julian made a fraudulent application for documents in Jamaica and was deported.

In October that year the driver of the getaway car, Mark Mann, decided to give evidence in return for a lighter sentence and this led to the trial of Julian, now back in England, and Igheawara in November 1990. Both men admitted two other robberies from branches of the Royal Bank of Scotland netting over £50,000 and conspiracy to rob the Security Express van. Julian received 22 years and his companion 20. Mann's sentence was a more modest eight years. The court had been told that whilst on remand he had been moved to six different prisons.

Odoha was now wanted for assisting Julian in his escape, so he decamped to London where he was helped by a man who was to become a close friend, Tony Johnstone.

Johnstone, who usually wore body armour, was originally a

Moss Side boy who committed a shooting just to prove himself before transferring his allegiance. By a curious coincidence his mother, Winnie, is also the mother of Keith Bennett, still missing from the time of the Moors murders. By now Cheetham gangs were more or less in control of the nightclubs in the city. One favourite trick in a raid was to take cash from the tills on the bar and then use it to pay for champagne.

Johnstone became 'the man', carrying guns and driving Ford Cosworths which, with an easy speed of 120 mph, made surveillance almost impossible. 'He just took off,' say the police who were trying to keep him under strict observation.

The night before he was killed in February 1991, he walked into a nightclub where the Cheetham Hill men had gone for a drink, grabbed the microphone and said words to the effect that whilst he would be happy to sort things out with them they were no match for him. Sensibly they declined the challenge. Although they were no doubt quite happy to see him go, thoughts that the Salford team had been involved in his death were red herrings. In the end Johnstone died over a quarrel which wasn't strictly his. The Salford comment was that if he had not died that Friday, he would not have lived six months.

He and three others did an armed robbery at Monksbridge in Oldham when the security van was literally kidnapped and some £360,000 stolen. A further £1 million was left on the van solely because the robbers were unable to carry it away. Within four hours of the robbery Johnstone and his friends were locked up, put on identification parades and then released.

All that was recovered were six £20 notes found in a Wendy House belonging to a relation of Craig Bulger. Bulger was charged and convicted of dishonestly handling the money. The police believe that Johnstone's serious troubles began when he then went to ask for £80,000, his share of the takings, and was told by Desmond Noonan, a member of a Cheetham Hill family, that there was only £40,000 left. Bulger was not pleased and told him he was going to complain to Tony Johnstone.

This, in turn, could not have pleased Noonan who that night went to visit Paul Flannery, then in a Southport hospital. Flannery had served eight years for an armed robbery. On his release he had made serious threats to a policeman and when other officers went to arrest him Flannery, possibly because he thought his visitors were from a rival organization rather than policemen, dived through a window seriously injuring his back.

A week later Johnstone was killed. He had gone out with his friend Tony McKie, who became a prosecution witness, in his new fine white Cosworth when he was flagged down by Desmond Noonan, so said McKie, near the Penny Black public house about 10.30 in the evening. According to his evidence, McKie saw a Ford Orion parked nearby with three men sitting in it, including Paul Flannery making his first ambulatory outing from hospital in the front seat. McKie told the court that Flannery nodded to Noonan and then fired shots at him, McKie. Clearly something was wrong and Johnstone tried to climb a wall to escape; he was shot in the back. At the trial in the summer of 1992 Noonan, his brothers Damien and Derek, Paul Flannery and a prison escapee Michael Sharples were all acquitted.

One of the hardmen from Moss Side was Delroy Brown, known by the police as Public Enemy Number One which, said an officer, 'isn't far from the truth'. Brown led a charmed life. In 1986 he was an unknown who appeared from Birmingham, 'dripping in gold and driving a BMW', and teamed up with members of the Pepperhill mob. The belief is that it was Brown who triggered off the war between Cheetham Hill and Pepperhill, not through any drug deal but simply over a domestic matter. Brown was seen out with the girlfriend of a Cheetham Hill man doing five years for robbery. The information relayed back to The General began a feud between the two. Brown's car was taken from him and he was held up at gun-point. He retaliated and then received a visit from four masked men at his home; shots were fired. And so began the Moss Side-Cheetham Hill war with Tony Johnstone a leading soldier.

One attack came in 1990 when Johnstone led a group of men into the International Club in Longside where Brown was drinking. Johnstone, according to accounts, emptied a .38 at the luckless Delroy. It was after this that Jonathan Quartey received a visit from the police at his home on the Alexandra Park estate where a Colt .45 automatic was found. He received thirty months' imprisonment, reduced on appeal.

Meanwhile Brown, together with a friend, had ventured into Cheetham Hill territory, the PSV Club in Hulme. There Stephen Jackson, a friend of the General, was shot in the testicles and Delroy (who did not do the shooting) was dragged into the car park where serious efforts were made to cut his head off. Eventually he escaped with the help of friends and fled to Liverpool where he treated the wounds with Dettol, hiding in Embledon Street off Granby Road in Toxteth until matters quietened down and his injuries healed. Jackson later received ten years for the possession of cocaine. He had objected to being tried in Manchester, but this did not help him. In 1990 the judge, known as 'Wacko' by the community, gave him the sentence in Liverpool.

The final Cheetham attack on Brown came when his car was overturned in Alexander Park. After that things quietened down, mainly because of Johnstone's problems with the Noonans. However, that was not the end of Delroy Brown's localized troubles. Once again it was almost a domestic matter.

One of the more popular shebeens on the estate where Red Stripe, curried goat and red snapper is on offer is off Gooch Close, and was a favourite haunt of Delroy Brown and his friends. It was from outside there that his car was taken by two 13-year-olds, driven away, damaged and dumped. Unfortunately the report to Delroy gave the perpetrator of the incident as another man entirely; in turn his car was attacked, with the tyres being slashed and the vehicle set on fire. This was now the start of the Gooch-Pepperhill war. Machete attacks became prevalent. A classic drive-by shooting resulted in a 14-year-old boy being hit in the eye and partially losing his sight.

After that, say the police, there was real war. There were mountain bike and motorbike attacks on people and property and then, in 1991, came the first death – that of Carl Stapleton. It was perhaps extraordinary that, with so many violent attacks, there had been no deaths before. Stapleton, who was related to a major player in the game, was found alone, out of his ground, and stabbed eighteen times with a survival knife. It was at this trial that the principal witness completely changed her evidence; she had been in what amounted to protective custody from which she had regularly absconded, returning time and again to the estate. At first she had identified a Stephen Morrison, who in a previous incident had himself been macheted, but at the trial she said she had picked him out from a parade because she fancied him rather than because she had seen him get out of a car at the place of the killing.

Delroy Brown was becoming increasingly suspect even

amongst his friends. There were rumours that he was an informant, and he was chased by a gang of Gooch into the Big Western public house in Pepperhill where he was attacked by a dozen youths. 'He is incredibly brave,' says one police officer with some admiration. 'If you see his body it is a mass of scars and holes.' He managed to grab the knife from one of his assailants and then barricaded himself behind the cellar shutters. When the police arrived he was the only one remaining. In his pocket they found fifteen rocks of crack which he alleged had been planted. He was charged with possession with intent to supply, and at the Manchester Crown Court in June 1993 he received six years' imprisonment.

In January 1993 one of the seemingly more horrific random killings took place in Moss Side when 14-year-old Benji Stanley was shot in the heart while he was queueing to get pies in the popular Alvino's Tattie and Dumplin' shop. The killer had driven up in a silver Rover and fired through the window at Benji; he then walked into the shop and shot the boy once more through the chest.

It was a crime which for a time provoked if not national outrage, then at least national publicity. All investigations showed, as Detective Superintendent Terry Smith told the inquest held in December, that Benji was not involved with crime or gangs. However, unfortunately for him he was wearing khaki clothing and a coloured bandana, a badge of one of the Moss Side gangs.[16] Detective Superintendent Smith said that Benji's clothing was part of growing up, and the coroner commented: 'He was a young man going about his normal life, getting some food with a friend and he was brutally murdered. The indications are that it was basically an assassination.'

The court was told that 16-year-old Tito Gunning, who had been with Benji when he was shot, had later told the police that a version of the events and description of the gunman he had given immediately after the killing had been made up.

There may have been a truce for a short while, but in the first seven months of 1993 there was a string of shootings which culminated in a sub-machine gun attack on a public house in

---

[16] Red for Gooch, blue for Doddington. In this way the gangs match the colours of the Crips and the Bloods from Los Angeles gang wars or, looked at another way, the respective colours of Manchester United and Manchester City.

Whalley Range district which borders Moss Side. Almost a year to the day of Benji's death, another killing dispelled any lingering doubts that it and the ensuing measures taken by the police might have brought a new and improved era to Moss Side. Despite the fact that he was wearing a bullet-proof vest Julian Stewart, aged 21, was found shot to death on 12 January 1994.

Not all the killings were shootings. When Ian Marriot, assistant manager of the Ritz – a club only a few hundred yards from the Hacienda – was attacked, a bottle of acid was thrown in his face one afternoon. He took seven hours to die. No one was arrested.

7
—

Cardiff
and the South West

Crime in Cardiff in this century is spanned by two murder cases –
one in which justice was demonstrably not done, and the earlier
one where many people still believe it was not done either.

'I was brought up being told they were innocent,' recalls one
old-time villain.

'They' were Edward and John 'Tich' Rowlands, accused of
killing a boxer turned bookmaker on 29 September 1927 in
St Mary Street, Cardiff. Dai Lewis, a former professional
welterweight boxer, ran the 'chalk and water' protection,[1] a
small-time protection racket at Monmouth races, and in doing
so fell foul of the Rowlands brothers who regarded that unnecessary service as one which they and their followers alone
would provide for the bookmakers. It appears that Lewis,
despite the protection racket he ran, was popular with the
bookmakers. Presumably they were happier paying private
enterprise than the local big machine.

The day before, he had been warned that the Rowlands were
not pleased with him and despite a certain amount of bravado he
took the precaution of staying away from home that night and
slept in a hotel in St Mary Street.

The next day was business as usual. He went back to the races
at Monmouth and in the evening returned to St Mary Street and
the Blue Anchor public house where he drank all evening,

[1] Providing chalk for the bookmakers to write the odds on their boards, and water for
their sponges to change them.

ignoring the Rowlands brothers and their friends Daniel Driscoll, John Hughes and William Price.

He was set on shortly after closing time outside the Blue Anchor. John Rowlands had previously warned Lewis about muscling in and he was the instigator of the attack, as he had been of many others. Lewis's throat was slashed in a wound seven and a quarter inches long and one and a quarter inches deep. As he lay dying on the pavement, 'prostitutes rushed to his aid, ripping off their petticoats in a desperate effort to staunch the flow of blood'.[2] He was taken to the Royal Infirmary hospital where the police went to his bedside waiting for him to name his attackers. It was while they were there that two calls came inquiring after the state of Lewis. The second was traced to the Colonial Club in Custom House Street, and there the police found the Rowlands, Driscoll, Hughes and Price.

In the early hours of the morning it became clear that Lewis was not going to survive, and a local magistrate and the Clerk to the Justices came to his bedside to take a dying declaration which could be used in evidence at any subsequent trial. A dying declaration was what was called an exception to the hearsay rule, which only admits in evidence statements made in the presence of the accused. In this case there would have been no breach of the rule because Edward Rowlands and Daniel Driscoll were brought to Lewis's bedside.

The boxer maintained the code of the Underworld: 'I do not know how I have been injured,' he said. 'I do not remember how it happened. There was no quarrel or fight. Nobody did any harm to me. I did not see anyone use a knife.' Then he added to Eddie Rowlands, 'You had nothing to do with it. We've been the best of friends'; and to Daniel Driscoll, 'You had nothing to do with it either. We were talking and laughing together. My dear old pal.' To his wife he gave £3.5s 0d – what was left from his earnings at the races.

The funeral on 5 October was attended by up to 25,000 people who lined the streets as the cortège passed. It was a week after that John Rowlands made the admission that he had stabbed the boxer. Lewis had, he said, attacked him with a knife, they had wrestled for it and Lewis was accidentally stabbed. Driscoll and Eddie Rowlands both said they had seen the fight but had made

[2] D. Thomas with R. Grant, *Seek Out the Guilty*, p.39.

169

off not anxious to be involved. At the magistrates' court John Hughes was discharged and the other men committed for trial at the Glamorgan Assizes.

The queue for seats in the public gallery began thirty-six hours before the trial itself commenced on 29 November, with Lord Halsbury prosecuting for the Crown: 'This was murder as cruel and beastly as you can possibly imagine, premeditated and carried out – I might almost say flaunted – in Cardiff's main street.' In fact, however, the evidence was confused; witnesses were not able to agree on what had happened. Some said that John Rowlands had the knife as he approached Lewis, but a police officer said Driscoll was holding Lewis whilst Edward struck him in the face.

Driscoll did not help himself. He called a patently false alibi, as a result of which he became one of thousands who have been convicted not for what they have actually done but for telling lies. His discredited alibi cannot have helped his colleagues. Although Price was acquitted, the jury found Driscoll and the Rowlands brothers guilty after an hour's retirement.

The jury may have been certain at the time but the public, the police and politicians were not. £600 was collected for an appeal and a petition mustered a quarter of a million signatures demanding that the Court of Appeal look at the verdict. That Court, with Mr Justice Avory amongst its members, was never likely to be over-sympathetic and the appeals were dismissed on 11 January 1928. On the way to the appeal hearing, however, John Rowlands went berserk and, certified insane, was sent to Broadmoor where he died many years later.

A Harley Street doctor returned from a holiday in France to give his opinion that Lewis had died from a heart attack rather than from loss of blood. Three Cardiff doctors who attended the post mortem supported him.

The case had already been raised in the House of Commons and two members of the jury travelled to see T. P. O'Connor, the Father of the House, with a petition from eight members of the jury:

We, the undersigned, hereby state that we are of the opinion that the sentence of death should not be carried out. There has been so much brought into the case at the Court of Criminal Appeal and in other ways, as to cause us great anxiety since we made our decision. Sentence of death should be waived as an act of mercy.

O'Connor managed to obtain an interview with the Home Secretary, but this did not produce any result. 'No regard can be paid to expressions of opinion by individual members of a jury by which a prisoner has been convicted.'

The night before the execution the man Driscoll asked for a bottle of port; Edward Rowlands told his family, 'I have told the truth all through. Don't forget me at eight o'clock tomorrow. They can break my neck but they can't break my heart.' Rowlands was apparently shaking and had to be helped when he went to the scaffold, but Driscoll remarked, 'Which is mine?' when confronted with the two nooses. Both maintained their innocence to the end and Driscoll's last words were said to be, 'Well, I'm going down for something I never done, but you don't have to pay twice.' Outside the prison a crowd of over 5,000 gathered and sang hymns.

The men were certainly unfortunate; their position reflected the Home Secretary's attitude towards racecourse violence. Two years earlier he had refused a reprieve for one of the Fowler brothers from Sheffield. Later a more liberal attitude prevailed, and it became the custom that if one man of two due to be hanged was found to be insane before the execution, then the other was reprieved. This was the situation in the famous Chalkpit murder case in 1947 when Thomas Ley, one-time Minister for Justice in New South Wales, and Lawrence John Smith, a joiner, were found guilty of the murder of John Mudie, a hotel barman. The body was discovered in the chalkpit which gave the case its name on 30 November the previous year. Ley, then aged 67 and clearly in a state of dementia, had fallen in love with a lady in her sixties but wrongly believed she was carrying on with Mudie, a much younger man. Smith was recruited to help obtain a confession from Mudie, who was later killed. After the trial Ley was sent to Broadmoor where he died on 24 July 1947. John Smith's sentence was commuted to one of life imprisonment.

Ex-Detective Superintendent Power took the view that Driscoll had indeed tried to stop the fight, and that if he had not given the false alibi he might well have been acquitted. As for Eddie Rowlands, the belief was that all he had intended was that Lewis should be marked rather than killed. The case became known in Cardiff as the Hoodoo murder. John Hughes died within twelve months, and one of the prostitutes who had given evidence committed suicide by jumping from a second-floor window. One of the detective-sergeants committed suicide, two other officers died – one from tuberculosis and another from cancer – whilst a third died from a stomach complaint. All were relatively young men. In September 1928, Harold Lloyd – the solicitor who represented Price – was sentenced to five years' penal servitude for embezzling clients' monies.

The most famous area of Cardiff crime was Butetown, better known as Tiger Bay, where the Lewis killing had taken place. From the end of Victorian times it had become the home for seamen whose boats docked in Cardiff. By the beginning of the First World War there was a black population of around seven hundred, and it was there in 1919 that the first race riot of the century broke out. The causes given are varied, but those who had returned from the War were angered that their jobs had been taken and worse, they believed, so had their women – even worse still, that they had been taken by the coloured men who were thought to be nearer the animal than their white counterparts.[3]

The flashpoint, so far as Cardiff is concerned, occurred on 11 June 1919 – although there were almost simultaneous riots in Liverpool and in the North East – and is described by PC Albert Allen writing in the *South Wales Echo*:

> I was the only PC on duty at the Wharf when it started and I was on duty the whole time it lasted in the Docks area. First of all I would like to point out the cause. In Cardiff there were quite a number of prostitutes and quite a number of pimps who lived on their earnings. When conscription came into force these pimps were called up. Then a number of prostitutes went to the Docks district and lived with these coloured people who treated them very well. When the war finished the pimps found their source of income gone as the prostitutes refused to go back to them. The night the trouble started, about 8.30 p.m., a person who I knew told me to expect some trouble. I asked why and he

---

[3] Editorial in the *Liverpool Courier* quoted by J. Williams, *Bloody Valentine*, p.18.

explained that the coloured men had taken the prostitutes on an outing to Newport in two horse wagons and that a number of pimps were waiting for their return.[4]

Fighting and rioting continued for some days, leaving one dead, numerous injured and very few men charged.

Bute Town was where the action was. In Bute Street alone in the 1920s, when the place was 'bad and dangerous', there were said to be 42 cafés, a dozen pubs and sundry brothels. In 1952 there were 106 convictions connected with prostitution; not exactly a high strike rate. In 1954 the whole community was 8,000 strong: white, coloured, Arab, Indian, Somali and Maltese. At the time of the murder of Lynette White in 1988, there were thought to be some 150 prostitutes working in the rebuilt area.

But while Bute Town may have been dangerous the crime was strictly small-time, fencing, prostitution and related offences, a certain amount of rolling and mugging drunken sailors, theft from the docks. It was the sort of crime associated with an economically poor area. There were, however, more talented people at work in the city.

On the afternoon of 4 December 1928, a mailbag bearing a pink label was placed in the luggage van of the train which left Cardiff at 3.15 p.m. for Paddington. The bag was later found, including all the unregistered packages and some of the registered ones, on the banks of the Thames near Cannon Street the next afternoon. £5,500 in currency notes and £600 in Bank of England notes were missing.

From the police investigation it seems that the guard did not leave his van except for five minutes near Reading, when he was spoken to by a man who complained of sickness and who rushed into the lavatory with his head in his hands. However, this seems to have been a red herring, for the package was received by a porter at Paddington. Police inquiries showed that some well-known faces had been travelling that day. A George Rogers was the man who had been sick and Danny Davies, a bookmaker – confusingly associated with a man giving his name as Daniel Davies but really James Foster – had been on the train. Foster had already been acquitted of a similar mail theft the previous

---

[4] Quoted by J. Williams, *Bloody Valentine*, pp.18–19.

year. Danny Davies was suspected of all the big coups in South Wales and of master-minding robberies.

George Rogers was also known as Bastable, as well as having the more engaging soubriquet 'Portsmouth George'. He had been licensed to stand as a bookmaker at Wembley greyhound track, but had been thrown out for bad language and had been arrested with Coleman and Jack Davies in 1925.

The following Sunday in the *Empire News*, and much to the fury of the police, Joseph Foster kindly explained how on a previous occasion he had been duped into being a 'staller' for the gang. A staller was the last man in such a scam, who would set up an argument with customers or officials in order to allow the men carrying the proceeds of a theft time to make their escape.

According to reports, the £5 notes stolen in the robbery were thought to be in Cardiff. It was believed that a wholesale effort would be made to launder them at a professional athletics meeting due to take place in Powderhall in Edinburgh in the first week of January.[5] Instead, the notes in the main turned up at dog tracks.

A letter very neatly written by a Mr George Evans from Lambeth Hospital arrived at Scotland Yard on 19 February 1929, offering to name the perpetrators. When he was seen by the police he named a totally different collection of men – 'Jeweller George', George Spiers, a man named Willis and another by the name of Ryan – from the ones whom the police suspected. Unfortunately for Evans' theory, Spiers was serving a sentence for a mailbag robbery and was in custody at the time of the Cardiff-Paddington snatch. 'There is no doubt that Evans' mental faculties are somewhat impaired and I am given to understand by the Infirmary Authorities that he is given to fits of delusion,' wrote a policeman who investigated the claim.

Davies, Foster and Co lived to fight another day. And, it seems, fight again they did.

A year to the day a mailbag containing £3,500 in bank notes was stolen between Swindon and Paddington. Marked for delivery to London, the bags were made up and placed in the last van on the train as it stood in Swindon station. Shortly before the train left Swindon a lady approached the guard,

---

[5] Amateur athletes such as Rugby Union players would run in masks to protect their non-professional status at these meetings.

Maurice Sherrick, and asked him to find her an empty compartment; she said she was feeling ill and asked him to look in on her during the journey. He found her a compartment three coaches away from his van, and during the journey he did indeed go and look her up and spent some minutes talking with her. This was the only time he left the guard's van. Bags were unloaded at Reading, but everyone questioned was adamant that the London bags were left untouched.

It is not difficult to guess whom the police had in mind for this little escapade. Davies, Rogers and three other men, including William Arnold – an ex-Superintendent of the GPO who had been discharged following a conviction in 1921 for stealing mailbags in Birmingham – were highly favoured.

A week later the police received an anonymous letter putting George Bastable firmly in the frame. He was, it was said, the originator of numerous Post Office thefts including a Cardiff job and one in Hull: 'He is hand in glove with every crook in London and in the provinces and was said to visit Cardiff once a week to keep a check on the progress of his war on the Post Office.'

The letter was signed 'One of Bastable's victims', and presumably was from a former member of the team with whom Bastable had fallen out. Watch was kept on the men but nothing came of it. The notes started filtering into circulation, all in the London and Essex areas, and a good number, as might be expected, from various greyhound tracks. Every tenderer was questioned, but each was able to account satisfactorily for his possession of the note. By 3 May 1930, the investigation was effectively closed. Davies, Rogers and Co., if indeed it had been them, appear to have retired.[6]

There were 2,000 people in the auditorium and a queue outside the Odeon Cinema, Bristol, on 29 May 1946 when cinema manager Robert Parrington Jackson was shot in the temple. The cinema was showing *The Well-Groomed Bride* starring Olivia De Havilland and Ray Milland, with a support of *The Light That Failed* starring Ida Lupino and Ronald Colman. Just at the moment when a boy actor in the film shoots a cap pistol, so did Jackson's murderer. Jackson died the next morning. Curiously Jackson had his own gun which was never found, but weeks later a gun was found in a static water tank in Bristol's Park Row. The

[6] PRO: MEP03/501/509.

175

police ran the usual 'developments expected' announcements, but it was all hot air. There was speculation first of all that this was a robbery, but the theory seems to have been discounted in favour of another that it was a disgruntled member of staff or a relation or perhaps a wronged husband or boyfriend. Jackson had the reputation of being a womanizer and it seemed all of the takings had been left behind. Yet another theory was that it was an American robber who went straight to the Midlands and was then shipped back to the States by the American authorities; and still another that it was the work of a local thief, Blackie Alan. There the case stood for nearly fifty years until, in October 1993, a man walked into Bristol police station to say that the killer had been his father.

Then *Today* revealed the name of the killer, Billy 'The Fish' Fisher, and the motive. 'The Fish' was so-called because he was so slippery.

Short of money, he and a friend, Dukey Leonard, had jumped on to a train from the South Wales coalfields and broken into Parrington Jackson's office. He had reached for the alarm and they had shot him before escaping with loose change. As is usually the case the police had retained a 'secret clue'. This time it had been revealed that Jackson had been shot once, but in reality he had been shot twice and the son who reported the killing knew this. Fisher told his family in the 1980s and died in 1989, by which time Dukey Leonard was also dead. Surviving members of the Odeon staff seemed pleased that it had been a robbery rather than a personal attack on Jackson.[7]

Another killing which is likely to remain unsolved for some time is that of former car dealer Wayne Lomas of Hengrove, Bristol, who disappeared in August 1988. Three years earlier he had been acquitted of attempted murder after it was alleged he had fired a sawn-off shotgun at a man outside a Bristol night-club. The day before he disappeared he had been arrested twice for fighting.

Six days later the police went to his home and found the dogs roaming loose in the garden, the tumble-dryer still switched on and five days of newspapers on the hall floor. An uneaten meal was on the table. The police suspected it was a gangland killing; Lomas had been thought to be involved in drug dealing and

[7] 3 November 1993.

protection. On 11 October 1993 the police received a tip-off and went to the house of a couple, not involved in the inquiry, who were away in America. There, eighteen inches under the dining-room floorboards, was a concrete block, and inside the remains of Mr Lomas. Four men were arrested and released without charge.

Not everything goes right all the time for armed robbers. David Lewis, who had a conviction in 1987 for robbery at a post office, obtained a job with Securicor as a guard; he had used a man he met in prison as a referee. One of Lewis's longer-term aims for 1993 was to hold up Bookers Cash and Carry in Leckwith, Cardiff, but unfortunately he and and his colleague and referee Paul were thwarted when, having taken £90,000, a rival organization opened fire and relieved him of the takings.

But the police maintain, perhaps with more justification than is often the case, that career criminals in Cardiff did not flourish as they have done in other major cities. They point out its relative isolation by road from the rest of the country until the late 1970s. Certainly London criminals were imported to carry out bank robberies, but because of the relatively low crime figures the CID was, they say, able to devote sufficient attention to big-time crime to make it unprofitable.

There was also the possibility that the local outlying communities might take the law into their own hands. In his book, *How Green Was My Valley*, based on stories he was told as a child about a mining community, Richard Llewellyn recounts the hunt for – led by the local minister – and subsequent killing of a child molester. The events of the first weekend in June 1992 were equally dramatic for the village of Penrhys near Tonypandy. There, in the garden of his home, Ronald Penrose was beaten so badly that he did not recover. His son Jason was kidnapped. After the attack on Penrose, who himself had a conviction for theft, Jason was apparently bundled into a car, taken to a quiet spot by a lake and roughed up. It was believed that the actions had taken place because of a heart attack suffered by an elderly lady who found her house being burgled.

This was not the first time that otherwise completely respectable members of a community have carried out their own brand of justice. There have been several such events in Wales, let alone other parts of the country. Indeed it had happened only the previous month. In the small community of Newborough in Anglesey some two hundred villagers, disheartened by the failure of the authorities

177

to deal with what they saw as the criminal activities of a local youth, met in the village square and decided to run him out of town. The youth was eventually taken into what amounted to protective custody. His family left the village shortly afterwards.

In recent years, perhaps the most extreme example of the vigilante in England, and the community's sympathy towards him, occurred when Stephen Owen was acquitted of attempted murder by a Maidstone Crown Court jury in May 1992. Owen, described as mild-mannered, had shot and wounded a lorry driver who had been responsible for the death of Owen's 12-year-old son in a hit-and-run incident. After serving twelve months of an eighteen-month sentence, the man had seemingly expressed quite the reverse of remorse.

The murder which stands at the opposite end of the century to the killing of Dai Lewis is that of the death of prostitute Lynette White, slashed to death on St Valentine's Day 1988. It had, however, been preceded by another killing in which arrests were made and, after a campaign by JUSTICE, two young men Wayne and Paul Darvell, local misfits, were freed.

The Darvell case occurred in Swansea. On 19 June 1986 they were convicted of the murder of a sex-shop manageress, Sandra Phillips. In June the previous year she had been sexually assaulted, savagely beaten, and her shop then set on fire in an effort to cover the traces of the murderer. Wayne Darvell, suggestible and with limited intelligence, was a compulsive confessor. He had earlier admitted to the murder of a dentist which he could not possibly have committed. Now he admitted this murder and implicated his brother Paul.

When the case was referred back to the Court of Appeal in July 1992 the defence alleged that there had been a planted earring, false sightings and a doctored confession. The Crown Prosecution Service did not contest the appeal.

One crucial piece of evidence, that of a palm print found on a pay-phone attached to the wall near the dead woman's body, was neither hers nor that of the brothers. This information was not passed to the defence; instead they were told that the tests had been insufficient for positive identification. Certain officers were investigated but there have been no prosecutions.

Lynette White, then aged 21, was killed in a frenzied attack on 14 February 1988. She had been the girlfriend of – and had worked for – a small-time pimp, Stephen Miller. The week or so before her murder she had fallen out with Miller. Most of her earnings, between £10 and £25 a time, were disappearing up his nose and she believed he was having an affair with another girl. She was also due to give evidence in two cases, one involving Francine, a sister of the powerful Cordle brothers, who was alleged to have stabbed a prostitute, Tina Garton, in the lung. Lynette had met Stephen when his older brother Tony was living with Francine. Tony had returned to London at the request of her brothers after he had beaten Francine once too often. Stephen and Lynette had begun to live together.

The English Collective of Prostitutes argues that it is desirable for a working girl to have a man who will protect her, and that such a person should not be prosecuted for living off immoral earnings. It is, they say, safer for the girl to have someone who knows where she is and may be in a position to help her if she gets into difficulties with a client. Certainly at the start of their relationship Miller seems to have been boyfriend rather than pimp. As her death approached, their relationship may have altered.

In *Bloody Valentine* John Williams interviews a lesbian pimp, Debbie Paul, who explains how such a relationship can work:

> Most of the girls are working for themselves. And some of the girls are working for themselves and their man as well. Round here the way it works is that if you've got a man dealing with drugs, and you've got a prostitute and they connect, then half of his money's with her and half of her money is with him, it's all mixed up together. If you've got a relationship with a pimp you've got to have some sort of agreement – I give you some of my money and you give me some of your money; you're making off drugs, you've got to compromise. But I don't think Stephen ever compromised, he would just take all the time.[8]

Lynette's body was found in the squalid Bute Town flat where she took her punters. She had been stabbed more than fifty times and, from the defence wounds on her hands, it was clear she had tried to fight off her attacker. Her head and one breast were almost completely severed, but there had been no rape nor mutilation of her genitals.

For ten months the South Wales Regional Crime Squad had

---

[8] J. Williams, *Bloody Valentine*, p.61.

no evidence except that it seemed a white man had been seen covered in blood a hundred and fifty yards from her flat shortly before her body was found. Then in December five black men, Stephen Miller, Tony Parris, Yusef Abdullahi and two cousins, Ronald and John Astie, were arrested. The reason for this was that two prostitute women Angela Psaila and Leanne Vilday suddenly told the amazing story that they had been present when Lynette was killed by the men, and they had been forced to participate in the slashing of her body.

What, if any, corroborative evidence was there? So far as Miller was concerned it was his own admission. He was questioned at length and, after denying the offence, he confessed. A supergrass, Ian Massey, said that Parris had confessed to him in prison and Abdullahi's girlfriend, Jacqui Harris, put him in the frame; she said that Yusef had told her he had been in the room when Lynette was killed. There was no corroborative evidence against the Asties and there was no forensic evidence against any of the men – this from a room which must have teemed with forensic material. The motive, the police decided, was revenge by Stephen Miller for Lynette's bad behaviour.

There is no doubt that from the start Psaila and Vilday told lies. Psaila seems to have had some racist feelings; in court she called the defendants 'black monkeys'. The police were so concerned about Vilday's evidence, and the changing of her statement between committal proceedings and the trials, that she was taken to a hypnotist, something which had been effectively discredited if not outlawed in both the English and American courts by the mid-1980s.[9] Vilday had named Martin Tucker as one of the killers and then withdrawn the allegation,

[9] Hypnosis has been used for a variety of legal and quasi-legal purposes including the obtaining of quick information by Israeli troops. There are two basic techniques, the crystal ball and the age regression. In the first the hypnotised person is invited to 'look into this ball and tell me what you see'. In the age regression the person is taken back in stages to the moment he is trying to recall. There are considerable difficulties in gauging the accuracy of the evidence obtained. Witnesses can lie deliberately or unknowingly and tend to guess at answers anyway. Once a person has been hypnotised the recollection, right or wrong, becomes that much stronger. Dr Martin Orne, a leading opponent of hypnosis in American courts, said at a Home Office conference in 1981 that 'hypnosis decreases reliability whilst making the witness more compelling'. In a trial at Maidstone Crown Court on 19 June 1987, the police had used a self-taught hypnotist who had learned his craft from reading books in the public library. The evidence he had obtained was ruled inadmissible. Earlier in 1987 the Home Office had issued guidelines to the effect that there be an uninterrupted video of the session, and that a witness who may be called to give evidence on material matters should not normally be considered for hypnosis.

and Psaila made and withdrew an allegation against another man.

For trials there were in the plural. The case was transferred to Swansea and the evidence had been heard by Mr Justice McNeil when, at the start of his summing-up in February 1989, he died of a heart attack. The second trial began in front of Mr Justice Leonard – the judge in the so-called Vicarage Rape Case – in the May and ended in November.[10] At 197 days it was Britain's longest murder trial. He warned the jury of the dangers of convicting on the uncorroborated evidence of the girls alone, and they must have listened to him because they acquitted the Asties. The others received life imprisonment.

Now began the campaign for the release of the Cardiff Three. It became known that the supergrass Ian Massey had given evidence against 'Ged' Corley, the Manchester policeman whose conviction was quashed by the Court of Appeal. Massey, a man with a record for violence, serving a fourteen-year sentence for robbery, was released after his first parole hearing. He had served a third of his sentence. Jacqui Harris retracted her evidence and made a statement saying that Yusef would often say weird things and that she had made her statement to hurt him. That left the confession of Miller, a man with an IQ of 75, a point above subnormal. It transpired that he had denied the offence some three hundred times before confessing. As Lord Justice Taylor said in the Court of Appeal:

> If you go on asking somebody questions, and tell him he is going to sit there until he says what you want, there will come a time when most people will crack. Oppression may be of the obvious, crude variety or it may be just by relentlessness.

How did the trial judge not exclude a confession obtained in these circumstances? It appears he was never asked to hear the transcript of the tape made of that part of the questioning. The solicitor who was with Miller during the interviews was blamed for not trying to intervene on Miller's behalf.

---

[10] Mr Justice Leonard was criticized over his sentencing in the Vicarage Rape Case in February 1987 when he handed down a substantially less severe sentence for the particularly unpleasant rape of a vicar's daughter than for a burglary (see R. Herridge and B. Hilliard, *Believe No One*, p. 1). He retired on the grounds of ill-health at the end of 1993, not long after the Court of Appeal decision in the White Case.

Twenty-nine days after the killing of Lynette White, the body of another prostitute, Geraldine Paulk, was found in the Fairwater area of Cardiff about two miles away from Lynette's flat. She too had been savagely slashed. No one has been arrested for her killing.

8

Birmingham and the Midlands, Sheffield and Yorkshire

On 1 June 1921 a team of thirty-eight, including some of Birmingham's most notable criminals, went for a day at the races. They were on their way to the Derby, as indeed every English racing gent should. But perhaps they were not exactly going to the Derby. They were going to waylay the Italian boys, the Sabinis, who had usurped the position of every rightful Englishman, that of racecourse bully. Believing that it was time the thieving Italians were taught a lesson, they had gathered, armed with an arsenal of weapons including razors, coshes, axes and knuckledusters, outside the Malt Shovel public house in Milk Street.

They had been geed up, if not exactly financed, by Horatio Bottomley, proprietor of the magazine *John Bull*, swindler *extraordinaire* and protector of all things British, and his equally opportunist friend Reuben Bigland, known as 'Telephone Jack'. Bottomley apparently began ranting about the scandal done to the British boys who had served so valiantly in the trenches, only to find that on their return the Sabinis had stolen their pitches at the racetracks. On the eve of Derby Day a Birmingham boy had been attacked in Covent Garden and had needed seventy stitches in his legs alone. The combination was irresistible.

It was certainly correct that the Sabinis, together with the backing of the Jewish team the Solomons, were running the Southern courses, but it was not correct to say that the British boys had been edged out by foreigners. Billy Kimber, the leader of the Brummagem Boys, was certainly British. But if the

183

Sabinis, with their Italian father and English mother were not, then how could the Birmingham-Italian Mancinis, some of Kimber's henchmen, be either?

A meeting was arranged in a hotel off the Bull Ring and instructions were given to attack the caravan of London book-makers taking taxis back home from the races. The aim was to ambush them in the Ewell Road. Steve Donoghue won the Derby on the courageous horse Humorist[1]; the Birmingham men left and duly blocked the road with their charabanc and attacked the first cab in sight. One of the men inside lost three fingers to a meat cleaver. The cabs were overturned and the occupants routed.

Unfortunately, somewhere along the road to Epsom the wheels of the Birmingham coach had become crossed and, instead of attacking the Sabini bookmakers, the Brummagem men waylaid some bookmakers and their friends from Leeds who until that day had been wholly sympathetic to the Birming-ham cause. There was worse to follow.

At first, when they heard of the affray, the police thought it was a Sinn Fein riot, but when PS Dawson arrived on the scene he found it was far more easily controlled. First he removed the sparking plugs from the charabanc and then he used the expedient of threatening to shoot the first of the men who moved. He was then able to keep twenty-eight Midlands ruf-fians (ten escaped) under wraps until help arrived.

Ruffians they were. Here is a small selection of some of the finer representatives.

John Allard had a conviction for manslaughter in March 1912 after pushing the point of an umbrella into his victim's eye and served seven years' penal servitude. For his part in the Epsom affray he received eighteen months' hard labour.

Edward Banks had been involved in the shooting (of Darby

---

[1] Humorist was indeed a brave horse. He began to haemorrhage shortly after the race and died within a few weeks. A post-mortem showed he had been running on only one sound lung. Bottomley and Bigland soon fell out. Bottomley was running a crooked Victory Bond draw and it was arranged that Bigland should receive a £500 prize. They met at King's Cross Station and according to the story Bigland asked where was his monkey. 'Up a stick,' replied Bottomley, displaying enormous wit. It was the end of their relationship. Bigland was so annoyed that he published a 2d pamphlet which Bottomley saw as defamatory, sued for libel and lost. He was prosecuted and received a seven-year sentence. In prison he is said to have retained his sense of humour. He was seen on the prison machine by a visitor who commented, 'Sewing?' He replied, 'No sir, reaping.' But the story is also told of Oscar Wilde. P. Baker, *Time Out of Life*, p. 35.

Sabini) at Alexandra Park the previous year, and there was a suggestion that he had been going to get some Mills bombs from Birmingham.

John Lea(e) had a conviction for manslaughter and three other cases of wounding.

William Graham was described by the police as a ruffian and bully known as Cockney Bill. He was living with Annie Moran, a well-known thief and prostitute, off the proceeds of robberies by her. On 4 March 1912 he had received five years at Birmingham Quarter Sessions for wounding. He was one of those acquitted of the affray. In all, seventeen out of the twenty-eight were found guilty. Two received three years' penal servitude and three eighteen months' hard labour.[2] Shortly after, following a raid on a public house in which shots were fired, the ringleaders at the Assizes received up to five years' imprisonment.[3]

If that was the end for a number of Birmingham trouble-makers, there was plenty going on in Sheffield. There had been for years. In the 1840s there had been an alliance between Sheffield men and others from Manchester, Nottingham and Liverpool to form the Northern Mob who had controlled betting at cock-fights, prize-fights and race meetings, and later there had been indigenous to Sheffield the Gutterpercha Gang and another led by a man called Kingy Broadhead whose speciality was a sort of protection racket involving gentlemen and tall hats. If they did not wish to see their headgear in the mud, they paid a tribute.

In the First World War in Sheffield there were the Red Silk and White Silk gangs, named after their neckerchiefs, who were principally muggers but who could, if roused, be persuaded to deal with local soldiers on leave at the Blonk Street fairground. Most towns and cities had such banditry. At the time Hull, for example, had the Silver Boys.

The early 1920s witnessed the bitter battle for the control of Sheffield by two rival gangs, the Mooneys and the Garvins. One of the principal reasons for their wish for supremacy and control over a large percentage of the working-class element in the town was simply that, in June 1921, 69,000 from a workforce of

---

[2] The Brummagem Boys eventually reached an accommodation with the Sabinis and the race tracks of Britain were divided between them on a rough North-South split. Billy Kimber is said to have ended his working life as the manager of a London greyhound track.
[3] PRO: MEPO/3/346.

512,052 were jobless. As a result betting was rife with, according to evidence given to the Betting Tax Committee in 1923, some 90 per cent of the adult working-class population of industrial areas either participating themselves or assisting others to do so. The potential takings were enormous, with a successful local bookie taking up to £100 a day and employing forty runners each receiving commission of up to two shillings in the pound.[4] This was nothing really new. It was estimated that in 1913, in a survey of four large works in the city, 486 out of 600 men were habitual gamblers.

Betting was not confined to horses and greyhounds. There was semi-professional athletics and, as in other large cities, bare-knuckle fights. There was also Pitch-and-Toss. This was one of the simplest of all gambling games, a variant of which is the staple Australian gaming diet of Two-Up. Generally three or more coins are spun in the air with betting on whether the majority fall heads or tails.[5]

The major Pitch-and-Toss rings in Sheffield, and there were many others around the countryside, were at Sky Edge, Wadsley, Five Arches and Tinsley. They were run by the rival gangs of Sam and Bob Garvin and George Mooney. The clientele came from a wide area, Rotherham, Chesterfield and Barnsley.

The Sky Edge ring was old-established. It had been run before the First World War by 'Snaps' Jackson and, when he went into the army, his brothers. Control then passed to a local bookmaker, William Cowan. After the War Cowan passed control to George Mooney, then in his late twenties and living in West Bar; his gang was much more a racecourse mob than a street gang, palming betting slips, running the protection of local bookmakers and beating up recalcitrant ones and their clerks. Indeed the Sabinis might have been proud to call him a brother.

Mooney drew the members of his gang from two separate areas of Sheffield – West Bar and the Park. Things worked well until the end of 1922 when profits began to slip. The reason for

---

[4] I am most grateful to Julian Bean for permission to quote from his books, *Crime in Sheffield* and *The Sheffield Gang Wars*. Both provide a detailed and fascinating account of life and crime in Sheffield in the 1920s.

[5] Pitch-and-Toss had as many variations as venues. It was also known as 'Nearest the Mottie' and 'Nudgers', 'Hoying' and 'Burling'. Playing had been banned on Sundays in Victorian England. It was played on any waste ground with rings on pit banks in Lanarkshire and on the beaches near Swansea. It survived in places as a regular sport until the 1950s. See C. Chinn, *Better Betting with a Decent Feller*, pp. 95–103.

this was first that the 'Sankey' money, a payment of 10 shillings a day added to the wages of 8/6d, was withdrawn, and second a determination by the welfare authorities to cut off allowances from families whose members were found gambling. The gang began to disperse with Mooney – who not unnaturally saw his position as leader requiring the most money – dispensing with lesser lights, particularly the Park mob.

They now teamed up with the slippery Sam Garvin. After all the Sky Edge ring was on their own horizon, if not doorstep. The Park Brigade was formed and within weeks, using superior numbers, ousted Mooney and his men from control. Reprisals were not long in coming and William Furniss, a former Mooney man, was attacked by Frank Kidnew and Albert Foster as he lay in bed. Furniss was dragged out of his home on 29 April 1923 and knocked unconscious with pokers. It is easy to see how matters escalated. This clearly could not go unpunished and three weeks later there was a full-scale riot in Corporation Street. Only one man was arrested, and on his appearance before the city magistrates he was fined £1 for assaulting a bystander who was hit by a brick and £6 for assaulting a police officer. He had, apparently, been at the Licensed Victuallers' Ball in the Cutlers' Hall. On 27 May it was the turn of Frank Kidnew to suffer. He was set on, receiving one hundred cuts which required a stay in hospital. Asked about his attackers he replied, 'Reckon they've spoiled my suit.'

Matters escalated from there onwards and on 16 June the police arrived at West Bar to find the Mooney house there under siege from the Park Brigade. They also found one of its members, George Wheywell, shot in the shoulder. Inside the house Mooney's small arsenal was revealed – two guns and three life-preservers. Mooney and his mates and the Park Brigade members were arrested this time. All were remanded in custody at their own request except for Thomas Rippon who, immediately he left the court, was chased and slashed by George Wheywell and part of the Park Brigade. This time they ended in custody – except for Wheywell.

A week later George Mooney pleaded guilty and the rest of his team not guilty. They ended by being bound over in the sum of £25 each, as were the Park Brigade. Then came the case of the attack by Wheywell on Tommy Rippon. Mr Rippon decided he did not wish to give evidence and the 'extremely dangerous' Wheywell lived to slash another day.

The Mooney team was back in court within the week. They were unable to find sureties until after Carpatheus won the Northumberland Plate, the Pitman's Derby, at 4 to 1.

Now it was suggested by the Watch Committee that stricter controls should be exercised by the police over the gangs. In turn they replied that they were under strength and not getting the support of the courts. On the Underworld front it was said that Mooney had been to Birmingham to reach an alliance with Billy Kimber and those of his boys who were left, whilst Sam Garvin and the Park Brigade were looking for help from Darby Sabini. Mooney also gave an interview to the *Sheffield Mail* explaining that there was no such thing as a Mooney Gang whereas the Park Brigade were a hundred strong. The troubles, he maintained, were because of a threat to his legitimate hold on Sky Edge. Unfortunately Mooney went on to name his five supporters, who were none too pleased to see their names in the newspapers. One of them, John James 'Spud' Murphy, had it out with Mooney in the street, as a result of which little altercation each was bound over in the sum of £5. Nothing was done about the clear breach of the previous week's £25 bind-over. The police had some justification in thinking they needed more help from the courts.

By the end of 1923 Mooney had become something of a pariah. His 'four supporters' had taken real umbrage about being named. In September Murphy had been sent for trial charged with an assault on Mrs Mooney; he had thrown a brick at the pregnant woman, knocking her unconscious. Again the police may have thought he got off lightly. The Assistant Recorder, C. Milton Barber, was long on homily and short on sentence.

> People in the city of Sheffield, be their names Mooney or Murphy or Smith or Jones, or anything else, must know that if they come up to these courts and are convicted of crimes of violence they will all be dealt with in a suitable manner. Taking into consideration all the circumstances you will be sentenced to six months' hard labour.

The Mooney family did not have a very happy Christmas. By now Sam Garvin's Park Brigade ruled supreme. On Christmas Eve Frank Kidnew led a razor attack on the house, but failed to find George Mooney hiding in a cupboard. Bail was allowed in the sum of £20 each to Kidnew, Sam Garvin, Sandy Bowler, a one-time boxer, and Robert Crook, but not before they had spent Christmas in the cells. In January Mooney had the humiliation of being protected by the police as he went to court to give evidence. Cross-examined, he admitted to fifty-three convictions. Curiously, although all four had, they said, been distributing tickets for a charity boxing tournament at the time of the attack, only two were believed. Garvin and Crook were acquitted, Kidnew and Bowler received a modest three months each. The damage had been done to Mooney. His close friend Albert Foster had already sought refuge in Birmingham. Now his brother John emigrated and in early January Mooney left the area. Garvin reigned supreme; at least for the moment.

Garvin was a man born in 1880 who had convictions around the countryside for assault, illegal gaming, housebreaking and theft. He was well-built and well-dressed, and popular not only with his followers but also for his assistance when he organized a boxing tournament for the relatives of men killed in a colliery disaster at Nunnery. Whilst on bail for the attack on George Mooney, with Kidnew as the referee at the tournament and Barlow as the secretary, he raised £130. He wrote to the *Yorkshire Telegraph and Star* thanking people for their support and, at the same time, pointing out just how many 'congratulations have been showered upon me'. It was an action which would be repeated over the year by any sensible gangleader who knew the benefits of some well-advertised charity work. He took an interest in politics, breaking up Labour Party political meetings, and his family was one of the first to move into the Walkley estate which had the unheard-of luxury of an indoor bathroom.

Over the next two years gangs roamed the streets of Sheffield stealing and mugging passers-by and fighting each other. As well as Garvin's Park Brigade who committed themselves – apart from some thefts and robberies – to the destruction of what was left of Mooney's team, there was now a Junior Park Gang and a rival organization, the Smithfields Gang, constantly at war with each other. The local magistrates seemed afraid to hand out heavy sentences and now the prospect of meeting violence with violence occurred to senior police officers.

At the New Year of 1925 an arrangement was made over the running of Sky Edge. Six delegates from the former Mooney organization and six from Park Brigade would supervise the division of proceeds. The public was pleased, the Mooney men were pleased, but what was in it for the Garvin team? On the face of it not much – after all, they were in control. Looked at a little closer, things became clearer. The price for the concession was the withdrawal of yet more summonses against Sam Garvin, Barlow, Kidnew and William Wareham. They had been in a bit of horseplay after which a Mooney man, George Newbould, had needed several stitches. Magistrates and defendants wished each other a happy New Year.

The troubles began again by the end of January. Four former Mooneys went – together with the assistance of a Birmingham thug Tom Armstrong – to Sky Edge to sort out their percentage and were told that any deal they might have thought they had was off. They were chased by about fifty Park Brigaders (should that be Brigadiers?) into a house from which they had to be rescued by the police. By now things were hotting up once more. George Mooney had returned from his abdication but his gang was being run by Foster (who had defected from Garvin), Wheywell and Tom Armstrong, one of Billy Kimber's Brummagem boys who was living at George Newbould's home.

Attacks and counter-attacks followed one another with frequency. Now George Newbould was seen as the leader of the forces opposed to Garvin. He had two pitching rings under his control and the police were raiding Sky Edge on a regular basis. Patrons were looking for other rings where there were no such tiresome interruptions. Apart from running the pitching rings, however, the gangs controlled the poor quarters such as the Crofts, Norfolk Bridge and the Park, collecting protection from the publicans and shopkeepers.

It was the death of a bystander which brought matters home to the citizenry of Sheffield. There has long been a tradition that the Underworld should be allowed to play by itself provided it does not cross the boundary dividing its representatives from decent folk. The line was crossed on 28 April 1925 when William Plommer, an ex-Sergeant in the First World War, a labourer and father of two children, one a three-week-old baby, was stabbed to death. A fight had taken place near Plommer's home in which a 23-year-old Garvin gang member, Wilfred Fowler, had been defeated. Plommer had only been a spectator, but the next night Fowler and his friends had toured the area threatening to do for Plommer and two of his friends.

Plommer came out of his house to meet them and was attacked by a gang of eight men. Plommer who, towards the end of the fight, was hit over the head with a child's scooter, had received stomach wounds which seemed to have been caused by a bayonet. A policeman in the vicinity found Wilfred Fowler, his younger brother, Lawrence, and a third man George Wills sitting on the steps of a shop. Plommer lay nearby.

Meanwhile the gang had gone looking for Plommer's friends and had caught up with Harry Rippon who was slashed with a razor. He identified his attackers as Sam and Bob Garvin and William Furniss.

In all eleven men were finally charged with the murder of Plommer. They included the Fowler brothers, Frank Kidnew, Sam Garvin and George Wills. In those days a coroner's jury was entitled to return verdicts of murder against named defendants and they did so in the cases of the Fowler brothers, with allegations of aiding and abetting against seven of the others including Garvin and Kidnew. The defence was that Plommer had run a tossing ring under the railway arches at Norfolk Bridge and had been the attacker of the Fowlers, going for them with a poker and razor. Efforts by the defence to substantiate either allegation in the police court failed. The men were committed for trial at the Leeds Assizes.

Plommer had indeed been unfortunate to be involved. Wilfred 'Spinks' Fowler had argued with a man called Harold Liversidge in the Windsor Hotel. Liversidge had been struck and had then gone to Plommer's house to get help. Quite clearly there were a number of spectators and encouragers at the fight because James 'Spud' Murphy was one of the watchers. Liversidge and Fowler had fought with the latter, ending on the floor. As Plommer helped Fowler up he was told, 'Jock, you have got to have a tanning for this tomorrow.'

The next day Plommer was advised by a friend to leave his home but he refused. Evidence was called that he was approached by seven men, each of them armed. He offered to fight them one by one and knocked down Lawrence Fowler before he was overpowered. It was the case for the prosecution that one of the Fowlers had struck the fatal blow.

Kidnew was acquitted on a submission of no case to answer at half-time. So was Robert Garvin. Sam Garvin was acquitted by the jury. George Wills and two others were found guilty of

191

manslaughter. Both the Fowler brothers were convicted of murder. Before sentence was passed the brothers were asked if they had anything to say and Lawrence replied, 'I spoke the truth. I only struck one blow with the poker. I am innocent. If his wife would only speak up. It is an impossible decision.' Wilfred said nothing. George Wills was sentenced to ten years' penal servitude on the manslaughter charge.

An appeal was lodged and unsuccessfully argued. The Court of Appeal took the view that, rather than the Fowler brother having been unfortunate to be convicted of murder, some of the rest had been fortunate not to be. There was still the hope of a reprieve, particularly when it was rumoured that Wilfred had made a last-minute confession exculpating his brother. Surely the Home Secretary had to act? He did not. There had been trouble during the summer at a series of Northern racecourses and law and order was in the air. The brothers were executed on consecutive days – Wilfred first – at Armley Prison, Leeds. Lawrence had asked to be executed with his brother, but for no clear reason this small act of clemency was denied him. Another man, Alfred Bostock, who had battered his mistress to death and thrown her in the river at Rotherham, shared the scaffold with Wilfred on 3 September.

What, meanwhile, had happened to Sam Garvin? The answer was that on Saturday 1 August, the day after his acquittal in the Plommer case, Garvin was back in the dock on a charge of wounding Harry Rippon, Plommer's friend. This time he was found guilty but, yet again, the sentence does not seem to have been the swingeing one which this old bully merited. He received twenty-one months' hard labour. His brother, Robert, received a modest nine months.

And what about George Mooney? On the day Garvin was sentenced he came unstuck on the way back from pony races at Worksop. He had the misfortune to find himself in a railway carriage with William Cowan whom he had ousted six years earlier from the Sky Edge ring, an action which could be said to have started off the whole present state of affairs. At the end of the journey Mooney was charged with grievous bodily harm; Cowan had three fractured ribs and a bitten ear. When questioned by the police, Mooney did not mention the ribs but denied the attempted cannibalism. He received nine months' hard labour.

Albert Foster received eighteen months' hard labour for a fight outside a boxing tournament Sam Garvin had promoted in the happier days when he was at liberty; and Peter Winsey, another Garvin man, struck old Patrick Mooney, George's uncle, splitting his head; he received two months' hard labour. Inroads were being made into the teams.

What was also breaking up the gangs was the attitude of the new police Special Duties Squad, formed four days after the Plommer murder. According to former Chief Constable Sir Percy Sillitoe, who is generally credited with the destruction of both the Sheffield and Glasgow gangs:

> I called my senior officers together and asked them to select very carefully for me some of the strongest, hardest hitting men under their commands. I had 700 policemen, each with a minimum chest measurement of thirty-six inches, all fit and healthy men, and none of them was disinclined to play the gangsters at their own game and meet violence with the strong arm of the law. It was not difficult to pick a dozen of the best of these to form a 'flying squad' specially to deal with the gangster problem. These men were taught ju-jitsu and various other methods of attack and defence, and it was surprising how little teaching they needed. They had just been waiting for the chance to learn![6]

The squad was led by ex-Coldstream Guardsman PC Walter Loxley, who weighed in at 19 stone 8 lbs and stood 6 feet 2 inches. Its other members probably needed no ju-jitsu lessons. Jerry Lunn was an ex-heavyweight boxer, and Julian Bean describes a third officer as 'another hardman well versed in the techniques of rough-house and back-alley brawling'. According to Sillitoe another member could not only hold seven tennis balls in one hand but could also pick up five loose tennis balls in his fist. They were soon in action against the gangs and dealt out heavy punishment in the bar-room and street brawls which preceded arrests. If cross-summonses were taken out suggesting that the officers had acted outside the scope of their authority, then help was at hand from the courts:

[6] P. Sillitoe, *Cloak Without Dagger*, p. 79.

On the other hand, if you are satisfied that at the time when this man Wheywell was assaulted, that he had begun by striking the officer, as, I believe, the evidence shows, and that what the officer did was after that, believing he was going to offer further violence, then you must find a true bill against Wheywell.[7]

And the jury did just that: Officer 0. Wheywell 3 months.

Sillitoe is undoubtedly mistaken when he recalls forming the Special Duties Squad. It had been done by the former Chief Constable Lieut. Colonel John Hall-Dalwood, who had fallen out with the Watch Committee in the autumn of 1925. There had been considerable difficulties in the force, with allegations of heavy drinking by senior officers. Hall-Dalwood retired in early 1926 and Percy Sillitoe took up duties on 1 May 1926, the first day of the General Strike. There is little doubt, however, that he honed the Squad. Perhaps like many another officer time had dulled the cutting-edge of his recollections. In this passage we are almost into ex-police officer Tom Divall's fond remembrances of Darby Sabini and Billy Kimber as 'good allies'.

The Mooney and Garvin gangs had a final clash, as a result of which both leaders were sent to prison. After George Mooney came out, when his sentence was completed, I sent for him and saw him alone in my private office. I spoke to him like a father. I said: 'Well, Mooney, you see what my attitude is. If you chaps do this sort of thing I am going to see that you go to prison, and it's not getting anywhere. Now what is the sense of it?'

Mooney did not answer. I went on: 'Why don't you stop this damned nonsense of fighting Sam Garvin's men? I shall stamp out his gang just as I shall stamp out yours, but if you have any decency in you, as I believe you have, you won't wait to be stamped out like some sort of dirty pestilence. You will come to your senses while there is time and keep your dignity.'

When he got up to leave I said, 'I really believe you will try to better yourself, Mooney, and I want to shake your hand.'

---

[7] Mr Recorder W. J. Waugh quoted in J. P. Bean, *Sheffield Gang Wars*, p.111.

He stood and looked at my proffered hand for a long moment without saying a word. As I was about to withdraw it, he burst suddenly into tears, grasped it and said: 'You are the first gentleman I have ever had the privilege of shaking hands with, sir.'

All good stuff from *Eric or Little-by-Little* or *Tom Brown's Schooldays*. There is no record, however, of Mooney and Garvin having been in prison over the same incident, but there were suggestions that they might have a man-to-man fight for control for a purse of £100. It was thought it would draw a bigger crowd than a Sheffield United *v.* Sheffield Wednesday Cup-Tie. It never took place; after all Garvin was 47 by now.

By 1927 the police had bent, if not broken, the gangs – there were still sporadic outbreaks by the Junior Park and Smithfields gangs – and indeed Mooney and Garvin went their separate ways. Both became bookmakers on the northern courses. Garvin, wearing a white hat, was Captain Mee, and Mooney metamorphosed into George Barratt, betting at the Owlerton Stadium until well after the Second World War. Perhaps the homily described by Sillitoe did happen and did take effect, for Mooney had no more convictions. Garvin, who had not had the benefit of Sillitoe's uplifting speech, continued to associate with thieves and pickpockets and added to his list of convictions until his death in the 1960s.

Although it was estimated that at the height of the armed robbery escapades the great bulk of large-scale criminal enterprises in the South of England and the Midlands were organised from London and carried out by groups which included London-based operators, this did not stop there being a very substantial number of local operators. A 1964 study showed that there would be 1 in 10,000 major full-time operators in a town of 80,000. Such an operator would of course be extremely low in the pecking order of London.[8] But it was to the Midlands and North West that London criminals turned when they had to leave 'the smoke' for some reason. For example, when Eric Mason received a bad beating at the hands of Frankie Fraser, could get no sympathy from the Twins and was also none too popular with

---

[8] J. Mack (1964) 'Full-time Miscreants etc', in *British Journal of Sociology*, vol. XV, pp. 38–53.

some other London faces, he went to Blackpool. There he was joined by some brothers who had also fallen out with the Krays. In turn they moved back through the Midlands where they ran some girls and owned a club or two.

On 31 October 1984 Police Sergeant John Speed was murdered in Leeds when he went to assist another colleague who had also been shot whilst investigating two men seen tampering with car-door handles opposite Leeds parish church. The gunman was chased for over a mile before he managed to escape by hi-jacking a car at gun-point. The killing led to suggestions that an 'affable and dangerous' Irishman had devised an ideal way of carrying out robberies in the United Kingdom and had carried them out for about fifteen years. The procedure was simple – that of hit and run. Within hours of the robbery the perpetrators were back in the Republic.

Inquiries led to the police interviewing 10,000 people and 18,000 leads being checked out. Finally, after an anonymous telephone call the police were pointed in the direction of Eamonn Kelly. Kelly, born in Dublin, had spent the greater part of his life in Leeds. Detectives flew to Dublin and it was found that there were a number of applications pending for Kelly's extradition on bank robberies. He was already serving fourteen years for his part in the kidnapping of Jennifer Guinness in Ireland. However, it became clear that so far as the killing of Police Sergeant Speed was concerned Kelly could not have been the killer.

Kelly was, however, linked to an Irishman who had lived in Yorkshire, Gerald Stone, and through him to Dave Graceworth, known as 'The Mechanic' because of his ability to soup-up all manner of motor vehicles. Graceworth was seen loitering in the car park of a supermarket and was approached. He took off and was killed in a high-speed chase when he lost control of the vehicle he was driving. His guilt was confirmed by an accomplice on the day of the robbery which led to the murder of Sergeant John Speed.

Anything Londoners can do Yorkshiremen can do better, including tampering with witnesses. In 1992 Judge Jonathan Crabtree lifted reporting restrictions at the Newcastle Crown Court and revealed a massive trial-fixing plot described with some justification as the 'worst in history'. After a six-month trial at Leeds Crown Court, Scarborough antiques dealer John Walsh had been convicted in 1989 of handing £1.25 million of antiques and valuables which had been stolen over a ten-year period in a series of often violent raids on country houses in the North of England. Walsh's haul had been discovered by some Scouts who camped on land near the home Walsh shared with his mother. The police dug up five beer barrels and freezer bags containing silver, porcelain and jewellery. He received seven years' imprisonment.

This was only the beginning of the story. The police set up Operation Judge to inquire into what they considered was perjured evidence given on Walsh's behalf. The defence had been that the witnesses had sold the items to Walsh. In fact many had been bribed with cash or gifts of clothing to give perjured evidence. Over a period of eleven months thirty of the witnesses, including a former Yorkshire cricketer, a Hatton Garden diamond merchant and other antique dealers were convicted. Sixteen went to prison for their part in the conspiracy and Walsh received a further three years and was ordered to pay £40,000 costs. His brother Ivor was sentenced to five years, and his sister-in-law Susan received twelve months.

After the last trial Detective Superintendent Ian Peacock, who had headed the twelve-strong team of detectives, commented:

> I think most of Scarborough must have known what was going on and it must have seemed for some that justice had just simply ceased to exist and the Walsh family were above the law.

Back in Sheffield, drugs have taken a hold not dissimilar to that in other cities. There was, however, a slightly unusual case in 1992. Another 'Mr Big' Craig Allen ran a drugs ring from a police cell block at Bridge Street. Described as 'short and flabby and not a user, something which gave him the power of ten over lesser mortals', he had already escaped from a prison bus in Grenoside in May 1991. Whilst on remand for a post-office break-in he used the now fairly liberal facilities which allow the use of the telephone to an inmate to keep in touch with his family, to mastermind a drug distribution centre. The cell block was being used at a time when prison cells were not available to remand prisoners because of overcrowding. Allen fed £30 a day into the telephone to organize a distribution network of couriers to deal in heroin, amphetemines and cannabis across South

Yorkshire, Nottinghamshire and into Manchester. Eventually staff at the cell block became suspicious of his almost total monopoly of the telephone and it was tapped. The police now heard how Allen's middle-aged parents had kept drugs in a dog kennel and in a specially built floor safe in the burglar-alarmed shed in the family home in Parson Cross.

Allen's mother, Marjorie, collapsed in the dock when she received two years. His father had half that sentence, Allen's girlfriend received five years. In all fifteen people received sentences and Allen himself collected ten years for supplying, eighteen months for the post office and twelve months for escaping from the prison bus. The police described him as having a mind like a computer. 'He rang all his contacts from memory and was able to work out weights and prices straight away,' said an admiring officer.

Any doubts that crime was not alive and well in Leeds were dispelled in December 1993. Apart from a place for local talent to thrive, it has long been one of the safe havens for London gangsters who need some time away from 'the smoke', and it was to this city that Jack Spot had fled in November 1943 after a small spot of trouble in a Paddington spieler. Here, according to his memoirs, he had protected a club owned by a man named Milky against the predations of a Polish mobster. This led to Spot being given a share of a book at a local dog track, and the general enhancement of his reputation.

Leeds was also a city which had difficulties with its police force in the 1950s which led to a series of prosecutions of serving officers and the eventual jailing of a former inspector for the manslaughter of an immigrant.

Now yet again clubs and drugs with linked dealing and protection have become rife in the Chapeltown area, the drug and red-light district of Leeds. In December it was alleged that two men, Robert Samuels and Clifton Bryan, were seriously attacked and wounded as a reprisal for their earlier behaviour. They had, Leeds magistrates were told, kidnapped a teenager, Mark Smith, and then blackmailed his associates into paying £2,900 as a deposit for his release. It was a complicated series of affairs with Smith being kidnapped for allegedly assaulting a Michelle Midgeley, a friend of Samuels and Bryan.

A further instalment of £7,000 was due to be paid for Mr Smith's release and arrangements were made to collect the money from a bank in Chapeltown. When Bryan and Samuels arrived on Monday 13 December they found no Mr Smith and instead, said Stephen Fox for the prosecution: 'Another car was parked further along. It followed them. They stopped, the car pulled alongside and someone fired off a double-barrelled shotgun.' It was the first of nine discharges that night. Samuels was badly injured and Bryan thought him to be dead. He drove towards the local hospital, pursued by gunmen who shot at the pair once more as they reached the hospital's Chancellor Wing.

Smith, however, was the one who ended in court when he appeared accused of conspiracy to murder. Reporting restrictions were lifted at the request of his solicitor.

This violent incident is not an isolated one. According to a report all the small Asian businesses live on their nerves. A fish-and-chip shop has lost its till twice during frying hours; robbers have simply walked in and taken it. The local community fears that, if things are not controlled and the disaffected young black community does not have its energies channelled in the right way, then Chapeltown could become another Moss Side.

The penchant for motor-cycle killing spread to Northamptonshire in October 1993 when John Reynolds, a local property dealer, was shot to death whilst walking his golden retrievers with his daughter. The motor-cyclist shot him five times.

Over the years Leicester has also had its share of troubles. In the 1960s the Lambrianou brothers, two of whom were convicted in the Kray trial, had what seemed to be an unhealthy interest in the mini-cabs in the city until they were spoken to on the subject by Charles Kray. That was the decade of the first hot-dog wars of which Bob Black, who used to work for burger baron 'Mr Big' Gary Thompson, said: 'In the Sixties there was a lot of rivalry. In those days a burger stand would get turned over, or if somebody stole someone else's pitch they would get a good hiding. Today, they are using shooters.'[9]

In the early 1990s things were much more serious. 'Mr Big' Gary Thompson, known by the soubriquet not merely because he weighed 25 stones but because of his control of the business, and his assistant, John Weston, died on 27 August 1990 outside Thompson's Victorian home in Oadby. They had been followed from the Thompson catering business in Aylestone Road, Leicester.

---

[9] *Independent on Sunday*, 2 September 1990.

Thompson had been shot three times with .22 bullets; one bullet had passed through his right leg and into his left. A second had gone through his arm before entering his spleen, and the third had been fired at close range into his head. His companion was found curled up, shot in the legs and head. The opinion of the pathologist was that both had been shot whilst on the ground. It was thought that a large sum of cash, certainly £30,000 and possibly as much as £80,000, had been taken from Thompson's Bentley.

Thompson, who had worked up his father's hot-dog barrow trade from the time he was 12, was undoubtedly the King of the Midlands burger business. In 1978 he had been fined £400 for assaulting a rival hot-dog salesman. He had seen off his main rival Geno Loizo by purchasing his business after a long-running battle in which Thompson had sent two men to steal all Loizo's hot-dog equipment, including not only his freezer but also 1,000 bread rolls and his tomato sauce. Now between 1981 and 1987 Thompson's business turned over £3 million. That year he went to prison for a VAT fraud involving over £400,000.

On the August Bank Holiday weekend that he died, Thompson had his vans at three local shows as well as at York races and in Devon and Essex. A little after midnight on the Monday, he and Weston transferred the substantial takings to the boot of his Bentley at the depot and drove home. They were followed by Terence Burke and Warren Slaney in a gold Ford Sierra. Weston was shot first and, according to Mavis Thompson who saw the fight, her husband was standing his ground against Slaney before he was shot. The men then drove off with the money.

The prosecution put the case as a simple robbery which went badly wrong. Slaney ran an alibi defence, whilst Burke said that he had been recruited with Thompson's knowledge to 'do an insurance job'. The gun had been taken to kill the Rottweiler guard dog; he, Burke, did not know there would be any shooting of humans. He said that while on remand Slaney had threatened to kill him and he had been warned to wear a bullet-proof vest while on trial at Northampton Crown Court in February 1992. Slaney did not give evidence but called witnesses to the effect that he was at the engagement party of his cousin at the time of the shooting.

Given what amounted to a cut-throat defence – Burke's counsel described Slaney as 'the cool executioner' – it was not surprising that the jury convicted both men. Slaney, a former professional boxer, cried out, 'They've convicted an innocent man – I've been framed.'

Were either of the versions of the case the correct ones or, as Mr James Hunt QC, counsel for Burke, suggested, were 'some very big men behind the scenes'? Certainly troubles continued in the hot-dog business for some time after the killings with Joe Persico – who ran vans and who had, at one time, worked for Thompson – finding them vandalized and daubed with graffiti. An unlit petrol bomb was found on the steps of his parents' home in Equity Road. Shots were fired through the front windows, and the windows of the car showroom belonging to Persico's brother, Tony, were smashed.

Then a dead pig with 'THE GRASS' and 'JOE' written on it was dumped outside Tony's garage. The pig had been artistically made-up with a receding hair-line and heavy facial scarring. Its eyelids had been cut off.

Joe Persico, who in the past had received a sentence of five years for kidnapping and grievous bodily harm, went into hiding after being warned there was a £25,000 contract on his head. Fly posters began appearing around Leicester suggesting 'Joe Persico sold Lee Oswald the gun'. Another more colourful one was a 'wanted' poster for 'Joe Per-Sicko' and suggesting he was impersonating Postman Pat, a hardman, a plank, a chicken carcass and that, amongst other things, he had 'tiny genitals'; 'a Max Wall lookalike trophy, no business (soon) and no chance'. The posters were signed by local body-builder Ramzy Khachik, who owned a gymnasium and provides doormen for clubs in the Midlands.

Persico was, quite understandably, extremely alarmed. He spent a considerable time at the offices of the *Leicester Mercury* putting his side of the case. One former reporter remembers him as being 'almost paranoid with worry'.

But paranoid or not, fight back he did. He sent videos of Thompson's funeral to his rivals and rang them to play dirges down the phone. Eventually he and Khachik met. There had been a problem with Persico's sister in the ice-cream van depot. Marie Persico believes a gun was pointed at her. Khachik says she held a knife and he leg-swept her to the floor to disarm her. The knife ended in the possession of the police and no charges were brought.

The Persico-Khachik confrontation came in the Holiday Inn, Leicester in April 1991. Names were called and Khachik invited Persico to sort matters out in a man-to-man fight. Apparently Persico did not move; instead he began to dial on his mobile phone, as did Khachik. The manager of the hotel called the police who 'arrived to witness the stand-off'.[10]

That had not been the end of the Persico troubles. In 1991 he was charged with reckless driving and threats to shoot his former business partner, Clifford Taylor. It was all part of a long-running feud in which a year earlier Taylor had obtained an injunction against Persico. Taylor had bought the vans of the murdered Gary Thompson and according to his counsel, Persico had raided his lock-up garage and made off with the mobile food stalls. Persico's counsel denied any involvement by his client in the incident. His explanation did not appeal to the judge, who said at a later hearing that he had 'an abundant opportunity' to reveal where the fleet had been hidden and had not done so. He received a four-month sentence for contempt of court and ignoring an injunction.

Earlier in the year Persico had been acquitted at Leicester Magistrates' Court when on 8 April 1991 the prosecution abandoned a case of common assault, criminal damage and threatening behaviour. Mr Walter Berry, prosecuting, said that two out of four prosecution witnesses had failed to appear and the other two were refusing to give evidence. Three were said by Mr Berry to be 'terrified'. Earlier Persico's counsel had asked for the matter to be adjourned because of a film the previous night on television. In the Cook Report on the mobile burger business Cook's hot-dog operation – established by Roger Cook for the purposes of the programme – was closed down and towed away by rival traders. The film appeared to show Mr Persico in a bad light. The magistrate declined to grant the adjournment, saying he had not seen the film.

Things were even better when at Leicester Crown Court on 27 November 1992, to cheers from the public gallery, he was acquitted of the threats to kill Clifford Taylor but convicted of reckless driving.

The Persico family had earlier had difficulties when in June 1985 Joe, then known as John, was sentenced to five years'

---

[10] *Independent*, 6 April 1991.

imprisonment. He was described by Mr Justice Hayden Tudor as the ringleader of a gang who had kidnapped and then tortured 18-year-old Mark Coulson following an incident in Tops nightclub in Leicester in which Coulson, said Persico's counsel, had challenged him to a fight. When Persico had declined he had been attacked by other people and a broken glass had been pushed in his face. The judge pointed out that according to Coulson he had never seen Persico before.

As Coulson and another friend left the Range Inn on the Melton Road, Coulson was kidnapped and his friend chased away. Coulson was taken to Persico's home where he was punched and kicked and a wire put round his neck. He had a finger broken and his feet were stamped on. Finally he was thrown in a canal, fortunately in a shallow part.

Yorkshire has not escaped the growing trend of the kidnapping of relations of workers who have access to substantial funds rather than being rich in their own right. Sometimes, however, the victims have been able to strike back. In February 1994 two masked men broke into the Huddersfield house of a security van driver, bound and gagged his wife and then took Polaroid photographs of her with a shotgun pointed at her temple. She was forced to write a message to him. They then approached him after he and a co-driver had picked up cash to deliver to a local sub-post office. As he left the van to make the delivery, one man passed the co-driver a note to be given to the husband. He recognized the writing and drove after the men who were in a BMW. Along the road he rammed the vehicle but, after a chase, it got away. Some hours later his wife was found shaken but otherwise unharmed in the boot of the BMW where she had been during the chase.

A new form of organized crime has crept into the Midlands. The usually law-abiding Asian community is thought by observers to have some of the smartest players in the game. Credit cards and cheques which have been stolen in Midland cities have appeared in Liverpool and Manchester as well as in Southall within a matter of hours. Traveller's cheques stolen by one member would be cashed by a second and used by a third to buy heroin in India. There has also been a thriving trade in illegal immigrants. According to former Detective Superintendent Roy Herridge, new recruits to the Asian gangs such as the Tooti Nung and the Holy Smokes were recruited from school: 'They will start off in petty theft, graduating to burglaries at about the age of 15, moving up into bigger crimes. It appears to be an organization where any criminal talents are used to the fullest.'[11]

The same observers worry what will happen when, rather than if, some of those players put more than just a toe into the water of the drugs market.

[11] *Evening Standard*, 2 August 1989.

9

Dublin

As is the case with most police forces, the Irish Gardai would have you believe there are no organized gangs in their territory and never have been. 'Have a good holiday but I can tell you you're wasting your time,' said an experienced and long-serving Detective Sergeant. He was speaking of professional, as opposed to political, criminals. Yes, there had been and probably still were a few small independent operators in the professional field such as Charlie Ainscough, a sort of Dublin version of Fagin, who had a few boys and prostitutes thieving for him. Poor Charlie had been found dead by a police officer, and when his body had been removed to the morgue it was discovered that £10,000 was sewn in the nightshirt. The Gardai who found him had never been allowed to forget it. There was another man who went round dressed as a policeman passing cheques and, of course, there was the famous MacArthur murder, the professor who killed a nurse in a park when she found him trying to steal her car and then shot dead a man from whom he was buying a gun. He was found at a football match sitting next to the Attorney-General, who later resigned. And the film *The Field* was based on the murder of a man called Moore. But these were all isolated incidents. What about the man they called 'The General' who was said to wear a pig's mask? Surely he was organized crime? Well, yes, but he was probably in retirement, following years of successful hounding by the Gardai. The Dunne family? They were simply small-time criminals.

Not everyone would agree with the assessment of the situation

205

and the bland dismissal of 'The General' and the Dunne family. What they would agree was that crime took off in a big way in the 1960s. Before then there had certainly been gangs. In the 1940s there was the Animal Gang, led by a former heavyweight professional boxer, from Sean McDermott Street, Buckingham Street and Gardiners Street in North Inner City. Like the Garvin and Moody gangs from Sheffield in the 1930s, they had been the heavy men at the Pitch-and-Toss rings and had done a bit of protection, thieving, and touting on the side. At one time they had challenged (and failed to oust) the box-man Sartini who ran a Pitch-and-Toss gang in the Greenhills wielding a short-handled dray driver's whip.[1] Their end had come after a baton charge by the Gardai at a Balldoyle race meeting. They were said to be the sons of people who had served in the British Army. Then there was the Hatchet Mob who were mainly a fighting gang, and the Red Hand gang who also dabbled in extortion. But, and on this there is a consensus, apart from these minor villains, until the 1960s there was effectively no professional crime in Ireland. There were family disputes, certainly, but there was no theft or robbery. Says former Gardai, Jim Ridge, now a barrister:

> People were so poor, they had no time to go out stealing, they were simply trying to make a living. And they had nothing to steal. When I was a young officer, we dealt with gas-meter bandits. You would stop a boy in the street and sniff the coins in his pockets to try to smell the whiff of gas on them. If you wanted crime you had to go to the cinema and watch James Cagney say, 'Top of the world, Ma.'[2]

But crime did take off in the 1960s. Armed robberies jumped. In 1963 there had been none; twelve in 1969 (which netted the grand total of £7,782). By 1981 there had been 306 robberies with takings of over £1 million. Killings, which were almost invariably domestic matters in the 1960s, rose from an average of six to over twenty by the late 1970s.

In 1982 the US Embassy said that up to twenty-three replacement passports a day were being issued to their citizens who had

---

[1] It may seem strange that a man with such a name held sway in Dublin's half-world, but there had long been a strong Italian community in the city. Later the amusement arcades would be owned by other Italian families, the Senezios and their relations the Dal Rios.
[2] This was in the film *White Heat* (1949).

been robbed in Grafton Street, the main tourist area. By the summer of 1993 Jury's hotel reported forty-five incidents of thefts from visitors on their premises, and representatives of the tourist industry complained that there was a group of known pickpockets operating in the St Stephen's Green – Grafton Street – Trinity Street triangle between 11 a.m. and 4 p.m. along with an organized betting ring (mainly of travellers) in the area from Trinity College to the Tourist Office. Children and young adults were being dropped off at various beats, and disputes over territory were sorted out by older males. The pickpocketing ring was thought to be well organized, with one woman in possession of a radio which picked up Garda messages. There were now 90,000 indictable crimes recorded annually.

The Garda Report on Crime in 1990 showed that the value of property stolen was £36,376,810, of which 8 per cent had been recovered. This compared with a total of £33,023,563 the previous year.

The reasons for the increase in crime are complex. From Independence until the 1960s the Irish economy had stagnated until with the social revolution things began to pick up. In the 1930s the old IRA had avoided commercial crime. Post offices were attacked, but only because they belonged to 'an illegitimate' state. Now the upturn in the economy coincided with the troubles in the North. In the late 1960s the IRA and Republican movement became radicalized and moved to the political left. Splinter groups such as Saor Eire (Free Ireland) rose and then waned. Political and criminal alliances were formed, so that the distinction between commercially orientated and political fund raising blurred. Some of the proceeds would go to the party and some would stay with the commercial arm of the temporary partnership.

It was also found that it was extremely easy to rob banks and this in turn coincided with the rise of the Dunne family. They were – and Christy, known as Bronco, in particular was, say admirers – the first to raise the motor-car robbery to an Irish art-form. The father Christopher, also known as Bronco, married in 1936. He came from the Liberties/Dolphin's Barn area and worked part-time as a docker. As a young man he had served twelve months for manslaughter after hitting a youth who had struck his mother.

At the time of his marriage his bride was 15 and worked a

clothing stall in Francis Street Market, and he was 22. She was to have twenty-two pregnancies and fifteen surviving children. Ten of them racked up 150 convictions between them, and eight of the eleven brothers went to industrial school for larceny. Hubert drowned whilst trying to save other boys who were in difficulties. His brother John saw the tragedy, and left Ireland to become a building contractor in England. By the time he was 18 Christy Jr, born in 1938, reckoned he had done two hundred burglaries. In 1960 he stole a judge's car. He would say of the family, 'We knew we could depend on one another with our lives. We are totally dedicated to one another.'

Henry Dunne, aged 8, and his elder brother, Larry, had caused a stir in May 1960 when they were found in London. A photograph was captioned: 'Anyone lost a son?' They were claimed by their father who had come to find work in England and told them, 'You can stay with me.' Wrong. They were packed off back to Dublin to begin a circuit of industrial schools and remand homes. In the September Larry was put on probation for theft and loitering and on 31 January the following year he was sentenced to two years' Borstal for attempted larceny. He did not last long on the outside after his release; this time it was for stealing from gas meters and he earned a year in Letterfrack.

By the time he had served the sentence his family had gone to Birmingham. One of Larry Dunne's closer friends was Eamonn Saurin, an accomplished armed robber who a decade later was wanted for questioning there for the murder on 6 November 1972 of pensioner Kenneth Adams. On 16 July 1981 Saurin was arrested over the murder of fellow armed robber Christy McAuley in an argument over a woman, an ironic situation as McAuley was a well-known homosexual. This was done in the full view of Lawrence 'Chickey' Maguire who, quite properly, refused to give evidence. The refusal did not help Saurin much; he was convicted at Birmingham in 1982 and received life imprisonment.

Larry continued to flit in and out of prison. Most years in the 1960s and 1970s there was a conviction or two. 1974, for example, was a good (or bad) year when there were eight, double the total for the previous year. In 1980 he was disqualified from driving for twenty years. By this time he had racked up ten convictions for traffic offences. Now he was chauffeured by other members of his family and friends. He said this was the best thing that could happen to him; now he could change cars at will and so confuse the Gardai. Dunne had returned to Dublin in 1969, by which time some of his brothers had begun to deal in drugs, something he seems to have avoided wherever possible. In the meantime, however, Larry Dunne concentrated on raids on banks and post offices to finance him and the rest of his family. Bank raids in which he was not involved also continued.

On 20 February 1970 seven men in a Cortina and Triumph 2000 cut all the telephone wires into the village of Rathdrum in Co. Wicklow and robbed the Hibernian Bank there of £1,500. In a particularly daring move, they stopped the local Gardai and ordered them to throw the keys of their car on to the road.

The influence of Saor Eire, which extended for only a two- or three-year period from 1967, more or less collapsed after the killing of an unarmed Gardai officer, Richard Fallon, outside the Royal Bank on Arran Quay, Dublin on 3 April 1970. No one was convicted. Previously the organization had staged a spectacular double bank raid in Newry in March 1969 when some £22,000 was taken.

The fortunes of members of the Dunne family ebbed and flowed towards the end of the 1970s, reaching a low point in 1977 when Larry was accidentally shot, and an even lower pitch when in 1980 Henry was asked to burn a garage and was trapped when it ignited prematurely. Rescued and taken to a doctor in Dun Laoghaire, he was given large doses of morphine, which was the beginning of his habit. Things picked up for him that year when he was later acquitted of a robbery at the Bank of Ireland in Finglas.

In a profile in the *Sunday Press* the Dunne family are seen as the first non-addicts who were able to organize the distribution of drugs, and as a result they prospered.[3] By 1981 Larry in particular had adopted a high profile, as did such other gang-leaders as the Krays and Glasgow's Arthur Thompson. He was seen at the ringside of boxing tournaments. When the daughter of a member of the family married, an invitation to a prominent newspaper editor was only declined at the last minute; and when his sister, Colette, needed bail on a drugs charge those queueing up to stand on her behalf included a barrister, a building contractor and a company director. She ultimately received two years. When Henry Dunne went down in February 1983

[3] 26 June 1983.

for drug offences Father Michael Sweetman, a prominent Jesuit, was there to give a character reference, before the judge handed down a ten-year sentence on firearm offences. Like Arthur Thompson after him, Henry, unemployed at the time of his arrest, lived in a council house, but it was one equipped with more than the bare necessities of life. Mock Tudor woodwork had been added to the porch and inside, along with a private bar there was a sauna.

Laurence Dunne did not stay around for the result of his second trial in 1983; he absconded on the second last day of the proceedings. He had been arrested not at his new house in Sandyford which had panoramic views of the city, but in his more modest establishment in Rathfarnham. When Drug Squad detectives broke in to his home in October 1980, under a pillow in a bedroom they found 70 grammes of heroin. In the living-room cocaine was discovered, and there was also cannabis in the house. Seamus Dunne, another member of the family, was in the house at the time; he had an envelope with £3,000 in it. Laurence Dunne said that he would accept responsibility for anything found in his home. The first jury disagreed.

In his absence, at the second trial the jury found Laurence guilty, and he was sentenced to fourteen years' imprisonment. He was retrieved two years later from Portugal, where he had been seen getting off the ferry at the little port of Villa Real de Santo Antonio in the Algarve. His wife, Lily, was sentenced to nine years' imprisonment. Two years later his house failed to reach its reserve of £220,000.

For a short while after Larry Dunne's conviction *in absentia* it seemed as though a small Northside operation, the Gang of Six, might take over his drugs empire. Unfortunately for the group it lacked anyone of sufficient stature to command respect, and heavies such as Harry McOwen were recruited to give the gang something of a presence. To finance a drug deal the gang embarked on the hi-jack of an ambulance, to be used in a raid on a cash consignment travelling from Belfast to the Central Bank in Dublin. But the hi-jack went hopelessly wrong when one of the ambulance drivers managed to get free and gave the alarm. The Army was invited to provide an additional escort and the raid was called off. Shortly after that McOwen, who had in the past had associations with both Saor Eire and the INLA, was shot outside the North Cumberland Street Labour Exchange.

But the consensus is that the nearest thing Dublin has had to a master criminal is the man known as 'The General'. Just as the identities of masked wrestlers have been common knowledge amongst the *cognoscenti* so, for some years before his unmasking, the name of 'The General' was well known and newspapers took to referring to him as 'the man who denies he is The General'.

Finally in October 1987 the *Sunday World* took its presses in its own hands and splashed the headline: Gardai name No 1 crime family.[4]

It told of Martin Cahill's sister Ann, serving eight years for possession, and her husband, Hugh Delaney, heavily involved in the city drugs trade; of the death of one brother, Anthony, in the Curragh military jail of a drug overdose and another, Pat, in a knife fight. Two other brothers were convicted in 1979 for an armed raid on the payroll at Smurfits in Clonskeagh. John, who during the raid was shot by Gardai, was sentenced to ten years' imprisonment and brother Eddie to twelve.

In 1975 Anthony had been charged with the murder of bank official John Copeland, found dead in his basement flat on the Palmerstown Road. The case against him had been that his fingerprints were found in Copeland's flat, and the theory was that Copeland had been stabbed when he disturbed burglars. Cahill was acquitted after accounting for the presence of his fingerprints by telling the jury that he had burgled Copeland's flat a few hours before the murder. Later Anthony was convicted of participation in an armed robbery. In prison at the Curragh military camp used for difficult prisoners, he repeatedly complained of being beaten up.

Brother Pat went down in Ballyfermot, stabbed to death in the summer of 1987. Anthony Quinn, charged with his murder, was acquitted after telling the court that Patrick had stabbed his father. The Gardai said that the Cahill family had given no help in the investigation and had declined to identify the body.

Martin Cahill grew up in the Holyfield slums, at that time some of the worst in the Dublin area. At the age of 11 he was convicted of housebreaking, for which he was given probation, and in 1965 at the age of 15 he was sent to St Conleths, again for housebreaking. Discipline was harsh. He recalls there was a

[4] *Sunday World*, 11 October 1987.

special strap known as the impurity strap for those caught in homosexual acts. Four years later he married Frances Lawless, whom he had met whilst working in Goodbody's making sacks. That was his last known job. He was next convicted of receiving cigarettes and a watch and was sentenced to four years' imprisonment, being released in 1973.

Now, when he was organizing the Prisoners' Rights Organization, Cahill ran up against Ned 'The Buffalo' Ryan when the latter was promoted to Detective Superintendent. According to Cahill, Ryan said he would be putting the squeeze on petty criminals who would be 'reduced to robbing grannies' handbags'. According to the *Today Tonight* programme, Cahill was responsible for the hiring of hitmen to assassinate Ryan.

Then in February 1988 it was announced that Cahill would be named in a programme by RTE. The announcement came after a £30 million dragnet the previous year when it was believed that 'The General' had got away with the Beit art robbery on 21 May 1986.[5]

The alarm went off at 2 a.m. and when Gardai officers arrived they were told by staff that everything was all right. The loss of the paintings was not discovered until 9 a.m. when the gallery opened to the public. Seven of the less valuable paintings were found discarded during the day. It is suggested that the gang had deliberately triggered off the alarm to lure the Gardai into a false sense of security.

The Beit collection had had an unhappy career. Begun by his diamond-mining uncle in South Africa, it had been brought to Russborough House in 1952 by Sir Alfred Beit, a former British MP who had retired to Co. Wicklow. On 26 April 1974 a gang of four armed men and the British heiress, Dr Rose Dugdale, had stolen nineteen paintings from the hundred-strong collection. Sir Alfred and his wife had been assaulted and tied up whilst the paintings – a Vermeer, a Goya, two Gainsboroughs and three Reubens – were removed.

Demands were made to the director of the National Gallery for £500,000 and the transfer from British prisons of the Price sisters who had been convicted of terrorist bombing offences. Eleven days later the paintings were recovered undamaged in Co. Cork.

---

[5] 'The General: The world according to Martin Cahill,' Michael O'Higgins in *Magill*, March 1988.

Rose Dugdale was sentenced to nine years' imprisonment for her part and was released in 1980. The raid had also been an effort to obtain the release of her husband Eddie Gallagher, sentenced for his part in the kidnapping of Dr Tiede Herrema. After the recovery of the paintings Sir Alfred donated his collection to the state under the care of the Alfred Beit Foundation, and Russborough House was opened to the public in 1976.

This time, under the possible supervision of 'The General', the stolen paintings included Vermeer's 'Woman Writing a Letter', which of itself was thought to be worth in excess of £5 million, and a Goya portrait.

The robbery had gone down in December 1987 and in an unconnected incident 145 files, including those relating to the highly sensitive cases of Malcolm MacArthur and Father Molloy, the priest found dead in a businessman's home, were stolen from the DPP's office in September 1987.

Five weeks later an attempt was made to steal Renoir's 'Les Parapluies' and Monet's 'Sunshine and Snow' from Dublin's Municipal Gallery. At least seven raiders entered the premises, hiding the staff and two early morning visitors at gunpoint. When they tried to remove the paintings the security alarm went off and the robbers fled. At that time it was thought that both raids were connected and they were the work of an England-based gang of international art thieves. The Gardai were strengthened in this belief because no demand was made for the return of the paintings from the Beit collection.

'The General' had first come to prominence in the £90,000 armed robbery at Rathfarnham Shopping Centre, and a decade later in July 1983 he was regarded as the prime figure in the £2 million robbery of the Thomas O'Connor and Sons' jewellery factory in Harold's Cross. It was a robbery about which the Gardai had advance information. On a number of occasions the premises had been staked out by them but no one had appeared. Now, on the night of 26 July, with only twenty-five of the 100-strong staff at work, the gang hid in a boilerhouse at the premises. As each member arrived they were locked in a lavatory, and when all had been accounted for the manager Dan Fitzgibbon was made to open the strong-room. It took thirty minutes for the gang to load their vans before they left, setting off a smoke bomb as they did so, something which led the locked-in staff to fear they would be burned alive. By the time the

Gardai were notified the jewellery was in parcels all over Dublin.

A reward of £25,000 was offered for information but not a single call was made. A fraction of the stolen property was recovered, some buried in a back garden in Terenure (a suburb near the Cahill home) and some more, but not much, in Norway. There were rumours that there had been an attempted drugs-for-jewellery swap in England, but Cahill maintains he has never been involved in drug dealing. The raid broke the company, which was insured for only £900,000 of its £2 million loss; it went into receivership four years later.

It was over this raid that the story grew up that when gold from the robbery had gone missing 'The General' had a suspect nailed to the floor. In an interview he commented, 'I've heard the story. I can only say there might be some truth in it, but I wasn't there at the time.' He went on to suggest that the blame for the incident could more properly be laid on some over-enthusiastic and undisciplined gang members. The gold was the stolen property dug up from the back garden in Terenure, and Cahill is said to accept that they nailed the wrong man.[6]

Six months later on 11 March 1984 Provos kidnapped Thomas Gaffney as he left the Park Inn public house at Harold's Cross, home of the famous Irish greyhound stadium.

The next, say Gardai officers, came in December 1984 after a robbery of £90,000 from the Quinsmith branch in Rosemount Shopping Centre in Rathfarnham. Cahill has persistently denied any involvement, but has been monitored by the Gardai from that date.

In the 1980s it was possible to lay the blame for almost every major operation at 'The General's' door, and his name was first in the frame when it was discovered that over a hundred sets of documents had been stolen from the offices of the DPP at St Stephen's Green in early September 1987. They included the files on Malcolm MacArthur, convicted of killing Bridie Gargan in 1982,[7] and the death of Father Niall Molloy who died

---

[6] Neil McCormick, 'Is this Ireland's most wanted man?', *GQ Magazine*, December 1991.
[7] On 12 January 1983 the socially well-connected Malcolm MacArthur, then aged 36 and who had just run through the money left to him by his wealthy father, was jailed for life for the killing of a 25-year-old nurse Bridie Gargan.

After he had run through his £80,000 inheritance MacArthur – who had a 9-year-old son by a girlfriend, Brenda Lyttle – planned to obtain more funds by armed robbery. His first step was to steal a car, and it was while he was attempting to steal Bridie Gargan's

at the home of Co. Offaly businessman Richard Flynn in 1985. In a sensational case Flynn had been acquitted of the manslaughter of Father Molloy, but the priest's family was taking action in the civil courts claiming £7,500 for mental distress under the Civil Liability Act.

It was, however, on the evening of 30 November 1988 that members of 'The General's' gang went too far in their escapades. Ann Gallagher, the postmistress at Kilmanagh, and her landlady were kidnapped from their home. The next morning she was made to go to Kilmanagh post office and withdraw cash and stamps worth nearly £30,000. With her was Myles Crofton, who had a radio-controlled bomb strapped to his chest. After the raid a high-profile seventy-strong surveillance unit was set up to monitor and harry the activities of 'The General', his henchmen and other target criminals.

In their turn the criminals did not make life easy for the Gardai. As they drove into housing estates they would be rammed by stolen cars. Shortly after Christmas, an informer told the Gardai that Detective Superintendent Ned Ryan, known as 'The Buffalo', was to be killed. The newspapers reported that his reaction was a characteristic laugh, but the strain of the following months told on his health.

One of the arrangements of 'The General's' gang was that associates were free to work on their own, and the surveillance on two worked well. On 23 February James 'Shavo' Hogan was found in possession of firearms and received eight years' imprisonment. Cahill was questioned and released without charge.

Four months later Eamonn Daly, one of 'The General's' most trusted lieutenants, went down for twelve years for robbery. The

Cont'd
Renault in Phoenix Park that she surprised him. She was returning to her car after sunbathing on a warm July day. He first threatened her with a replica gun and then hit her over the head with a hammer. He then put her in the back of the vehicle and drove off. A passing ambulance driver seeing a hospital sticker on the nurse's car presumed MacArthur was a doctor with a patient and, sounding his siren, led the vehicle to St James's Hospital. MacArthur did not however stop, but drove out of the exit gates and abandoned the car two miles away. Nurse Gargan died four days later.

MacArthur was arrested in the flat of the senior law officer, the Irish Attorney-General, Patrick Connolly, whom he knew through Ms Lyttle. After MacArthur's arrest Connolly, seemingly blind to the implications of his action, went to America on holiday, but was recalled by the Prime Minister, Charles Haughey. The affair contributed to the defeat of the Haughey-led Fianna Fail party in the next general election. Another allegation of murder, that of a farmer from whom it was suggested MacArthur went to buy a shotgun, was left on the file.

adopted son of a Crumlin schoolteacher, he had sixteen convictions dating back to 1973 and was already on bail for a 1985 robbery on the Equity Bank in Grafton Street (which had netted £13,000) when, on 26 March, he was arrested by Dun Laoghaire Gardai during an attempted robbery at Sandyford. Martin Cahill's brother, Michael, eventually pleaded guilty to receiving the proceeds of the Grafton Street robbery.

Daly was one of two men wearing false beards and moustaches who followed a Securicor employee into the Atlantic Homecare centre. In turn he was followed by plain-clothes detectives. When a gun was seen to be pointed at them by Daly, they jumped on him; he was found to have a loaded 9mm semi-automatic pistol in his pocket. Two other men escaped following a shoot-out.

In court, the financing of Daly's £40,000 house in Terenure was explained. He had done it with £17,000 damages from a car accident, a £5,000 government grant and a £5,000 corporation grant. After his conviction he went on a 'dirty protest' in the maximum security prison at Portlaose, complaining that he was being housed with subversive prisoners. Also protesting were the Border Fox, Dessie O'Hare, and two members of his gang, Fergal Toal and Eddie Hogan, along with Michael McHigh serving forty years for the murder of a Gardai sergeant.

The war with 'The General' has produced tales of valour from both sides. At one time when the police were surrounding the house, something they appear to have done over long periods in the 1980s and 1990s:

> He wouldn't let us in; came to the door with a great big butcher's knife. One of our lads shot a dog which he thought was attacking him. Meanwhile a girl with a baby in a pram left and after that Martin came to the door and in we went, peaceful as anything. The lad said he was sorry about the dog but Martin didn't seem to mind and said he was no fucking good anyway. Of course the girl should have been stopped. Talk about Homer nodding.

Cahill maintains, 'You must never, ever look at them [the Gardai]. Their presence must never be acknowledged.' To this end, like Orphée, he had removed the reflecting glass from his wing mirrors.

Sometimes the Gardai won an engagement. Sometimes the wins were shortlived. On 13 August 1991 Cahill appeared, hooded and handcuffed, to face charges of dangerous driving, obstruction and a breach of the peace. He had been remanded in custody for a psychiatric evaluation after the arresting Garda officer Ciaran McCarthy had alleged his actions had been those of a completely irrational man. According to the officer, Cahill had stripped off on the road and again at the station.

According to the papers no report was available and Cahill was released on £100 bail. When he emerged from the District Court in Dublin, he had on a white nightshirt, and had a mask and a model of a bird's nest strapped to his forehead. 'One Flew Under the Cuckoo's Nest' was handwritten on the front and back of the nightshirt. Cahill blew a duck decoy, asked one of the many reporters whether he was a chicken and, after enquiring whether a nearby bicycle was a boat and whether the street was the River Liffey, rode off in some triumph.

As mentioned earlier, in January 1986 the theft of some £30 million paintings, including works by Vermeer and Goya, took place from the state-owned Sir Alfred Beit collection housed in Russborough House, Co. Wicklow, and sixteen months later John Patrick Naughton of Templeogue, Dublin was remanded in custody in London, charged with dishonestly handling £12.5 million of the paintings which were bound for Geneva.

In the autumn of 1987 the Gardai received what was a humiliating setback in their efforts to retrieve the paintings and arrest those responsible for their disappearance. A Dutch criminal and informant was contacted with a view to the disposal of some of the paintings. He contacted the Dutch police, and was later given a relatively small-value painting to prove the bona fides of the vendors. A 'sting' operation was set up and a Dutch detective posing as a French art dealer was shown one of the Beit paintings in a Dublin hotel. The meeting was monitored by the Gardai, and a further meeting was arranged when the detective was told to travel alone to the Kilakee Woods. Over thirty armed detectives were in the area, with about half a dozen following the buyer to his rendezvous; the remainder waited for instructions in a nearby hotel. At a crucial moment in the surveillance, the electronic state-of-the-art surveillance equipment failed and a detective had to phone a near-by bus depot for directions. The gang disappeared on their high-powered motor-bikes and no arrest was made. What apparently had happened was that two paintings were produced in the Kilakee Woods at about 2 p.m.

on Sunday 27 September 1987. A series of false trails had been laid to divert the Gardai surveillance unit, and when the Gardai on the ground radioed for assistance they were unable to secure direct contact. By the time the Gardai had made their way through the boggy ground of the woods the vendors had gone. The Gardai did, however, carry out an unsuccessful search of the woods to see if any paintings had been left behind. The force had had similar troubles four years previously when in the Don Tidey kidnapping in 1983 in Ballinamore, Co. Antrim, armed men had also evaded a Garda dragnet.

'The General's' reputation soared when in February 1988 as part of the reprisals for surveillance and damage to his own car, twenty cars belonging to the Gardai were damaged at Stacksdown Golf Club, used almost exclusively by Gardai. Eleven greens were also dug up. A few days earlier a group of men had attacked a Nissan Bluebird belonging to 'The General'. The Gardai accepted that they were at the time keeping 'The General' under surveillance, but would not confirm they were in the area.

In April 1988 Cahill was bound over to keep the peace in sureties of £1,500 for a year, having been found by the court to have been threatening both neighbours and members of the Gardai. Evidence in the case was that detectives had been offered £20 notes by Cahill whilst his son stood by with a camera. This was not an altogether new technique: 'Once or twice we'd stop him and he'd pull out a tape recorder and start dictating his protest into it. Then he'd pull down his trousers and show us his Mickey Mouse underpants. Several times we left him without them.'

In court for the hearing Cahill wore a wig, a false moustache and glasses. Outside he immediately donned a ski-mask. 'There's nothing wrong in that,' says a Garda. 'He's an ugly-looking fucker.'

In *Magill* Cahill is described as bearing '. . . a close resemblance to Bob Hoskins in *The Long Good Friday* or to Del Boy in *Only Fools and Horses*'.

In June 1988, acting on a tip-off, detectives went to Cahill's house where after a search the Gardai say they found a loaded .45 Colt in the water-tank. The subsequent decision of the DPP not to prosecute angered senior officers, who believe this was a cast-iron opportunity to score even a minor triumph. The thinking may have been, however, that someone with a grudge against Cahill may have planted the gun himself and then given the tip-off.

By 1993 'The General' seemed, by all accounts, to be slowing down in the scale of his operations.

On 24 April 1993 at about 8 p.m. the Gardai received a complaint from a Mrs Sile Holmes of Swan Grove, Ranelagh, that Cahill along with his son, Christopher, and armed with sledgehammers, had forced open the front door, and smashed three television sets as well as windows and mirrors.

Shortly afterwards both 'The General' and his son, the latter noted to be sweating heavily, were stopped near by and taken to the police station. Not long after that, along came Frances Cahill together with Glen Holmes. Later Mr Holmes ordered the Gardai from his mother's house and prevented them from taking the sledgehammer for examination. The matter was dropped.

But there are now more violent players than 'The General' even at his most tiresome, and a series of killings has all the hallmarks of gang warfare. In July 1992 it was apparent that the fragile peace which had established territorial boundaries between the six major warring gangs in the city had been fractured; fatally for Mick Travers, shot with four bullets from a pump-action shotgun outside his shop in Darndale. In December 1991 hairdresser Patrick 'Teasy Weasy' MacDonald had been executed in his salon in Fairview. Now, said the Gardai, Travers' death had the hallmarks of a gang killing – shotgun, motorcycle – as did that of MacDonald. MacDonald, armed robber and Irish National Liberation Army renegade, was believed by the Gardai to have run a one-man crime wave in a series of robberies on pubs and shops in the North Inner City. He was gunned down in front of customers in his shop; the lone gunman then stood over him and fired further shots into his body. It was the second attempt on the life of a man who had been into protection in the North City centre. Informed observers believe that his death was the result of his interference with the drugs scene controlled by Northside brothers.

They were quick to rule out four of the gangs, including that of 'The General' whom it was thought was now more devoted to tyre-slashing than other crime. A second family-based gang thought to control the heroin trade in the South of the City, and being investigated in connection with the importation of a large quantity of chemicals into Dublin that month, was ruled out on the basis that it was 'well organised, everybody knows which is their turf and they have never had to resort to serious violence.'[8]

The other Southside gang eliminated from Garda inquiries was one controlled by a Donnybrook man who specialized in protection rackets in parts of Dublin 2, as well as Ringsend and Irishtown in Dublin 4. He had been questioned over the killing of Jackie Kelly in Pearse Street in the 1980s, and was thought to have handled some of the Beit paintings as well as being a fire-raiser in the South Docks in 1990.

So far as the Northside was concerned, the position was more complicated. There were thought to be two major criminal organizations: the first operated by a man living in Swords, north of Dublin, and the second, and far the more organized and dangerous, run by a family from the North Inner City. The two units had co-operated on various projects. It was the North Inner City family who were believed to have been behind the 1990 Finglas mail-van robbery, as well as hiring the killers who shot Patrick MacDonald in Marino in December 1991.

There was, however, also the possibility that karate-expert Travers had been the subject of an independent contract as he worked in his shop in Darndale. He was not a well-liked man; he liked to hit and hurt people. According to one comment:

> He hit people he knew and people he didn't. People who knew him knew better than to fight back but in a pub he would spill a drink on somebody deliberately or push somebody. When they reacted he would ask them to step outside. If they did he invariably beat them up. If they didn't he would nab them at closing time.

Another said, 'He would kick you as soon as look at you.'

After MacDonald's death the Gardai drew up a list of operators in the city whom they believed were capable of contract killings. It included two ex-paramilitaries who had, at one time, had links with the INLA and were associated with the North City gang. One was suspected of the killing of Danny McKeown outside a Dublin labour exchange in 1982 and the murder, the following year, of Gerald Horrigan in Ballymun.

---

[8] Diarmaid Doyle quoting a Garda officer, *Sunday Tribune*, 19 July 1992.

Horrigan, who died in a drug war raging at the time, was chased into a block of flats by a motorcycle passenger and shot in the head and chest.

June 1993 saw the temporary end of Eamonn Kelly, regarded by the Gardai as one of the most organized and intelligent of criminals in Dublin, and one who at the time of his conviction was assuming Mafia-style status. His downfall, as is the case with so many, was drugs. Born in 1949, one of nine children in the Summerhill district of Dublin, he had already been convicted four times at the age of 19. Then two of his brothers, Matt and Des, offered him the chance to get out of crime, and he became the managing director of Kelly's Carpetdrome on Dublin's North Circular Road. Des left the business to go on his own in 1976, and five years later Matt and Eamonn Kelly's company went into receivership. The brothers were held personally liable for debts approaching £2 million.

Fire-raising is a particularly Dublin activity and the Kelly business had been bedevilled by arson attacks. On 14 June 1982, the evening before the High Court liquidator was to assume control of the premises, the group's headquarters on the North Circular Road was destroyed by fire. This was by no means the only misfortune the group was to suffer. The next month up went the Fiesta club in Talbot Street, whilst a year earlier Matt Kelly's Silver Shadow Rolls-Royce was set on fire and, sadly for children, two haulage containers full of Christmas toys went up in flames whilst parked outside the Glasnevin cemetery.

Three years later Eamonn was in some difficulties, and he was sentenced to ten years for stabbing a union official. The verdict was set aside on the basis that one of the main witnesses against him had a conviction for manslaughter which had not been disclosed to the defence. On the re-trial Kelly was convicted of an assault and sentenced to three years' imprisonment. The Gardai maintain that on his release he became a major player in Dublin's underworld. Investigations into his involvement with forged currency and drug importations came to nothing until a three-month surveillance in the summer of 1992 ended in his arrest over possession of one kilo of cocaine, which would have a street value of £180 a gram. At the time, the father of nine children was unemployed and receiving £140 social security per week, but he had raised £20,000 necessary to enter the game. The drugs were smuggled by Cuban Elisabeth Yamonoha, taped in folds of fat to her stomach, and the pair were arrested in Jury's hotel. She received a sentence of four years.

At the time of his sentence in 1984, Kelly's lieutenants were brothers from another Dublin family, but by now they were breaking out on their own. In early 1987 they were suspected of involvement in the £1 million Securicor robbery in Fairview. One, a successful grocer, was investigated, to no effect, with regard to fire-bomb attacks on rival premises.

According to Patrick Hickey, who pleaded guilty to receiving £191,000 taken in an armed raid from guards when they were loading cash-bags from the bank at Marino Mart on 27 January 1987, he had been pressured by one of the brothers into helping launder the money, making trips to Newry to pay the money into an account kept by a brother which had been opened just eight days after the robbery.

The van, which did not have a Gardai escort, had just completed thirteen collections when it was attacked outside the Bank of Ireland. Another of the receivers, Francis Sheridan, who had been found with £220,000 in a bag in the attic of his Swords home, received a sentence of twenty-one months.

The undercover Gardai exercise to nail the robbers themselves had aborted when detectives moved on Hickey as he was passing a package containing £80,000.

In November 1984 a fire destroyed the fittings and furnishings of Edward Hutch's home at Portland Place on the North Circular Road, Dublin. Three years later Mr Hutch was awarded £1,250 out of his claim for £20,000 against the Dublin Corporation. Hutch had told the court that he was an inept thief, being caught every time he pulled a job. Not so, thought Judge James Carroll who branded him as 'an idle and dishonest character'. Hutch, who produced receipts for the furnishings, had claimed he had earned his money by breeding German Shepherds and bulldogs, selling colours and hats at sporting events and from gambling.

There was success for the Gardai when John Gilligan was sentenced to four years for receiving. The Gardai believed he was leader of the so-called Warehouse Gang, operating as all good thieves should by specializing in identifying a ready market for a particular brand of stolen goods, whether it was animal drugs, videos, video games, or children's clothes. The gang, which had operated almost unchecked for ten years, would raid the target

The queue for the public gallery for the Cameo Murder Trial (*Liverpool Daily Post & Echo*)

Herbert Balmer, doyen of Liverpool Detectives
(above)
(*Liverpool Daily Post & Echo*)

Places to cache your drugs: in Alma Grove, Bermondsey, a stash of heroin was found under a gnome
(below)
(*Martin Goodwin*)

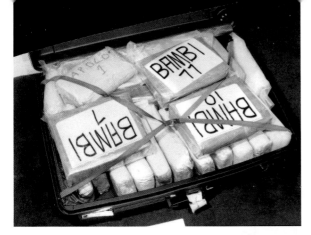

Or try a case of Bambis
(above)
(*Enterprise News*)

Floated in on a surfboard
(right)
(*Enterprise News*)

**Be careful what you eat,
these are not yet more
bread rolls**
(below)
(*Topham*)

Jimmy Nash (centre), **Ronnie Kray and Christine Keeler out on the town**

Micky and Linda Calvey
(left)

**Johnny Rice, friend
of Jack Spot, at
Brighton races**
(below)
(*Syndication International*)

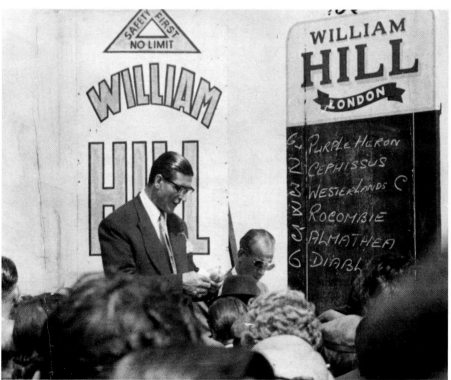

**Tommy Falco,
'victim' of another
gang slashing**
(*Syndication International*)

**The Cardiff 3 outside
the High Court
16 December 1992**
(*Enterprise News*)

Viv Graham(left)
shot in Newcastle on
New Year's Eve 1993
(with his friend Rob
Armstrong)
(*Newcastle Journal*)

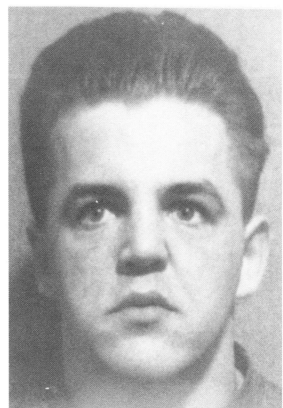

Lee Duffy
(*North News &*
Pictures)

Joe Persico, victim of the beefburger feud
(above)
(*Leicester Mercury*)

A 'bubble' of supergrasses with their warders in Bedford Prison
(below)
(*Rex Features*)

factory on a Friday night, and by the time the loss was noticed the goods would have been distributed throughout Dublin; they were then sold to small-time dealers or shops, and on occasions would be sold back to the losers.

Gilligan was trapped when he was seen unloading hardware goods from a lorry in the Walkinstown district. At a previous sentence hearing, the 38-year-old former seaman had been described in court as having no other income than from crime. In 1988 he had been living on social security of £50 a week, from which he was maintaining three ponies at livery in a local riding school. By the time of his conviction in November 1990, he had acquired a house and stables in Co. Meath.

Just as the mainland has been the scene for drug trafficking, so has the South West of Ireland where because of the particular terrain surveillance is difficult. At one time or another Howard Marks (see pp. 294–296) and James Humphreys – the porn king of Soho in the 1970s – have been alleged to have operated there along with Mark's friend James 'call me the Shamrock Pimpernel' McCann.

After the successful Operation Julie in England in 1977, which broke a ring operating out of Hampton Wick in Middlesex, said to be producing £20 million of LSD annually, the price of a microdot soared from £1 to £5. Humphreys saw a gap in the market and along with two other Londoners went to Ireland to set up operations. There in Knocklong, a small village on the Limerick-Tipperary border with the nearest local Gardai point three miles away, and with Shannon in easy reach, he posed as a greyhound breeder and dealer. Jack and Donie Ryan, who owned the local pub The Cross, were in some financial straits and agreed to store chemicals for him. At the end of the day they were the ones to suffer. Humphreys fled to Spain. Donie Ryan received three years for aiding and abetting, and Jack committed suicide by injecting himself with a humane animal killer. The other Londoners were acquitted after a re-trial.

Just as the Gardai had found it difficult to adjust to the modern car bandit, so they found difficulties in coping with the increase in drug trafficking. One man who was a shining example of humanity was Garda officer Dinny Mullins. People describe him as a true Christian who understood and wanted to help junkies, drug dealers and their problems. It is substantially due to him that there was a crackdown on the estates against

223

drug dealers, but this did not occur before a number of families were ruined by the trade.

Prostitution has recently been more of a problem in Dublin than in cities in Great Britain. In 1983 John Cullen, a protector, was killed in a dispute over the protection of a girl, and four years later it was said that it cost £200–£300 (Irish punts) for a girl to get free of a pimp who was estimated to take 80 per cent of her wages. The cost was to hire a group to deal with the pimp and explain the facts of life. Prostitution continued to flourish around the canals, and of the approximately one hundred working around Fitzwilliam Square thirty were thought to be from Britain, remitting their earnings to that country. English girls kept such brothels as there were mainly for political and foreign clients.

Outside Dublin it seems the professional criminals kept their grip on such country sports as dog-fighting. In 1988 there was said to be a ring at Ballyfermot with thousands of punts being gambled on dogs which cost £600 plus for a male pup.

One breeder who refused to sell his dogs and threatened to report those involved was persuaded not to. He said:

> . . . these guys are deadly, they are far more dangerous than all the drug pushers and shotgun merchants around here. Everyone knows who they are but fear grips the community. The money these guys gamble each week is enormous and anyone who tries to stop them is simply asking for trouble.[9]

On perhaps a wider but less dangerous note, there has been a concerted attempt by gangs to shake down the Dublin Corporation. When one man claimed he had fallen on an uneven pavement, records showed that three out of four of his brothers and sisters and six cousins had all made claims over accidents on the particular corner where the man had fallen.

[9] *Magill*, March 1988.

10

Women

Towards the end of 1992 a conference on professional crime was organized under the auspices of the University of London. At the end of the afternoon when there was a general audience discussion, there was considerable support for the view that women were moving out from what has been seen as the traditional supporting role of their brothers, fathers and lovers and into independent operator status. Indeed, there was some admiration and support for this change. It was almost as if it was now politically incorrect to suggest that women criminals were dependent upon men for their livelihood. The feeling seemed to be that women could and should be as bad as or, preferably, worse than their male counterparts.

Yet as a general rule, certainly in Great Britain and Ireland, and even in America where criminal history is littered with such formidable women as Kate Barker and Bonnie Parker, with few exceptions the role of the little woman in professional crime has been supportive rather than pro-active. Even the position of Kate 'Ma' Barker as an organizer of crime is debatable. The official FBI version of the woman who as a child saw Jesse and Frank James and possibly died under a hail of bullets in 1935, is that she was a great organizer who planned the kidnapping of millionaires William A. Hamm Jr and Edward Bremer, and killed her lover Arthur Dunlop. The distaff version is that she was more in the traditional mould as provider for and shelterer of her certainly lawless sons. There is also an argument that, far from wielding a machine-gun in the final battle in which she and her son

Freddy died, she shot herself early in the contest. Of Bonnie Parker's active participation in a series of raids in the Middle West there is no doubt. She was killed along with Clyde Barrow in a gun battle with a Texas Highway Patrol led by Captain Frank Hamer on 23 May 1934. A notable nineteenth-century American woman who played more than a subservient role in a criminal partnership was Jeanne Bonnet. She ran a gang of women – escapees from a San Francisco brothel in the 1970s – who survived on the water-front by a series of thefts and robberies. The gang did not last long after the death of their leader who was found shot in 1876. A twentieth-century example is Barbara Graham who ran with a gang of robbers in California in the 1950s. She tortured and then killed an elderly crippled widow, Mabel Monahan, in a failed jewel snatch. Graham was executed on 2 June 1955.

Rarely have women set up shop on their own so to speak. In America, where there has been more of a tradition of a female gang, those such as the Battle Row Ladies Social and Athletic Club, better known as the Lady Gophers, were only auxiliaries of the male all-Irish Gopher gang who ran Hell's Kitchen, the district around the 8th and 9th Avenues in Manhattan, in the early years of the century. The Lady Gophers sank along with their male counterparts when railroad police put a stop to the looting of freight cars along Eleventh Avenue.[1]

Of course there have been notable exceptions where wives, girlfriends and mistresses have played an equal part, but generally their activities have been confined to hiding and caretaking the spoils, obtaining sureties and keeping the network in touch when an arrest has been made, providing comforts so far as prison regulations allowed or they could evade them, and weeping during pleas in mitigation. The girls who attached themselves to Glasgow gangs were also useful in another way, and they were probably not alone in this. They would cache the weapons of their boyfriends when they were searched on entering dance halls and later, after the inevitable fighting was quelled, during further searches by the police. They rarely were searched themselves. It was easy for a girl to cause a great deal of trouble for an officer by making a complaint of indecent assault.

---

[1] Again, in more recent years such New York female gangs as the Dagger Debs were affiliated to the Daggers, whilst the Dragon Debs were associated with the Dragons, the Emperor Ladies with the Emperors etc. See K. Hanson, *Rebels in the Streets*, p. 15.

From time to time women such as the prostitute Marthe Watts could be relied on to mind the shop whilst the master – in her case the vice-king Carmelo Messina – was away. She could also be relied upon to set up diversionary tactics, as when she and Blanche Costaki made allegations against the journalist Duncan Webb when he was at the height of his investigations into the Messina brothers' prostitution empire. They complained to the police that Webb had threatened that if they did not part with £50, photographs just taken of them would appear in the *People*. They had offered £7 and he had refused. The police would have nothing to do with the complaint except to enter it into Webb's file.[2]

Occasionally, instead of playing the lure in the Murphy or Badger game[3] women would participate on their own terms. In modern times one woman conducted a blackmail racket of her own devising. She would accept a lift from a male driver or force her way into a car and then threaten to cry rape if money was not handed over. On one occasion she stripped naked in the back of a taxi-cab and the driver had a heart attack. She received a sentence of three and a half years at the Old Bailey.

[2] Duncan Webb, the journalist, had a career during which he seems to have worn both black and white hats. So far as the white hats are concerned, he undoubtedly brought down the Messina brothers with his crusading articles. Wearing his black hat, he acquired a conviction at Plymouth Magistrates' Court for communicating the movement of His Majesty's Ships. He had telephoned the *Daily Express* and spoken so loudly he had been overheard. He was fined £50 on 26 January 1944. More peculiar was his conviction at Marlborough Street on 8 August 1946 when he was bound over under the Prosecution of Offences Act and ordered to pay 2 guineas costs. A charge of grievous bodily harm was reduced to common assault and the magistrate dismissed a charge of impersonating a police officer. According to the evidence, Webb had picked up prostitute Jean Crews and agreed to have intercourse for £2. Mrs Crews told the court they went to her flat where he 'had connections with her and then went to the bathroom to cleanse himself'. He then would not leave the flat and she said she would call the police. In the street they met Herbert Gardner Wadham, and Webb allegedly showed him a press card, masking it as a police warrant card. He seems to have arrested Wadham and then struck him in the face. As they marched along Tottenham Court Road Wadham approached a temporary reserve police officer for help. At the police station Webb denied ever having seen Wadham before. Webb later married Cynthia Hume, wife of the murderer Donald of whom he remained in fear all his life. He died of a virus.

[3] The Badger game is a variation on a confidence trick. The victim goes to a hotel with a girl who is either very young or looks it. Shortly before intercourse takes place, but when both are undressed, the 'father' or 'uncle' of the girl bursts into the room and demands compensation for the violation of his under-age daughter or niece. This compensation may enable her to be sent away to boarding-school to forget the experience, and the mark can be squeezed for a lengthy period. If an older girl is used the 'father' can be replaced by the 'husband'. The Murphy game is the simple robbery of a client during or after intercourse, often by a ligger who has remained hidden during the proceedings.

At the end of the last century and during the early years of this, a genuine transatlantic example of independence was May Sharpe. Born in Dublin in 1876, she spent six years in a convent school before running off to New York at the age of 13 with £60 of her father's savings. She seems to have been a genuine operator on her own account. Of course she was obliged to rely on male help but, in her late teens, she was clearly the dominant and financially successful partner. In New York she met and married Dal Churchill, 'robber, highwayman, safe-cracker and rustler' who rode with the Daltons and was hanged near Phoenix, Arizona in 1891. May, now 15, went to Chicago where she became queen of the Badger game. During her career she would use the names of May Wilson, May Avery, Lilian White, Rose Wilson, Mary Brown, Margaret Smith and May Latimer, by which name Eddie Guerin, the safebreaker, knew her. At the age of 17 she had accumulated the astonishing sum of $300,000. Travelling to New York she is said to have teamed up with Charlie Becker, the corrupt police officer, before she moved on to Guerin in 1901. It does seem highly likely that she was under the protection of Becker because although whilst in New York and Detroit she was convicted in fourteen cases, including dealing in revolvers and larceny as well as the more mundane prostitution and disorderly conduct, she 'seems to have escaped so lightly as to have suffered practically no punishment at all'.[4]

Chicago May was a beautiful woman, very resourceful and courageous, what Hollywood would nowadays describe as a gunman's moll . . . [She] was no mere ornament of the alliance, but took her share of the planning and execution in many capacities. Seducing a bank-manager – to get impressions of his keys – or standing guard with a revolver while a safe was blown, or 'taking the dairy' [diverting

---

[4] Lieutenant Charles Becker (1869–1915) followed in the great tradition of corrupt New York policemen such as Inspector Alexander 'Clubber' Williams. After a re-trial Becker was convicted of complicity in the murder of the gambler Herman Rosenthal, who refused to pay protection money and was believed to be about to blow the story to Herbert Swope of the *New York World*. There is little doubt that the District Attorney Whitman bribed witnesses to secure the conviction. Becker was electrocuted in the most clumsy manner at Sing Sing on 7 July 1915. His wife attached a silver plate on the top of his coffin: *Charles Becker Murdered July 7 1915 by Governor Whitman*. (The District Attorney had clearly benefited from Becker's conviction.) She was persuaded to have it unscrewed when it was pointed out she might be prosecuted for criminal libel.

suspicion] in a counting house, all came equal to Chicago May.[5]

It is difficult to know how Guerin and May Churchill teamed up. In her book she says it was at a thief's funeral, but there is no doubt that within weeks they were working together.

On 26 April 1901 she, Guerin and a man known as 'Dutch Gus' removed £50,000 in francs and cheques from the Paris branch of the American Express Company, where they and their accomplices overpowered and gagged the attendant and blew the safe. Guerin and 'Dutch Gus' were sent to Devil's Island from which Guerin made his famous escape in 1905.[6] She and Emily Skinner, also a mistress of Guerin, had gone back to France to see what they could do to help. Both were arrested. Skinner was released after a week but Churchill received five years. As seems customary in those days, she did not serve the sentence out and was released early.

They met again in England, quarrelled at Aix-la-Chapelle – although Guerin was wanted in France he seems to have skipped across the Channel with impunity – and met up yet again this side of the water. It seems she was now blackmailing him, threatening him that if he did not look after her she would inform on him to the French authorities. It would certainly be her stock in trade. The officer in the attempted murder case which would follow, Inspector Stockley, described her as 'one of the most notorious women in London, whose chief business is to compromise and blackmail men. She has driven men to suicide by these means.'

At the committal proceedings of Churchill and Charles Smith on a charge of attempting to murder him, Guerin gave evidence that she said, 'You dirty bastard. If you don't take care of me I will send you back to Devil's Island where you will die like a dog. If I can't do you that way I will do you another.'

According to Emily Skinner, who it must be admitted may not have been a wholly disinterested witness, within ten minutes of that conversation Churchill was on her way to Tottenham Court Road police station.

Guerin went to prison to await an extradition to France to serve the remainder of his Devil's Island sentence. It was there he

[5] J. Phelan, *The Underworld*, p. 111–12.
[6] Ibid., p. 107 *et seq*; PRO: MEPO 3/346.

met Charles Smith, also Irish, a tinsmith by trade and, wrote May, a 'good prowler' by vocation who 'reminded me of my first husband'. He had been thrown out of Cape Town the previous year. He was also known as Cubine Jackson or Clarence Coldwell, and had clearly known May Churchill at some earlier time in their lives.

He was also capable of mixing things up. According to him, Guerin had wanted him to throw vitriol over Mrs Churchill and had told him to go to Pat Sheedy, 'a well-known sporting man who lived in New York' – in fact he owned a gaming house – who would give him $200 and then he could blind her. According to Guerin it was Smith who wanted to throw the acid of his own volition. He was apparently complaining that Mrs Churchill had not done enough for him while in prison.

Sir Richard Muir, for once acting on behalf of the defence, obtained Guerin's release on Friday 14 June 1907. Guerin spent the night with Emily Skinner and next day he had to go to see his lawyers and then the newspapers in Carmelite Street who were after his story. May had clearly patched things up with Smith – if indeed they needed patching – and was living with her new companion.

There is little doubt that Guerin was a violent man and May Churchill had every reason to be afraid of him. She and Smith took matters into their own hands and went looking for him. On 16 June 1907 they went to the Hotel Provence in Leicester Square where Guerin and Emily Skinner, who may have been Churchill's maid some time earlier, had been within the hour. An acquaintance there said it was just as well Guerin had gone. May said she was afraid he might throw acid over her; Smith said that if Guerin was a bad man he could be one too. They learned that the pair had gone to Bernard Street near Russell Square tube station, and they went after them in a hansom cab.

The whole episode was a blunder from start to finish. At the corner of Marchmont Street May called out, 'There he is.' Smith got out and fired six shots at Guerin at almost point-blank range, managing to hit him once in the foot. He hadn't finished firing before a police constable arrived and arrested Churchill. Guerin said, 'When you could not succeed in sending me back to Devil's Island you stoop to murder.' 'Yes,' she replied, 'and I am sorry we did not succeed.' Smith managed to get only a short distance before he was surrounded by police and civilians. He tried to shoot again, but the gun was now empty and he merely threw it at one of the bystanders. At the trial he alleged Guerin had fired at him first and had then tried to throw vitriol over Churchill. There was absolutely no evidence to support this. Churchill, arrested by the solitary constable, was taken to the police station followed by a rough crowd, some of them kicking the officer. During the mêlée she dropped her handbag and a witness, Robert Ward, who picked it up, noticed it had an open knife sticking through the side. 'I carry it for my own protection,' she replied when questioned about it. Smith tried to do the decent thing by her; when charged he replied, 'She has done nothing wrong. I don't see how you can charge her.'

Whilst in Holloway prison awaiting trial she did her cause no good. She wrote a letter to a Mr Thompson which was intercepted by the authorities.

Dear Ted,
I wish you to retain Purcell, otherwise I am done. They will not let me have bail everything has been kept back. As far as you are conserned (sic), those letters of yours would help me where you warn me of this man, will I use them, as your name would not appear. Good bye you might never see me again. This fellow Smith was the one Eddy got to throw the vitriol so you see I lost no time, turn the tables.

Yours as ever,
May

You can hear all from Arthur Newton.[7] Help me.

Smith received twenty years in the days when twenty years meant just that, and Chicago May had fifteen for her pains. She appears to have been a model prisoner and was released from Aylesbury when she had served a little over ten years. Smith served fifteen and, according to May Churchill's book, he was released early after the efforts of Lady Astor on his behalf. May was deported back to the United States where she was a source of trouble to the police until her death. She clearly held no hard feelings towards them, for she dedicated her book *Chicago May* to the great reforming Californian police officer August Vollmer '. . . who first showed me a practical way to go straight'.

---

[7] Arthur Newton was a fashionable if dishonest lawyer of the time. He defended the murderer Crippen and later went to prison for fraud. See PRO Crim 1 108/2.

231

For part of the time May ran a small house in Philadelphia and then, before her death in 1929 in hospital there, she announced that at long last she was going to marry Charles Smith. She was 53 at the time. However, she may have lived on. Some accounts have her arrested for soliciting in Detroit in the early 1930s, when she was said to be charging $2, and give the year of her death as 1935.[8]

Her one-time lover, Guerin, was an interesting character. He was probably born in Soho of French parents, although police reports have him as being born in Chicago in 1860. He first came to the notice of the American police at the age of 26 when he was arrested for burglary and shot an officer in an attempt to escape. The British police first arrested him in August 1887 when, under the name of George McCaull, he was given three months for possessing housebreaking implements. Next year he was back inside for burglary, and he attempted to escape from Holloway prison. On 19 May 1899 he was sentenced to ten years at Lyons for larceny from a bank; he tried to avoid extradition by endeavouring to establish that he was born in London, but failed. He cannot have served much of his sentence, for he was next arrested in Paris in 1901 for the American Express case. This was when he received a life sentence at Paris Assizes and was sent to Devil's Island in French Guiana. He escaped in either 1904 or 1905 and was arrested here on 20 April 1906, most likely on the information of Chicago May. This time he successfully pleaded that he was a British subject and was released on 14 June 1907 after thirteen and a half months in Brixton prison. There was also another technicality. In theory the French authorities had abolished Devil's Island before Guerin was sent there – it was something they did on a more or less annual basis at the time – and so he could not have escaped from there.

After the jailing of Chicago May his career was principally that of safebreaker and hotel jewel thief. According to police files, January 1908 found him with Matthew Carr aka Springate, committing a heavy jewellery larceny at Starlings the pawnbroker's in Great Portland Street. He was never charged.

On 9 April 1908 Guerin was discharged at Guildhall for frequenting banks, and on 24 April of the same year he was again discharged at Westminster Police Court when a charge of

---

[8] C. Sifakis, *The Encyclopaedia of American Crime*, p. 144.

throwing corrosive fluid in the face of Alice Mahoney was withdrawn. (Chicago May was clearly right to fear for her beauty.) In Glasgow in January 1912, a charge of frequenting the Central Station Hotel for the purpose of theft was found not proven. He had been loitering in the hotel on 18 October 1910 when several bags were found to have been ripped open and jewellery stolen. He was arrested with eight skeleton keys and a contrivance for obtaining wax impressions on him. The stipendiary magistrate accepted Guerin was a known and reputed thief, but despite the equipment he had with him gave him the benefit of the very little doubt. After that his career was downhill. He was convicted of being a suspected person (loitering with intent to steal) at Bow Street in September 1920, and appealed against that charge and one of assaulting a police officer. His appeal, financed by the swindler Horatio Bottomley, was dismissed. A year later, as Thomas Garen, he was accused of stealing jewellery and a dressing-case from a guest at the Hotel Metropole, Brighton. He died in a Poor House in Bury, Lancashire on 5 December 1940.

Guerin is, however, best known for that escape from Devil's Island – one of the few men to do so successfully – along with some companions. He alone was picked up by a steamer near what was then British Guiana; he was exhausted but fairly well nourished. He was brought back to London and the French government commenced extradition proceedings. They had problems first because Devil's Island had, legally, been abolished. How then could Guerin have escaped from it? Secondly, he had a British birth certificate. The authorities refused to return him. Unfortunately, later in his criminal career Guerin let slip that on the voyage he had eaten his companions, and from then until he died he was regarded as an outcast in the Underworld. He was, according to the Home Office file, 'one of the most daring and expert criminals who has ever come under the notice of the police'.

An early British counterpart of May Sharpe was Mary Milliner, the prostitute mistress of the celebrated thief-taker and receiver of stolen property, Jonathan Wild. In 1708 he was imprisoned for debt, and when he was discharged four years later he set up house in Drury Lane with Mary whom he had met in prison. Initially he was what was called a twang, the pickpocket who would take the wallets of Milliner's clients; in those days intercourse with prostitutes was almost invariably undertaken vertically. Wild began his criminal apprenticeship proper with a Charles Hitchin, a City Marshal who taught him the trade of receiver which Wild was to perfect. For twelve years he was able to maintain such a successful double life that by 1724 he petitioned to be made a freeman of the City. His end came when he was indicted for receiving ten guineas as a reward for helping a Mrs Steham to recover stolen lace, the theft of which he had arranged. Convicted, he was hanged on 24 May 1725. He had tried to commit suicide the night before, and still drowsy was pelted by the mob on the way to Tyburn. He was survived by both Mary Milliner and Charles Hitchin. Milliner, whose ear had been sliced off by Wild in a temper, had been paid a pension by him to the date of his death.[9]

In the 1820s the Connaught circuit in Ireland had a woman hangman:

Who think you, gentle reader, officiated upon this gallows high? A female! a middle aged, stout-made, dark-eyed, swarthy-complexioned, but by no means forbidding, woman! – The celebrated Lady Betty, the finisheress of the law, the unflinching priestess for the Connaught circuit and Roscommon in particular. Few children born or reared in that county thirty or even twenty-five years ago were not occasionally frightened into being good by the cry of 'Here's Lady Betty!'

This woman (who had been previously convicted of a horrible murder) officiated, unmasked or undisguised, under the name of Lady Betty, as the hangwoman for a great many years, and she used often to flog publicly in and through the streets as part of her trade or profession, being always extremely severe, particularly on her own sex.[10]

There have been, of course, a number of women who were convicted or acquitted of murder – Florence Maybrick and

---

[9] Wild was born in Wolverhampton in 1683 and apprenticed to a buckle-maker. Hitchin remained a City Under-Marshal for a further three years, when he was tried for sodomy. Acquitted of the capital offence but convicted of a kindred misdemeanour, he was sentenced to a term in the pillory, as well as six months' imprisonment and a fine of £20. For a full account of Wild's life, see *The Thief Takers* by Patrick Pringle. The character MacHeath in John Gay's *The Beggar's Opera* was based on Wild.

[10] *Dublin University Magazine*, January 1850.

Adelaide Bartlett are Victorian examples of each – but these were generally poisoners of unwanted husbands rather than participants in organized crime. The sad Ruth Ellis, part Welsh-part Belgian, good-time girl, model and part-time prostitute is another, convicted of shooting her faithless lover and a passer-by in the evening of Easter Sunday, 10 April 1955, outside the Magdala public house in Hampstead. By no means was she a gangster's moll or pro-active in crime, but she belonged in the twilight world of Mayfair and South Kensington drinking clubs and the Edgware Road and Paddington abortionists. She lived at a period where a gay time in the old-fashioned slightly shrill sense of the word was had in the days after the War by slightly soiled men, often with RAF ties and moustaches, who bought and sold things cheaply and, from time to time, cashed dud cheques.

In 1946, after she had a child by a Canadian soldier, she began to work for Morris Conley, the owner of a number of clubs including the Court Club in Duke Street and the late-night Hollywood in Welbeck Street. Shortly after the Ellis shooting Duncan Webb named Conley as '. . . Britain's biggest vice boss and the chief source of the tainted money that nourishes the evils of London night life'. This was really rather going it a bit, since the Messina brothers still had part of their operations intact. Perhaps because they were Maltese this didn't count. Conley lasted another six years before the *News of the World* reported his conviction for keeping a brothel in Westbourne Terrace, Paddington. The police had seen eighty-two men go to the address over a three-day period and, best of all, there was 'the nature of various paraphernalia one associated with these types of premises'. There were four known prostitutes amongst the tenants. Conley, who initially said, 'I did not know what was going on,' had £400 in his pocket at the time of his arrest. He was fined £100 and ordered to pay 25 guineas costs.[11]

Ruth Ellis drifted from club to club and man to man, ending with racing-car driver David Blakely with whom she had a relationship for two years. She still continued her work as the manageress of the Little Bottle Club, entertaining men in her flat above the premises, and Blakely had other girlfriends. In February 1955 they began to live together in a flat in Egerton Gardens. The relationship was stormy and Blakely left shortly

[11] *People*, 11 December 1955; *News of the World*, 10 September 1961.

before Ruth Ellis had a miscarriage at the beginning of April. There is some evidence that he hit her in the stomach, which led to the miscarriage. On Good Friday, driven by a man Desmond Curren, described as her alternative lover, she went to see Blakely where he was staying with friends in Tanza Road, Hampstead, and the police were called twice to remove her. On Easter Sunday there was a party at the house; Blakely left about 9 p.m. with a friend to go to the Magdala. When he left the pub she shot at him six times. One bullet hit a Mrs Gladys Kensington Yule in the hand, one missed and the other four hit Blakely who died instantly. She was immediately arrested.

There was no real defence proffered by Melford Stevenson QC who led for the defence. She was asked only one question by Christmas Humphreys for the prosecution:

– Mrs Ellis, when you fired that revolver at close range into the body of David Blakely, what did you intend to do?
– It is obvious that when I shot him I intended to kill him.

The judge, Mr Justice Havers, told the jury, 'Even if you accept every word of it [her story] it does not seem to me to establish any sort of defence to murder.' In view of the judge's ruling Melford Stevenson made no closing speech to the jury, who retired for fourteen minutes before returning a guilty verdict.

There was a very real campaign to save her from the gallows. She was an attractive woman who by now had two young children. Her mother told her story to *Woman's Sunday Mirror*, and the *Empire News* had a few words from Mrs Jackie Dyer who had been a barmaid in the Little Club. Sidney Silverman, the campaigning MP, put together a petition which carried 50,000 signatures for her reprieve. It was in sharp contrast to the recent executions of two other women, both of them ugly and with whose crimes it was impossible to sympathize. Grace Merrifield had poisoned her employer thinking she would be left money in her will, and Styllou Christofi, a Cypriot lady who spoke little English, had strangled her daughter-in-law and set fire to her body in the garden. The brilliant journalist William Connor, writing as Cassandra in the *Daily Mirror* on 30 June 1955, had this to say:

Ruth Ellis does not matter any more than her two recent

female predecessors to the hangman's noose – Mrs Merrifield and Mrs Christofi.

But what we do to her – you and I – matters very much, and if we continue to do it to her sad successors then we all bear the guilt of savagery untinged with mercy.

Mrs Yule certainly didn't feel that way. She wrote to the *Evening Standard*: 'Don't let us turn Ruth Ellis into a national heroine. I stood petrified and watched her kill David Blakely in cold blood, even putting two further bullets into him as he lay bleeding to death on the ground . . .'

The efforts of Silverman and the others were to no avail. The fact that a passer-by had been injured is said to have influenced the Home Secretary against granting a reprieve. Ruth Ellis had taken little interest in the efforts to save her, regarding the matter much as a life for a life. She was hanged at Holloway prison on 13 July 1955, the last woman to be hanged in this country. She was, said a prison officer to the *Daily Mirror*, '. . . the calmest woman who ever went to the gallows'.

Within two years the law was changed and the Homicide Act 1957 was passed. Now under s. 3 there was an extended defence of provocation by words as well as deeds. In 1958 Ernest Fantle, who had shot his wife's lover after verbal provocation, was sentenced to three years' imprisonment under the section. It is inconceivable that a jury would not have found the same provocation in the case of Ruth Ellis had the defence been available.

One modern example of a woman criminal who possibly killed for money other than by using poison was the admittedly unbalanced 42-year-old Margaret Allen. Formerly a bus-conductress living in Rawstensall, Lancashire, she falsely boasted that she had had a sex-change operation. On 28 August 1948 she battered a 68-year-old woman, Nancy Chadwick, to death. The elderly lady was believed to have been in the habit of carrying large sums of cash with her, and her new red purse was never recovered. Allen had thrown her bag in the river.

Since the body was found outside Allen's house at 137 Bacup Road, it was not surprising that the police wished to speak with her. At first she denied any involvement, but soon admitted battering the old lady with a hammer, putting the body in the coal cellar and then, in the early hours of the morning, dumping it in the street in the hope that it would look as though the injuries were from a motor accident rather than from nine hammer blows. Allen never admitted stealing the purse:

I was in a funny mood and she seemed just to get on my nerves. I saw the hammer and on the spur of the moment I hit her with the hammer. I looked in her bag but there was no money. I didn't actually kill her for that. I had one of my funny moods.

At the Assizes a defence of insanity was put forward with no success. The Home Secretary ordered a special inquiry into her mental condition, but this did not save her. The one real friend she had in the town, Annie Cook, endeavoured to put together a petition for clemency but could only raise a hundred signatures. It too failed, and she was hanged on 12 January 1949. Apparently Allen kicked over the tray on which her last breakfast was brought to her, remarking that no one else was going to enjoy it. In his book[12] Edward Robey, who appeared for the Crown in the magistrates' court, wrote that of the people he had prosecuted and who had died on the scaffold she was one of three whose sentence might have been commuted to penal servitude on the grounds that she was mentally abnormal.

A female sideline was baby-farming, or angel-making as the French called it. Unwanted children would be given to the baby farmer along with a lump (and possibly an additional weekly) sum. The child would not live long. On 3 February 1903, Annie Walters and Amelia Sach became the first women to be hanged at Holloway prison which had originally been built to house prisoners of the Boer War. Amelia Sach, the younger of the pair, was the one who negotiated with the mothers, and Walters killed them.[13]

---

[12] E. Robey, *The Jester and the Court*, p. 131.

[13] Another slightly earlier example was in 1896 when Amelia Elizabeth Dyer, then aged 57, was hanged at Newgate prison by James Billington. She had been convicted at the Old Bailey before Mr Justice Hawkins of the death of four-month-old Doris Marmon, after the body of another baby, Helen Fry, had been found strangled with white tape and wrapped in weighted brown paper in the Thames near Reading. Dyer was traced because the name and address on the paper was one of her aliases. It was clear she had killed a number of children but when questioned would only say, 'You'll know all mine by the tape round their necks.' She ran a defence of insanity which the jury rejected in five minutes. She had been mistress of her profession for some twenty years. The woman who had promised the babies 'mother's care' went to the scaffold praying not for herself but for her 'persecutors'. Baby-farming became less common as the twentieth century progressed.

Nevertheless, although women have kept – possibly because of social pressures as well as physical strengths – mainly to 'womanly trades' of prostitution, nightclub hostessing, shoplifting, passing cheques and dishonestly handling stolen goods, there have been one or two notable exceptions, but even they have generally been working in partnership with a man or in some supportive role. In the summer of 1903 a particular one, the American con-woman Sophie Beck, managed to swindle the Story Cotton Company of Philadelphia out of $2 million, after which she retired to Paris where she lived in some style.

One British woman who seems to have cracked the mould was Louisa Wright, who for eight years from 1902 was the country's top woman jewel thief. Her speciality was using her undoubted good looks to obtain jewellery on credit or on approval, and then vanishing with it. She was caught in 1905 when in a moment of weakness she went along with a plan of her current husband and tried to chloroform a jeweller. The effort failed miserably. She was arrested, charged and acquitted, possibly because she stood in the dock with a baby, rented for the day, in her arms. Defendants in those days were not permitted the luxury of a seat.

Louisa Wright was born in 1880, the only daughter of a Bedfordshire farm labourer and a cook, and came to London as a housemaid. Initially she teamed up with a small-time crook, but she had her sights on better things. By 1902 she had eradicated the traces of her upbringing and had become in all but reality a well-bred lady. Invited to country houses, she left the windows unlatched for an accomplice.

After her acquittal her position in society was gone, and so was the husband. She moved to Paris, but in 1910 was back in London where she tried another scam. This time she became Lady Campbell of Hans Crescent, SW1. A young jeweller was summoned and persuaded to leave jewellery worth some £4,000 with her, on the pretext that her aunt who was ill wanted to choose a piece for a wedding present. She had rented the house on forged references the day before. Wright was arrested at Dover as she tried to leave the country. She served seven years of a ten-year sentence, and on her release left for France where she lived on the Mediterranean coast, to all intents and purposes a thoroughly respectable and conservative woman. During her imprisonment efforts were made by members of the Underworld to find the place where she was believed to have cached her wealth. They were unsuccessful.

In Britain the best-known individual woman criminal of the first three decades of this century was undoubtedly Lilian Goldstein, known as the Bobbed-Haired Bandit, a lower-middle-class Jewish girl from North-West London who was the driver and nurse for Charles 'Ruby' Sparks, the celebrated jewel thief who later became a smash-and-grab artist. By some accounts it is she who suggested he turn from the country house burglaries at which he had been a master to the less skilled trade of throwing bricks through jewellers' windows. She was regarded highly not only by Sparks and his friends but by the police. Detective Chief Inspector 'Nutty' Sharpe described her: 'She usually drove a big Mercedes car. Sitting at the wheel with a man's raincoat collar turned up around her close-fitting hat, there wasn't much to see of her.'

Increasing interest by the Flying Squad in the smash-and-grab raids persuaded Sparks to return to burglary, and she was caught with him at Manchester in 1927. He pleaded guilty to protect her and received three years' penal servitude. In return, she waited outside Strangeways when he escaped during the first few months of his sentence. Unfortunately he was hampered climbing the wall and she was obliged to drive off without him. Sparks went on to serve ten years' imprisonment and was involved in the Dartmoor mutiny. He escaped from the Moor on 10 January 1940, together with Alec Marsh and Dick Nolan, after serving two months of another five-year sentence; Marsh was recaptured in six days and Nolan after four months.

In the *Sunday Pictorial* of 3 March 1940, and for a number of weeks thereafter, readers were treated to the tale of the Bobbed-Haired Bandit and her renunciation of the devil in the shape of poor Ruby and all his works. She was now going straight, and to prove it she was bravely prepared to own up to what she had done – 'I can take my punishment so that I can finish with my life of degradation' – and indeed to give her correct name, Joyce Powys-Wilson. She told of smuggling money into Brixton for Sparks, of the raids and how once a fence came from Birmingham to price the stolen jewellery. She also wrote an open letter to Sparks, pictured in a prison photograph screwing his face into the shape of a gargoyle on a minor French cathedral.

I know you will be surprised to hear from me in this way. I know you will wonder how I have had the courage to do this, after all these years. But, Ruby, I have HAD to do it, because, as I told you, I want to finish for good with the past.

I want to know what it is to have a night's sleep without waking up in terror every time I hear a strange noise. I want to walk the streets in the daylight [and much more of the same until . . .] If you want to write to me for the last time you can do so at the *Sunday Pictorial*. I shall wait for that letter, because I want to know that you understand, and have forgiven me. Then I can face the future with the same courage that I showed in those nightmare days of crime together.

And so goodbye – for ever. Joy.

The cunning little vixen. It wasn't at all.

The police were puzzled. They were convinced that the Bobbed-Haired Bandit was Lilian Goldstein, not this society lady Joyce Powys-Wilson. More was revealed in the next article, in which Joy said her parents separated soon after she was born and her father (who had worked on the Stock Exchange) disappeared. She had worked in the First World War with a very select Mayfair party in a Red Cross Unit.

She had, she said, fallen in love with a peer whom she was to marry but whom she chucked because he was a snob. (His name was not mentioned 'as he is happily married and an important figure in the land'.) Then came Peter, who was a Jew.

Now, funny as it seems now I can swear that I did not know what the word Jew meant. I thought it was some small religious point. And I was simply flabbergasted when my mother told me that my association with him was impossible.

Then she met Ruby, whom she was told was a bookmaker: 'In a few moments I decided that Ruby was just the man for me.'

Notes appear on the police file written after the publication of each article. The officer who knew her in Manchester was convinced that it was all hogwash. 'The woman known as the Bobbed-Haired Bandit is Lilian Johnson aka Lilia Goldstein or Lilian Rose Goldstein,' he wrote firmly, adding that she had convictions for shoplifting and soliciting in 1926, both at Marlborough Street.

He was able to give more details of her early life, which did not include a father on the Stock Exchange.

Her mother's maiden name was Kendall and she was born on 4 August 1902. Her brother is Victor Kendall, with convictions for housebreaking. On 15 July 1920 Harry/ Henry Goldstein was ordered to pay 10 guineas costs and 3 months' hard labour for living off her immoral earnings at Old Street Police Court. On his release from prison on 9 October 1920, she married him and became a prostitute and saleswoman in the West End.

After the next article appeared they decided that Joy Powys-Wilson was someone who barely knew Sparks personally but had access to details of his career. Ms Powys-Wilson was an adventuress, they deduced, and they were partly correct.

On 6 June 1940 Joyce Powys-Wilson aka Jeska, a film artiste, received five months' hard labour for stealing from Harry Barley, a cardboard-box manufacturer who had befriended her after reading the *Pictorial*. Whilst at her flat at the Mount Royal off the Edgware Road, Mr Barley had gone to the lavatory and on returning he found that she, and his dressing gown, wallet and other items, were gone.

Interviewed, Ms Joyce Powys-Wilson said she had been Sparks' mistress. The police did not believe her, and again they were correct not to do so. It was all a double blind.

With help Sparks had made his way to Lilian Goldstein's home in Wembley Park where he hid out, supporting himself by doing jobs with Billy Hill. He rather touchingly describes his reunion with the Bobbed-Haired Bandit.

She looked older and tired and there was grey in her hair and the beginnings of lines down the sides of her mouth. I saw she was screwing up her eyes to see me, and I asked her: 'Lil, do you wear spectacles now?' She looked a bit uncomfortable, and said, 'Yes, sometimes – but only for reading.'[14]

---

[14] R. Sparks, *Burglar to the Nobility*, p. 117.

When Hill was caught after an unsuccessful raid on a jeweller's in Bond Street, Sparks found difficulty in obtaining work. To Goldstein's revulsion, he decided to set up an armed robbery. Before it was carried out Sparks was arrested by DS Ted Greeno, who had disbelieved Goldstein's protestations that she knew nothing of Sparks and had had her followed. It was not easy, she was adroit in shaking off a tail.

Alas, it was by no means a simple assignment and she led us a merry dance. To follow her with anything like consistency you needed to be a combination of athlete and acrobat, as she knew most of the answers on how to avoid being trailed. Her normal method of losing any 'shadow' she thought might be around consisted of catching a bus and travelling a little way, jumping off when it slowed down, dashing across the road and boarding one going in the opposite direction. Often she would repeat this process in reverse. Many a seemingly discreet observer found he was strictly on his own when she had done this several times in quick succession. If he did manage to hold on and keep her in view, there were more tricks to come. She would run into an Underground station, buy a ticket and be well down the escalator before the man shadowing her could reach the barrier. Then, as he too was riding down the escalator he would quite probably see her travelling up again on the other side![15]

Goldstein was also arrested and sentenced to six months' imprisonment by Sir Gerald Dodson, the Recorder of London. She served less than three weeks because the Recorder, after a homily which would no doubt today infuriate the politically correct – but which defendants will happily endure provided it means walking into the daylight at the end of it – substituted a probation order:

I have decided to reduce the punishment, for I think I can understand the human element in this case. He was an escaped convict to the rest of the world, but that is not how you may have viewed him. In doing what you did, although it was breaking the law, you followed a natural womanly

[15] R. Higgins, *In the Name of the Law*, p. 67.

instinct in trying to succour and protect this man with whom you had intimate relations over the years.

Sparks left behind a newspaper article which the *Sunday Pictorial* published. They had, it appears, paid over £400 for the series. Goldstein, who was, by the time of what proved to be Sparks' last escape, already involved with another man, disappeared from the scene sending a proper and traditional 'Dear John' whilst he was serving his sentence to which an additional twelve months had been added. The police were not pleased with her and a 'discreet watch' was kept on her. Some months later it was reported that she was still living in the Wembley area but was not associating with the local criminals.

Not all women have been as fortunate in their involvement in crime as the Bobbed-Haired Bandit. Eighteen-year-old Elizabeth Maud Jones, whose career lasted less than a week, was lucky to escape the hangman. She was convicted along with Karl Gustav Hulten of the murder of a taxi-driver, George Edward Heath. Hulten, then aged 22, a Swedish-American deserter from the Parachute Regiment of the US forces in Britain, met her in a café in October 1944. He was posing as Lieutenant Ricky Hulten and she as an actress. In reality she was working as a strip-tease artiste under the name of Georgina Grayson, and lived in a room in King Street, Hammersmith, near the Broadway. He fancied himself as a gangster and she as a moll. Together they set out on a nightly campaign of robbery, attacking pedestrians and cyclists. One woman, hit repeatedly with an iron bar, was then nearly strangled and thrown in the nearby Thames. Their reign of terror in West London was shortlived. On 7 October 1944, four days after their meeting, they hailed a cab driven by Heath and during the journey Hulten shot him. Jones said of the robbery: 'I knew the meaning . . . he wanted me to go with him to rob a taxi-driver . . . I saw a flash and heard a bang. I was surprised that there was not a loud bang because Ricky had told me it would make a big noise.'

The proceeds of this robbery yielded precisely nineteen shillings, a silver pencil and a cigarette case.

The pair drove on to Staines where they dumped the body in a ditch. Despite the fact that the body was found the next morning and a description of the missing Ford V8 cab circulated, Hulten and Jones continued to drive around for a further three days until on 10 October Hulten was arrested in the Fulham Palace Road with the gun and ammunition still in his pocket.

Jones did not last long on the outside. Speaking to a policeman friend who had commented that she looked pale, she said, 'If you had seen someone do what I have seen done you wouldn't be able to sleep at night.' They were both sentenced to death – with the jury recommending mercy for Jones – on 16 January 1945 after a trial lasting six days at the Central Criminal Court. Despite strong representations by the American Ambassador who visited the Home Secretary, Lord Morrison, and spent an hour arguing for a reprieve, Hulten was hanged by Albert Pierrepoint on 8 March. Jones was reprieved on the grounds of her youth – a decision apparently regretted by Sir Winston Churchill – and released from prison in May 1954. In 1992 a film was made about the case.[16] Called *Chicago Joe and the Showgirl*, it starred Kiefer Sutherland and Emily Lloyd.

The 1950s saw the rise of one of the better-known English women criminals who achieved a certain notoriety and press attention. Zoe Progl, known as Blonde Mick and, for a time, the 'Queen of the Underworld', was the first woman to escape from Holloway prison. In July 1960, during her fourth term of imprisonment when she had served one month of a two-and-a-half-year sentence for housebreaking, a rope ladder was thrown over the wall and up she went, down the 25-ft ladder on the other side and into a waiting car. She then sent her prison clothes to the *Daily Mail*, to be returned to the Governor at Holloway.

She was recaptured in Notting Hill in the October after touring the south coast with her small daughter, Tracey, her boyfriend and one of the women who helped her escape. She was traced when a police officer noticed a car number WOP 598 which he knew did not exist[17]. Inside was Progl's driving licence with her address. She was found asleep either in bed or on the kitchen floor, depending on which of the rival newspaper reports was accurate.

Whilst out, she had given an interview to the *Daily Express* and was pictured drinking gin in the Pier Hotel, Chelsea, offering

---

[16] The case became known as the Cleft Chin Murder, a characteristic of the taxi-driver Heath.

[17] In those days licensing authorities did not allow a car number which made 'an unfortunate word'.

to give herself up if the Home Secretary knocked a year off her sentence. Otherwise, she said, she was planning to have plastic surgery to mask a five-and-half-inch giveaway scar under her left eye.

Progl had eighteen months added to her sentence. The friends Barry Harris, her boyfriend, and Bryanna O'Malley received nine months apiece. They had financed the last few months with a series of cheque frauds. Adelaide de Boer, described as having a soft heart and eighty-three convictions for prostitution, also went down for nine months although she denied being involved in the escape. Whilst in prison Progl sued the Commissioner of Police, Sir Joseph Simpson, over a solitaire diamond ring, a gift from her former lover, the now long-dead Tommy Smithson. The police did not oppose the application; it had been confiscated on her arrest in 1960. After completion of her term of imprisonment Progl sold her story to a Sunday newspaper and announced she was going straight.

Four years later in April 1964 Progl, now aged 35, who had previously been married to US Master-Sergeant Joseph Progl, by whom she had three children, married 24-year-old salesman Roy Bowman. She had gone to the United States with Progl at the age of 16, but left after a year and returned home. When he traced her she was serving a Borstal sentence for receiving: 'Roy knows about my days as a burglar, as a rich man's mistress, as a gangster's moll. He has decided to give me a chance to become a respectable woman. I don't intend to let that chance go.'[18]

It is believed that the pair emigrated to Australia. Certainly this particular Queen of Crime has made no reappearances in the newspapers since.

Shoplifting has always been a woman's sport. It was from the Elephant and Castle that the female shoplifting and pickpocketing team known as the Forty Thieves originated in the 1930s. Ex-Detective Superintendent John Capstick wrote in his memoirs:[19]

Dressed to kill, those girls would descend on a West End store like a swarm of locusts. They would roll up in taxis and chauffeur-driven limousines and practically clean the place out in an hour.

[18] *Daily Mirror*, 17 April 1964.
[19] J. Capstick, *Given in Evidence*, p.114.

London shops were not their only raiding-grounds. They worked impartially from Carlisle to Exeter, and from the coastal towns to Birmingham. Some would stay in the South while others dropped in on the Midlands or the North.

Capstick, known by the girls as Charlie Artful, went on to describe the leader of the Forty Thieves in their hey-day:

> . . . the life and soul of their parties, was a woman said to be the sister of a notorious Soho gangster king. She was one of the slickest thieves I ever tried to follow. Utterly fearless, she knew every trick in the book and she could put away three fur coats and a bolt of cloth in the time it took any of her team-mates to snitch a pair of cami-knickers.

Libel laws probably prevented him from naming her as Maggie, 'The Little Elephant', sister indeed to Soho gangster Billy Hill.

Shirley Pitts was given a great funeral when she died in 1992. A member of the powerful South London family of Pitts, one of whom was responsible for throwing acid into the face of a man he believed had informed on him, she was a noted shoplifter in her own right.[20] She could literally strip a jeweller's shop, says a contemporary admiringly. She was a very good-looking girl, and she and a colleague would pick a good jeweller's with one male staff member. She or the colleague would take it in turns to make a play for the salesman, and the other would strip the shop. Outside her brother Aggie would be in the car acting as a minder.

Forgery is also a crime at which women can excel. Edna Dorothy Thatcher, known as 'Edna the Pen', was one who did so until she received eight years' preventive detention at the Old Bailey in October 1959. She had left school in the early 1920s,

---

[20] The Pitts family had a long-running feud with a John Goodwin and in 1983 two members kidnapped his wife, taking her to a caravan park in Essex where she was held hostage. She was eventually released and on 22 June 1984 Charles Pitts received an eighteen-year sentence. His son-in-law, Sean McDonald, received eight years. Goodwin had long been a thorn in the side of the police and had received a seven-year sentence for jury nobbling, quashed by the Court of Appeal. Whilst on bail for a bank robbery of which he was subsequently acquitted, Goodwin had taped up his Christmas tree to record detectives receiving money. At their subsequent trial two were acquitted. The third man ran the ingenious defence that although he was taking money he would still not allow this to influence his evidence and so would not have committed perjury. He was convicted but, in turn, his conviction was quashed by the Court of Appeal.

where her neat writing had led to predictions of a rosy future as a copy typist for a solicitor or accountant. Unfortunately she was soon bound over for two years for theft, and then went straight until the early 1930s when she received nine months for embezzlement. Another sentence followed in the mid-thirties and then another in 1943 when she served two years, again for forgery. In 1951 she remarried – her first husband had died on active service – and this time it was seven years for forgery. She was released in May 1956.

Edna then became the bookkeeper for a firm of gown-makers and almost immediately obtained a job with the firm's accountants so that she could cover up her fiddle. She was caught when she added a nought to the £60 personal cheque of one of the directors. Even on bail she continued 'working'. Preventive detention carried no automatic remission.

When women went on armed robberies, their role was almost always that of the driver. One such was Sheila Porritt née Tobias, daughter of a leading North Country criminal, who had married into the powerful South London Porritt family. She was convicted as the driver in a wages snatch back in her home town of Manchester. She had taken her child from a former relationship along with her on the blagging because she could not find a childminder. Later when she did find a babysitter for an evening, she paid her £2 wage with some of the stolen money. Sheila Porritt received five years whilst others in the team drew up to fifteen. One of them, Albert Reddans from another South London family, collected ten years, but this was made consecutive to another ten-year sentence he had received the previous month.

There have been persistent rumours of women who have actually been 'on the pavement' in armed robberies. The sister of a number of Irishmen from Paddington of whom an admirer said '[she] was like a man' – presumably in courage rather than physique – was said to be one of them, as was another girl from Notting Hill. So far, however, the best-known London female armed robber has been Linda Calvey, who boasted she was the original of one of the characters in the popular ITV series, *Widows*. Linda – one of nine children in an East London family which made dockers' hooks – became involved with Micky Calvey. A long-time friend of Mickey Ishmael, thought by some to be capable of being a serious contender for the top of the league, in 1953 Calvey received eight years along with Ishmael for robbing Marks & Spencers. Linda had married him in 1970, when he was taken from Wandsworth prison to a local register office. In 1977 he was acquitted of charges of burglary brought on the evidence of supergrass Charles Lowe.

Micky Calvey died on Saturday 9 December 1978 in a shoot-out when he tried to rob Caters supermarket in Eltham, South-East London. Four men had attacked security guards as they carried a box containing £10,000. The other three men fled after discharging a shotgun over the heads of the crowd. On hearing of his death Linda said, 'Micky has been in trouble before, I know, but he's been trying hard since he came out of prison a year ago.' Some two hundred people attended his funeral at the East London crematorium, to which Mickey Ishmael sent a wreath in the form of the letters 'PAL'.

Linda earned her nickname of the Black Widow[21] by shouting 'murderer' at the police officer who stood trial for the shooting. There had been some evidence that Calvey had been shot in the back, but the officer explained that this was the way he had been standing rather than that he had been shot whilst fleeing. He was acquitted and given a bravery award.

Shortly after that Linda became involved with robber Ronnie Cook, going with him on trips abroad including one to Las Vegas when it was said they spent £30,000 in just over a week. He lavished gifts on her – clothes from Harrods, jewellery, money, a car, even £4,000 for cosmetic surgery. There was, however, a down side: Cook was obsessively jealous, forbidding Linda to speak to other men, beating her savagely and, according to reports, subjecting her to sadistic sexual practices.

Three years later he was jailed for sixteen years for his part in what was described as one of the 'most spectacular and well-planned robberies in the history of crime'. Now while that is a phrase quite often used by prosecuting counsel opening the case to a jury, this did have the hallmarks of brilliance. It was in fact Billy Tobin's Dulwich raid, when a hijacked mobile crane was rammed into the back of a security vehicle containing almost £1 million near a school in Dulwich.

---

[21] An American version of the Black Widow and a very pro-active one at that was Griselda Blanco, who headed a drugs empire running the length of the Americas. Her three husbands, a number of lovers and rivals have all died and she is credited with originating the drive-by motorcycle killing. Jailed in Florida, she is likely to serve at least twenty-five years from 1990. *Daily Star*, 5 November 1990.

Calvey promised to wait for him and, as a mark of her fidelity, had 'True Love Ron Cook' tattooed on her leg. But, it seems, she could not now give up the lifestyle to which she had grown accustomed. Almost certainly Cook had had money salted away and she began to spend it, taking up with one of his friends, Brian Thorogood, whom Cook had arranged to act as a 'minder' for him whilst he was inside. Thorogood left his wife, bought a house in Harold Wood, Essex and moved in with her. Later he too was sentenced, receiving eighteen years for a post office robbery. Linda, who seems to have supplemented her income by being the armourer for various robbery teams, served three of a five-year term for conspiracy to rob. That was the end of Thorogood, but now Cook was due for release. What could she do?

Fearful that he would find out about both her infidelity and her dissipation of his money, she planned to kill him, offering a £10,000 contract. Finding no takers, she turned to Daniel Reece, a convicted rapist whose evidence had assisted the police convict David Lashley, the killer of Australian heiress Janie Shepherd. Quite apart from the money, Reece too was enamoured with Calvey and agreed to do the job.

In theory Ron Cook had a cleaning job outside the prison but, as with so many before him, he took to more agreeable days out. On 19 January 1990 Linda Calvey collected him from Maidstone Prison and drove him to London whilst Reece, whom she had already collected from another prison, waited outside her flat. Cook brought in the milk and as he stood holding it Reece followed him in and shot him in the elbow. He could not, he later told police, bring himself to kill the man: 'I could not kill him. I shot to his side and he fell backwards into the kitchen. I moved forward and stood over him. I could not kill him. I have never killed anyone.'

Linda Calvey had no such qualms. She grabbed the gun from him, ordered Cook to kneel and then shot him in the head.

Reece took a train back to the West Country to continue his thirteen year sentence for rape, buggery and false imprisonment.

At first it seemed as though Calvey had been successful. The police appeared to accept her story that an unknown gunman had burst in and shot Cook while she cowered in a corner. Then it was discovered that Reece had been with her over the weekend and had been her lover. It was curious that he had not been mentioned in the statement. Under questioning Reece cracked first, telling all.

Reece, who was not notedly popular in prison following the evidence he gave against Lashley, thought twice about squealing again and withdrew his confession in court. Linda Calvey told the jury his confession was a fabrication. 'Ron meant everything to me,' she said. This gesture of solidarity did him no good; he too received a life sentence for murder.

Just as the men in Fay Sadler's life ended up dead or in prison, so did those in the life of Linda Calvey, a classic gangster's moll turned gangster.[22]

Perhaps the delegates at the 1992 conference on professional crime were right, women were taking a more active role. They certainly had been in terrorist offences. The first traces of women as gang leaders came in August 1972 when security expert Peter Hamilton told a Council of Investigators in Brighton that, 'It is well known that there are principal leaders of guerilla organizations in Britain, Germany, and America who are women.' He went on to add, 'Women are playing a bigger part in muggings and few gangs are without them.'

In 1975 a United Nations Geneva conference was told that girl football hooligans in Britain have become as commonplace as the vicious female muggers of the States. There is little doubt that females can identify with and lead a cause, e.g. the IRA, or the Weathermen for whom Bernadine Dohrn undertook a sexual as well as political revolution. But can they actually take a pro-active part in heavy career crime? The research into women criminals is, if anything, against the proposition, but it may be misleading.

The criminologist Pollak suggests that the low crime rate of women is more apparent than real, and is largely due to the masked or hidden character of female crime. He sees the crux of the sex differences in criminality as qualitative rather than quantitative, and argues that women commit crimes which by their very nature remain unreported in criminal statistics, e.g. shoplifting, domestic theft and criminal abortion. He estimated that in New York City the prosecution of abortionists and shoplifters would reduce the crime ratio man to woman from 10:1 to 4.7:1.

---

[22] Fay Sadler was the mistress of Selwyn Cooney and also Tommy Smithson, as well as Elephant and Castle villain, Jack Rosa. Cooney and Smithson were shot, Rosa died in a car accident (see J. Morton *Gangland*).

Other reasons are social controls. Crime amongst women is much higher in the more emancipated countries. There are genetic factors as well as physique and physiological ones. In a survey by Lombroso and Ferrero in 1892, amongst eighty women arrested for 'resistance to public officials' a high proportion were menstruating. Pollak quoted a similar survey of Parisian shoplifters in the 1890s, but a 1962 survey of London shoplifters found no such correlation.[23]

In 1991 Diana Hutchinson interviewed a girl who might almost be making the First, if not Premier, Division. Jenny had taken to cheque frauds rather than go on the game, had carried a gun, slashed people, and driven the getaway car. She had a minder and was able to write a four-figure cheque for a suit for her son rather than steal it.

Mind you, I don't think I've heard of an all-girl gang going out to rob a bank. Girls want the quick thrill. They are not prepared to put in the months of planning, driving past the place, checking every movement like the men do. They are not so professional as the men yet. But the way women are taking to crime, that will come. It's only later women find out the hard side.[24]

Jenny had clearly not heard of the Hibbert sisters. On 10 March 1966 Eva (aged 21, with a two-year-old daughter and a pile of debts) and Christine (depressed from the death of her boyfriend and out of work) took a black air-pistol to the Barclays Bank branch in Vauxhall, South London and demanded money from the cashier. The effort was not a success; the girl simply pressed the alarm bell. They tried the same half an hour later at a sub-post office near Clapham Common with the same result. At the Old Bailey, Judge Brian Capstick (son of 'Charlie Artful' Capstick) told them, as he gave them two years apiece, 'I hope women considering offences of this sort will not think they will be treated leniently because they have small children or are pregnant.'

---

[23] K. Dalton (1961), 'Menstruation and Crime', *Brit Med. J.*2. 1752–1753; T.C.N. Gibbens and J. Prince (1962), *Shoplifting*, London, Institute for the Study and Treatment of Delinquency; C. Lombroso and G. Ferrero (1894), *Das Weib als Verbrecherin und prostituierte*, Hamburg, O. Pollak (1950), *The Criminality of Women*, New York.
[24] D. Hutchinson, 'The Godmother', *Daily Mail*, 30 May 1991.

At least they fell into the pattern suggested by Jenny that women generally will not put in the required amount of research.

Slightly more successful was Susan Bussey, acting in cahoots with her lover Paul Byrne. She had fantasized all her life over the prospect of being a bank robber and she, Byrne and three others carried out six successful raids in the summer and autumn of 1986, pulling in some £60,000. Bussey, aged 22, would be the blonde businesswoman wearing a pin-striped suit and carrying a sports bag, waiting patiently in the queue for the teller. It was she who wielded the gun and gave the orders. In a role-reversal situation, Byrne was the driver. Again the planning was not what it should have been. They used one of their own cars on the raids. The end was inevitable and came on 7 November 1986 when they raided another North London bank. This time the research was significantly wrong. They arrived late and when they returned to the getaway car they were ringed by the police. Bussey and Byrne each received a ten-year sentence.

For a time Helen Windeller was a moderately successful criminal, leaving her husband and daughter at home when she went to rob a sub-post office in Orpington, Kent. She ensured that the mothers and children had left the premises before she pulled out an air-gun and demanded and received just over £200. When her home was searched she had a stash of cannabis valued at £16,000. She was jailed for five years.[25]

One unlikely combination, in which by reason of age alone the woman must seem to have been the dominant character, was that of mother and son, Mabel Jacqueline Miller and Thomas Larvin, who in the summer of 1990 were jailed for a total of eleven years at Newcastle Crown Court. They had been caught red-handed carrying out the last of six building society armed robberies which had netted £11,500. When questioned, Mrs Miller said she knew nothing of her son's activities when out of the car; she had merely been giving him driving lessons.

There are now accounts of very young all-girl gangs dealing in cocaine and crack in South-West London. Kelly, 16, a former member of a South London female gang, said she was forced to smoke crack as an initiation test. 'Some of the girls were vicious but a lot of it was to compete with the boys. We were all armed and I carried either a machete, an army knife or a gun under my jacket.'

---

[25] Lois Atkinson, 'It's a Woman's Underworld,' *Woman's World*, June 1988.

The report in the *Sunday Times* went on to say that:

. . . the female gangs were formed by women drug dealers who were tired of handing their profits to male gang leaders. Some of the women arm themselves with 'zip' guns designed in America for women and small enough to fit into a handbag.

The women's aggression has shocked even experienced police officers. One detective in Brixton, South London, said, 'These girls who work in gangs are tough because they are constantly under threat of attack from rival gangs, former employers or boyfriends. They are streetwise and they know the law inside out.'[26]

In the early 1980s Elaine Player, now lecturing at King's College, London, undertook research into groups of girls between the ages of 16 and the late twenties. She found that the black girls she interviewed had established themselves into collectives rather more than their white counterparts and, without any apparent male support, some were engaged in organized shoplifting, cheque frauds and the occasional rolling of males brought back to their flats.

They have some way to go before they match the girls' gangs of California, such as the Lady Rascal gangsters who are the female equivalent of the Vietnamese and Cambodian male Tiny Rascal Gang. Where, say, ten years ago the function of the girl gang member was that of 'ho' or girlfriend, now they are starting to participate in drive-by shootings. In Chicago girls on the South Side seem to have adopted the traditional supportive role until 1992, but evidence is now emerging that they have become perpetrators. Charles Brown, the assistant director of a rehabilitation project for female gang leaders, says:

These girls feel like they have been in the dark ages for many years, just having babies, doing drugs. Now that they have the expertise, they want recognition, they want control. They want to start shooting. They feel they can control the gangland scene. Killing is now as much a girl's privilege as a boy's. There is no distinction between the sexes when a gun is in the hand.[27]

---

[26] *Sunday Times*, 19 December, 1993.
[27] Esther Oxford, in the *Independent*, 1 December, 1993.

The latest available Home Office statistics (at 30 June 1991) show that twenty-nine women were serving sentences for robbery, not necessarily armed. This was out of an adult female prison population of 1,038. By far the highest number, 260, were serving sentences for drug-related offences, and 170 were serving sentences for violence to the person, 166 for theft or dishonest handling of property and 161 for what were called other offences. Thirty-four were serving sentences for burglary, some of which may have been aggravated burglary – which broadly means that violence was used whilst on the premises or weapons carried. Eleven women were serving sentences for non-payment of fines.

Statistics are not necessarily a great help. It may be that women are indeed more adroit at evading arrest or conviction, or that judges are more reluctant to send them to prison than their male counterparts. Even so, if British women criminals have started to come out from behind the washing-machine and into pro-active major league crime, it is with some hesitation.

11

This Sporting Life

So far as horse-racing, and for that matter greyhound racing, is concerned, gangland activity falls into three separate but not wholly unconnected segments. The first is concerned with the animals themselves – ringing, doping and generally fixing the races for betting purposes. The second is the control and manipulation of the bookmakers, and the third is peripheral activities such as pickpocketing and short-con tricks which are worked at the racecourse or on the trains taking punters to and from the races[1].

Daniel Dawson makes a convenient historical start. In 1812 he was convicted, after a second trial at the Cambridge Assizes, under an almost forgotten statute of George I making it a capital offence maliciously to destroy cattle and horses. He had poisoned a number of valuable thoroughbreds when he impregnated the drinking water at Newmarket with a solution of white arsenic.

There was heavy wagering in the London clubs as to whether a man could be hanged for poisoning a horse, but those who said

---

[1] A short con is one which requires only a few minutes or, even better, seconds of the victim's time. The rewards are limited to the amount the victim has on him when the trick is worked. A long con, of which the Big Store is the classic example, requires time and patience but the rewards are likely to be much greater. The Big Store was worked particularly in the West and Southern States of America. A complete bogus business or illegal gambling joint was set up in which the proprietors, salesmen and other customers were all part of an act designed to swindle possibly only one man. If this seems incredible, then read of an example in Philip S. Van Cise's *Fighting the Underworld*. There are two classic Big Stores operated in the films *The Sting* and *The Grifters*.

he could be won the bets when Dawson was executed in front of Cambridge Castle on 8 August 1812. He was visited during the period between trial and hanging by a number of noblemen, but Dawson remained silent about those who had paid him.

In 1892 the Duke of Westminster's horse Orme was suspected of having been poisoned to prevent his running. If an effort had been made it was not successful, and the horse won £33,000 for his owner.

The turn of the century produced a number of scares of doping and allegations of foul riding. A number of American horses had come over along with American jockeys, the leading rider being Tod Sloan of whom, because of the regularity with which he finished in front, the phrase 'on your tod' (Tod Sloan = alone) was coined. Sloan, a man of immense talent, and a brilliant shot who won international events at Monte Carlo, was in the hands of the bookmakers. He won and then lost even more thousands and so was an easy prey. The jockey Jack Leach, when writing of him, said:

> . . . flagrant dishonesty ended the fabulous career of Tod Sloan. Tod had the ball at his feet, but kicked it the wrong way so often that he had to be got rid of. Here was a man who had everything needed by a top jockey, but a kink in his brain unbalanced him.[2]

It was then that the allegations of doping were rife. It was suggested they were done with a mixture of cocaine and a weak solution of nitroglycerine under the mane; it was applied on the way to the start and the effect lasted five to ten minutes. This could cause a problem because if the start was delayed the effect could have worn off and the horse, reacting to the stimulant, would come home half-asleep. In one French case, where the fashionable dope of that time was strychnine and ether, the horse lay down and slept at the starting post. The other way was in the form of a pill, made of ginger or cayenne and cocaine, which took much longer to act.[3] It was also suggested that a small shot of

---

[2] It is said that when he died in California his coffin was put in a room at the funeral parlour next to that of a celebrated gangster. Sloan did not have too many floral tributes but when the boxers Jim Jeffries and Gentleman Jim Corbett went to pay their respects, Corbett removed most of the gangster's flowers and put them on Sloan's coffin. 'Tod always travelled first class,' he said to Jeffries. J. Leach, *Sods I Have Cut on the Turf*, p.40.
[3] *Pearson's Magazine*, 8 August 1914.

strychnine applied between rounds could generate enough energy for a boxer being beaten on points to go for a knock-out.

There were also suggestions that mechanical aids were being employed, including a mechanical saddle which stimulated the horse by its vibrations, and an electric spur. In the forefront of these allegations was Sloan. It was said he kicked the ball into his own net once too often, and shortly afterwards was returned to America.

In 1914 the Jockey Club caused a sensation by demanding that three horses had their saliva tested for drugs. In 1930, after Don Pat trained by Charles Chapman won the Bedfont High Weight Handicap at Kempton Park, it was found that the horse had been doped. There was never any suggestion that Chapman had been involved in any way, but in accordance with the severe penalties handed out by the Jockey Club in those often unenlightened days, the horse was disqualified from all further races under Rules and the unfortunate Chapman warned off Newmarket Heath. No appeal lay against the Stewards' decision, and Chapman's only remedy was an action for libel claiming that the words that he had been warned off implied he had been a party to the doping of his horse. Patrick Hastings appeared for Chapman and Norman Birkett for the Jockey Club. The jury found for Chapman and he received £13,000 damages, but the Court of Appeal overturned the verdict on the grounds that the Jockey Club's statement was privileged. The dopers were never discovered.

After the Second World War a number of trainers automatically lost their licences when their horses were found to have been doped. These included John Beary, Ernest Street – whose horse Rock Star was doped in the Clarence House stakes at Ascot in September 1950 – Morgan Scannell, Cecil Ray, Harold Isom – whose horse Compassion was doped at the meeting at Kempton Park on Boxing Day 1951. All fell foul of the rule that even if the trainer knew nothing of the doping it was his responsibility.

George Allden was one of the small trainers, who in 1949 had a yard at the fifteen-roomed Beechwood House, Newmarket. Then at Pontefract on 28 September his filly Luxuriant, trembling and sweating, won the Upton Selling Handicap by a length and a half at the price of 100–6. It does not appear that the stable had been betting heavily on the horse; the owner had had £35 each way and Allden £15 to win and £10 a place. The subsequent tests showed traces of cocaine and strychnine. In December Allden's licence was withdrawn and he was ruined. Efforts to clear his name failed and two years later, then aged 54, he was working as a production clerk in a Manchester factory.

In those days the drugs were: the stimulant cocaine; atropine, another stimulant but which in large doses could also act as a depressant, and which was found in Rock Star; strychnine; Benzedrine, which staves off fatigue, found in Woolpack, a steeplechaser which fell at Doncaster, killing its jockey, in 1948; caffeine, a stimulant, which cost Mark Collins his licence when Quizzical Miss proved positive after a saliva test, also at Doncaster, in 1950; cortisone, used for treating rheumatism, also used on greyhounds; adrenalin, a gland extract; and two stoppers – morphine, also found in Rock Star, and barbiturates, more effective with greyhounds.

The year 1952 produced another flurry of doping stories.

Dopers, their syringes charged with the costliest products of medical research, prowl British racecourses. Others lurk in roadside cafés waiting to stand coffee to the drivers of horseboxes, while they themselves step outside for a word with their charges.

Various anti-doping measures were suggested against them. Remedies offered included, 'Light chain-mail blankets to be worn on race days; horses to journey to race meetings in convoy, and proper planning for the future (the breeding of a strain of dope-immune horses)'.[4]

It had come about because of the doping of one of Lord Rosebery's horses in training at Newmarket with Jack Jarvis. He declined to name the horse or the race, but offered £1,000 reward for information. Jarvis, protected by Lord Rosebery, was immune from the wrath which fell on the small trainers. It was the first glimmer of a relaxation of the draconian rule.

Then in 1955 ex-trainer Harry Lowe, who had sent out winners both on the Flat and under National Hunt rules from his Stockbridge yard, announced his retirement and also that he was going to tell all to the *People*.[5] 'All' meant how he had doped

---

[4] *Daily Mail*, 16 February 1952.
[5] 13 March 1955.

his horses: 'I had to do it and I am not the only one by a long chalk.'

Things had changed by 1960 when the fashionable trainer John Dunlop's horse Red Letter was to finish fourth in a field of five at Kempton Park in July. The sprinter Skymaster was also got at and beaten at Ascot. Sing Sing was got at before the July Cup at Newmarket. Getting at a favourite before a big race is more likely to be the work of a bookmaker than a punter, because the defeat of the favourite in the big race is almost invariably to the bookmaker's rather than to the punter's gain.

Charlie Mitchell, bookmaker and moneylender, was one of the great dopers of the 1950s and 1960s. He was also a member of the Krays' gang. Charlie Kray, with whom he went to Montreal in an unsuccessful visit to collect stolen bearer bonds, describes him as 'a small broad-shouldered man with a fresh face and a full set of sparkling white teeth; he was also completely bald'. He was arrested with the Kray twins and later turned Queen's Evidence, a great feather in the cap of Nipper Read and a great blow to the Krays who had thought that Mitchell of all people would remain staunch. Mitchell told Read that there had been a contract out on him and also Leslie Payne in the sum of £50,000 each. Mitchell had, he said, been the one required to find the money and arrange for a man to come from New York to carry out the hits.

He later compounded his bad behaviour by prosecuting two men with whom he had had a row in the North End Road, Fulham, near where he had his bookmaking business. As he put his head through the car window one of the men had wound it up, and Mitchell was dragged along the road. He was later shot dead in the south of Spain; his killers were never found.

He had an even less attractive side. He was what is called a thieves' ponce (a man who couldn't do the job himself and took a cut from the men who were regarded as having the guts to do so) and one of his victims was the great con-man Charles Da Silva, who deeply feared Mitchell, to whom he would give 75 per cent of his earnings. For a time Da Silva appears to have been protected by the Kray twins, but after their arrest and conviction his luck ran out.[6]

---

[6] According to Derek Raymond in his book *The Hidden Files*, pp. 111–12, Charlie Da Silva was killed in case he talked to the police rather than face a further prison sentence. He was one of the greatest con-men of all times, a man who once sold a fleet of ships to a Yorkshire farmer on a train between Hull and King's Cross.

In one of the first doping scandals of the 1960s, the police interviewed Bertie 'Bandy' Rogers at stables in Oxfordshire. He shot himself that night, and so missed the trial at Gloucester Assizes when a former jockey was found guilty of attempting to dope a horse and, despite the pleas of Sir Gordon Richards, received an eighteen months' sentence. The ringleaders received four years.

Three years later in 1963, at Lewes Assizes, William Roper, as ringleader, received three years for conspiracy to dope horses. A pretty Swiss girl had toured stables on the pretext of buying a horse, and of the twenty-one stables she had visited twelve favourites had been got at. She received a sentence of twelve months' imprisonment, but her punishment was lightened because she had already taken the precaution of selling her story to a Sunday newspaper to be published on her conviction. Another defendant, Edward Smith, known as the 'Witch Doctor' because of the potions he carried with him, had unfortunately fallen to his death from a landing in Lewes prison on the eve of the trial and so missed the proceedings. Another of the gang was Joe Lowry; his convictions dated back to 1930 and he received two years. It was never made clear for whom he and the rest of his team had been working. By 1966 he was at it again; this time he tried to dope Spare Filly, a horse in Lambourn trainer Bob Read's yard, and was given five years. The police had hidden out after a tip-off.

Doping steeplechasers is tantamount to attempted murder. When Staghound was doped in a novice steeplechase in the 1960s at Birmingham with Fred Winter up, he was a red-hot favourite from hurdling. Winter knew what was in store for him at the first fence. The horse never saw it. He 'went straight on', unseating Winter as he performed a somersault, then ran blindly at the second fence at which he again fell. He never ran in a steeplechase again.

It was not as if the racecourses were not trying to protect their charges. In 1952 a secure area became mandatory at every racecourse to which no outsiders were admitted for twenty-four hours before racing. For a time 'this was so successful that no racehorse has since been got at, so far as is known, in racecourse stables', wrote Roger Longrigg. Trainer Gavin Hunter was equally enthusiastic. 'It is virtually impossible to dope successfully, in a yard or in racecourse stables. Nowadays trainers go to the races happy in their minds that their horses will run on their merits.'[7]

Sadly the last years have shown their confidence has been misplaced. In 1957 efforts were made to get at the Derby favourite, Crepello. The owner, Sir Victor Sassoon, was followed on his visit to his trainer's stables in an effort to identify which box he visited. Crepello had been switched boxes, but the substituted animal had almost certainly been nobbled.

The next year Alcide was heavily backed for the Derby and then got at; he did not run. In 1959 Sing Sing, the undefeated champion two-year-old the previous year, was nobbled and withdrawn from the July Cup; he never ran again. In 1961 Pinturischo, favourite for the 2,000 Guineas, was given a very powerful purge thought to be used for elephants; he recovered, and the poor animal had to be doped again to ensure he did not run. Ribofilio was tailed off in the 1969 2,000 Guineas. The hot favourite 'could never raise a gallop', said Lester Piggott, his jockey.

By 1984 there were fears by the trainers that Gorytus, Forgive 'n' Forget, Gambir and Gaye Brief, all from top and different yards, had been got at. In 1988 Playschool put up a lifeless showing when favourite for the Cheltenham Gold Cup; he never won again.

The early 1990s produced another series of doping scandals. In 1990, nasal spray was used to dope two class horses, Norwich and Bravefoot, at the Doncaster St Leger meeting. They finished fourth and last in their respective races. The ITV racehorse commentator John McCrirrick had been vociferous in pointing out the betting patterns for the races and the fact that the favourites were being opposed in the market. In Bravefoot's race the second horse was heavily backed. Speaking after the Norwich doping, the Queen's trainer Ian Balding said that he thought between six and thirty horses a year were got at.

In July 1993 a BBC television programme *On The Line* showed how easy it was to walk in and out of the 'secure stabling' of at least one racecourse. In the programme, former top jockey and later trainer Dermot Browne told how he had doped a number of horses – possibly up to eighty – with the drug acetyl-pronazine just before they ran. In 1992 he had been given a ten-year ban by

[7] Roger Longrigg, *Daily Telegraph*, 21 July 1976.

the Jockey Club for telling a jockey to pull a horse and passing information to a bookmaker.

The switching of horses was for years one of the mainstays of the racetrack. As far back as 1844, Running Rein which won the Derby – the premier classic for three-year-old horses – was in fact Maccabeus, a four-year-old. At level weights a three-year-old because of its inferior physique could not be expected to defeat an older horse of reasonable quality. Maccabeus had been switched as a yearling for the foal Running Rein. Running as a two-year-old there had been doubts about his age. When he won at Newmarket one writer put it, '. . . to speak plainly, the colt is as well furnished as many of our *bona fide* three-year-olds.'

The running of that Derby was unhappy. The favourite, Ugly Buck, was the subject of deliberately foul riding; the second favourite, Tatan, was not only got at the night before but also pulled by his jockey Sam Rogers, who was warned off for his riding. Leander, who was leading at the time, was struck into by Running-Rein/Maccabeus and injured so badly that he was destroyed. An examination of his jaws showed he too was a four-year-old. His owners were warned off, and in a rage one of them announced that Leander was not four at all but six.

Switching has continued intermittently throughout this century. In the 1920s Coat of Mail was nothing if not moderate and was sold by Leech, his trainer, for export. A month later he won at Stockton by four lengths and the jockey, Billy Griggs, described him as being one of the best two-year-olds out. This was not surprising, since the horse Griggs had ridden quite innocently was Jazz, a smart four-year-old. Curiously the horses did not even look alike: Jazz was a tough little brown horse, and Coat of Mail a narrow washy bay. The coup had been organized by the notorious 'Ringer' Barry, who after his release from prison wrote in a Sunday paper how he used to paint horses to resemble one another. In his career he switched and doped horses to great effect. After his prison sentence he became a racing tipster advertising his credentials as 'The man who wrote his reminiscences in the *People*'.

One of the great switches at a racetrack occurred on 16 July 1953 when Fracasal won the Spa Selling Plate. The jockey, Billy Gilchrist, who had picked up a spare ride, reported that, '[I] picked up the stick, gave him one and he went right away to win by two lengths.' That Fracasal was unfancied in the betting was not surprising. He had been placed third in one race and unplaced in his other five. His odds of 10–1 reflected support for him on the course. What was not known at the time, however, was that there had been heavy betting on him in London, Wales, the Midlands and Scotland. Normally when this happens the money is 'blown' back on to the course and so the off-course betting on the horse is reflected in the starting price. It didn't on this occasion. The 'blower' wires had been cut at 1.30 p.m. and the bookmakers could not hedge their bets.

It all came out at the trial of Harry Kateley, Gomer Charles, Maurice Williams and Colonel Victor Dill. Fracasal was in fact Santa Amaro, a very smart French horse. Kateley, as the ringleader of the coup which should have netted at a minimum £60,000, received three years' imprisonment after a re-trial. Charles and Williams went down for two and the ex-Etonian, Victor Dill, got nine months. At one time during the case Reginald Spooner, the detective investigating the affair, was offered £20,000 if no charges were brought. Billy Gilchrist never received his riding fee.[8]

A later case of switching came in the 1980s with Flockton Grey, another three-year-old who ran as a two-year-old, again not surprisingly winning.

It has not simply been what has gone on with the horses that has caused the trouble at racecourses; it has been the peripheral 'sports' of welshing, bookmaker protection and intimidation, punter intimidation and the whole fairground of the short-con artist with the Three-Card-Trick, Crown and Anchor, Banker, Pitch-and-Toss and the Spinning Jenny or Spinner, let alone the pickpockets.[9] For a time Jack Spot ran a racecourse 'Take a Pick' contest in which the punters were invited, at sixpence a go, to pull a straw with a winning number from a cup. Even if they were successful they only received a cheap prize, whilst Spot received up to £40 a day. The Three-Card-Trick has flourished around the world under a variety of names and guises. Its origin lies in the Cups and Balls, one of the world's oldest conjuring tricks which

---

[8] There is a long account of this complicated affair in I.Adamson, *The Great Detective*, Part 4, Chapter 6.
[9] Banker was a very simple way of losing one's money. Bets were laid out in lots and it was a question of drawing a higher card than the banker whose sleight of hand would have been good enough to give him a winning edge.

manifested itself into Thimbles and Peas and the Three Shell swindle. The object of the exercise was for the punter to guess under which of three shells the operator had put a pea. There is a painting by Hieronymous Bosch of the operation of the Cups and Balls trick. To the left of the picture is a pickpocket at work.

The Three-Card-Trick, Find the Lady or Three-Card Monte are all pasteboard versions of the shell game. The three cards, usually including the Queen of Spades, are laid face down on a table or board and shuffled; the public is then invited to nominate which is the Queen. Each has the same set of devices, such as the bent corner (the pea off the board is the shell game equivalent) which can sucker the mark into believing that he has chosen the Queen of Spades.

In 1912 the Three-Card-Trick was held by the Divisional Court to be a game of skill – as of course it is by the operator.[10] If the game were a question of the sleight of hand defeating the eye then it might be so, but the operators have long taken precautions to make sure that the mark is misdirected by assistants in the crowd. If by any mischance he still picks the right card, there are still a number of options open to the operator, including the use of the assistants to claim the bet as their own, or to cry 'Police', or simply to overturn the board and rough-handle the punter. A spinner, now rarely seen, was a cross between the Three-Card-Trick and a roulette wheel. It consisted of the punter betting on which suits of cards came up. It was, of course, fixed by using a stick, known in the trade as a Haley, to stop the wheel. Pitch-and-Toss was a gambling game in which the punters laid bets on whether a number of coins would fall head or tail up. Banker was a simple form of *chemin de fer*, whilst Crown and Anchor was another board game.

The police were warned to be alert for these short-con artists. Occasional magistrates' courts were held, often in a room behind the stands, after the last race of the day, and it was usual for the local force to provide a 'racing book' for any plain-clothes officer on duty. This would contain photographs and records of all the local dips and other rogues, so that if an officer arrested one of them the man could be dealt with without delay.

---

[10] R.v Brixton Prison Governor, ex p Sjoland (1912) 77 JP 27. Two years later it was held that where there was cheating during play this was an offence under s.17 of the Gaming Act 1845. R. v Moore (1914) 10 CAR 54.

Welshers, as Evelyn Waugh put it, the name given to thieves on a racetrack, operated either as pairs or sometimes as a gang. In 1933 one of the great 'welshing coups' occurred at the Derby meeting at Epsom. A fake totalisator was constructed on the course on the chassis of a lorry hired for the day for 30 shillings. There was no sight of the giveaway chassis itself because it was decked out in posters, banners and flags. Set next to the site of the St Dunstan's Derby Day Service near Tattenham Corner, it was grandly called the St Dunstan's Tote and with 5/-, 10/- and £1 windows did big business. Once the off was signalled the crowds rushed to the famous corner to watch the horses come down the hill, and in their absence the gang disappeared; it is said they cleared over £1,600. There was a repeat effort at the Grand National meeting the next year, this time with the grandly named 'The National Totalisator'. This time, however, their efforts were thwarted by racecourse security officials and the team decamped.[11]

Bookmakers have always been at risk from fraud or violence. In 1848 the Glasgow fancy used brute force to obtain a levy from the owners of stalls at Paisley Races. By the turn of the century the Glasgow fancy had metamorphosed into the Redskins, so-called because of the knife scars on their faces. They had the run of the Scottish tracks whilst the Newcastle Boys held control over those of the North East. Indeed, in the 1870s a number of small tracks were closed down in and around London because of the activities of the gangs, and in 1893 the Brums, a Midland gang, demonstrated an early version of steaming when they raided the principal enclosure at Scarborough. Together with a gang from Leeds, they rushed the turnstiles stealing what they could. This diverted the racecourse police and so a second front was able to climb over the rails which separated the paddock area. Watches and money were stolen with impunity.

Later, in the twentieth century, the Aldgate mob acted in the same fashion as the youths on the London Underground today.

---

[11] W. Bebbington, in his book *Rogues Go Racing* (Chapter XXIV), has a number of stories about welshing bookmakers, including one who hired heavyweight boxers to knock down punters with winning tickets as they made their claims, and another of a Midlands bookmaker, Sam Isaacs, who decided to decamp after the Derby was run and shammed an epileptic fit. The punters on whom he was welshing assisted him to escape by calling for an ambulance. Isaacs had already given the takings on the race to his confederates.

Old-time bookmaker, Sam Dell, talking to Carl Chinn,[12] had this to say:

They were all pickpockets, they used to walk around, a gang of pickpockets. They were led by a face amongst them called D. Right villain and he was the leader and they used to operate mostly on Bank Holidays and High Days and Holidays and they'd be twenty-handed and this new thing that goes on called steaming – when they rush in and knock you – well they did that sixty years ago. They, what they would do, they would lift a guy in the air, someone would take his money . . .

The 'D' referred to may be the great Jack 'Dodger' Mullins who was a well-known Aldgate pickpocket and hardman. Born in the 1890s, he was regarded as a tearaway and 'ignorant as hell and bloody brutal with it'. In the 1930s he served a six-year sentence for demanding money with menaces from the old villain, Arthur Harding, with whom he had worked a protection racket at one time. Harding had apparently gone straight after his marriage, but Mullins often called on him to go out to do a bit of protection work with him. When Harding finally refused, Mullins took to tapping him for money. He is reputed once to have kicked a dog to death because 'It bit me.' He served a further five after he was arrested, tooled up, going to Brighton to deal with the Sabinis on the free course there. He was later a leader of the Dartmoor mutiny.[13]

If horseracing had been more or less cleaned up during the 1920s, at least from the protection of bookmakers, the same certainly could not be said for greyhound racing. Many of the racecourse bookmakers' protectors drifted over to this new and lucrative pastime. They included Alfie Solomon, released after serving his three years for the manslaughter of Buck Emden, and old 'Dodger' Mullins.

On his release Alfie Solomon went to live not all that far from Sir Edward Marshall-Hall KC in Maybury Mansions, New

---

[12] C. Chinn *Better Betting with a Decent Feller*, p.197.
[13] Mullins lived until his seventies, when apparently he was injured in a car crash. He was taken to hospital but died from pneumonia. There are references to Mullins in a number of books, including Raphael Samuels' *East End Underworld* and Reg Kray's *Villains We Have Known*.

Cavendish Street. Life was clearly not kind to him in his efforts to find decent honest work; he was beset by villains. In February 1930 he wrote to the Director of Public Prosecutions saying that he had gone straight since his release, working on the greyhound and racetracks:

> . . . A month ago I happened to go to Clapton dog races for the first time. After racing I went into the bar with a man named Bernard Dorrie, who owns and runs dogs there. A conversation was overheard while having a drink. A man named Luper took the biggest part in this, and he is a confidential friend of Superintendent Brown, who are always to be seen together. On leaving the Clapton Stadium, this particular night I was followed by a gang of men with Luper the leader under the protection of Inspector Pride. I was followed through a number of turnings, my life was threatened by a gang who is now on remand at Marlborough Street, who 'Dodger' Mullins is the head. I can't say that Inspector Pride was there then, but he was in the Stadium drinking with them until 11 o'clock at night. The words I heard used this night was, 'Let's do him,' and 'We've got the Big Five behind us now.'
>
> The appeal I am making to you is, as this man Luper is working under the protection of Superintendent Brown, what protection have I got. If necessary to hold an inquiry into this affair I am quite willing to come and give evidence in front of you, as I have got further news to tell you, that will surprise you, and I can bring witnesses.
>
> Hoping you will give me your protection as I don't know which way to turn.
>
> Yours faithfully,
Alfred Solomon.

Sadly Alfie never seems to have been given that chance and so we shall never know what surprises he had in store for the Director. The letter was passed to Sir Trevor Bigham at Scotland Yard, who soon discovered that things were not quite as they appeared from Mr Solomon's letter. It was clearly intended as something in the way of a pre-emptive strike, but the Yard had already had a prior anonymous telephone call which warned that there was likely to be trouble at several dog-tracks between rival gangs run by 'Dodger' Mullins and unfortunately the 'going straight' Mr Solomon. Perhaps Solomon was unlucky in that the senior officer against whom he complained was invited to deal with the allegations.

On 7 February Solomon, Jack Burman and what Superintendent Brown (to whom the matter was passed for his attention) described as 'several other criminals' had visited Clapton Stadium and demanded money from the bookmakers. Solomon was seen in the club room with Bernard Dorrie, a bookmaker, and asked by Mr Luper, the track manager, to leave. Solomon was eventually ejected. 'I am assured by Divisional Detective Pride that although he was present at the grounds, in accordance with his duties, he saw nothing of the incident to which Solomon refers,' said Brown, who added that after Solomon was ejected he and his associates decided to take their revenge on Luper when on 18 February he and his wife went to Wembley. He was set on by Jack Burman, who attacked him with an iron bar. Burman received two months for his pains and was bound over to keep the peace for six months in the sum of £100.

Now the Gospel according to Superintendent Brown came out in a note on the file dated March 11:

Alfred Solomon is one of four brothers; the other three obtain their living, as far as I know in a legitimate manner, as Bookmakers on Race Courses, usually under the name of 'Charles Lewis', but Alfred is nothing better than a member of a gang of thieves who blackmail Bookmakers for a living. I had the conduct of the enquiries in the case referred to by Solomon when he was last sentenced to Three Years penal servitude for manslaughter, and it was generally considered at the time that he was extremely fortunate not to have been convicted of the capital charge. During the course of the proceedings in this case, and since, he has shown considerable antipathy towards me, and no doubt he has often seen me in the company of Mr Luper and upon whom he is now endeavouring to vent his spite.

Mr Luper I have known about 18 years. First as a licensed victualler at Woolwich, at Lambeth and afterwards at Hackney. He has on many occasions rendered other Police officers and myself valuable assistance by giving us information gleaned by him in his business which

269

has led to the arrest of thieves and recovery of stolen property. Since giving up business as a licensed victualler abut three years ago, he became interested in the promotion of the Clapton Dog Racing Track, is now the manager, has heavy financial interests in the concern, and his aim is to keep the Track clean of such as Solomon and his associates, and he has legitimately sought the aid of the police to this end.

There is no truth in the suggestion that Luper is working under my protection, and I venture to express the opinion that Solomon's letter to the Home Office was written out of spite. It was brought to my knowledge that he did, in fact, broadcast amongst his undesirable acquaintances, some days before he wrote, the fact that he was writing to the Home Office.

That was about the end of the matter. A later note reads:

Alfred Solomon is a dangerous and violent person who is the last person in this world to want protection. On 27 April 1921 he was acquitted at the Central Criminal Court of shooting and wounding a man named Kimber with whom he had quarrelled, the defence being that it was an accident. On 6 July 1923 he was again acquitted of conspiracy and occasioning actual bodily harm.

It was also noted that he had the conviction for manslaughter. The note dated 14 March 1930 to the Home Office, returning their papers, reads: 'He is a dangerous rascal and his enemies are far more in need of protection than he is.'

Bernard Dorrie surfaced in July of the next year when he endeavoured to stand bail for Soloman Small, described in the police memorandum as a share pusher (also close associate of undesirable persons), who was on bail for an Aliens Act offence of not registering a change of address. Dorras was told that the police would object if he persisted in proffering himself and he withdrew.

What was sometimes a source of worry was any other things police officers got up to during their service and after their retirement. Betting and policing very much went together. For example, Detective Superintendent Ted Greeno wrote in his autobiography that on the first day of the Ascot meeting one year he had lost almost £50 and 'the next day was just as bad'. The third day he had a further £50 on a horse which fortunately won. This was in the thirties, when his pay would amount to a few pounds a week. His superior 'Nutty' Sharpe had just retired when on 6 July 1939 an ill-written anonymous note was received by Scotland Yard complaining that pensioned policeman ex-Inspector Sharpe was in a bookmaking business in The Final public house, King William Street. Signed 'On the Beat', it alleged that he was now in partnership with bookmaker Tommy Williams and Phil Lee, the guv'nor of a pub.

The note, written in capital letters, read:

A FINE ADVERT FOR THE POLICE SHARPE A BOOKMAKER NOW – AS BAD STILL AS EVER HE WAS WORSE WHEN IN THE POLICE HE GOT AWAY WITH IT TO THE DISGRACE OF ALL OF YOU WHO SHOULD HAVE KNOWN THE GAME HE WAS HAVING FOR YEARS ONE OF THE WICKED SCOUNDRELS IN THE POLICE FOR YEARS.

At least the poison-pen writer had his facts right. Discreet inquiries were made and it was apparent that Sharpe was associated with T. Williams & Co at 1 Thames Chambers where a *bona fide* commission agent's business was carried out and that he was an associate of Phil Lee, licensee of The Final. There was, however, no evidence of any offences under the Betting or Licensing Acts. Sharpe was also a ring steward at Wimbledon greyhounds.

The police did see Sharpe:

Although it has been generally understood that one of his partners in the commission agent's business is the notorious Tommy Williams this is not the case. It turns out that the Thomas Williams in question is a son, said by Mr Sharpe to be of good education and reputation. When I saw him, Mr Sharpe mentioned that there had been a re-adjustment of matters and that the partnership now consists of Williams and himself only, Philip Lee of the Final Public House having ceased to be a partner on 14th July 1939.

Even as it stands at the moment, the business association with the son of Tommy Williams is not as nice as it might be. I know Mr Sharpe fairly well and whilst I am satisfied that he would not consider any business association with Tommy Williams senior, or anyone like him, I am of the opinion that having gone into partnership with the son he sees nothing wrong in it, and would be prepared to contest it if it was suggested, as well it might be, that such a connection is inclined to be unworthy of an ex-Chief Inspector of the CID of the character and principle of Mr Sharpe (Memo of 12 August 1939).

Sharpe was sent a message and the rules of the game were spelled out to him. No one could say he must not do this, but he was letting the Force down. He said he would re-consider the matter.

Next year there appears a note on the file: 'On Sunday March 30 1940 I met Mr Sharpe and in general conversation he informed me he was no longer associated with the betting business referred to.'

A further handwritten note on the file reads:

Whilst not doubting the word of Mr Sharpe I feel it right to mention that there have been rumours that he is still connected with T. Williams & Co. and it might be as well to have the matter reviewed in say another month when flat racing is re-commenced. A Bell, Supt.

A final note suggested that things should be let lie as horseracing was likely to be suspended during the duration of the War. It was not.[14]

In any event there was dog-racing to which the ex-Chief Inspector could have turned his attention. He might have cared to cast an eye on what was the first ever dog-doping prosecution in London in 1942. The usual method of dealing with a race was employed. Generally there are six dogs in the traps (five at tracks with smaller circuits and, just to make the betting more competitive, eight in America) and the standard procedure is to dope three fancied dogs, leaving the rank outsider and the two on whom the bets are to be placed alone. The betting is then done on what is called the reversed forecast (known in betting terms as 'about'), one of the undoped dogs to win with the other undoped

---

[14] Public Record Office MEPO3/759.

one to come second, and then the bet is reversed. It pays a much higher rate than a straight win, particularly if they are unfancied in the betting as is likely. Sometimes the third dog will be included in a 1–2–3 bet combination.

The standard way of getting to the dogs (apart from through the trainer) is through the kennelmaid. All that must be avoided is a kennelmaid who develops scruples at seeing the dog for which she cares in considerable discomfort. In one early case in 1942 the girl was found a position in a kennels attached to Wembley Stadium and given the not inconsiderable sum of £50 as a retainer to dope the dogs in her care. She would be allowed to settle in for three weeks, then after she had done the first dog she would receive the sum of £400, sufficient then to buy a house. In fact the man had overplayed his hand. The girl was frightened, went to the police and was infiltrated by them into the Wembley kennels. Money was sent to her but she was not for the time required to interfere with the running of any of the dogs. Over a period of weeks she was introduced to other members of the team and finally to a woman. It was agreed she would give capsules to the animals four hours before the race and let the syndicate know she had done so. The financial arrangement was changed slightly, and now in return she would get £25 a week and then £300–£400 per race depending on the winnings.

Now an arrangement was made for her to meet a man at a West End hotel, where she was given a package and later asked to hand it back. She became cross and said she wanted to back out of the doping arrangement, but the man said that this had been a test. There was nothing in the parcel, but he wanted to see if she was being shadowed by the police.

The next time she was given the capsules it was arranged that the dog should be withdrawn from its race. The girl went to a meeting place to be paid, and as she left gave the signal that everyone was there. Three men were convicted and the woman acquitted.

Greyhounds owned by members of the public are in general sent to a trainer who is attached to a track. It is that trainer's duty to supply, fit and well, a certain number of dogs for each meeting. The owner pays the trainer for the dog's keep but receives a small sum every time the dog runs. He has no say in which races it will be placed. Unless the dog is absolutely useless there is a tacit agreement that by handicapping the various dogs – placing them

273

in traps from which it is easier or more difficult to win – the owner can expect to see his or her dog win every few weeks. However, it does not always work that way. I remember talking to an old racehorse trainer who also raced dogs and had what amounted to a matched pair of dogs; the only difference was that one had a mole under the fur of its belly. He was not convinced that he was being given a fair crack of the whip at his local stadium, and said that unless things improved next week he was going to switch dogs as the one with the mole was a good length faster than his litter brother.

In fact switching was rife. At Southend in 1949 Red Wind won an Open puppy race (dogs came from outside tracks to compete) over 500 yards in less time than it had taken to cover 460 yards in a trial four days earlier. In greyhound racing a second is worth sixteen lengths. It had been backed to win £4,000. On a check of its details it tallied, but inquiries in Ireland showed the owner had bought a dog named Waggles. When the trainer's wife came over to England and went to see 'Red Wind', Waggles recognized her at once. The owner was convicted at the Old Bailey, when the judge said there should be a cleansing of greyhound racing stables:

> That is in the interest of this recreation in which thousands of people find pleasure. It is most desirable that it should be as clean as any other form of English sport.

By 1950, only 72 of the 209 greyhound tracks in Britain were licensed; the rest were flapping tracks. On 9 June 1955 Harley Street doctor Adam Clark, together with Charles Green and Benjamin Selby, was convicted of conspiracy to cheat and defraud by doping dogs with hydrocortisone. Each received fifteen months at the Old Bailey. The doctor's mitigation was that they only operated at flapping tracks, of which there were still a high proportion.

Tote frauds were rare. In 1955 the only money known to have been obtained by fraud from the tote was less than £19 on a turnover of £25 million. There was, however, one splendid scam. It was that at certain provincial tracks there was a good view of both the tote window and the starting traps from a high point in the stands. If a particular dog trapped well, it was bound to win. The confederate went to the tote window shortly before the hare started and asked for 50 £1 tickets. By the time the race had started some thirty had been punched. The man then claimed that his wallet had been stolen and he could not pay for the tickets. What had happened was he had received a signal that the dog on which he had bet had trapped badly and could not win. Had he received the all-clear signal, he would have bought all the tickets.

On 24 June 1957, the crowd went wild at Harringay when the even money favourite Billycan Sprint bit the 10–1 outsider Ruben's Commission who was declared the winner. Protesting that they wanted the race re-run, the crowd smashed the tote board and set fire to the judge's box, starting traps and seats in the grandstand as well as stealing drinks and cigarettes worth £1,000.

An offshoot of greyhound racing was terrier racing in Ireland in the mid-1950s. As always betting was to the fore, and there were reports that a home-brew alcohol was rubbed on the dog's skin to make it run faster. According to *Everybody* in March 1958:

A dog's weight must not vary by more than 2 lbs from its registered weight. Whether you're a regular punter or only attend a dog meeting occasionally, you can rest assured that dog-racing on reputable tracks today is one of the cleanest sports in the country.

This was one of the ways the authorities could guarantee the sport would be run cleanly. It was, of course, still possible to deny the dog its walk the night before the race, give it a bowl of water or even put elastic bands on its toes. And from an outsider's point of view, quite apart from doping the animal, the traps themselves could be greased.

In December 1958 Johnny Coulon revealed all in the *People*. He maintained he smeared aniseed over the traps, which caused a dog to hesitate and not leave until it actually saw the hare. In this way, he said, in 1944 he smeared five traps at Carntyre, Glasgow, leaving Gladstone Brigadier to win handily in the Scottish Derby. In another example in 1951 in Monmouthshire, he did three dogs with hexamethomium, leaving three dogs. One, Battledore, the rank outsider, he ignored and bet on the other two in the forecast. Five dogs staggered out of the traps – a rival concern had doped his two dogs. Battledore won. Other schemes in Glasgow including trying to dye a dog black with hair dye and racing a dog over its racing weight – over the years dogs were run in weighted muzzles. He was convicted on 5 December 1958, but had sensibly left his story behind with the *People*.

Along with John Coulon, Daniel Swain, Patrick Arnold, Kenneth Collishaw and his wife Daphne, a former kennel-maid, Samuel and Charles Hoare went on trial along with other kennelmaids. Dogs had been doped at Charlton, Wandsworth and Park Royal with meatballs laced with pheno-barbitone. The tip-off had come in May when a girl at the Sunbury Kennels told the kennel manager she had been asked to dope a dog. Daphne Collishaw received a year, the other kennelmaids six months, Coulon three years, Daniel Swain two, and Kenneth Collishaw eighteen months. The girls had received between £20 and £30 a dog. Kennelmaid Barbara Baker had blown the whistle because she could not bear to think the dogs might suffer. She disappeared shortly before the trial and was thought to be in Ireland.

In the late summer of 1964 came the Dagenham Coup, following which bookmakers sued Romford Stadium as the owners of the Dagenham track. It was over an ingenious coup which partially succeeded.

The sixth race on 30 June 1964, the 4.05 p.m., was an Open over 840 yards flat. Seven tote booths and every tote window taking forecast bets was blocked. By backing eighteen out of thirty combinations the conspirators fed money into a pool by making certain losing bets. The other twelve combinations were backed to one unit on each. The odds produced were phenomenal and one punter, John Turner, claimed £987.11s. 9d. on a 2-shilling bet. It was claimed that the stadium should have refused to declare a dividend on the race. The winning odds of the second and third favourites, Buck Wheat and Handsome Lass, coming first and second were 10,000 to 1. The favourite was third, so this effectively eliminated any doping allegations. The bookmakers said the market had been rigged.

There had been examples of bookmakers involved with a market which didn't add up. On 28 June 1947 a Major 'Mac' McKenzie had laid a bet covering a three-year-old horse named Glendower to win £2,000 in the Chepstow Stakes. He expected that the horse, ridden by Gordon Richards, would cost him £4,000 if it lost. Unfortunately one of the only two rivals withdrew, and with the placing of many more bets by the blower service the odds at starting were 20 to 1 on. McKenzie lost £40,000, had to sell shares in the GRA of which he was then a director and never recovered.

The Dagenham bookmakers screamed when next day Turner told how he had masterminded the coup with 125 helpers each paid £5, and £50–£100 if it was successful. He borrowed £3,500 from a local bookmaker as a stake. The bookmakers announced they would not pay; the debts were not legally enforceable and all Turner could do would be to object to the renewal of their licences. The triumph was temporary; Mr Justice Paull's judgment was overturned by the Court of Appeal. John Turner was prosecuted for conspiracy to defraud, along with Terrence Orwell and Henry Cohen. The winnings, had they been paid out, were thought to be between £7 and £10 million.

There had been other coups. In 1963 Mrs Mary Martin had successfully objected to a bookmaker's licence after placing 25 15-shilling place-only accumulators at tote odds with William Hill. The matter went to arbitration and against Mrs Martin because accomplices had put large bets on other dogs to inflate the dividend (400-1 was the biggest ever paid out on a forecast).

On 7 November 1965 the *People* named Peter Phillip Hubbard, Ronald Maxwell and Judith Hubbard as the masterminds of greyhound doping plots. Mrs Hubbard was the owner and looked after the store of dope, and dogs were doped at what had been seen as impregnable tracks such as Harringay and White City as well as Belle Vue and Glasgow. The *People* said that dogs were being doped in such quantities that it was decided to allow them to run rather than cancel the races, or even the whole meeting, and observe betting patterns. A young boy was planted into the Northaw Kennels and Irish girls were imported. At one time Hubbard maintained that out of six kennels at Walthamstow, he had girls in four. The plan was the standard Dope Three-Bet Three.

By 2 February 1966 they were all at the Old Bailey. There was Kray-man Charles Mitchell, Peter Hubbard, Ronald Maxwell and Peter Curtis (described as a security officer, who acted as Hubbard's sidekick over the years), along with two girls Claudette Hamilton and Josephine Carroll. Girls were softened up with the bright lights of London.

The prosecution alleged that at least fifty dogs from five tracks

277

had been doped by the ring. During the course of the first trial one witness admitted she received £390 to lie to get Charles Mitchell off. The jury was discharged from giving a verdict and, in a second trial in April 1966, Margaret Fletcher gave evidence that she was promised a dog called Monday's Ranger for her father if she doped other dogs. Mitchell and Hubbard went to prison.

In 1989 warned-off trainer Jerry Fisher was alleging he had doped dogs with cocaine, put caffeine into meat-balls and piddled in the dog's bowl to avoid detection. Dogs were being stopped at trials to lengthen their odds when they actually ran in a race, and were run at flapping tracks to regain their interest in racing, he said. In the last three months of 1993, seventy positive dope tests were recorded and nine trainers were struck off. Positive samples exceeded the total for 1992.

The old tried and tested methods still seemed to be working, even though the NGRC have recently switched from using Glasgow University for testing to the Jockey Club's sophisticated analysis centre at Newmarket.

Ex-trainer David Haywood, fined for using an illegal substance to doctor one of his dogs, said, 'A high percentage of dogs are doped to slow them down and cocaine, amphetamines and steroids have been used. Some trainers will hide a bottle of dog's urine up their sleeves so if a steward asks for a test he can bend down and pour the "clean" stuff into the sample jar.'[15]

So far as boxing is concerned, the British Boxing Board of Control has had things fairly well under control for the past sixty years. Even so things could go wrong. Nothing to do with organized crime at all, but in a contest between Steve McCarthy and Tony Wilson in September 1989 Minna Wilson, seeing her son getting a beating, climbed on to the apron of the ring and began hitting the unfortunate McCarthy with a shoe. He sustained a cut on his head, refused to fight on and was disqualified. He appealed to the Boxing Board of Control, who upheld the referee but ordered a re-match. Mrs Wilson was not at the ringside on that occasion.

More seriously, one of the Board's principal preoccupations has been the illegal prize fight which might bring the anti-boxing lobby down on its head yet again. In 1936 the fear nearly became the reality. There had been an argument between two Wands-

---

[15] The *People*, 9 January 1994.

worth labourers outside a pub over a remark passed about the wife of one of them. A blow was struck but not returned; instead a challenge was issued for 8 a.m. on 23 August 1936 at King George's Park, Wandsworth. An audience of between 200 and 300 turned up – one newspaper said 1,000 people were there. A bookmaker had gone to bet on the park fight, illegal bookmaking being common at fights between ordinary people settling a quarrel.

Now a local boxing promoter decided to hold a gloved contest. William Hillsley, Catch as Catch Can (29) *v* Ernest Simmonds, The Battling Dustman (36) at Wandsworth Stadium in September 1936 as a supporting contest to Maurice Strickland, the New Zealand Heavyweight Champion, and Pancho Villa. Jim Wicks, witness to the Montecolumbo killing, was now the matchmaker for the Stadium. He had said he could get the men a licence each and expected they would get between £25 and £50 nobbins.[16] He anticipated the bout would add £100 to the night's takings with these 'local sportsmen' on the bill. Proceeds were going to Battersea General Hospital.

The police sought to interfere on the grounds that it was undesirable. There was no knowledge of whether the men were evenly matched – there was a seven-year age gap – and they didn't want a promoter to unjustly enrich himself. Moreover the police were clearly sceptical as to whether all the proceeds would end up in the hospital. They thought the fight could also draw a partisan crowd, and requested the advice of the Director of Public Prosecutions as to the legality of the whole affair. When it came to it, the promoter withdrew before a ruling could be made.

Two early prize-fight champions, Bill Stevens 'The Nailer' and Bill Darts, threw their fights in March 1761 and May 1781 respectively. Stevens was paid £50 by Jack Slack whom he had already defeated, and lost in a very quick seventeen minutes to George Meggs. Darts threw in the towel for £100 against Peter Corcoran. In this century, however, there have been few instances of fixed matches, certainly at championship level. Dai Dower and John L. Gardiner were champions who unknowingly benefited from an arrangement struck with their opponents.

---

[16] Nobbins were coins (and occasionally notes) thrown into the ring at the end of a close and well-fought contest. Traditionally they were divided evenly between the boxers, but usually the winner gave the loser all the money. The biggest sum of nobbins ever recorded was over £150.

There are stories that Jack Spot had a hand in fixing fights and it is inconceivable that, from time to time, money has not changed hands at a number of the smaller tournaments over the years. This is more likely to have been done to promote a boy's career rather than for betting purposes. In general, however, the way of massaging a boy's reputation in this country has not, as in America, been to pay the opposition but rather to select non-punching opponents with weak chins. Nor is there any real evidence that money has been paid to referees and judges, however peculiar the scoring of some contests has been. From time to time the British Boxing Board of Control has down-graded a referee whose conduct of contests has given rise to concern, but this has more usually been because the referee has not intervened to prevent a boxer taking too much punishment rather than because he has been signalling his intention to betters at the side of the ring or deliberately favouring a contestant. This had not always been the position in the earlier days of unlicensed boxing; one sporting journalist was invited to be a judge for a bout at a promotion: 'I was told quite firmly which boy was going to win and I didn't dare do anything but score for him.'

One boxer who temporarily benefited from a fixed fight was Tony Mella, a promising heavyweight after the War. His friends bought off an opponent at the Mile End arena, but in his next contest he was matched against the Southern Area champion who would have none of it and gave Mella a bad beating. Mella went on to own a number of clubs in the West End before he was shot by his friend Alf Melvin, who immediately committed suicide.

In June 1990, however, it appears that the scales at a tournament at the Royal Albert Hall were tampered with, although it was never made clear by whom. Mark Reefer came in as a late substitute in a title match with Pedro Gutierrez. Reefer weighed in on the limit, took a bad beating and was knocked out in the last round. The promoter was later sent a letter by the managing director of the manufacturers of the scales, saying he was distressed to learn that his company had been asked to calibrate the scales short. 'Somebody asked a member of our staff to do it and he foolishly acceded to the request.' There is no evidence that the promoter knew of the matter, which was reported by the Board of Control to the police. No action was taken against anyone.

Perhaps it is looking at things through rose-tinted glasses to say that although boxing and the criminal fraternity go hand in hand, the latter – many of whom have been in the game themselves – like it too much to try to interfere with the matches on a regular basis. More often the troubles arise when boxers have to retire and have not been able to put away sufficient money during their careers. They are then recruited into the twilight world of the nightclub bouncer, and some into the even darker world of the enforcer and the robber. One prime example is the former lightweight champion Sammy McCarthy, who has served several sentences for armed robbery.

There has always been a certain amount of unlicensed boxing, in the sense that it was not under the auspices of the British Boxing Board of Control, and also some bare-knuckle fighting around. In the 1970s there was a genuine and properly organized fledging rival establishment run by Frank Warren, but when he became successful he applied for and was granted a Board licence. Since then unlicensed boxing is the place where boxers who have grown old, had poor records, or recent criminal convictions and had lost their licences, find a home along with young talent who have been persuaded against going with the Board. Boxers fight under pseudonyms – 'Tyson', 'The Duke' – and the punters like the illusion of being on the margins of the law. Unlicensed boxing has its other uses:

This fellow's amphetamine business went down the toilet when M escaped [from prison] and set up a factory of his own. Suddenly everyone wanted to deal with M. They wanted a slice of his rep. He had to get back to basics – get back on the streets, do the rounds of the unlicensed boxing, the greyhounds to get it on its feet again.

Bare-knuckle fighting is alive and well. The old stars such as Donny 'The Bull' Adams, Lenny 'The Governor' or 'The Mean Machine' McLean[17] and Roy Shaw are now relatively old men, but their exploits on the cobbles have become legends.

In 1992 McLean served a sentence of eighteen months' imprisonment for assault after the death of Gary Humphreys who had stripped naked, urinated on the stage and played with

[17] *Sky*, December 1992.

himself at the Hippodrome nightclub in London before being hauled away by the bouncers, including McLean who was acquitted of his murder. Humphreys suffered from a hyperactive condition and had run out of tablets to control it. 'You knew he would be defenceless against you,' said Judge Richard Lowry QC, 'but you decided to teach him a lesson.' During his time on remand McLean had been seen by psychiatrists who described him as tearful and suicidal.

After the case, as often happens, he recovered his old ebullience. During his sentence he is reputed to have told his young, and nervous, cell-mate that there was to be no breaking wind. He himself immediately did so twice and then said, 'That's for both of us.' He had served a previous sentence of four years for an attack on youths in the street, a punishment he regards as unfair:

> I came out of a nightclub and there was a woman in a car with a kid and three drunks around the car going, 'Show us yer fanny' and all that. If I'd done what 90 per cent of the public would've done and walked away, those guys would've raped the woman.

McLean's most famous unlicensed fight against Brian 'The Mad Gypsy' Bradshaw was recorded on video. Mr Bradshaw was out for forty-five minutes after unwisely beginning the contest before the bell with a head-butt. McLean is said to have received £20,000 on a winner take all against the 'Old Guv'nor' Roy Shaw. He describes his technique in another contest in awesome terms: 'I broke his jaw in seven places, bit half his ear off, half his cheekbone off, half his nose off and his bottom lip and then I'm going at him like a lunatic.'

A film of McLean's life was being shot in 1993.

There is now a new generation of martial arts men who will fight for promoters in Birmingham and London, where there are three manors. The venues are parks, clubs and warehouses, where the purses are winner takes all, if he is lucky, and there is heavy betting. The rules are even more basic than in the Shaw-McLean days. A foul takes place when one of the fighters is unconscious and his opponent still damages him. The fighters are hardmen and minders who will carry out a beating as a side contract or in the guise of a contest. One warrior reported being offered £1,500 to participate in a dog-fight. This is not so bizarre as it may seem. Man *v* Dog fights have been around for many years. In Wicken, in the Fens, the first policeman sent there in Victorian times was murdered by a mob including Pitt Fletcher. Fletcher, known as 'The Fen Tiger', in one Dog *v* Man fight bit off the dog's snout, but not before he himself had lost an ear.

Football on the field, as opposed to the transfer market, has always been the subject of whispers of game fixing, often to help out friendly clubs to avoid relegation, obtain a bigger gate in a cup replay and sometimes for betting purposes. Few of the allegations and rumours have been substantiated.

In 1913 a man was imprisoned for five months for trying to bribe the English full-back Jesse Pennington to make West Bromwich lose or draw against Everton. Before the Second World War there was an attempt by the former Celtic and Scotland player Archie 'Punch' Kyle to bribe Hamilton Academicals to lose a home game against Leith Athletic, a match they should have won with some ease. He first approached the Academicals' captain Willie Moffat. Moffat contacted his Board, who called in the police.

A second approach took place with a police officer Robert Colquhoun hiding behind some curtains recording the conversation. Kyle's defence was that he was arranging the transfer of Moffat to an English club for whom he scouted. What he had meant to suggest was that if Moffat did not play to the top of his form the transfer fee might be reduced. Kyle received a short sentence. Hamilton played well that Saturday and lost.

One of the unconfirmed tales is the story of the Division Three (North) club whose players put their wages on the opposition but omitted to tell the new, young and very keen centre-forward of their bet. He equalized in the last minute.

In the 1960s, however, there was an increasing number of stories that games were being fixed for betting purposes. It began with the suspension by Bristol Rovers of two of their players, and followed with a series of stories in the *People*[18] which named players involved in bribery allegations. This was bad enough but, worse, some were household names. The black day for English football had been 1 December 1962 at a time when the players, earning £60 a week, were bribed over a First Division match. The attitude of newspaper reports of the time is curious. It seems as

[18] 12 April 1964.

though a bit of skullduggery in the lower divisions was to be
expected (although it could dramatically change who won the
hundred thousand or so on offer by the pools companies), but
that when teams reached the pinnacle of the First Division then
the game must be sacrosanct. The allegation was that David
'Bronco' Layne (he was nicknamed after a popular television
Western hero), Sheffield Wednesday's star centre-forward, Peter
Swan their centre-half and Tony Kay, later transferred for
£55,000 to Everton from Wednesday, were guilty of backing
their team to lose an away match at Ipswich, who had in fact
(and unexpectedly) won 2–0. The players, said the article, had
received £100 each. The man behind the fix was former Everton
and Charlton player Jimmy Gauld, who had broken his leg
playing for Mansfield Town at the end of his career. He had
apparently met Layne in the stands at a Mansfield evening
match, put the proposition to the centre-forward and in turn
he had contacted Kay and Swan. According to the *People*, two
other matches were fixed by Gauld on the same day. Lincoln City
were to lose at home to Brentford and York City away at
Oldham Athletic. Everything went well. Ipswich had won,
Brentford beat Lincoln 3–1 and Oldham beat York 3–2.

Once the allegations were out in the open other reports were
forthcoming. In 1962 the Oldham players had refused to accept a
bribe from Gauld, who had been fined a derisory £60 for the
attempt.

The financial success of such a fix would depend on the
appropriately named fixed odds offered by bookmakers on
single matches. The bet would be for doubles on the unfancied
teams, which could pay off at odds of 10–1 or even better. To
make this successful the fixer would have to involve tame
bookmakers who would lay off the bets and invest some of
their own money rather than by trying to spread the bet over
several bookmakers, something which might attract attention.
One of the two bookmakers named in the *People*, Joe Hancock
(52) from Mansfield, committed suicide in a local reservoir when
a police investigation seemed inevitable.

The fixing had been going on since the 1959–60 season.
According to Gauld, he received a letter saying that certain
players were being paid by Tranmere Rovers to deliberately
lose their next match and so help that club avoid relegation.
He then arranged for Swindon, for whom he was playing in the

1959–60 season, to lose to Port Vale so there could be a 'double'.

Ten players and former players were served with summonses to appear at Mansfield. They included Gauld, Layne, Swan and Kay and Jack Fountain, once captain of York City. The case was eventually heard at Nottingham Assizes in January 1965. Matches rigged had ranged through the divisions during the years 1960–1963 and included the Scottish match of St Mirren *v* Dundee United. All were found guilty of at least one offence. On 21 January 1965 Gauld received four years and was ordered to pay £5,000 costs. Fountain received fifteen months; Layne, Kay and Swan each received four months. On the release of the players from prison, the Football Association banned some of them for life.

Rumours of attempted fixing lingered on. Arthur Ellis, the referee, disclosed he had been offered the princely sum of £35 to make sure Preston won their 1959 cup-tie with Stoke. In October 1960, amidst a flurry of reports of bribery, with players naming each other and five players from a Northern club reporting matters to the police, one former player admitted to the *Daily Mail* that he had tried to rig the Chelsea *v* Everton match and had offered another player £500. From then on allegations of match fixing died away.

Violence at sporting fixtures is as old as sport itself. Chariot drivers in Constantinople under the Emperor Justinian wore the Blue and the Green racing colours which led to clashes between their rival supporters. Racing was banned for five years after a battle between the fans of the rival charioteers.

However, the mainstream football crime has been on the terraces. Football hooliganism has long been part of the game, with English 'supporters' being at the forefront. At the end of the last century grounds were regularly closed after rival supporters had fought, but in more recent years the travelling of fans to away matches has masked a variety of crimes and has provided a legitimate explanation for criminals to be out of their home ground.

At the beginning of the 1993–4 season Superintendent Adrian Appelby of the National Anti-hooligan Unit spoke of rape, armed robbery and fraud being carried out under the cover of a hard core of some five hundred football fans as they travelled to cities where the local police did not know them.

The top tier of gangs – Chelsea, the Inter City Firm from West

Ham and the Arsenal 'Gooners' – were all investigated in the late 1980s, and there had been prosecutions most of which had collapsed amidst allegations of police impropriety.

The new generation of gang members had grown up in the belief that they were untouchable and, said Appelby, the largest gang, the Chelsea Headhunters, had alliances with supporters of other teams including the seemingly unlikely ones of Colchester and Heart of Midlothian. When Hearts had played Standard Liege in Belgium, their supporters had called on Chelsea for help in the violence which was likely to ensue. The police had also found links between Chelsea supporters and the British National Party.

Professor Dick Hobbs of the University of Durham carried out research in the 1980s into members of football gangs:

> I worked with a group from 1981 onwards. They were neighbourhood men of violence and several were prominent members of a group of organized football hooligans. In 1987 Ecstasy was re-discovered in Ibiza and the Acid House party scene took off. Security was needed – not from middle-aged dinosaurs but from people the same age as those who were going to the parties. The football hooligan was ideal. Some were already appearing on television on chat shows. They had become minor media stars. Their reputations had been made overnight.
>
> Young men like them were obvious sources for security at raves and so on. The organizers turned to them for help. In turn they began to collaborate with people dealing with drugs on the premises. It was quasi-extortion. They would let people in to deal and soon in turn they cut off the middleman and sold the drugs themselves. Very quickly they made enormous sums of money.
>
> They then began to sell the goods outside the raves and sought out importers. Ten years later they no longer operate security but have set up legitimate people to run that for them – sporting and music venues. They've on the face of it gone legitimate and they'll move about – Liverpool, Manchester, wherever. They have moved into time-share, property abroad, clubs, sweetshops, car dealerships – a wonderful front. They are constantly mutating: several have opted out, whilst others are in professional crime of a more complicated sort.

12

The Drug Trade
– Soft and Hard

Writing in 1952 in *The Truth about Drug Addiction in Britain,* Kenneth Allsop was convinced, or at any rate his publishers were, that there was no problem of teenaged drug addicts in Britain:

> We are not going the way of America. But the fashion for drug-taking is on the increase, and it is a social danger that should be watched.

He cited the lack of an organized drug market ring as the haphazard price for the cost of dope. Reefers, he found, cost from 2/6d to 7/6d. Loose in paper packets, the going rate was 2/6d a gramme. A heroin taker 'once firmly addicted' will need 30–50 tablets a day at a cost of between £30 and £50 a week.

Throughout the century there has always been a drugs presence in Britain, but certainly for the first fifty years it had been a limited and relatively controlled one. Indeed, in the late nineteenth century drugs were the province of the intellectual. Opium, for example, was not made an illegal substance until 1916. A little morphine never did Sherlock Holmes any harm and, while Freud eventually destroyed his nose with cocaine, would he have been able to write quite so influentially without it?

Shortly after the First World War a five-foot Chinese, Brilliant Chang, trafficked in both women and drugs. He was almost certainly the supplier of the drugs which led to two well-publicized deaths. After the Victory Ball held at the Albert

Hall, Billie Carleton, a pretty young actress, collapsed and died. The inquest showed she had died of cocaine poisoning and was addicted to opium smoking. It was common knowledge that Chang had been a close friend, but although her companion of the night before, Reggie de Veuille, was charged with manslaughter nothing was ever proved against Chang. Then in March 1922 Freda Kempton, a dancing instructress, was also found dead from an overdose of cocaine. This time Brilliant Chang did feature; he had been with Freda the night before, and faced a hostile series of questions at her inquest. 'She was a friend of mine, but I know nothing about the cocaine,' he told the coroner. 'It is all a mystery to me.'

Chang, gap-toothed with dark hair swept back, was apparently the son of a well-to-do Chinese businessman sent to England to pursue a commercial career. Instead he opened a restaurant in Regent Street and started drug trafficking on the side from his private suite. He operated more or less unchallenged until 1924 when two carriers were arrested. Letters in their possession linked them to Chang. Despite police surveillance nothing was established against him although, in the flurry of unwelcome publicity after Freda Kempton's death, he withdrew his operations to Limehouse where in 1924 the police raided his premises. They found not only a mandarin's palace in the grimy building but more importantly, in a secret cupboard, a large quantity of cocaine. He was deported after serving a fourteen-month sentence. During his six-year reign it is estimated he made over £1 million from drugs trafficking.

When he was driven out of Soho Chang's empire there was taken over by another dope pedlar and white slaver, balding and hollow-eyed Jamaican-born Eddie Manning, who had come to Britain in 1916, worked in a munitions factory before an accident invalided him out and then played the drums in a touring company for three years. From 1919 he does not seem to have worked again and, the police thought, ran a dozen prostitutes, using them to sell cocaine at 10 shillings an injection from his flat in Lisle Street and the Berwick Street cellar café he owned with his Greek woman friend. In 1920 he had served a sentence of sixteen months for shooting at Frank Miller at Cambridge Circus. He was a trifle unfortunate; from the evidence, it does appear that on this occasion he was more sinned against than sinning. He was being pressured by Miller, known as 'American

Frank', known bully and blackmailer, and his brother Charles Tunick to hand over some of his gambling winnings. When the matter came to court there was no appearance by Miller and, in a plea bargain, the attempted murder charge was whittled down. He received three years' penal servitude for possession of opium on 19 July 1923. Efforts to deport him as an American failed. Manning claimed to have been born the son of a freed slave in 1882 in Jamaica, but inquiries there failed to substantiate his claim. Eventually the authorities abandoned their efforts and he continued to survive until he received his final sentence in 1929. By now he too had been chased out of the drug-dealing world and was into receiving. Property worth £2,000 was found at his flat. After serving his sentence, he dropped out of sight.[1]

As a rule morphine, heroin and cocaine were smuggled over from Germany in small packets. Then personal searches by the customs were the exception rather than the rule. Distribution was in the hands of the likes of Manning and also those of 'newspaper boys' who pretended to be selling the evening papers and distributed cocaine under this cover.[2]

In the middle 1950s the main area for drug dealing was the home of the musicians, 'Tin Pan Alley', Archer Street, along with Piccadilly Circus, Brixton, Westbourne Park and Aldgate. Dope was peddled at the greyhound tracks around London, and the economy showed a profit of around £200 per pound weight of marijuana.

By 1957 *The Times*, for one, was still dancing to the tune of the Black Peril. It was not our health but our morality which was at risk:

. . . Of the people convicted, seven out of eight are coloured men, mainly West Indians. The hemp problem has been with us now for about ten years. Will it become more serious? The market in Great Britain will continue extremely tempting while it contains so many coloured people. The Home Office and police tend to lump together . . . white offenders as band leaders who specialize in the more exotic types of dance music, or even as musicians who

---

[1] There is a fairly full account of his life and death, including his pathological fear of owls, in V. Davis, *Phenomena in Crime*, Chapter 7.
[2] S. Felstead, *The Underworld of London*, VI.

specialize in exceptionally 'hot' music at 'modern music clubs' in the West End of London . . . White girls who become friendly with West Indians are from time to time enticed to hemp smoking . . . this is an aspect of the hemp problem – the possibilities of its spreading amongst irresponsible young white people – that causes greatest concern to the authorities. The potential moral danger is significant, since a principal motive of the coloured man in smoking hemp is to stimulate his sexual desires.[3]

Girls were being lured to smoking parties, where they were being charged 5 shillings a reefer at Swindon. On 1 July 1960 three Turkish Cypriot youths were convicted. Writing in a column for the *Empire News* in 1957, Robert Fabian, the great detective, had already warned that it was the 'easiest, newest weapon of the West End white slaver. Every pound of marijuana can make 1,000 cigarettes. They sell for 7s. 6d. each.' This appears to back up Kenneth Allsop's belief that there was no international organized ring. Either that, or the police and press did not have a clue what was really going on.

There was a bit of a home production market on which the courts were quick to stamp. In 1959 Reuben Ritchie and John Luton were convicted of unlawful possession of cannabis resin. The defence was unusual. Apparently they had bought a sixpenny packet of budgerigar seed at a pet-shop near their homes in Tiger Bay, Cardiff. Usually this was harmless, but because of an extraordinarily fine summer they were able to harvest a crop weighing six pounds – worth, said the prosecution, £2,300. They were jailed for nine months each. It all seems so innocent now but, as Tom Lehrer sang in the nightclubs of the 1960s, 'Today's young innocent faces are tomorrow's clientele.'

Early in 1961 *The Times* was confident that headway was being made in the world battle against drug addiction. There was a decline in the use of heroin. In 1956 – the latest year for statistics, but there was no reason to suppose things had deteriorated in 1957 – only three countries manufactured heroin: Britain with 37kg, Belgium with 11kg and Hungary 12kg. Some of this was made into non-addiction forming drugs and so the net world production of heroin could be counted at 39kg.

[3] 'Haunt of the Reefer' in *The Times*, 1957.

The effect of the controls had been to reduce almost to vanishing point the possibility of drug addicts obtaining narcotics from legitimate sources, so now they had to have recourse to illicit sources. The Permanent Central Opium Board thought this was really rather a good point. The Board, which was largely concerned with the fight against illicit traffic, had advanced some conclusions from the figures:

Traffic in opium was most active in the Far and Near East. The largest seizures in heroin were in North America, the Mediterranean basin and Hong Kong. The trade in morphine had not declined and most was seized in the Near and Far East. Traffic in cannabis was largest in Africa. The importance of cocaine as an illegal drug had considerably declined whilst synthetic drugs hardly featured. In no country or territory did the amounts of any synthetic drug seized, if at all, exceed one kilo.

Six years earlier Duncan Webb, writing in the *People*, ever worried about the dark menace, was able to have 'London's Drug Fiends Exposed'. It was from East London that the majority of 'coloured marijuana agents' worked: 'I gained access to a Negro who was the chief market supplier to the entire East London area. He gave his name and address in Stepney, alleging that this was one of the busiest distributing points in London.' Webb also interviewed one of the man's sub-agents, who told him that most of his supplies came in through Liverpool: 'Whilst they were quite content to peddle marijuana "Negros" apparently recoiled from supplying heroin and this trade was almost wholly in the hands of white men.'[4]

Of course, organized crime was involved and there is little doubt that the Messina brothers, those Czars of London vice, were also involved in the drug trade. There is a report that in 1955 Carmelo, using the name Gino Miller, was dealing in 'silk', the trade name for heroin, in Germany. He was set up to deal in a scam with an Interpol officer, but the deal never went through because the Messinas were arrested in London over vice matters.

July 1960 had the *Sunday Graphic* speculating 'through the eyes of Ace reporter, Charles Wighton' why there was no big-

[4] *People*, 13 June 1954.

scale dope traffic in London – amongst the capitals of Asia, Europe and the New World he believed this was the only city free of drugs. The answer as to why it had escaped the predations of Dope International, the worldwide criminal drug conspiracy, was not hard to explain. London was the centre of this huge undercover organization whose . . .

> supply lines spread from the opium-growing lands of Turkey, right across the world. And for that reason, the higher executive of Dope International does not want the British authorities in general – and Scotland Yard in particular – to change their present official attitude of, 'It doesn't happen here, it can't happen here.'

There was, he said, considerable evidence that payments for consignments of dope were being made through branches of foreign banks in London, and deals were being transacted in West End hotels by 'businessmen from the Lebanon, Syria and Turkey and their associates from the other side of the Atlantic'.[5]

It was not until the 1960s with a so-called swinging London, a Conservative government pointing out that we had 'never had it so good' and political scandals such as that of Ivanov-Profumo-Keeler that the so-called soft drugs market took off, to be followed by the hard market a decade later. Yet then, Howard Marks – soon to become a millionaire from marijuana dealing – and his kind were regarded by the population not as criminals but more as Robin Hoods risking their liberties to spread a little happiness. In 1964 it was noted that drug taking was on the increase and three years later Regional Drug Squads were formed to combat the 'drug problem'. Now there were signs of a moral panic and it was too late.[6]

By October 1966, despite assurances to the contrary over the previous years that dealing was not prevalent in the city, it was accepted that Liverpool was one of the principal centres of trafficking. The next year nationwide saw over 3,000 convictions for drug offences. In 1973 Customs officers had captured nine tons of cannabis, worth more than £8 million to the pedlars, in what was recognized now to be a desperate struggle against

[5] *Sunday Graphic*, 10 July 1960.
[6] See *inter alia* Steve Chibnall, *Law and Order News*.

importers. Scotland Yard arrested 700 wholesalers and middle-men in London, and with the Customs chipping in with another 500 arrests the total throughout the country rose to around 2,000 dealers as opposed to users. Cannabis was costing £500 a lb on the streets and hash oil was now a major currency. Although heroin and cocaine deals – costing £500 an ounce – were on the increase, the backbone was still in cannabis.

Fifteen years on, by the standards of the early 1970s and even by those of the previous year, seizures had become astronomical. They included 189kg of heroin and 358kg of cocaine (261 per cent increase on 1986). One seizure of 208kg in Southampton and bound for Holland was the largest ever in Europe. It was soon overtaken, however.

The smugglers were also becoming more imaginative. In his book *Snowblind*, Robert Sabbag describes the ingenious ways in which dealer Zachary Swan arranged drug shipments whilst protecting his sometimes innocent couriers. They included Aztec statues, dolls, teddy bears and rolling-pins stuffed with cocaine. On one occasion his innocent mules were given free trips to Colombia with all expenses paid. They had, however, to bring back gifts (supplied by Swan), to be photographed with them at the office of the 'tour company' through which they had won the trip. They were taken out to lunch and identical souvenirs were switched for the drug-laden ones.[7]

Sometimes things were more prosaic, as when five Colombians were found at Heathrow with £2 million (16kg) in book covers and between the two vinyl sleeves of gramophone records. At the Isleworth Crown Court, members of the team received terms of fourteen years for the women and sixteen for their minder. The couriers had been paid £550 and their expenses.

The garagers of the drugs when they arrived here were also fairly ingenious, even if it did not always do them much good in the end. One cache was found in a collection of garden gnomes, and after another swoop caretaker Ian Berry pleaded guilty to conspiracy to supply 40kg of cocaine. He had placed it in a burial chamber. Edward Coakley, also caught in Operation Basket, was found within minutes of leaving the caretaker's lodge. He was jailed for ten years and Berry for seven at the Inner London Crown Court on 25 March 1988.

[7] R. Sabbag, *Snowblind*, pp. 140 *et seq.*

Sometimes the drugs were simply floated over from the Continent unsupervised, to be collected later. Sometimes they floated to the wrong place. On 5 June 1988 £4 million of drugs were found on the beach at Saltdean near Brighton.

That year saw the end of one of the great cannabis smugglers of all times. Howard Marks (Garw Grammar School and Balliol) went down, betrayed by the then Lord Moynihan who was under extreme pressure from the Drug Enforcement Agency because of his own nefarious activities.[8]

Marks' first entry into the dealing scene was handling small amounts in Notting Hill and later in Brighton before, in 1970, taking over the smuggling route to replace a friend, Graham Plinston, another Balliol man who had been caught in Germany with 100lb of hash under the back seat and in the door panels of his car. Marks travelled to Germany to pay the fine, but he could not resist a stupid piece of small-time smuggling, a bottle of perfume on the way home. Questioned, he admitted he had been travelling on behalf of Plinston and so went down in someone's little black book.

From then on he first worked for Plinston and subsequently joined him as a partner, importing ever-increasing amounts through Shannon and into England. The first shipment was 200 lbs and the third a ton. Marks and his partners turned their attention to America. He fell out with the American authorities three years later when on 14 September 1973 he was waiting in Newport Beach for a load of hashish. He saw the bust on television and fled through New York and Montreal back to Europe. Two months later he was arrested in Amsterdam, told the Customs officers he was working for MI6 (which he just about had been after being recruited on a temporary basis by a former Balliol chum), was granted bail, was on his toes once again and was finally arrested in the Swan Hotel, Lavenham in Suffolk in May 1980.

---

[8] Lord Moynihan died in 1993, leaving several claimants to the title including a son by his fifth wife Jinna, a former Manila hotel receptionist. Another claimant, Andrew, is the son of his fourth wife, Editha, a Manila massage parlour manageress. A third claimant to the title is Moynihan's half-brother, the former conservative MP and one-time Minister for Sport Colin Moynihan. In March 1994 Colin Moynihan was reported to be petitioning the Queen because his request for a writ of summons – official document necessary before a peer may take his place in the House of Lords – had been rejected by the Lord Chancellor. This aim is that the Queen will refer the matter to the Committee for Privileges. (*The Times* 12 March, 1994.)

His conduct at the ensuing trial at the Old Bailey was a masterpiece of suggestion, innuendo, and downright lies. It ran along the lines, 'Yes, he had been drug trafficking but it had all been done under the supervision of MI6.' He was even able to produce a Mexican 'secret agent' to back up his story. Against his own expectations and certainly those of his solicitor and counsel, Marks was acquitted. The defeated opposition described itself as 'astonished, disbelieving and incredulous'.

In a curious way, however, his acquittal was his undoing. Generally police and Customs officers accept losses with something approaching fatalism. The fault of a stupid jury, crooked lawyer, senile judge are some of the more common reasons trotted out for the failure of a prosecution. This time, however, they were really upset not only by the acquittal but by the book of memoirs which followed. Marks had hoped to persuade the novelist Piers Paul Read – who, ten years earlier, had written *The Train Robbers* – to write the book. Read declined the task and Marks settled on the *Observer* journalist, David Leigh, who put together a vastly entertaining romp *Howard Marks, His Life and High Times*, which first, along with many a book, did not sell as well as the authors had hoped, and second and more importantly, had infuriated the Customs officers. In particular one Drug Enforcement Officer, Craig Lovato, made the destruction of Howard Marks and his empire a prime commitment.

After his acquittal Marks, based in Majorca, was to meet his nemesis in the shape of Lord Anthony Patrick Andrew Cairnes Berkeley Moynihan, son of an English peer who had squandered a good part of the family's wealth and who died shortly before he was due to appear on a charge of gross indecency. He had been introduced by a business associate, Phil Sparrowhawk, who had interests in massage parlours in the Ermita district of Manila. Moynihan and Marks put together a scheme to improve the quality of Manila-grown marijuana. As they did so, discussing the project over the telephone, Lovato listened on a telephone tap he had been allowed by the Spanish authorities to set up.

Moynihan was an Achilles heel. He had left England in the early 1970s, closely pursued by Scotland Yard who wanted to talk to and charge him in relation to a number of commercial frauds. Over the years he had been involved with a number of disreputable schemes closely related to Filipino prostitution.

Now Lovato was able to pressure him into turning against Marks. First there was the threat of an American Grand Jury indictment for conspiracy to smuggle drugs into the United States against Marks and also Moynihan; and, second, Moynihan was beginning to pine for England and his mother. Moynihan was provided with a wire, with instructions on how to turn the tape off after twenty-nine minutes so that Marks did not hear a worrying bleep. The rest, as the saying goes, is history.

Marks was arrested in his home at La Vileta in Majorca. In due course he was extradited to America and when he learned that his former partners would give evidence against him he pleaded guilty, earning himself twenty-five years.

As the end of the 1980s approached, the courts began to dish out consistently heavy sentences in an effort to deter drug trafficers.

On 9 January 1988 three Israeli army reservists and James Greenfield – a one-time member of the Angry Brigade, who once served ten years for bombing plots – were found guilty of a drugs-for-arms deal intended to provide the IRA with surface-to-air missiles. They smuggled premier quality Lebanese Gold cannabis resin worth £5 million into Britain. For their pains the sentences totalled thirty-six years.

And as they went to prison, so others came out. There was widespread belief that a gang dubbed the 'A team' and named after the actors in the popular television programme, organized the escape of drug smugglers Klass Karte and Wolfgang Oestmann who broke out of Channings Wood in Devon in February 1988. A police spokesman said: 'We have information that there are people who will supply the plans, getaway cars, hideouts, forged passports, the lot to help top villains get free if the money is right.'

It was the third escape of major criminals in six months. Six-figure sums were on offer to teams who could organize successful break-outs.[9]

One of the problems in the drug war has long been the rivalry between police and Customs. In the past they have kept things secret from each other to reap the kudos of the capture. There has also been a long-held belief that if the police are allowed near a consignment of drugs, not all of it will be recorded. The

---

[9] *Daily Star*, 19 February 1988.

remainder will be siphoned off for a variety of purposes, something which Customs officers would not countenance.

Now a senior police officer said, 'The battle against the drugs menace facing Britain is far too important for us to be distracted by fighting between ourselves.' This was in March 1988 on the conviction of Francis Cook at Chelmsford for importing cannabis in lorry containers. The owner of Le Fez restaurant in the Edgware Road, he had wanted to do one run a month for a year and then retire. The surveillance operation had taken two years and Cook had been on the run for four.

A senior Customs officer made a similarly laudatory statement:

> If we don't work together the only people who will benefit will be the drug dealers. Operation Quest shows just what can be done. We are proud of the way Customs and police have worked together in this investigation.

It was not always the case, and one of the most spectacular busts in the history of drug trials ended in mutual Customs–police recriminations. At the beginning of 1994 there was a major disaster in the case of Joseph Kassar, a Manchester businessman, convicted of a plot to smuggle £67 million of cocaine imported amongst lead ingots from Venezuela. The shipment had gone through and had been distributed through sources in Liverpool, but the planners tried a second time. On this occasion Customs and Excise found nearly £150 million in street terms of 95 per cent pure cocaine at a warehouse in Stoke-on-Trent. They removed the drugs from the crates of thirty-two lead ingots which, this time, had come in through Felixstowe and were on their way to Liverpool. The Customs tried to prove that the £67 million had gone through Kassar's hands, but in the end they were only able to show £300,000 had passed that way.

That was bad enough, but the full story of the investigation and its repercussions was yet to come out. When it did, it showed a complete lack of co-operation between the Customs and the police. The success story which turned to ashes had begun on 26 June 1992 when the Customs were waiting as Brian Charrington landed in his private aircraft at Teesside Airport. Six months previously Customs officers had drilled into the lead ingots stored in the Stoke warehouse, and they believed Charrington was the organizer of the shipment.

At his home was £2 million in cash contaminated with traces of almost all major drugs. It is interesting that some of the notes had been passed through cash machines in the South of England in the previous fortnight; this gives an example of how quickly drug money can leave street level and end in the hands of top men. There were also details of a £4.5 million payment to a salesman known to be working with a Colombian cartel.

Charrington had been fancied as a major player since 1989. One of his runs had been to smuggle cannabis in beer crates with the aid of day-trippers to France. Drugs to the value of £500,000 were confiscated. In 1990 a Danish skipper convicted of trying to export £5 million of drugs from Denmark named Charrington as being implicated in the scheme. There was also a tale that he had been smuggling cocaine into Britain by using corrupt airport baggage-handlers to remove the bags containing the cocaine from the baggage conveyor and so thwart any investigation. It appears that members of the drug wing of the Number Two (North East) Regional Crime Squad had been working with Customs to prepare a case against him. Unfortunately, what appears not to have been mentioned is that quite apart from his being Target One, or Numero Uno as Gene Hackman playing 'Popeye' Doyle would have described him, Charrington was just about the Numero Uno police informant. The moment he was arrested the police went to his rescue; if need be they would give evidence in his defence. In fact this is not uncommon practice. For example, in January 1989 Detective Superintendent Martin Lundy was allowed to give evidence *in camera* on behalf of his protégé, supergrass Roy Garner.[10]

The Customs complained that far from producing major drug-related arrests Charrington had only implicated small-time if professional criminals. Gilbert Gray QC, the barrister for Charrington, asked for and was granted a meeting with Sir Nicholas Lyell, the Attorney General. Five weeks later, on 28 January 1993, all charges against Charrington were withdrawn by the Crown Prosecution Service; he and ten others were due to be committed for trial to the Crown Court. In their turn, the

---

[10] There has been considerable speculation as to the extent of Martin Lundy's involvement with his supergrasses. The extremely interesting Lundy saga is recounted from opposing points of view in A. Jennings, P. Lashmar and V. Simson, *Scotland Yard's Cocaine Connection*, and Martin Short's *Lundy*. He himself has written an article 'Bent or brilliant?' which appeared in the *News of the World*.

police complain that the bust of Charrington had pre-empted a major strike against a Colombian cartel.

In January 1994 the only person to be convicted for his part in the whole affair was Kassar, described by the trial judge, Mr Justice May, as 'not one of the principal organizers, but very much a middleman'. It is interesting to speculate on the sentences which would have been passed on the leaders. His solicitor complained that the case had been surrounded by secrecy and that the press had been deliberately gagged to prevent the truth being known. John Merry, who runs a news agency in Darlington, claims that a local Member of Parliament telephoned him urging him not to publicize the case. At the time of Kassar's trial Charrington was believed to be in Hong Kong. According to the *Observer*, one of the police officers involved in thwarting the Customs inquiry left the force in January 1993 and in the September drove to Spain with his wife, a serving police constable, in an £87,000 BMW registered to Charrington.[11]

Sometimes the Customs have to make do with just the seizure. Towards the end of 1993 friends and relations cheered as six men accused of one of the biggest drug-smuggling operations were cleared by a jury at Southwark Crown Court. The allegation had been that they had smuggled 796kg cocaine worth £125 million into Britain aboard a 115-ft yacht, *Foxtrot V*, which docked at Durham Wharf, Charlton, South London in November 1992. The organization, said Anthony Glass for the prosecution, had 'taken months to plan, months of preparation, and vast expenditure'. *Foxtrot V* had been bought in the United States in 1992 and had been provisioned and fuelled before it was crewed to London, from where it sailed in October to a rendezvous off the Venezuelan coast. The cocaine, alleged Mr Glass, was air-dropped into the sea and collected by the boat which then returned to London.

At the end of a three-month trial which itself cost around £2 million, the five men who had been involved with equipping and the sixth who was said to have rented space to store the drugs were discharged. The man who had rented the space told the jury he was forced to do so at gunpoint by people who have never

---

[11] The *Observer* was about the only newspaper to carry what would appear to be a major story. See David Rose and John Merry, 'Drugs Bust Victory Turned to Dust' in the *Observer*, 16 January 1994.

been caught. The other five said they did not know there were drugs on board. Three men who were named as being prime movers in the plot, including the financier, were never caught.

Sometimes they had to make do with nothing. In 1993 Customs officer Richard Holywell was jailed for nine months for breaching the Official Secrets Act by supplying information from Customs telexes which enabled a suspect to pull out of an alleged international drugs ring.

Unfortunately he had fallen in love with the suspect's 20-year-old daughter and came across a telex which said the suspected smuggler might return from Europe with drugs. The man's car number was listed. Holywell told the sister of the girl that her father was under suspicion.

The deaths of drug dealers continued to pile up. One of the earlier and more spectacular ones had been that of Marty Johnstone, whose handless body had been found weighted and dumped in a flooded quarry at Ecclestone near Chorley, Lancashire in October 1989. Just about the only identifying mark was a charm worn around his neck with 'Good Luck' in Cantonese. He had been stabbed in the stomach and shot in the head; it took a considerable amount of talent before the police could issue an identikit of the face.

When it all came out, at a trial which at 123 days was then the second longest murder trial in Britain, the late Mr Johnstone was revealed to be a former leading member of an international drug syndicate. It had been run by New Zealander Alexander Sinclair, described unsurprisingly, in the time-honoured words of the judge, as 'ruthless and dangerous'. Johnstone had been found to have short-changed the worldwide syndicate and as a result had had to go. Mrs Justice Heilbron, who in her years at the Bar had defended, amongst many other celebrated criminals, George Kelly, the Cameo Murderer, and Jack Spot, sentenced Sinclair to life imprisonment with a recommendation that he serve not less than twenty years. It was said by the prosecution that he was worth £25 million, 'give or take a number or two'. He was also ordered to pay £1 million towards the prosecution costs, which were said to be at least £1.32 million. There were heavy sentences for other members of the organization including those who were only charged with, or convicted of, being involved with the drug side. One woman, described as the syndicate's banker, received thirteen years.

At the same time as the police were searching for the body of Gary Pettitt in Chorley there was news of two shootings in London. On Friday 28 May 1993, small-time dealer David Edwards fell foul of another dealer and was killed at his home in West Norwood, South London, with a single shot to the heart.

There were suggestions that the killing might be linked to the death of Chris 'Tuffy' Bourne, an illegal immigrant who died in a hail of fifteen bullets in a squat in Vassal Road, Brixton. He had been hit at least three times; ten bullets were found embedded in the wall behind him. His own revolver was later found by the police. Helped by the false passport racket, Mr Bourne was a frequent visitor to this country. He had been deported twice to Jamaica and was back in this country only because he had escaped from immigration officers at Birmingham airport in the February by vaulting a barrier and sprinting off towards the Bull Ring. Bourne's death was the second of the weekend.

In fact Bourne had been sentenced to two counts of life imprisonment in Jamaica. The sentence had been reduced to fifteen years on appeal, and he had been paroled in 1985. Despite his leap for freedom, the police knew where he was and had been keeping him under observation. The squat in Vassal Road was known to be a crack house, and one theory is that Bourne and colleagues met more resistance than they had anticipated when they turned up to warn the occupants off what they regarded as their turf. Bourne was a senior member of the Shower Posse and in Jamaica reprisals against their rivals the Spanglers were swift. One man was killed and dozens were injured.

One dealer from Leicester was fortunate to survive a row over crack proceeds. He was thrown fifty feet over the balcony of a block of flats in the Wessex Gardens estate off Westbourne Park Road in Paddington, but survived with multiple injuries.

Over the last five years the Yardies have established a substantial presence in the United Kingdom. Quite apart from their activities in Manchester, they have bases throughout London and every other big city, with the exception of those in the North-East of England and Scotland. 'They are ruthless killers, butchers – and in the United States they have even scared off the Mafia from their traditional trafficking grounds,' says one senior London officer.

The rewards are enormous. On every kilo of cocaine bought

from Colombia there is around 800 per cent profit, something which when translated means billions of pounds a year.

The police now fear an even larger Yardie presence in the United Kingdom, and cite two grounds for this. The first is the disbandment of the specialist unit Operation Dalehouse on 'political' grounds. It is difficult to understand the reason for this move. The unit may not have smashed the Yardies, but it certainly made substantial inroads into their activities, and had almost completely disrupted the Spanish Town Posse with a total of 267 arrests. Moves were also made against other Kingston, Jamaica, gangs including the Shower Posse, the Spanglers and the Gulley men. Just as the defeat of Michael Manley's People's National Party in 1980, whom the Yardies had supported, led to their moving their operations into America, now the success of the People's National Party in March 1993 may have had the same effect. The People's National Party seems to be one of law and order, and it may try to exercise some control over the Yardies' presence in Jamaica which is discouraging tourism.

On 29 July 1993 the decomposed body of Craig Swann was found by a family mushroom-picking near Loch Tummel in Perthshire. He had been missing for over a year.

Swann had an engineering degree from Edinburgh and was studying languages at Southampton before going back to South America. He was not known for excessive drinking or going out with married women; he was, so his family said, a very ordinary bloke. On Sunday 9 August 1992, he went out for an evening in Edinburgh and never returned. A couple were later seen abandoning Swann's car in the driveway of a house in Ruchazie Road in the East End of Glasgow, scene of the Ice Cream Wars of a decade earlier. During the investigation into Swann's disappearance, the police learned that his working holidays in South America could have been covers for drug dealing. It was feared he was the subject of a contract killing by members of a South American cartel he had double-crossed.

A rather more curious killing took place in September 1993. It was that of Andrew Birchcroft, or Birjukove, who was shot in the Two Brewers at Perry Hill, Catford. Again it was a contract killing, but this time possibly with a slight difference. The style was the usual one. The killer, in black leathers, shot Birchcroft with a .22 automatic and then ran from the pub to a waiting motorcycle. The motive may have been the difference. Birchcroft had been told not to deal in drugs in the locality, and for some time it was suggested that the killing was a punishment for defying community wishes. Said one man who knew him:

This is a nice neighbourhood here – it's not North Peckham – and Andy was told not to bring cocaine into it. He ignored the warning and came back. It's not so much vigilantes as what you would call pest control. It's to keep the neighbourhood respectable.[12]

Of course, that may be fanciful; it may just have been that another dealer wanted the territory. Seriously injured in the shooting was Bobby Campbell, the former St Mirren footballer. He had run the nearby Rutland Arms until it was temporarily closed by the brewers after complaints of drug dealing which Campbell had tried unsuccessfully to prevent.

It took some time before the traditional London criminal ventured into drugs. At one time it was regarded, along with living off immoral earnings, as something which lowered a man's status in the criminal hierarchy, but one by one the old villains turned to the more lucrative and safer – than running across a pavement towards a Securicor van where armed police might be waiting – pastime of drugs.

And down they went one by one. Joe Wilkins, nephew of the redoubtable Bert, and a prince if not King of the Soho escort trade of the 1970s; Train Robber Charlie Wilson, killed in Spain by a contract killer; Train Robber Tommy Wisbey along with his partner, fellow Train Robber James Hussey, were also sentenced to long terms of imprisonment, as was a man whom many had thought to be a potential King of the Underworld after the downfall of the Krays, Mickey Ishmael.

Others thought Ishmael didn't really have the luck necessary to go right to the top. His seemed to run in increasingly short bursts. Ishmael, who had had troubles as a bank robber, found life as a drug dealer not that much easier.[13] On 1 March 1988 he was arrested for possession of drugs. He had been planning to distribute amphetamines. There had been a round-the-clock surveillance on him and he

---

[12] Duncan Campbell in the *Guardian*, 16 September 1993.
[13] See J. Morton, *Gangland*, p.205.

was seen to go to a house near his home. Some sixty-five officers were involved in the raid and Ishmael claimed he was being fitted up. He received thirteen years for conspiracy; other men in the plot received up to seven years.

Not only – as Charlie Wilson found – was the South of Spain not completely safe, nor was the South West of Ireland. It was there that English criminal Charles Brooke Pickard was abducted, either in a drug deal which went badly wrong (more popular theory) or because he was an informer (he had received a surprisingly light sentence after a eulogy by a Garda official).

He lived at Castlecove between Sneem and Caherdaniel in South Kerry. In 1988 he had been arrested by detectives in Dun Laoghaire after coming to Dublin to collect a £4,000 debt from a man named Marty, who in turn said another owed him the sum. Pickard, armed with a .22 revolver, went looking for the second man. He had served eighteen months in 1972 for drugs and firearm offences, and in 1976 five years for drug supplying.

It was thought that he might have fallen foul of a Mr Big who had masterminded a major shipment of Moroccan hashish which had landed by Derrynane. A man and woman were jailed for that operation, but the mastermind was never arrested.

On 26 April 1991 Pickard was seen being bundled into his van by balaclavaed men. On 16 May this was found burned out in the Kerry mountains. Penny Pickard, his wife, denied any involvement in drugs. Since his suspended sentence Charles had, she said, been 'born again'.

On 17 January 1994 the Customs had a spectacular seizure. Into Manchester Airport along with a consignment of flowers from Amsterdam came six boxes containing 250kg of cocaine. The drugs had come from Cali, which has replaced Medellin as the powerbase of the Colombian cartels. The Customs officers knew of this; they had been involved in an elaborate four-month-long sting operation in which two of their number had travelled to Colombia posing as wealthy buyers. At one stage in the operation they had been obliged to produce £2 million, funded by the Greater Manchester Police, to prove their *bona fides*. Two men were arrested and Pat Cadogan, an assistant chief investigator, claimed:

We have broken an attempt by a major cocaine importer to set up a distribution network in the North West of England.

We must have destroyed their credibility in the UK and a seizure of this kind must be a major setback for them.

The next day it was reported that tainted heroin had been the source of a series of deaths in and around Bristol. It transpired that the heroin was not tainted, merely 60 per cent pure and too strong for the bloodstream. Heroin is normally 'cut' with chalk or bicarbonate of soda to around 35 per cent purity, otherwise the lungs of all but the most hardened drug users are damaged. Breathing stops very quickly.

A similar problem occurred in the King's Cross area of London between the 11th and 19th of March, when seven addicts died in nine days. King's Cross, once the fiefdom of Alf White in the 1930s and 1940s, has passed through a number of controlling hands, including in the 1980s a group of Scotsmen, before becoming a dealers' paradise in the 1990s. Now King's Cross is in the hands of the Italians and the Jamaicans. The problem, as in Bristol, was not necessarily impure heroin, rather a too pure strain.

July 1993 saw a police crackdown on the area which had been the venue for a quarter of all the crack-cocaine seizures in 1992. The crackdown had resulted in the closure of some 24-hour take-aways and mini-cab firms following undercover surveillance and secret filming of dealers. One film showed the bizarre sight of a young man pulling (with some effort) a bag of drugs from his rectum, washing the package, storing it in his mouth and then transferring it by seeming to kiss a young girl. Until then dealers had been relying on the Police and Criminal Evidence Act 1984 which prevented officers forcing open a suspect's mouth. As a result 60-milligram balls of heroin (£10) or the rather more expensive 90-milligram balls of crack cocaine (£25) could be wrapped in clingfilm and kept in the mouth. Sentences of up to nine years were handed out. No longer, said Commander John Townsend, was it possible for a drug dealer to make £700,000 a year in the area.[14]

Dealing at street level might still be strictly small-time, with a bag of heroin going for £50 to be cut into eleven portions: one for

---

[14] Speaking at the Association of Police Officers' conference in Birmingham, 7 July 1993. Nick Cohen, 'Purity that kills in the darkness', in the *Independent on Sunday*, 11 April 1993.

the buyer and the rest to be sold at £10 a time. In January 1994 a take-away in the King's Cross area was doing a hot trade if not in butties at least in DIY kits of spoon, syringe and candle for £1.75. A local Salvation Army worker did not appear to think much had changed after the purge:

> King's Cross is definitely a Yardie enterprise. Its organized crime and violence constantly erupts between ethnic groups, to determine who's actually running the place. The Afro-Caribbeans will disappear for a while. And then all hell will be let loose one night and you'll find it's the Italians who are being chased through the streets by a new gang wielding everything from guns to crowbars.[15]

A habit in the area costs £150 a day which, added up, amounts to between a half and three-quarters of a million for a dealer – profit figures more or less identical to those before the purge.

Drug dealing continues at a high level in Clapham. In October, the local community officer Patrick Dunne was shot dead as he went to investigate a burglary in the neighbourhood. A number of men were arrested for the killing, but after consideration the Crown Prosecution Service decided there was not sufficient evidence to seek a committal to the Crown Court for trial.

In January 1994 the Customs and Excise released the figures for drug hauls during the previous year. Heroin seizures had risen slightly over the previous year to around 570kg, enough for five doses for every man, woman and child in the country. On the other hand cocaine seizures had fallen substantially from over 2,000kg to under 1,000kg. This was because in 1992 there had been two seizures of huge consignments of 900kg and 800kg respectively. Cannabis had risen to a record 53 tons and amphetamines had gone from rather under 20kg in 1989 to over 500kg in 1993. It was a similar story with Ecstasy. The amount seized in 1989 had been negligible; now nearly 600kg had been confiscated.

Douglas Tweddle, the Chief Investigation Officer for Customs, said he found the rise, particularly in synthetic drugs, very worrying. Most Ecstasy came from mainland Europe, with 90 per cent manufactured in the Netherlands which was also a

---

[15] Trudy Culross in 'Heart of Darkness', in *Midweek*, 20/24 January 1993.

major source of cocaine. For heroin, the old-fashioned overland Balkan route from the heroin-producing areas on the Afghanistan and Pakistan borders was still popular. One seizure had been of £20 million found in a lorry on the M1.

Since the Spanish authorities have tightened up the Morocco-Algeciras route for cocaine coming to Europe, direct import to the United Kingdom has become more popular. Another reason is that the Californian market has been saturated and the Colombian cartels are looking for new growth areas. Drugs have been floated and boated in to England, with the Channel Islands as a popular route. Once in, it is reasonably easy to remit consignments to the rest of Europe.

Postscript

Perhaps it would not go amiss to look at some of the theories criminologists have, and have had, about the causes and cures for crime and why people join gangs.

An immediate problem arises. Just who or what is a criminologist? Some would say that those who write true-crime books which show that Major Armstrong could not possibly have murdered his wife and tried to poison a rival solicitor are criminologists. Those who teach social science and policy courses at Universities where degrees in criminology are handed out would disagree. Their interest would be in why the Major turned to crime, and whether he was influenced by the fact that a neighbouring solicitor Mr Greenwood had been tried and acquitted of the murder of his wife a few months earlier.[1] For

---

[1] In 1922 Major Herbert Armstrong, a solicitor at Hay-on-Wye on the Welsh borders, was convicted of the murder of his wife. His practice was not doing well and there is evidence he had tried to poison another local solicitor. Nevertheless the evidence was not strong, and Sir Henry Curtis-Bennett who defended Armstrong believed he would obtain a not guilty verdict. The Court of Appeal was dismissive, with Mr Justice Avory remarking, 'To find a packet of three and a half grains of arsenic in a solicitor's pocket is surely rare'. An application for a retrial, following the disclosure of the discussions by a juryman to a newspaper, was rejected. Armstrong, who continued to protest his innocence, was hanged by John Ellis who himself later committed suicide. Harold Greenwood, who had a practice a few miles away, had been acquitted in November 1920 of the murder of his wife. Greenwood, who was by no means popular with the locals, was said to have poisoned her. He was acquitted principally on the evidence of his daughter who said she had drunk from the same bottle of wine with which Greenwood was said to have tampered. Greenwood, ruined by the case, died a few years later. In an interview he commented, 'I am the victim of gossip, of village scandal and if you know Welsh village life you know what that means.' There are a number of accounts of the two cases including John Rowland's *Murder Revisited.*

the purposes of this short essay I would adopt the attitude of the second group.

There have been theories about the causes of crime since crime itself existed but, to try to keep matters in a time frame, I propose to start with the theories from the eighteenth century onwards. Necessarily they will be in a potted version, and it may be that I shall be accused of over-simplifying, and possibly mocking, what appeared at the time to be perfectly good theories.

In defence of the over-simplification, sometimes it appears that sociologists equate incomprehensibility to all but their own inner circle with success. I hope the only time a sentence such as this appears in this book is as follows:

> With respect to the study of crime ethno-methodology, like symbolic interactionism, treats crime as a matter of definition or, more precisely, as a product of members' methods of practical reasoning. However, unlike symbolic interactionism ethno-methodology is concerned with the situated production and use of these definitions rather than treating these as given in the fabric of local settings.[2]

Quite.

So far as the mocking is concerned, well, most of the theories proffered over the last 150 years have subsequently been discredited by a rival theorist either with cause or simply because he, or occasionally she, wished to gain fleeting attention and propagation for the theory which he held at one time and was then voluntarily or compulsorily forced to abandon. Or, from time to time, they changed their social or political stance and with it the theory.

The Italian, Cesare Beccari, can be credited with the creation of what is known as the classical school of criminology. In 1764 in the so-called Age of Enlightenment – a time which housed such thinkers as Voltaire and Jeremy Bentham and such charlatans as Casanova – at the age of 26, Beccari wrote *Of Crime and Punishment* in which he argued that a person consciously chose to adopt an unacceptable or illegal pattern of behaviour. 'Invisible' causes such as poverty had nothing to do with the exercise of the man's free will. It was a belief which held sway for a century and which still has its adherents today.

[2] S. Hester and P. Eglin (1992), *A Sociology of Crime.*

Another early theory was that of Quetelet, who argued that crime was cyclical and based on the phases of the moon. The thinking behind this was the old lunatic theory – the person who loses the ability to act rationally during phases of the moon – but I have always thought Quetelet had something which can be applied to modern crime even if not in quite the same way. Professional crime is, and always will be, cyclical. Take a calendar year. After Christmas there is the need to earn money and pay off the debts incurred. The nights are dark; it is the time for the housebreaker. When spring comes there is a fall-off of nocturnal crime as the nights get lighter. As summer follows spring criminals, pickpockets (except those who stay behind to deal with the foreign tourists here), shoplifters and hotel thieves transfer their activities to the Continent as tourists go abroad stuffed with travellers' cheques and currency. When the summer holidays are over, the shoplifters are back in town and with dark nights coming on burglary is that much easier. November and early December is the time for lorry hi-jacking and warehouse breaking. For a start, they are full with goods for Christmas and money has to be earned for presents. By the second week in December there is a fall-off. No one wants to be in custody over the holiday and the cry becomes, 'I must have bail for Christmas to be with the kids.' It is rarely pointed out that all they will see of their father is his backside disappearing towards the pub. After Christmas, there is the need . . . Simplistic, perhaps, but probably with a grain of truth. I have to admit, however, that through a lack of statistics or willpower or both, I have never conducted anything more than what is rather grandly called empirical research, which more simply means my own experiences, to back up my modest effort to support Quetelet. However, the theory did receive some support on 30 December 1993. Firearms were carried in six separate London robberies. £1,300 went in a raid on the Leeds Building Society in Kingston, a robber was thwarted at the National Westminster Bank in Battersea and another fled empty-handed from the branch in Baker Street. Two men robbed the Leeds Building Society in the Walworth Road; a man waved a pump-action shotgun in a failed robbery at a sub-post office in the Hertford Road, Enfield, and an armed robber netted £92.75 from a betting shop in the Harrow Road.

One of the earliest members, indeed a founding father, of the so-called and rival positivist school of criminology was another

Italian, Caesare Lombroso, in the 1870s. He made a study of criminal types amongst prisoners by taking skull measurements and other physical details. His theory that cranial features pointed to a criminal mentality, and that women with excessive pubic hair were more likely to become prostitutes than those less well endowed, held fashion for some years until it was discovered that the skulls of officer cadets at Sandhurst were the same as those of Lombroso's prisoners. I have never seen whether a study of undergraduates at Girton was undertaken to disprove his other theory.

Even after his basic theory was discredited, Lombroso spawned a whole series of arguments as to the causes of crime based on the human body. There were suggestions that twins were more susceptible to crime than single children, and that if one twin became a criminal his sibling was sure to follow. There were other arguments in the 1920s, that certain physical types divided into mesomorphs (strong and lean), endomorphs (short and fat) and ectomorphs (tall and skinny) were predisposed to certain forms of crime. A parallel research produced a similar theory. A study of over 4,000 criminals produced the argument that leptosomes (long and skinny) committed petty theft and frauds, athletic types (well developed) were violence-prone, pyknics (small, round and fat) were predisposed to fraud and possibly violence, whilst dysplastics (those with mixed characteristics) favoured sex offences. Another later study by Sheldon and Eleanor Gleuck in the 1950s, of some five hundred delinquent boys matched against a similar number of non-delinquents, suggested that:

> [it] is quite apparent that physique alone does not adequately explain delinquent behaviour, it is nevertheless clear that in conjunction with other forces, it does bear a relationship to delinquency.[3]

This was one of the theories which was promptly walloped by rivals. The Gleucks were said to have developed 'a new Phrenology in which the bumps of the buttocks take the place of the bumps on the skull'.

But even now the great man is not forgotten. In the 1970s came

---

[3] Sheldon and Eleanor Gleuck (1956), *Physique and Delinquency*.

the revival of the theory, tracing directly back to Lombroso, that women are more likely to commit crime when suffering from pre-menstrual tension.

In the 1920s in Chicago, attention shifted to the relation between urban growth and urban problems. As a result a good deal of research was done by members of what became known as the Chicago School. Their findings included the confirmation that there was more crime in the inner city than in the suburbs. It was also found to be the case that this level of delinquency existed no matter how much the population shifted with an influx of immigrants. Transposed to London, the theory works reasonably well. Certainly in the past Soho could be deemed to be the centre and there, over the years, there has been a high level of criminal behaviour whether the English, French, Corsicans, Maltese, Cypriots or Italians have been the ascendent nationality. As a general proposition, if the city is divided into circles those furthest from the centre have the least level of crime, although more crime occurs in outer circles such as Brixton, Hackney and Tottenham than in Highgate and the rest of North London. The Chicago School coined a phrase, differential association, the theory of which dated back a good seventy years. The reasoning goes along the lines that criminal behaviour is explicable not by the needs and values of the community but is learned by individuals in small groups. This often criticized argument would go a long way to dismember the next – and superficially most attractive – theory, which is that poverty breeds crime.

There is certainly evidence that when times are hard people, and women in particular, will turn to what is seen as petty crime such as shoplifting and prostitution in order to obtain food and to pay off the debt collector. There are plenty of studies which will show that poverty is an influence in criminality. But it is impossible to say that poverty is anything more than a con-tributing factor. One of the problems is the lack of a clear definition. Is the person truly poor or does he merely see himself as poor? If it were otherwise, why would all poor people not commit crime? There is a theory that a criminal's memoir is one of the most worthwhile studies of crime. It is here that the sociologist tends to exercise a certain amount of tunnel vision. A criminal's memoir is more likely than not to be full of self-justification. Francis Fraser, once one of London's leading criminals, wrote that his family was dirt-poor and that poverty had been the overriding reason for his career; yet Leonard Read, the police officer who was largely responsible for the downfall of the Kray empire, wrote in his memoir of his own poverty-ridden childhood:

> People say the Krays had a deprived upbringing and that this could have turned them to crime, but I reckon there was more money coming into their house than into ours.[4]

It is also interesting to note that of Fraser's brother and sisters, one became a nurse and emigrated to America, where she rose high in her profession, and his brother was in work all his adult life and has no convictions.

The poverty argument supports what is called the strain theory developed by American sociologists in the 1960s. The argument runs that both individuals and whole groups find their efforts to attain desired success in society to be blocked. As a defensive mechanism these groups develop a sub-culture which has a different series of values from that of the rest of society, and it is amongst these groups that the greatest amount of crime occurs. A classic example of this is in Moss Side, Manchester today where:

> More than a quarter of the population is long-term un-employed: it is not unusual to find families with three generations who have never worked. The crisis is worst amongst young blacks, up to 80% of whom are unem-ployed. Overall, more than half the children in Moss Side schools face the certain knowledge that they will not find work when they leave school.
>
> 'It is very difficult to appeal to young people on a moral and intellectual basis,' says Councillor Iqbar Seram, 'when they feel they have no stake in society.'
>
> In these circumstances it is not hard to understand the attraction of joining a gang and dealing in drugs. Where else can you find instant status, glamour, excitement and easy money?[5]

---

[4] L. Read and J. Morton, *Nipper*, p.1.
[5] *The Sunday Times*, 7 March 1993.

However, critics of the poverty variant of the strain theory suggest that 'it would be prudent to assume a low causal role for poverty specifically'.[6]

As the century went by there developed another theory, that of *anomie*, which originated in the last century with the French sociologist Emile Durkheim and was developed by the American Robert Merton. In essence it runs that a state of lawlessness in society or in an individual is caused by loss of belief and purpose. It is easy to see how it overlaps with the strain theory. According to Merton, rebellion is the last of the reactions resulting from *anomie*, and this includes the desire to substitute new goals in place of the conventional ones. The street gang, or for that matter the freedom fighter, would fit neatly into this category.

In essence it is not too different from the Marxist theory which was propagated in a slightly different form in the 1960s by the so-called radical criminologists. The Marxist theory sees the under-class as victim. The argument goes that the implementation of pure Marxism would overthrow capitalism which in turn, since there would be the reality of the promised land (to mix religions and cultures), would mean there would be no need for crime. In the meanwhile criminal activities (as defined by a capitalist society designed to keep the poor under the rich man's heel) such as theft can be related to the economic struggle, whilst prostitution is related to the weak economic and political status of women. The thoughts of the radical criminologists have shifted considerably since their heyday thirty years ago.

After the death of the two-year-old James Bulger in Bootle in early 1993, and the conviction of two eleven-year-olds for his death later that year, there was an outcry against video violence which, the trial judge said, might have led at least one of the boys to commit the crime. It was not a new theory. Similar ones have regularly been advanced about books. 'Is this the sort of book you would wish your wife and maidservant to read?' asked Mervyn Griffiths-Jones, prosecuting in the Lady Chatterley case. The implication was clear. The book would so influence them that a number of women of hitherto impeccable morals would abandon an afternoon's tennis on a Thursday and indulge in more unseemly sport with the part-time gardener. The behaviour of the maidservants would no doubt be even more appalling.

[6] Dermot Walsh in *A Dictionary of Criminology.*

Indeed, this has been the case whenever there has been a copying of behaviour in a book or film. The film director Stanley Kubrick withdrew *A Clockwork Orange* from distribution after reports that young men had emulated the film's anti-hero and had set fire to tramps. There were allegations that the French film *Je crache sur votre tombeau* and the video nasty *Driller Killer* had led to similar antisocial behaviour. In 1993 cuts were made to a Walt Disney production when it was found that young men had been injured and in one case killed when playing a game of chicken, lying in the road and letting lorries drive over them. The complaint was nothing new. It had been made about the 1953 James Dean film *Rebel Without a Cause*. Perhaps it is just as well that few young people read the Bible nowadays, or Scout camps might be littered with tent-peg murderers.[7]

Indeed, probably what can be seen from this brief review is that many of the theories have attractive aspects but no single one can satisfactorily explain why one person or group of people commits crime whilst others in a similar position do not. If they did, perhaps there would be no further need for criminologists to agonize over the causes of crime. The likelihood is that there are a number of combinations of circumstances, both physical and environmental, which will dispose a person to crime, but that not all will succumb.

But what of the punishment meted out to criminals? Surely there is some way – preferably imprisonment is today's thought – which will prevent re-offending and stop young men and women in the tracks of their chosen careers. On the other hand, do we not read in the newspapers on a weekly if not daily basis about the fact that probation costs less, that electronic tagging and custodial sentences don't work? Wasn't there a scheme in America where young criminals were taken to see men serving forty-five years who explained in simple terms and gestures what life in prison would be like for them? Can't people be made to stop committing offences? Sadly not. It is probably appropriate to quote from a handbook given to magistrates and judges:

The almost invariable conclusion of the large amount of research which has been undertaken (in various Western

[7] I cannot claim this thought is an original one. The argument was advanced by Irving Wallace in his novel *The Seven Minutes*.

countries) is that it is hard to show any effect that one type of sentence is more likely than any other to reduce the likelihood of re-offending, which is high for all. Similarly, longer periods of custody or particular institutional regimes do not seem to have a significant effect. Studies comparing the reconviction rates of offenders given community service orders with those given custodial sentences have shown little difference.[8]

Even in the last two years since *Gangland* was published times have changed, as indeed crimes have over the century. Gone are the days of the angler or thief who used a rod and hook to steal items from the inside ledges of windows left open by house-holders. Gone too are the Oysters, society women who would wear stolen jewels as advertisements for the receivers for whom they worked. Now goods are knocked out in the often less salubrious circumstances of the car boot sale where no questions are asked of the vendors and the sales themselves provide the opportunity for theft and protection racketeers who offer 'security services'. Modern technology has defeated, and a lack of willingness to serve a criminal apprenticeship has almost completely eliminated, the safebreaker. Because of social attitudes and legislation, the baby farmer has gone and the back-street abortionist has become almost obsolete. There are no great families such as the Messina brothers who control prostitutes, although there are still echoes of the white slavers in the men who run agencies for girls of little talent and less sense who wish to become members of a continental dance troupe and find it is prostitution under another name. There are, of course, still pimps and one recent, old-fashioned case was that of Kimberley Johnson-Laird and his 20-year-old pregnant and prostitute wife, Melissa, who ran a nation-wide team of prostitutes from the unlikely haven of Bury St Edmunds. He had set up a stable of fifty girls across the country from Weymouth in Dorset to Bradford, masking their activities with stripogram and kisso-gram assignments. He was jailed for eighteen months on 16 July 1993 for living off immoral earnings. Melissa received three months' youth custody. Johnson-Laird had run a similar operation out of Peterborough in 1989.

[8] *The Sentence of the Court*, HMSO, p.7.

Now, as often as not, there are women running one or two of their girlfriends as prostitutes. This is not completely new. In the first case of its kind known to the Metropolitan Police on 2 June 1939, Ida Parry of 46 Old Compton Street, then aged 61, had been controlling Doris Booker who lived with her. The police arrived just as Miss Booker returned with a client who had agreed to pay her 7/6d.

The Marlborough Street magistrate, E.C.P. Boyd, sentenced her to four months' imprisonment. She had been a prostitute herself for many years and was described in reports as a 'vile and violent creature'. The women lived together at the address in the names of John and Doris Parry. 'She just lives here with me and we muck in. I pay for the food and I take her to the pictures now and again. If she wants a shilling I give it to her and if I want one she gives it to me,' said Ida Parry, but the magistrate did not believe her. The Home Office papers say it was a pity she couldn't have been deported.

The great days of the jewel thief who would wait patiently for hour after hour to steal a film star's jewels when she went on set or to a première are long over.

On the other hand, at the turn of the century there was no such thing as the motor-car theft, nor the use of the motor-car in crime. Without cars the smash-and-grab raid was unknown until the Bonnot gang in France began the practice in the early 1900s. Now we have a great increase in white collar crime – or was it always present but undetected or unremarked? Certainly there was no such thing as credit-card fraud until the 1970s, and until the chequebook became a universal prop for the handbag or inner pocket, little of that either. Credit-card frauds cost around £165 million in 1993 or, put more graphically, £5 a second. Over 1.8 million of the nation's 80 million cards went missing. But, in 1925, according to the Official Receiver, long-firm fraudsmen were getting away with between £5 and £6 million annually.[9] Nor could there have been any such thing as a British Telecom swindle. On 8 February 1994 four members of a gang, Nisar Batha, Talat Kayeni, Shoiab Mahammed and Javeid Iqbal, who had helped criminal organizations in France and the Netherlands make calls which could not be traced, were jailed for up to two years. They had rented properties in false names and then asked

---

[9] Philip Knightley, 'Gang Warfare: How to thaw the freeze', in *King*, November 1956.

BT to install facilities allowing conference calls. The calls mainly went to Colombia and Pakistan. BT lost just under £448,000. It was made clear that the British end of the scam had no idea of the nature of the calls to these countries. It is an example, however, of the growth of Asian-orientated crime in Britain.

There have been other new crimes, from the one-off type run by squatters who demand £1,000 to leave a house rather than force the owner to go through the costly and time-consuming process of the civil courts.

A new form of theft which has grown up in the 1990s is that of mobile phones and the associated fraudulent use of registered users' air time. Over 12,000 mobile phones are stolen monthly. In some parts of London cars are attacked whilst standing at traffic lights or in traffic jams by youths on roller-blades. The car-jack (the forcible removal at gun or knife point) of the car from its owner has flown over from across the Atlantic. On Friday 28 January 1994, the body of accountant Grant Price was found on a deserted beach at Lee-on-Solent, Hampshire. It is thought he had been abducted at a car park in Gosport on Saturday 22 January by men who wished to steal his car. Two hours earlier an electronics student had been stabbed in nearby Fareham, in another apparent attempted car-jack.

An interesting variation on an earlier type of crime has reappeared. In January 1994 a motorist stopped to assist an apparently injured man near the centre of Plymouth, having been flagged down by a youth who pointed to the motionless figure. No sooner was he out of his car than he was attacked by a gang of up to eleven youths who beat him with a stick and broke his arm when he did not hand over his money. Warning motorists to be on the look-out for this trap, the police commented that this was a 'new kind of street robbery'. But the trick is not really a new one; it has merely come round again. It was popular in France in the 1930s, and was played by Alain Delon and Jean-Paul Belmondo in the film *Borsalino*. Perhaps someone in Plymouth had hired a video of the film?

It is probable that the police in Britain and Europe did not realize the full extent of Hell's Angels involvement in drug dealing and organized crime until the beginning of the 1980s. Until then the height of the ambition of these bearded, tattooed and dirty outlaw bikers was thought to have been the public performance of oral sex with an old-age pensioner. But, even before then the British chapters of the Hell's Angels had amassed a fairly impressive record of violence, rape and killings over the twenty or so years of their existence. Now in Germany the movement, with its involvement in prostitution, arms running, drugs protection and extortion, has been declared illegal. Here they were recognized as a mini-Mafia, one of the major controllers of the soft-drug trade and, it was believed, controlling two factories manufacturing amphetamines.

The movement appears to have started in Fontana, a depressingly dull steel town fifty miles from Los Angeles, in the late 1940s. The Angels there liked to refer to themselves as the One Per Cent – something which indicated that whilst 99 per cent of motorcyclists in the States were well-mannered and well-meaning, in no way did this squeaky-clean tag refer to them.

By the late 1960s when they rode into public and press view, the London chapters of the Angels would have two or three satellite chapters in cities such as Birmingham, Manchester and Sheffield, and in October 1970 two massed and augmented gangs had met on Chelsea Bridge to determine who ran London. Ranged on one side were the Essex and Chelsea Nomads, and on the other the Road Rats whose tag team partners were the Windsor Angels and the Jokers. For over a decade the Windsor Angels saw themselves as the kings of the English chapters. Whilst others wore red and white insignia, they wore black on white death's-head patches.

It was not the only power struggle amongst rival Angels. A month later in November 1971, Kenneth Sparkes was detained for five years after being found guilty of causing an affray in which Stan Megraw, who headed the Scorpios in a battle with the Windsors, died.

Estimates of the strength of the Angels varied wildly, with Gerard Kemp reporting the next year that there were nine chapters in Britain.[10] A year earlier it had been thought that there were chapters in up to forty British towns, but the press and public has long been confused over the difference between the pure Hell's Angel – if that is not an oxymoron – and the simple outlaw biker. What everyone did agree upon was that under whichever jacket they rode, they were evil, loutish, raping, pillaging monsters. This was an image the Angels of the time did their best to cultivate. When in March 1972 the allegations of

[10] Gerard Kemp, 'Inside the Mind of an Angel', *Sunday Telegraph*, 9 April 1972.

an Army nurse that she had been raped by up to sixteen Hell's Angels, members of the Wessex Free Wheelers, in a candle-lit garage in Aldershot, failed to convince a jury, the Angels were reported as saying they were going to have a 'gang-bang celebration tonight'. Asked if the acquittal would stand them in good stead with other Angels, their spokesman said:

> It will certainly stand us in good class. We'll be known as a classy gang by other chapters. Our status has gone up as a result of this case because no other Hell's Angels have been to court for something like this and been cleared. We have never had any trouble finding birds. When birds hear there are Angels in town, they come flocking out of interest. But now some parents may lock up their daughters. But we'll still get birds.[11]

It was at about that time the Angels moved into the protection game here, albeit on a very small scale – a move which would be repeated ten to fifteen years later with more skill and success by the football gangs such as The Firm of West Ham. On 29 August 1972 at the Weeley Pop Festival near Clacton in Essex, the organizers paid seven Angels £4 each for 'security work'. The previous year the local Round Table which organized an annual event for charity had run a Donkey Derby. This year they had been more ambitious, but the money given to the security Angels was not well spent. Other Angels leaped on to the platform, elbowed off a pop group and announced over the microphone, 'We're in charge here.' Fighting broke out and the 130-strong group of Angels armed with knives, chains and shotguns battled with local security men who were themselves armed with sledgehammers and mallets. By the time the Angels were removed, three hundred people had to be treated for minor injuries and another twenty were in hospital.

Retribution from the local magistrates was swift. Two days later thirty-nine Angels, including a former policeman who had, it was said, become their legal adviser, appeared charged with possessing offensive weapons and using threatening behaviour. All were found guilty. Three disappeared for six months, three were remanded in custody for reports and the rest were fined between £25 and £35 each. The confiscated weapons disappeared into the Essex police museum.

[11] *Guardian*, 23 March 1973.

In 1973 the Angels, following American tradition, gathered for an Easter Bank Holiday run from Birmingham to the West Country. Then it was feared that there would be a similar run for the August Bank Holiday. Again the spectre not only of damage to property but of mass rape was floated in the press.[12] On balance the turmoil did not materialize, although the Hell's Angels battled it out with some black youths (to whom the organization would traditionally have had some antipathy) at Ramsgate. But it was all pretty small beer and only one man was arrested.

But there were warnings that the Angels were trying to become something more than just wild men:

The only future they see is with the club [The London Chapter]. They dream of making the big time through the club 'like in the States'. There's a scheme to organize pop concerts and make money that way, like in the States. There's a plan to move into drug dealing in a big way, like in the States. Above all else, they want a united Hell's Angels Chapter throughout the country, like in the States. Nine months ago an attempted merger failed. But they still hope that they can get together with the only other clubs they respect, the West Coasters, the Windsors, the Cotswolds and the Roadrats.[13]

Two years later the Wessex branch were again in trouble; they may not have been organizing a pop concert, rather the reverse. A group set upon the Troggs pop group who were playing at a dance at Farnborough Technical College. Two of the Angels seized the carpet on which the group was standing and 'literally pulled the rug from underneath them', said the prosecutor happily. The leader received four years' imprisonment. The same year and the next, Angels battled it out with rivals and the police at motorcycle meetings at Silverstone. Hell's Angels were again active at Silverstone in 1986, when they rioted at the Motorcycle Grand Prix meeting.

But, seemingly, the pinnacle of Angel violent activity occurred with the battle of Cookham Dean on 18 September 1983 when there was yet another so-called peace conference ostensibly to celebrate twenty years of the Angels in Britain. It seems that, at

---

[12] *People*, August 1973.
[13] William Cran in *The Listener*, 12 July 1973.

the time, the All England Hell's Angels – divided into seven chapters, each with 10–15 members – were under pressure from chapters in the United States who thought they were not sufficiently strong and organized to deal with the drug trade. The Chapter was looking for a showdown amongst unruly minor chapters such as the Slaves, the Rats and the Mojos. There had been troubles for the Chapter over the past few years. In 1979, for example, the All England – aided by two Americans and two Dutch Angels – had dealt severely with a group of fifteen Windsors sleeping off a booze-and-drug jag in a car park near Brockenhurst, whilst in 1983 the Hell's Angels North Carolina had had a conference with the All England Chapter to discuss the difficulties they were facing. In theory, the idea of the meeting that September had been the drawing up of boundaries with the Windsor Chapter, whose President had been imprisoned for plotting the assassination of a rival, Richard Sharman – he was shot three times, once in the head, but survived. Sharman had reportedly refused to take part in the so-called peace talks. It indicated that the stronger Angel Chapters were hoping for more discipline between the chapters. With their quasi-company structure, there had never been any doubt that in an extra-curricular way there was discipline in the chapters themselves.

The troubles at the two-day meeting, which had until the Sunday been relatively well-behaved, broke out between the Rats and the Slaves when a woman was staked out and, it was said, sexually abused. Another cause of the fighting was that some Angels objected to being photographed in their colours. Now the Road Rats and Satan's Slaves from Exeter fought with axes and knives. The newspapers reported that two, Colin 'Cowboy' Hunting and Michael 'Ozzie' Harrison, were dead, and four were 'horribly wounded'. The police arrested fifty-one others.

Ozzie's funeral took place at St Agatha's Catholic Church in Kingston, attended by four hundred bikers including some from Germany. Then it was on to Kingston to bury Harrison, where girls were reported to be clawing lumps of soil out of the ground to fill the grave before six Angels took over the job. Threats of retribution was fairly swift, even if they did not materialize. The Road Rats wrote to the Slaves saying they would be making the 200-mile trip to the West Country over the Easter weekend. A week before, 100 armed police in riot gear had broken up fighting at Cheddar Gorge between the Rogues from High Wycombe, the

Slough Motorcycle Club and the Griffins from Coventry on one side, and the Chosen Few from Devon and the Dark Horses from Wiltshire on the other. Again the actual cause of the problem seems to have been over women attached to the chapters rather than a territorial feud.

Retribution by the courts was a little longer in coming. In December 1984, by which time charges against two Slaves over the deaths had been dropped, John Connolly received a sentence of eight years for riot.[14] As for the allegations of sexual indecency, the girl refused to make any complaint and at the time of the trial was believed to be living with the Windsors (the chapter as opposed to the family) in Slough.

There have been continual sporadic outbreaks of violence between Angels and other outlaw bikers. In May 1988 Stephen 'the Rabbi' Brookes, a member of the Pagan Outlaw bikers from Warwickshire was shot dead.

Meanwhile, if there was any doubt that the Angels had moved into the propery market Mrs Patricia McSorley, who lived in Maidenhead Road, Slough, was swiftly disabused of the idea. With the help of a mortgage swindle – in which two Angels Alan Kraft and Graham Geard who had posed as well-paid executives of a Watford company and who were sentenced to eighteen months' imprisonment each – the Angels now had a clubhouse.[15] They had put down £4,000 on the property and obtained a 95 per cent mortgage. The house now included a dormitory, juke-box and pool table. The McSorleys had the misfortune to live next door. When in December 1987 she sued Kraft and Geard for damages she claimed that the Angels subjected her to a reign of terror. Angels, she said, had had all-night drunken parties, lined up and exposed themselves to her, banged on her walls thoughout the night, called at 3 a.m. supposedly to borrow spray to drive flies from the body of a murdered Angel, and removed bricks from the wall which led into her attic. She believed that whilst she was out, Angels had got in through the unbricked attic and slept in her bed. The parties had become worse when Angel John Mikkleson died in

---

[14] In 1975 he had been convicted of an affray when the Road Rats were refused entry to a club in Barry, Wales. A petrol bomb had been thrown and the club manager received a fractured skull. The manager's son was set alight.

[15] It was reduced on appeal to nine months, of which six months was suspended which effectively meant their immediate release.

police custody on 16 July 1985.[16]

Meanwhile the Council had reduced the rates on her home from £500 to a nominal £1. The club-house was sold at a profit of £30,000. They had asked £118,900 for 125 Maidenhead Road, but the price had been reduced because of dry rot, woodworm and 'extensive damage'. The Council ordered the Angels to remove their insignia from a large sign above the front door and they complied by nailing it to the front door itself.

In the witness-box Geard denied these allegations, describing the exposure as a total fabrication, and a spokesman said, 'We never wanted trouble here and we never caused anyone any problems. We just wanted to get on with our own lives and stop other people messing us about.'[17]

On 12 January the Angels were ordered to pay Ron and Pat McSorley £23,632 damages. Mr Justice Drake ruled that the Angels had made the McSorleys' home uninhabitable.

When the Guardian Building Society called in the £58,000 loan on their club-house the Angels collected the money and redeemed the mortgage. Eventually a High Court judge granted the local Council what amounted to an order for possession.

By 1993 the National Crime Intelligence Survey reckoned that although there were only two hundred active Hell's Angels in chapters of eighteen members, compared with several thousand Outlaw Bikers, nevertheless the two hundred had, it was believed, been responsible for more killings and woundings in the previous year than all of the other organized crime groups in the country put together. Over the years during which it had been believed that they were a spent force, the Angels instead had become a financially strong, self-contained unit with strong legal representation who

[16] The High Court quashed a coroner's verdict on John Mikkleson, a Hell's Angel, and ordered a new inquest. LJ Watkins said he reached the decision 'with considerable reluctance'.

Mikkleson, aged 34, from Windsor, died in police custody after being involved in a fight at Bedfont, Middlesex in July 1985. He had been hit on the head with a police truncheon, put unconscious in a police van and left on the charge-room floor of the police station before being taken to hospital. He died without regaining consciousness. The jury returned a verdict of unlawful killing in March 1986. A number of officers were suspended from duty and eight of them challenged the verdict.

Lord Justice Watkins said it was unthinkable that the jury, who added a rider to their verdict that the killing was due to manslaughter as a result of the degree of care given to the man after he was overpowered, should have been satisfied beyond reasonable doubt that a criminal offence had been committed. A new inquest was ordered before a different coroner and jury. *The Times*, 19 December 1986.

[17] *Today*, 21 November 1986.

had sued more newspapers and magazines than any other group. The NCIS members regarded the Angels as major traffickers in amphetamines, and had moved into credit-card frauds with international links to white-collar crime. They were regarded as an organized crime unit in its purest form.

Perhaps it is because we have been made more aware of it by the press, but crimes have seemed to become more violent. People are not merely robbed but are badly beaten at the same time. Take the example of a jewellery dealer and his wife who were tortured by a gang who lashed her hands together with metal strips before kicking, punching and threatening them to make him reveal the combination of his safe.[18]

In 1992 ex-paratrooper John Calton, who had already served three years for robbery, now turned to kidnap and extortion. He told his victims he was wired as a human bomb and asked one mother which of her children she would choose to die. Another family was invited to nominate which child should be drugged and locked in the boot of a car. Calton's robberies were another in the series of kidnapping by gangs up and down the country in order to extract money from supermarket managers and those with access to large amounts of their employers' money. All in all he pocketed some £96,000, but Calton's run came to an end when one of his associates tried to sell the radio from a stolen getaway car. His girlfriend also went to the police after finding three guns hidden in her kitchen. Calton received a sentence of twenty-five years, and his associates Sean Wain and Robert Moore twenty apiece.

But there again, is the behaviour any worse than the 1936 case of Max Mayer, a dwarf who hanged from the bedstead the fox-terrier dog of an elderly lady whose house he was burgling and whom he also killed? Edward Robey, who prosecuted the case in the magistrates' court, wrote:

> I remember when Counsel opened the case he said to the Lancashire jury something like this: 'Look at photograph No 5'. They did so; he went on, 'That was this poor old lady's only companion; when the accused was savagely hitting her with a tyre lever her faithful fox terrier tried to defend her; he kicked it and then tied a piece of string round its neck, hung it on the bedpost where it was slowly strangled to death.'

---

[18] *Evening Standard*, 20 October 1992.

I shall never forget the faces of that jury as they stared stonily in the direction of the dock. There was absolutely no defence; but whatever it was Haslam had no chance after that opening statement.[19]

In 1989 there was a particularly nasty series of robberies, rapes and murder on and around the M25 which amounted to a reign of terror. The police believe that in the second half of the year the M25 raiders committed ninety-two offences. In one raid the jury found the men had pulled a 56-year-old man out of his car, than stripped and battered him before dousing him with petrol. He died of a heart attack. Three men, Johnson, Davis and Rowe, were ultimately convicted although they have continued to deny their guilt. Indeed there were certain disquieting features in the evidence. For instance all the defendants were black, although one witness who gave evidence at the trial stated that one if not two of the assailants were white and that one of them had blue eyes and blond hair. The Crown in fact had called as witnesses three young men who had also been resident at the hostel where the defendants had been living. Each of these witnesses admitted to having themselves disposed of property coming from one of the robberies; fingerprints of two of them were found on the cars used in the offences, and one of them had blond hair and blue eyes. Finally, one of the defendants had an uncrackable alibi, something prosecuting counsel acknowledged in his closing speech as 'one of the mysteries of the case'.[20]

Today the stench of drugs is everywhere. In April 1992 the police formed the National Criminal Intelligence Service at a cost of £25 million to counter career or designer crime, as it is now fashionably known. The aim has been to collect and maintain intelligence back-up and to handle informants as opposed to supergrasses. The organization had something of a major hiccough in its teething years. In 1993 an officer was arrested after a television programme was shown which gave the appearance of his batting on both sides of the fence. It cannot have helped the claim being made by members of the Service that they should not merely be information gatherers but should also be allowed to be an operative squad.

---

[19] E. Robey, *The Jester and the Court*, p.127.
[20] See Sean Enright, 'The M25 Three' in *The Criminal Lawyer*, November 1993.

In August 1993 Albert Pacey, the former Chief Constable of Gloucestershire, took over as head of NCIS. During its existence the service had, he said, identified the top 500 criminals living in Britain and a further 2,000 who needed targeting. The majority lived in the South East. It had also developed dossiers on 450 criminal operations through informants, which had led to 330 arrests, and had provided information through its drug liaison officers which had resulted in more than 760 people being arrested worldwide. In addition, it had helped in the recovery of more than £100 million in drugs. It had examined 16,000 disclosures from banks and financial houses on suspicious transactions. One in eight led to further investigations.

NCIS sees organized crime in the United Kingdom coming from the locals dealing in drugs, robbery, fraud, forgery and car theft as their staple diet. It also foresees considerably more attention being paid to this country by foreign criminals, with the Mafia interested in drug trafficking, fraud and money laundering; the Colombian cartels with cocaine and laundering; the Triads dealing almost exclusively with the Chinese community; the Asian element again interested in laundering and heroin; West African criminals dealing in fraud and drugs; the Caribbean element perhaps not as powerful because of an overall lack of structure; and from Russia and the Ukraine, criminals trafficking in firearms. At least the white-collar branch of the Yakuza from Japan, the Sokaiya, have not moved into Britain. Their speciality is extortion. Unless a fee is paid, they will appear at a company's annual general meeting and ask embarrassing questions about the potential misuse of company funds and the sexual activities of the directors. Steps have been taken to counter this, and now in order to attend a company meeting an individual investor must purchase 100 shares in that company. In 1992 1,824 companies held their annual meetings on 26 July to defeat the Sokaiya's efforts at disruption.

Guns move around at an alarming rate of knots, and they always have done. Back in the 1920s when Inspector George Cornish of the Yard was sent to Cheshire to investigate a country-house robbery – 'Brummy' Sparkes was well in the frame but was not picked out on an identification parade – a gun was found in the shrubbery, discarded by the thieves. Cornish had extensive inquiries made and it transpired that the gun, which had been made the previous year, was Spanish and had been sold to a dealer in the Argentine.

Gone in the 1990s except for the very young, the unsophisti-
cated and the semi-amateur, is the sawn-off shotgun. In its place
is the Astra .357, a Spanish gun originally designed for police
work, a Walther 7.65mm PPK or a sten gun. The silencer is now
being used by the hitman, and it is feared by the police that
machine guns will be the next stock in trade.

The National Criminal Intelligence Service also fears that guns
from the broken-down Eastern bloc will soon be on the market at
bargain prices of a few hundred rather than thousand pounds for
sophisticated weapons. Even in 1993 NCIS estimated that AK 47
Kalashnikov rifles were going for £100s rather than £1,000s.
Weapons on offer were not all ex-Russian army surplus. In
September 1993 the *Sun* purchased an Army issue Bren gun
for a modest £1,400 from a dealer named Billy outside the Globe
public house in Deptford, South London. The gun may have
been somewhat old-fashioned, but it was still capable of blasting
through a wall at 60 yards. The *Sun* reporter had suggested that
he needed it because he was having some trouble with Yardies,
and the vendor was most sympathetic.

> You've got us on your side if you are up against the Yardies.
> They are only trying to tread on our patch here and we are
> going to show them they can't f*** us about. We've had this
> trade sewn up for years and we're not letting it go.[21]

In a raid on a house in Everton on 6 February 1994, a complete
arsenal – including seven sub-machine guns, three Kalashnikovs,
an Armalite and an Uzi along with nearly 140 rounds of ammunition – was found under a sofa bed and in a wardrobe. It was, said
the police, not an IRA stack but one bound for the drug wars.

In five years' time perhaps the threat will be from Central
Eastern criminals as well as Asian ones. It seems a long road has
been travelled from the days of the Odessans and Bessarabians of
Whitechapel at the turn of the century; perhaps the circle has
turned fully. Two Armenians, Mkritch Martirossian and Gagic
Ter-Ogannisyan, were charged with the February 1993 murder in
London of Rusland Outsiev, the self-styled Prime Minister of
Chechenia, and his brother Nazerbeck.

Outsiev had been spending money like water during his time in

---

[21] *Sun*, 24 September 1993.

London – £2,000 restaurant bills, £100 tips for waiters and a string of prostitutes visiting his flat in Marylebone. The Prime Minister, who was ostensibly in London to organise the printing of stamps and currency and was also in the market for missiles, was shot in the head, as was his younger brother. He had been invited by the Armenian KGB to desist in his negotiation for Stinger missiles but had declined.

Martirossian told the police: 'The murders were planned by the KGB. I had no choice but to obey the KGB. They would have harmed my family'. Apparently a hit-man from Los Angeles had originally been recruited but, rather prosaically, he could not get a visa. When Martirossian was searched on his arrest he was found to have snake venom hidden in a bandage. He was to use this if he was caught. Instead, after a visit by an Armenian KGB agent to Belmarsh Prison in South East London where Martirossian was on remand, he hanged himself. Ter-Ogannisyan was sentenced to life imprisonment for murder in October 1993.

The matter did not, however, end there. Ter-Ogannisyan had married Alison Ponting, a BBC World Service producer, in 1988. On April 30, 1994, Karen Reed, Alison Ponting's sister, was shot dead on the doorstep of her home in Woking, Surrey. It is thought that Mrs Reed was shot by mistake for her sister, Alison, who had been staying with her following the imprisonment of her husband. Again a professional hit-man is thought to have been used. A fortnight previously the sisters had been warned by the police that they might be the target of an attack, when a car was abandoned after a chase and a gun was found together with a map marking the area of Woking where they lived.

In the old days it was possible to count on one hand, or certainly two, the number of famous British criminals who died with their money in the bank. Billy Hill definitely, Arthur Thompson, but not the Sabinis or Billy Kimber and not, although they are still alive, either Jack Spot or Frankie Fraser. Remember how the Train Robbers lost most of their money? I recall talking to a retired bank robber from the 1960s who said that as his share he had had over £1 million through his hands. That was real money then. Even allowing for exaggeration, he must (from the number of cases on which I defended him) have had a very substantial amount in his pocket tax-free. 'I pissed it out the window,' he said. It had gone on money, clothes, cars and particularly nights at the Astor where he said you could run through £1,500 at one sitting.

Few put their money away and when they did so, they did not always benefit from their investments. They had never heard of off-shore companies, tax-free havens and the like. Cash was King. Once I introduced a thief to a solicitor, from whom I rented an office, to buy a house. The afternoon before completion was due to take place, the client had still not produced the balance of the purchase price and the solicitor rang me on the intercom. 'He's coming in at five. You'll have to tell him I'm not going to take a cheque.' He needn't have worried. At five-past five the intercom buzzed again. Would I come down and help count the money? When I arrived the client was still pulling bundles of used notes from pockets imaginable and unimaginable.

The bank robber Jackie O'Connell put some of his into launderettes, but he was shot on the way to stand trial for the Bank of America safe raid and his wealth did him little good. Another man I knew invested his money in property, and then when charged with a jewel theft could not explain how he had come by the initial capital to set up his development. Perhaps pissing it out of the window was the sensible thing to do.

Now there are, say the police, around 400 'respectable' crime lords masterminding most of the illegal activities from drugs to gun sales on the streets of Britain. A report in the *Sunday Telegraph* said that these hardened crooks had now developed a respectable façade. The career criminal had usually started in drugs, dabbled with guns (almost obligatory in the drug trade) and then shifted smartly into money-laundering using a front company, possibly haulage or possibly a retail concern, to launder the illegal money.

A senior police source is quoted as saying:

It can take just four or five handshakes to move from being a school drugs supplier to a top-level dealer. If they are violent, unscrupulous and treacherous, they can maintain their parities.

The theory is that the higher they go up the crime ladder, with more money at their disposal, the more likely it is that they can distance themselves from the chain of events. But occasionally they get close to the action and have to prove their hands-on skills. From there, the article suggests, it is difficult for them to act alone. Trusty henchmen with whom they have previously worked are recruited, but these hoped-for allies may prove to be their undoing.

Apart from the standard use of the informer, surveillance is a tool in the police armoury, but it is expensive and some of the equipment may be used only once. The designer criminal, particularly in the drug field, and even at a very low level, is furnished with counter-surveillance equipment. These are the days of the designer criminals who live behind well-manicured hedges. According to Judge Gerald Sparrow, writing in 1969 at the tail end of the Richardson-Kray era, and rather against the burden of my thesis, they have been around for a long time:

> All the trappings are acquired, the luxurious centrally heated house either in London, or in nearby Surrey or Sussex, the young and smart companion often promoted to the status of wife, the Jaguar for him and the Mini for her. Golf as a recreation with all the gadgets. a well-stocked cellar accompanied by a passion for vodka which appears to be a status symbol.[22]

Peter Watson writing in the *Sunday Times* supported this view in July 1973. In his experience, designer criminals commuted from the Midlands and as far away as Cornwall, where when not working, they led elegant lives amongst their unsuspecting neighbours.

Perhaps both the police and Watson and Sparrow's versions are wishful thinking. I know of few relatively successful criminals' homes which match this description. Just as likely, you will have to send your clothes to the cleaners after you leave.

What is also certain is that today's career criminals are educating their children to another life. Just as a decade or two ago, in America, 'Mob' leaders sent their sons away from the waterfronts and districts where they themselves had been brought up, and to private schools and on to universities, so now are the very top criminals doing the same for their children. 'Company Director' listed against the occupation of fathers of pupils at the great public schools can cover a multitude of crimes. The interesting question to be answered is whether this and the next generation will go straight, or will they put their education to even better use? And the answer? Surely the latter. Damon Runyan wrote, 'The battle is not always to the strongest nor the race to the swiftest, but that's the way to bet.'

[22] G. Sparrow, *Gang Warfare*, p. 112.

331

Bibliography

Adamson, I., *The Great Detective* (1966), London, Frederick Muller
Baker, P., *Time Out of Life* (1961), London, Heinemann
Ball, J., Chester, L. and Perrott, R., *Cops and Robbers* (1979), London, Penguin Books
Bean, J. P., *Crime in Sheffield* (1978), Sheffield, Sheffield City Libraries
———— *The Sheffield Gang Wars* (1981), Sheffield, D. & D. Publications
Bebbington, W., *Rogues go Racing* (1981), London, Good & Betts
Beltrami, J., *The Defender* (1980), Edinburgh, W. & R. Chambers Ltd
———— *A Deadly Innocence* (1989), Edinburgh, Mainstream
Beveridge, P., *Inside the CID* (1957), London, Evans Brothers
Black, D., *Triad Takeover* (1991), London, Sidgwick & Jackson
Bland, J., *True Crime Diary* (1986), London, Futura
———— *True Crime Diary, Volume 2*, (1989) London, Futura
Booth, M., *The Triads* (1990), London, Grafton
Borrell, C. and Cashinella, B., *Crime in Britain Today* (1975), London, Routledge & Kegan Paul
Boyle, J., *A Sense of Freedom* (1977), London, Pan Books
Brady, C., *Guardians of the Peace* (1974), Dublin, Gill & Macmillan
Bresler, F., *Reprieve* (1965), London, Harrap
———— *Scales of Justice* (1973), London, Weidenfeld and Nicholson
———— *The Trail of the Triads* (1980), London, Weidenfeld & Nicholson
———— *An Almanac of Murder* (1987), London, Severn House
Brillett, D., *Sussex Murders* (1990), Southampton, Ensign Publications

Campbell, D., *That Was Business, This Is Personal* (1990), London, Secker & Warburg
———— *The Underworld* (1994), London, BBC Books
Cannon, J., *Tough Guys Don't Cry* (1983), London, Magnus Books
Cannon, E., *Gangster's Lady* (1993), London, Yellow Brick Publishers
Capstick, J., *Given in Evidence* (1960), London, John Long
Cater, F. and Tullett, T., *The Sharp End* (1988), London, The Bodley Head
Cherrill, F., *Cherrill of the Yard* (1953), London, Harrap
Cheyney, P., *Making Crime Pay* (1944), London, Faber & Faber
Chibnall, S., *Law and Order News* (1977), London, Tavistock
Chinn, C., *Better Betting with a Decent Feller* (1991), Hemel Hempstead, Harvester Wheatsheaf
Churchill, M., *Chicago May; her story* (1928), London, Samson Lowe
Cole, P. and Pringle, P., *Can You Positively Identify This Man?* (1974), London, Andre Deutsch
Colleran, G. and O'Reagan, M., *Dark Secrets* (1985), Tralee, The Kerryman
Colquhoun, R., *Life Begins at Midnight* (1962), London, John Long
Cornish, G., *Cornish of the 'Yard'* (1935), London, The Bodley Head
Cox, B., Shirley, J. and Short, M., *The Fall of Scotland Yard* (1977), Harmondsworth, Penguin
Darbyshire, N., and Hilliard, B., *The Flying Squad* (1993), London, Headline
Darling, Lord, *Lord Darling and his famous trials* (no date), London, Hutchinson & Co
Davis, V. *Phenomena of Crime* (no date), London, John Long
Dew, W., *I Caught Crippen* (1938), London, Blackie
Dickson, J., *Murder without Conviction* (1986), London, Sphere
Divall, T., *Scallywags & Scoundrels* (1929), London, Ernest Benn
Dobson, B., *Policing in Lancashire* (1989), Blackpool, Landy Publishing
Dow, P.E., *Criminology in Literature* (1980), New York, Longman
Dunne, D. and Kerrigan, G., *Round Up the Usual Suspects* (1984), Dublin, Magill
DuRose, J., *Murder Was My Business* (1971), London, W H Allen
Eddy, P. and Walden, S., *Hunting Marco Polo* (1991), London, Bantam Press
Fabian, R., *London After Dark* (1954), London, The Naldrett Press
———— *Fabian of the Yard* (1955), London, Heirloom Modern World Library
———— *The Anatomy of Crime* (1970), London, Pelham Books

333

Felstead, S., *The Underworld of London* (1923), New York, E P Dutton
———— *Shades of Scotland Yard* (1950), London, John Long
Finmore, R., *Immoral Earnings* (1951), London, M.H. Publications
Flynn, S., and Yeates, P., *Smack* (1985), Dublin, Gill & Macmillan
Fordham, P., *The Robbers' Tale* (1965), London, Hodder & Stoughton
———— *Inside the Underworld* (1972), London, George Allen & Unwin
Fraser, F. and Morton, J., *Mad Frank* (1994), London, Little, Brown
Fry, C. with Kray, C., *Doing the Business* (1993), London, Smith Gryphon
Goodman, J., *The Burning of Evelyn Foster* (1977), London, Headline
———— and Will, I., *Underworld* (1985), London, Harrap
Greeno, E., *War on the Underworld* (1960), London, John Long
Grigg, M., *The Challenor Case* (1965), London, Penguin
Guerin, E., *Crime, The Autobiography of a Criminal* (1929), London, John Murray
Hancock, R., *Ruth Ellis* (1985), London, Weidenfeld & Nicholson
Hanson, K., *Rebels in the Streets* (1964), Englewood Cliffs, New Jersey, Prentice-Hall
Hart, E.,T., *Britain's Godfather* (1993), London, True Crime Books
Hester, S. and Eglin, P., *A Sociology of Crime* (1992), London, Routledge
Herridge, R. with Hilliard, B., *Believe No One* (1993), London, Little, Brown
Higgins, R. *In the Name of the Law* (1958), London, John Long
Hill, B., *Boss of Britain's Underworld* (1955), London, The Naldrett Press
Hinds, A., *Contempt of Court* (1966), London, The Bodley Head
Hobbs D., *Doing the Business* (1988), Oxford, Oxford University Press
Hoskins, P., *No Hiding Place* (no date), Daily Express Publications
Jennings, A., Lashmar, P. and Simson, V., *Scotland Yard's Cocaine Connection* (1990), London, Jonathan Cape
Johnston, M., *Around the Banks of Pimlico* (1985), Dublin, Attic
Jones, E., *The Last Two to Hang* (1966), London, Macmillan
Kelland, G., *Crime in London* (1986), London, The Bodley Head
Kennedy, L., *A Presumption of Innocence* (1976), London, Gollancz
Knight, R., *Black Knight* (1990), London, Century
Knox, B., *Court of Murder* (1968), London, John Long
Kray, C., *Me and My Brothers* (1988), London, Grafton
Kray, Reggie, *Born Fighter* (1991), London, Arrow
———— *Villains We Have Known* (1993), Leeds, N.K. Publications
Kray, Ronnie, *My Story* (1992), London, Sidgwick & Jackson
Kray, R. and Kray, R., *Our Story* (1988), London, Pan Books
Lambrianou, T., *Inside the Firm* (1991), London, Smith Gryphon
Laurie, P., *Scotland Yard* (1970), London, The Bodley Head

Leach, J., *Sods I Have Cut on the Turf* (1961), London, Gollancz
Leeson, B., *Lost London* (1934), London, Stanley Paul & Co.
Leigh, D., *Howard Marks* (1988), London, Unwin Paperbacks
Lewis, D. and Hughman, P., *Most Unnatural* (1971), London, Penguin
    Books
Lucas, N., *Britain's Gangland* (1969), London, Pan Books
Mack, J.A., *The Crime Industry* (1975), Farnborough, Saxon House
Mandelkau, J., *Buttons – the Making of a President* (1971), London,
    Sphere
Mark, R., *In the Office of Constable* (1978), London, Collins
Marshall, J., *The True Story of the Ollie Murder* (1988), Lewes, Seagull
    Books
McConnell, B., *The Evil Firm* (1969), London, Mayflower
Meehan, P., *Innocent Villain* (1978), London, Pan Books
Merrilees, W., *The Short Arm of the Law* (1966), London, Long
Millen, E., *Specialist in Crime* (1972), London, George G. Harrap & Co.
Morris, T., *Crime and Criminal Justice Since 1945* (1989), Oxford, Basil
    Blackwell
Morton, J., *Gangland* (1992), London, Little, Brown
———— *Bent Coppers* (1993), London, Little, Brown
Murphy, R., *Smash and Grab* (1993), London, Faber & Faber
Napley, D., *Not Without Prejudice* (1982), London, Harrap
Narborough, F., *Murder on My Mind* (1959), London, Alan Wingate
Nott-Bower, W., *Fifty-two Years a Policeman* (1926), London, E. Arnold
Parker, R., *Rough Justice* (1981), London, Sphere
Patrick, J., *A Glasgow Gang Observed* (1973), London, Eyre Methuen
Payne, L., *The Brotherhood* (1973), London, Michael Joseph
Pearson, J., *The Profession of Violence* (1985), London, Grafton
Phelan, J., *The Underworld* (1953), London, George G. Harrap & Co.
Raymond, D., *The Hidden Files* (1992), London, Little, Brown
Read, L. and Morton, J., *Nipper* (1991), London, Macdonald
Read, P., *The Train Robbers* (1978), London, W. H. Allen
Richardson, C., *My Manor* (1991), London, Sidgwick & Jackson
Robey, E., *The Jester and the Court* (1976), London, William Kimber
Rowland, J., *Murder Revisited* (1961), London, John Long
Sabbag, R., *Snowblind* (1978), London, Picador
Samuels, R., *East End Underworld* (1981), London, Routledge &
    Kegan Paul
Samuels, S. with Davis, L., *Among the Soho Sinners* (1970), London,
    Robert Hale
Scarne, J., *Scarne's Complete Guide to Gambling* (1961), New York,
    Simon & Schuster

Shew, E. S., *A Companion to Murder* (1961), New York, Alfred Knopf
———— *A Second Companion to Murder* (1962), New York, Alfred Knopf
Short, M., *Lundy* (1991), London, Grafton
Sifakis, C., *The Encyclopaedia of American Crime* (1982), New York, Facts on File
Sillitoe, P., *Cloak Without Dagger* (1956), London, Pan Books
Simpson, A. W. B., *In the Highest Degree Odious* (1992), Oxford, Oxford University Press
Skelton D. and Brownlie, L., *Frightener* (1992), Edinburgh, Mainstream Publishing
Slipper, J., *Slipper of the Yard* (1981), London, Sidgwick & Jackson
Smith, P. G., *The Crime Explosion* (1970), London, Macdonald
Smithies, E., *Crime in Wartime* (1982), London, George Allen & Unwin
Sparks, R., *Burglar to the Nobility* (1961), London, Arthur Barker
Sparrow, G., *Gang Warfare* (1988), London, Feature Books
Stockman, R., *The Hangman's Diary* (1993), London, Headline
Taylor, K., *The Poisoned Tree* (1990), London, Sidgwick & Jackson
Taylor, L., *In the Underworld* (1985), London, Unwin Paperbacks
Taylor, R., *Murders of Old Sussex* (1991), Newbury, Countryside Books
Thomas, D. with Grant, R., *Seek Out the Guilty* (1969), London, John Long
Thompson, H. S., *Hell's Angels* (1966), New York, Random House
Thurlow, D., *The Essex Triangle* (1990), London, Robert Hale
Tietjen, A., *Soho* (1956), London, Allan Wingate
Tullett, T., *Murder Squad* (1981), London, Triad Grafton
Van Cise, P. S., *Fighting the Underworld* (1936), London, Eyre & Spottiswoode
Walsh, D. and Poole, A., *A Dictionary of Criminology* (1983), London, Routledge & Keegan Paul
Ward, H., *Buller* (1974), London, Hodder & Stoughton
Watts, M., *The Men In My Life* (1960), London, Christopher Johnson
Webb, D., *Deadline for Crime* (1955), London, Muller
———— *Line Up for Crime* (1956), London, Muller
Wensley, F., *Detective Days* (1931), London, Cassell & Co.
Whittington-Egan, R., *Liverpool Roundabout*
Wickstead, B., *Gangbuster* (1985), London, Futura
Wighton, C., *Dope International* (1960), London, Muller
Wilkinson, L., *Behind the Face of Crime* (1967), London, Muller
Williams, J., *Bloody Valentine*, (1994) London, Harper Collins
Woffinden, B., *Miscarriages of Justice* (1987), London, Hodder & Stoughton

Index